THE BIRTH OF THE CHURCH

ADRIENNE VON SPEYR

THE BIRTH OF THE CHURCH

Meditations on John 18–21

TRANSLATED BY DAVID KIPP

IGNATIUS PRESS   SAN FRANCISCO

Title of the German original:
Geburt der Kirche
Betrachtungen über Kapitel 18–21 des Johannes-Evangeliums
© 1949 Johannes Verlag, Einsiedeln

Cover by Victoria Hoke Lane

With ecclesiastical approval
© 1991 Ignatius Press, San Francisco
ISBN 0–89870–368–9
Library of Congress Catalogue Number 90–85550
Printed in the United States of America

CONTENTS

THE ARREST

18:1. *When Jesus had spoken these words, he went forth with his disciples across the Kidron Valley, where there was a garden, which he and his disciples entered.*

The Lord leaves the place where he had spoken with his Father. He goes *forth* from there. He does not, however, go alone, but in the company of his disciples. It is a company in which many things are not explicitly stated. Within it, the Lord is the one who knows everything; he has communicated his knowledge to the disciples, but they have comprehended only a little of it. Still, they have not been estranged from him through this gap in insight. They are the archetype of a true Christian communion, in which much is passed over in silence and each remains at peace even if not knowing everything about the other. For the Lord, something of the highest, most decisive sort is taking place: he has spoken with the Father, and now he goes forth. The disciples scarcely notice the enormity of this transition. They just go along with him. Thus the Lord goes with the Bride, the Church: she follows him, wordlessly, simply, in a sense colorlessly, but without revolt, in calmness in him.

They go into a garden, to a pleasant location that in no way corresponds to the event. What is now to be played out, the suffering, will be so beyond measure that no earthly scenery could reflect it.

18:2. *Now Judas, who betrayed him, also knew the place; for Jesus often met there with his disciples.*

The Lord chooses a place where he has often spent time with his disciples before. He does nothing out of the ordinary; he effects no transition from the everyday to the suffering. And at the same time, he shows the disciples how much they have to be, in any given situation, both trusting and on their guard. It seems like an old habit when they go into the garden. Yet today the new will come to pass. Thus man must always stay alert: any time can be the first, and any time the last. The Lord had spoken at length with the Father, and had commended all the disciples to him. That seemed to them to be a kind of confirmation and intensification of their previous Christianity; now, everything apparently slips back again into comforting everydayness. The Lord himself almost seems to lull them into security precisely by choosing the garden. And yet they ought to be able to see through the everydayness to the extraordinary thing that they have been prepared for. They have not made the most of the preparatory graces. And that, too, is a timeless situation in the Church. By going into the garden, the Lord shows her that she will never really be alert and ready, will never comprehend, as he himself experiences it, the ultimate seriousness.

Judas knows the place, he knows it so well precisely because he is a betrayer. The evil man often sees through things Christian better than does the Christian himself. His calculating forethought regarding the Church's position often proves more correct than the forethought of the Christians. The other disciples would probably not have known where Jesus would go. Judas knows where. They are still but small in spirit; they hardly yet know the Holy Spirit. Judas, however, is filled with the evil spirit. The devil is sly and clever; he is like a mirror-reversed image of the Spirit in God. And yet the devil knows God's intentions only from the outside; he cannot oppose them with adequate means, but only with partial, indirect, hindering means, yet never blocking ones.

18:3. *So Judas, procuring a band of soldiers and some officers from the chief priests and the Pharisees, went there with lanterns and torches and weapons.*

These preparations are so far from being adequate as to be, basically, absurd. The devil can work out the place where the Lord is to be found, but the means that he deploys in order to trap him are quite inappropriate. Such is the intelligence of evil: its point of departure is amazingly sharp and precise, then it immediately goes astray. The disciples, however, are intimidated by this. That one of their number who turned apostate should possess such power, could surround himself with such an assemblage, makes an impression on them. They feel that on their side is weakness and on the other side strength; if they needed means for support of the Lord's cause, they could never move in with the same show of force as Judas. The spiritual and the worldly run up against one another here: a poor Church, in whose midst, however, the Lord is present, and strong enemies who lack only one thing— the weakness of the Lord.

18:4. *Then Jesus, knowing all that was to befall him, came forward and said to them: Whom do you seek?*

The Lord steps forward. It is a mystery of his communion with the Church that he steps forward. Hitherto, he has not separated himself off from the disciples. Now, as something momentous is taking place, he steps forward. He detaches himself from the disciples in order to give account of himself, and also to set himself apart from the communion. When it is a matter of life and death, then, as now, the Lord steps forward. He appears. He need not do so through signs and miracles. It can be an invisible, yet effectively forward-stepping presence in the midst of the Church. Never in times of danger does he let his disciples down; he is the first to confront the danger. And every time that someone wants to strike at the Church, he first strikes the Lord. Even temptation and sin strike the Lord first: he is struck by sin even before the soul is harmed by it. The sinless Lord guides the gaze of sin toward himself; he takes it upon himself. Thus he steps forward and creates a distance between himself and the Church. For the disciples, the consequences of this are shaming. They will never be able to boast of having gone with him at the decisive moment. It will always be the Lord who, representatively, did everything alone. And yet, precisely by stepping forward as an individual, he imparts cohesiveness to the disciples. Through his being thrown into relief, they, too, stand out in relief; we see who they are and what unites them: they are sinners and they are redeemed.

The Lord knows what the persecutors are after. Nevertheless, he has to put the question: *Whom do you seek?* He requires the quite simple, quite plain answer. It is not enough for him to step forward. He wants to show that he is evading nothing. He wants to give evidence of his total consent to what is to come. His enemies fail to understand why he does not try to conceal himself in the crowd instead, why he steps forward almost challengingly and even questions them. They can have no idea that this question, which the Lord directs to them and, in particular, to the betrayer, is simultaneously a final reinforcement of the vow that he has taken before the Father. And both hear the question: Judas hears it as if it were the question of one who is ignorant and unsuspecting; the Father, however, hears it as the sealing of their pact. It is like a renewal of a vow, a strengthening of the validity of something that was agreed, the sign of consummate loyalty. At the same time, it makes manifest how unexpected the ways of loyalty and obedience can be and how little the bystanders are able to see through to the implicit obedience that can inhere in an action. Even to the disciples, the question must sound like a provocation that can only aggravate the precarious situation. For the Lord, it is the befitting thing: the question to the betrayer and the answer to the Father.

18:5. *They answered him: Jesus of Nazareth. Jesus said to them: I am he. Judas, who betrayed him, was standing with them.*

For the bystanders, the persecutors' statement and the Lord's answer have a purely human character. They all know that it is he. The statement comes at a late moment, when nothing more can be rescued. The Father alone knows the real content of these words *I am he.* He knows with the whole of his fatherly feeling how much the Son stands by him, declares himself for him, and how, therefore, at this decisive moment, he declares his divinity: his coming from the Father and his going to the Father. How, within the human words, the entire declaration of the sonship is contained. How nothing could fill the Son with more pride and joy than this awareness: I am the Son of the Father. How, for the last time before the suffering, the Son allows himself to be flooded by the fullness of the Father's love and his own love of the Father, in which the love of all mankind is included. He speaks to men who are betraying him and sees in them those who are helping him to complete his mission of love in the Father. He almost sees in them those who are fulfilling the Father's will by preparing the way for his return to the Father. The words are those of the strongest and most loving loyalty of the Son.

Judas, who betrayed him, was standing with them: Judas, who embodies everything that is against the Lord. Judas, who also gives him the opportunity to declare himself for the Father at the moment of danger. The Lord has known him all along as the betrayer. Now, when Judas stands before him, he almost overlooks him, so much is he filled with his declaration for the Father. Love and hate stand eye to eye here, but the Son's love outweighs Judas' hate so much that, at this moment, it scarcely takes notice of that hate. On the Cross, he will be virtually flooded by evil's hate because then he will wish it to be so. Here, we find the other Christian possibility: to be hated and yet to love, to love the hater to his face.

18:6. *When he said to them: I am he, they drew back and fell to the ground.*
They draw back in helplessness. They stand suddenly before something infinitely great, something unfathomable, a world that they do not know and that discloses itself to them for the first time. But they have no possibility of access to it; it stands before them as something utterly strange. Thus they embody not only mediocrity and evilness, but also limitedness, that which is hemmed in from every direction. They have always been content with themselves, have lived in a closed-up world of gratification. What transcends this world has never affected them, not only as a spiritual problem but also in their elementary existence. They deny that there is any kind of unfulfilment in them; they are so convinced of the validity of their human environment that they seek, and find, an answer to every question within themselves. Perhaps they have conceded to God a place that, in their view, is befitting for him, a place without influence, for the time after death. If they have a religion, its festivals, its prayers, all of its encounters with God are completely devoid of life. What is alive in them is sin, while God and death together form the remote boundary of their existence. And now, in God's answer, they suddenly encounter something completely unexpected. They stagger back, without making the least attempt to adjust to those words, to bear up under them. And they fall *to the ground.* They fall upon that which is familiar to them and within their reach, upon the ground that lies beneath them, upon that which, for them, signifies firmness and boundary. Lying on the ground, they can fall no further. That is the characteristic response of the flesh to the spirit. In the end, it clings fast to materiality, which offers it support and refuge. Nevertheless, something in them has been shaken: their narrowness, their sensuality has received a jolting premonition of the incomprehensible,

of the spirit. One might almost think that they had seen something rapturous in order to fall as they did. But it is more terror than vision, the terror that flees and calls for no clarification. They will not forget their fall. But coming to terms with it is not now possible. If the Spirit has touched them, they nevertheless possess no opening for him; their self-sufficiency covers them over.

18:7. *Again he asked them: Whom do you seek? And they said: Jesus of Nazareth.*

The Lord sees the effect of his answer. But he asks a second time. He persists with the question. Once again, in the same way, he seeks to communicate with them. That he does so with the same words that he used the first time indicates an accommodating attitude. One more time, in simple human words, he presents them with the entire magnitude of his spirit. In so doing, he shows them that he is not only the Ever-Greater, who must always demand more in the name of love, but just as much the steadfast, the unwaveringly faithful. If it is true that he always towers above them, then in that distance is contained not only the tension between the relative and evil and the absolute and good, between sin and love, but no less, too, the possibility of a reposal for man in God. Through the repetition of his words, they ought to become aware that a real relationship exists between them and God, that he himself is the love that never grows impatient, but has time and permits approach. The love that not only incomprehensibly demands too much but wishes to begin a process.

But the opponents, too, reply with their same words. They, too, persist in their demand. Although they have fallen, although they have this experience behind them, they are still incapable of modifying their answer. If the Lord asks the same thing twice, his question nevertheless contains something new each time. The second question plainly contains his will to draw closer, a clear reference to his love. They, by contrast, only barricade themselves all the more behind their answer; their second response no longer admits of interpretation: they intend, more intransigently than ever, to carry out the order that they have been given. They are now less open to the love of the Lord than before because they have suffered a defeat, and, indeed, a material one; they see in their fall nothing more than a sign of bodily weakness that annoys them, and not at all a symbol of their failure in general. They want to offset that reversal at once through a display of force.

18:8. *Jesus answered: I told you that I am he; so if you seek me, let these men go.*

The Lord declares once more that it is he. But all the exultation that was contained in the original statement, when he was testifying more to God than to men, is now clouded over. This time, his answer is more to men than to God. He is moving further on into the darkness of the coming Cross. Through the fall of his persecutors, he has realized how little his spirit can achieve against the vigorousness of their sin. Hence, there is no way left but that of redemptive suffering. He sees how urgent the sacrifice has become: only it can overcome the hate. He sees how closed they are, how little their fall and their contact with God's superior might has affected them. So hard is their sin that only the most extreme sacrifice can soften it, so deep their darkness that he himself must enter wholly into that darkness. He sees, quite humanly, what it costs to convert an unwilling man to a willing one. They are able to see in the good nothing other than a hindrance and an external constraint because it does not originate from their own center. They have their closed world view; they relate everything back to their preconceived opinions, which derive from their sins. In their self-satisfaction, they are incapable of recognizing anything at all that they have not themselves decided and laid down. The Lord's twice-given answer, into which he had put the whole of his love, bore no fruit; they remain as stubbornly averted as before.

So if you seek me, let these men go. In their eyes, he is a man, somebody or other. Somebody who disturbs them and is an annoyance to them. Not the Son of the Father. But he nevertheless gives himself over to them as the one that he is: as simultaneously the Son of Man and the Son of God. *If you seek me,* he says, me, one who comes from the Father and is on the way back to the Father, me, one whom you could apprehend and who, precisely through your apprehending him, becomes inapprehensible in the Father. In this *me* he sums up all that he is: what they see of him, and what he has prophesied to them about himself; what he knows of himself in the Father, and what the Father is in him. If, therefore, they are really seeking him as the one who he is, then they ought to take him and let these, who are his, go free. Thus the act of separation at the beginning of the scene, when he stepped forward, repeats itself, but in a different sense. Now, it is to the world that the Lord distinguishes himself from those who are his. The world should not confuse him and those who are his. He and his disciples strive together toward the unity of the Father, but the world should distinguish between them. The Lord himself requires that he be distinguished. He is not the Church—he is the Son, and he has the Church as his Bride. He is the head, they are the members. He is God, they are men. This is spoken directly to the world, but also indirectly to the Church. As the body of the Lord, she should know herself to be one with him, but she should take care not to confuse herself with him. *Let these men go:* it is not just simply the task of the Church to share in the Lord's suffering, neither as observer nor as joint sufferer. Not only do head and body diverge in that respect; their missions, too, are different. And the Church's mission is indicated here by the Lord himself. Among the disciples there is, perhaps, one or another who would be prepared, even if he could sense in advance what sharing the suffering meant, to tread the path to the Cross. There is also the majority for whom the burden would be too great. The Lord will select those few whom he wishes to take with him to the Cross. The remaining ones will be dismissed. It is not part of his plan to have a lot of overtaxed people around him. All the paths of his life are his paths: since he lived in obscurity for thirty years, was publicly active for three years and suffered for three days, all possibilities are contained in imitation of him. And precisely because all paths are different, they all require the same thing: readiness. Even if someone prepares himself for a certain path and outwardly aspires to something, he is still not certain when and how he will tread it. The Lord alone decides, and in fact does so continually, just as the Father continually decides over him during his sojourn on earth. At this point, he already chooses John, the friend whom he loves, for the path to the Cross; others will follow later, when it will suit him. The allocation is not solely a matter of divine predestination, but also one of affinity, of adaptedness. John has the love that permits him to prevail in love over obstacles; the others do not have this love. When undergoing surgery, a person does not take all his friends and acquaintances along into the operating room, but at most, perhaps, his best friend, so that he can stand by him, knowingly and strengtheningly accompany him. Through love, John has become another person: one who has been included, selected. If all those who loved the Lord in one way or another would have to suffer immediately as well, then everything would be distorted. The Lord has need of the unreflected, solid existence of the other disciples for the future, for the apostolate. He also has need of the intimacy of John, which, precisely because it is intimacy, remains the exception. Everyone has his office; if he fulfills that, then he stands in the right place. And the Lord wishes to protect the disciples from the crowd. There is a kind of economy of sacrifice.

18:9. *This was to fulfill the word which he had spoken: Of those whom thou gavest me I lost not one.*

The Lord does not want to squander the sufferings of those who are his. One should not concede to the rabble any more sacrifices than are absolutely necessary. Whoever has been chosen to suffer should bear the sacrifice; but if one can satiate the people's rage with less, then one should do so. In the Church, there is no self-chosen martyrdom simply for the purpose of filling a quota.

With this, a saying of the Lord is fulfilled. For he founded Christianity not primarily as a religion of dying, but as one of living. The world should not be given the impression that imitating Christ and dying are one and the same. The apostolate of action, of planning and carrying out, of committing one's personality whether in dangerous circumstances or not, is not to be regarded as inferior to the apostolate of contemplation and suffering. But the saying of the Lord is fulfilled in a still deeper sense. It is the sole point behind his Incarnation that none of those whom God has given him should become lost, but rather, that they should all be saved in him. In this redemption, the fact should be visibly proclaimed that it is really *he* personally who redeems us. It must not turn into some sort of blurred collective redemption. He alone is the Redeemer, and he alone determines, as he freely sees fit, who should follow him on the path to the Cross and have the experience, without dying, of his death. The surviving witnesses should not consist of unbelievers. Just as freely, he determines who, in a special way, should participate in his inner suffering; that, too, is the Lord's free choice, attesting as such to the distance between head and members. Thus he allows no one to become lost: he delivers them, not only up into heaven but also over to his cause, and both cause and heaven form an inseparable unity.

18:10. *Then Simon Peter, having a sword, drew it and struck the high priest's slave and cut off his right ear. The slave's name was Malchus.*

Seen in human terms, Simon Peter does something quite reasonable. He attempts to defend the Lord with his bodily powers. Seen in divine terms, however, his human reason is unreasonable. He has not comprehended that the struggle taking place here has only one end: redemption. His redemption, the redemption of the other disciples, the redemption of the persecutors. Peter makes use of his strength and of a particular chance weapon. Through his act, he embodies those who are capable enough of distinguishing the Lord from the world but not his will from theirs, who still think that they could achieve some insight on their own that could then be acted upon in the service of the Lord. The question was directed to the Lord, and therefore it is not the part of any servant to intervene. The servant may not answer on his own unless he is questioned as such, that is, as an envoy of the Lord. Not in every instance when the Lord is attacked does the Christian have a mandate to answer. He must not confuse himself with the Lord and his spirit. He possesses only as much of that spirit as the Lord communicates to him. The initial answer and reaction is always the part of the Lord; only the second, following one is the part of the Christian, even if there need be no passing of time between the first and the second.

Simon Peter engages a subaltern. The Lord, however, intends to engage them all with his responses, not just the subordinates. And yet, his action is related to ours not only as the matchless to the wrong-headed. He wants to grant us the right to have a real say within the context of his work. He has to reprimand us only if we take the expression of our good will beyond the limits of his grace, forge our own plans for redemption and wish to carry them out. The good will of man must also be suffused with the grace and will of the Lord. Everything, including the independent plans and actions of the Christian, must occur in obedience to the Lord; if the Christian has submitted his plans to God and his intentions have been approved, then he should act freely and confidently.

18:11. *Jesus said to Peter: Put your sword into its sheath; shall I not drink the cup which the Father has given me?*

The deed has already been done. But, in the midst of carrying out the act, Peter is called upon, through a strict command of the Lord, to stop it short. What he wants to effect with his "good will" is the decided opposite of what the Lord wants to effect. The will of the Lord is always to fulfill the Father's will and to remain within the bounds of his mission. Peter's act would have had the potential to hinder him in carrying out his mission. For a long time, Peter has lived as a follower of the Lord. He knows his teaching, he has listened to his talks, he has also heard the prayer to the Father. But he has heard it all as if from the outside; he has still not made the Lord's attitude of mind his own. Precisely for that reason, he does not understand that he was not allowed to identify himself, through his act, with the Lord. He is not tied closely enough to the Lord to know when he must separate himself from the Lord. He forgets the distance that distinguishes him from the Lord. He sees in the Lord the representative of the Father and in himself the representative of the Lord. For the Lord became man and thus possesses the same qualities as he. He forgets that the Lord is of one nature with the Father and that he remains a divine Person even in becoming man. He sees the man in the Lord to such an extent that he would also like to defend him as a man. He thinks that the Lord's entire task is exhausted in his being a man, that the Incarnation as such is sacrifice enough. He does not understand that the great sacrifice, the renunciation and the suffering as the way of return to God, is still to come.

So it is necessary for the Lord to remind him: *Shall I not drink the cup which the Father has given me?* He intends to drink it to the dregs, not a drop of his mission must be lost. Nothing of it may be altered or deflected by human means. Just as fully as it was conceived by the

Father, so fully must it also be carried out. Through no purely human—and thus in one way or another blind—love may the Father's commission be thwarted, the suffering postponed or even made impossible. Thus two viewpoints stand opposed here: the human one of the believing Peter and the divine one of the Lord. Already there exists a tension between the body of Christ and the head. Already there is evidence of how difficult it will be to realize the unity. Men will always be confronting the Lord with short-sighted earthly arguments. But there is just as plainly evidence that the Lord makes no accommodations and intends to make none. He converts the sinners, he suffers for them, he loves them and takes them up with him into his mission; but he takes them with him only as those entrusted to him by God whom he is to bring back into unity with the Father. He can never make the concession to them of sharing their limitations and human views when these do not coincide with his. He allows them freedom of belief and insight, but only if they find their truth in him and the Father. Whenever they begin to put their own truth in the place of his and to regard this as advantageous, he is forced to oppose them and to reproach them with the foolishness and inadequacy of their sin-darkened insight. He does not do this in the form of a dispute in which he might set his superior reasons against their inadequate ones. He avoids any show of being in the right. Quickly and calmly, he deflects everything back toward the center: toward his relationship with the Father. He overcomes their position not with arguments but with living proofs of his love; and he seeks those proofs there where they are most burning, where they originally arise: in the reciprocal love that unites him with the Father. If it is necessary for him to oppose a believer who is of good will, then he does not do so without drawing the believer toward a special grace: vision of his relationship with the Father. No dispute occurs between the Lord and those who love him without an immediate enlargement of this love, which he causes to grow into love of the Father. That is how he acts, above all, toward the Church as a whole: she will often want to embark on paths that are not his paths; however, he will not allow her to come to ruin on such paths, but will make use of the false path in order to anchor her more firmly in love. Because of this experience, Simon Peter will later be richer in love. Thus the principle holds good: better to have erred through love than not to err without love.

It is the Father who has given the Son the cup. Hence, the Lord makes Peter see that he is living not his own destiny but the life that was given him in the Father, and thus that the obedience he demands of Peter is rooted in the obedience of the Son to the Father. If the Lord had given in to the disciple, then he would have been, in the deepest sense, untrue to the pledge he had made to the Father. In upholding his loyalty to God, however, he draws Peter into that loyalty as well. Here, the Lord must demonstrate fully that he is the Son of the Father and disclose the qualities of the Father to Peter. He must also show Peter the righteousness that inheres in his love. He could have given in to Peter through love of an apparently human and amicable sort, using his grace to supplement and cover over what was defective in Peter. But his love comes from the Father and is grounded in the Father, and thus it must be transparent all the way up to the Father. Here, too, tensions will arise again and again between the purely human vitality of the Church and the divine vitality of her head. Again and again, men of the Church will incline to disobedience through thinking that they know better. Perceptible human action seems to them more valuable than prayer. If Peter had asked the Lord before turning to action, that is, if he had prayed instead of striking out, then his action might perhaps have been blameless. In the event, despite believing that he is defending the Lord, he is actually struggling against the Lord. He does so every time that he exchanges the weapon of the Spirit for the weapon of this world. He means well, yet it is not at all his own view that he should have but the Lord's view. Every time that the Church forgets the Lord, she will resort to this same, typical solution, through which she separates herself from the Lord.

18:12. *So the band of soldiers and their captain and the officers of the Jews seized Jesus and bound him.*

The evil accumulates a power that the good does not have. It runs up against no bounds, knows no scruples. The Lord abandons himself to that power after he has detached himself from his followers. He wants to be the weak one, the single one, the one who is overpowered from the start by superior numbers; it is his weakness that must ultimately triumph. He freely withdraws his own power and moves for the first time into the full passivity of his commission. He allows himself to be bound. No mention is made of whether the bonds were strong or weak; that is a matter of indifference. Whether, in a soul, the Lord is bound strongly or lightly amounts to the same thing: as long as one puts bonds on him, he is not free and cannot move. We do not know whether his human strength would have sufficed to break the bonds or not. For him, this binding means: being in the freedom of God, in the Father's commision, in the passivity that the Father has willed, in consummate love. Thus he makes no attempt of any kind to escape. He intends to allow himself to be brought back to the Father bound by our sins, bound as far as to the death, and this binding by sin will be the expression of his consummate binding to the Father. This initial bodily binding is almost more a symbol than a reality. Opposed in it are: love and sin, freedom and being bound. The Lord is free in his love, the world is bound in its sin. Before God, the truth is precisely the reverse of what man sees. That very one who allows himself to be bound will later release man from sin. He takes boundedness upon himself. In this, the truth of God and the truth of the world collide with one another. The world binds God in order to keep his will from growing strong, in order to obstruct his mission. And it will torture the bound one to death. It sees in that the expression of its complete freedom, which knows no limits but those it imposes itself. For it, the situation is plain: it holds power over the Lord, who is bound in weakness, whose life its word of command will put to an end. For the Lord, the truth is a quite different one. He allows himself to be bound by the unfreedom of sin in order to bring the world his consummate freedom and purity and thus to fulfill, in love, the Father's commission. For him, it is the highest intensification of his freedom and power when he submits to the unfreedom of being bound in order to suffer weakness and humiliation through to the depths and thereby lead sinners into the freedom of the Father.

THE QUESTIONING BY
ANNAS AND CAIAPHAS

18:13. *First they led him to Annas, for he was the father-in-law of Caiaphas, who was high priest that year.*

They lead the Lord to human justice. Neither their preparedness nor their hatred nor their inveterate Pharisaism nor their personal considerations will be the perceptible occasion for bringing the Lord to his death. They take the path of justice. Not for the sake of their personal peace of mind, but because of the effect they expect his death to have. They want to put an end to the whole movement, a legal end. It must be proven beyond objection that this was not the Messiah. The opinion of each individual is already fixed, but it still needs strengthening through numbers and mass, and thus the passing of a humanly just judgment. Their inner deliberations are subtle, intricate and full of guile; their outer path is an apparently straight one.

18:14. *It was Caiaphas who had given counsel to the Jews that it was expedient that one man should die for the people.*

Caiaphas represents the view taken by the enemies of the Lord and the enemies of the Church. The Lord's death is to be a frightening example that will force the rest of those involved to change their ways. It will serve to prove the justness of the judges, but will also bring to light their magnanimity in being content to go no further than punishing the main troublemaker. To be sure, what Caiaphas desires is not that *only* one should die, but that, at all events, someone should *die.* For his magnanimity is, in truth, merely politics. He sees no other way to put down the movement than to kill the Lord. Against his will, however, he fulfills by his action the will of the Lord. With all his freedom, he is so unfree that, through what he does, he has to round out the freedom of the Lord. He helps him to fulfill his commission. Caiaphas does not wish to kill the disciples; they are to be induced by the judge's magnanimity to return to their previous ways of life and thought. Here, too, Caiaphas merely rounds out the plans of the Lord, who does not want to take his disciples with him into his isolation.

18:15. *Simon Peter followed Jesus, and so did another disciple. As this disciple was known to the high priest, he entered the court of the high priest along with Jesus . . .*

Two disciples follow the Lord, and without having been asked to do so. One, because he embodies the Church and because the Church, as Bride, feels that she has a right to accompany the Lord. That she clings to this right, makes use of it, is not in itself surprising, to the extent that Peter here embodies the human, and not the supernatural, side of the Church. He cannot yet embody the latter because the sources of the sacraments are not yet flowing, because the living ties of the Holy Spirit do not yet exist between the Lord and the Church. In this order of events, the Lord and Peter are related to one another not as enemies, but still as strangers. The Lord is now living wholly in his hiddenness within the Father's commission; the only aspect of that commission to appear externally will be his weakness. Peter and the Church do not comprehend this hiddenness. It is as if the supernatural were now living in total seclusion within the secret between Father and Son. On the side of the believers, there are only the stirrings of faith, which are not adequate to penetrate the unfathomability of the divine secret. They know, at a theoretical level, about a relationship between Father and Son, but that truth still has no force in their insights and decisions. The place for that in their spirits has not yet been vacated by the Lord. Rather, the Church must endure a period of testing in order to become receptive to what the Lord wants to give her through his suffering.

The Lord had not asked Peter to come. Nevertheless, he goes too. His action is not disobedience, but still less is it obedience. At that moment, neither the one nor the other exists. It is not relevant. Outside of the sacraments, the Lord has established no obedience for his Church. Ecclesiastical obedience is born out of the sacraments and is conceivable only in connection with them; it is virtually a summary of sacramental life. A Christian obedience apart from confession would be meaningless. Although there can also be, besides

Christian obedience, a purely human type—for example, as protection against temptation, as reinforcement and human support—that human aspect must still be tied into the sacramental one if it is to be Christian obedience, that is, boundedness in the Lord. Without having been asked, Simon Peter does what seems to him humanly right but is not divinely provided for. Only in the supernatural—and within the Church that means: in the power of the sacraments, in their conferment and in their reception—arises the power of obedience in Christian life.

Peter, wishing to act as mediator, accompanies the other disciple because the latter knows the high priest. Peter wants to intervene as a private believer. He embodies powerless good intentions. He has no idea that, by acting in this way, he is attempting to interpose himself between God and the suffering Lord. His action is condemned to failure from the start. He is an example of the fruitlessness of every human interference in divine matters. Through his attempt to control things and to bring them into unity, he sets himself against the unity of Father and Son, into which they intend to draw man. Father and Son do not allow themselves to be drawn into any outside unity. The unity of Father and Son, the Trinity in unity, contains all the power of unification in itself. If someone takes another track and attempts to pave the way for the Lord in accordance with his own human judgment, to force the Lord onto human pathways, then he sins against the spirit of unity. Here, of course, the disciple does not know what he is doing; he is, however, a cautionary symbol. God has lived as a man among men to such an extent that wanting to weave him into the net of other human aspirations could occur even to those closest to him. The warning is intended more for later Christians; they are given a lesson: whoever follows some human impulse not put into his soul by the Lord not only acts wrongly but takes a course that can lead as far as denial. The falsely-trodden path that Peter embarks upon here contains the germ of the denial that follows. Every wrong-headed action can be traced back to its origin, indeed must be retraced afterward, in critical retrospect, so that man may recognize the point at which he began diverging from the Lord's path.

18:16. . . . *while Peter stood outside at the door. So the other disciple, who was known to the high priest, went out and spoke to the maid who kept the door, and brought Peter in.*

Peter remains standing outside. He would not have been capable himself of going inside; his self-confidence, by virtue of which he had accompanied the Lord, is not sufficient to allow him to accompany the Lord any further, nor does his determination suffice for carrying out the service he had envisaged. Only by virtue of a divine mandate would he have been able to follow along. His plight is similar to what happened before, when he wanted to strike a telling blow but hit only the slave's ear. He must realize that the steps he took on the basis of his own deliberations were less than fully successful. Thus there now reigns in the Church, in the closest proximity to the Lord, disorder and helplessness. Again, Peter has to learn to subordinate his own insights to those of the Lord. And in order that he not do so unwillingly, he must first gain an insight into his own inadequacy. Both in the coming to life of faith and in the choice of one's course in life, the human will must freely subordinate itself to the will of the Lord. But only he is free for the Lord who has recognized his own unfreedom. Peter was given a twofold experience of this.

The other disciple, however, comes out to get him. He acts as the complementing element between the Church and the Lord. But in so doing he interposed himself between the Church and the Lord. Bride and Bridegroom should not, at this point, be brought together. Only through the experience of suffering will the Bride grow mature and be led, through the Resurrection, to the Bridegroom. Whoever mediates at the wrong time does not recognize the power that is given to the Church. Later on, when the Church will really be the Bride, this mediation will come to exist in truth: there will be men charged with leading the seekers, those yet to be faithful, yet to be received, across the threshold. It will be a mediation that passes the seekers on to the Church, and one that ceases to exist as soon as Peter has been admitted and the Bride has found the Bridegroom. In this respect, too, Peter is the Church, but as not yet recognized, as the Church that stands at her own door, the Church outside of the Church. Here, he is almost the thing that is lacking in order that the

Church can be recognized as such. Thus, the other disciple mediates in a twofold way: he brings the Church herself to the Church, and then again, in his role as apostle of the Lord, brings the individual seekers and awaiters to the Church. In the first case, he provides something complementary; in the second, he transmits the conditions for being received, namely, the form, the framework, the order. For even before the convert enters the Church he participates in the Church's order.

This order is embodied still more visibly in the maid who kept the door. She directs the coming and going between inside and outside. She decides whether Peter enters or not. She herself does not command, but she knows who is to give commands. In the court, she is the level of first appeal, but that, too, exists, and she must be obeyed. There is no provision for selectivity within the hierarchy. The other disciple speaks with her. As a part of the Jewish court, she has a hostile attitude toward the Lord. And yet the disciple must negotiate with her. He comes to an agreement with the worldly power; he does this because he has seen that the Lord was led inside while bound and had thus, for the moment, accepted this power. The Lord did that in order to be able, through so doing, to serve the Father more strongly and better. The disciple does not, perhaps, know this; he sees only that the Lord has done it, and for that reason he too wants to do likewise. In that, he may hit upon the right thing, and his agreement with the worldly power may be made as a commission from the Lord. But since he has no clear insight into the Lord's motivations, yet nevertheless presumes to act as the Lord does, his agreement with the worldly power may also be something wholly misguided. Making a right agreement under commission from the Lord and making a wrong one that runs contrary to his commission stand, as on a knife's edge, balanced in sharp opposition.

18:17. *The maid who kept the door said to Peter: Are you not also one of this man's disciples? He said: I am not.*

The maid questions Peter, perhaps out of curiosity, perhaps also out of a certain duty-related orderliness; she perhaps wants to know how many of these men she has to let pass through the door. She belongs only to the worldly order; she possesses no spark of Christian faith. Only through rumor has she heard of the Lord and his teaching. It is not part of her duties to question Peter. Yet she does so, and in clear expectation, in fact, of an affirmative reply. Almost by chance, she has clothed her knowledge that Peter belongs to these people in the form of a question.

Peter answers No. To a completely inconsequential question he replies with an absolute betrayal. It was no wrong for the woman to have asked. But it is the grossest wrong for Peter to answer in this way. The young Church, just coming into being, suddenly shows nothing but her human side. A very short-thinking side. We see her foundering in her weakness. Scarcely arrived in the world, she has already lost her justification for existing, since she herself denies herself. Peter, who embodies the office, denies the office, but also denies his own person. He wants to be numbered among those who do not have faith. The first encounter between Church and world ends in catastrophe for the Church. The Bride denies the Bridegroom when she has hardly yet been chosen by him, when she has just begun to comprehend that she has been chosen and called by him. She denies him out of cowardice and fear, for nothing else is contained in what Peter says. He has had enough. This being a Christian is becoming too dangerous for him. All his preparedness for sacrifice and his devotedess are exhausted.

18:18. *Now, the servants and officers had made a charcoal fire, because it was cold, and they were standing and warming themselves; Peter also was with them, standing and warming himself.*

Warming themselves is their main concern. Peter, who has given his denial, joins them in order to warm himself too. All of them together form a kind of communion: through feeling cold and warming themselves—and through saying No to the Lord. This No has receded for the moment into the background; the officers have paused for a rest. They have done their job, taken the Lord prisoner. Peter, who has denied him, nestles himself into this pause like someone wishing to be as inconspicuous as possible. After the various harsh confrontations between world and Church, he now presses into the tepidness of this pause. He all but disappears amidst the officers. He warms himself, and in so doing begins to emerge in a new way from his paralysis. He feels bodily comfort. A new confrontation begins: it will be played out within himself. In his bodily comfort, his spiritual discomfort is brought to light. He is standing amid a group to which he does not really want to belong. In the easy familiarity around the shared fire, he becomes aware of the disparity. Earlier, it was overhastiness; now, in the pause, it is anxiety. A sense of dread arises within him. He feels his cowardice; he sees how far he has sunk. But there is as yet no remorse; first his body recovers from the paralysis, but not yet his soul.

18:19. *The high priest then questioned Jesus about his disciples and his teaching.*

The high priest asks factual questions in order to complete his records. He asks about the disciples and about the Lord's teaching, being aware that both—the disciples and the teaching—somehow form a unity. He knows that this teaching finds its realization in men, that the disciples signify a confirmation and enrichment of the teaching. Here, the high priest has understood something very essential, and in this respect he has perhaps understood more, in an objective sense, than the disciples. But his understanding moves outside the sphere of faith, and is therefore fixed and motionless. The Lord's teaching is movement; and what men bring to that teaching, so that it can become moving and alive in the world, is faith. Although the Lord's teaching is true even if man disregards it, it still seeks, because it is the teaching of love, after men, and its fully-developed truth consists in making men participants in love and thus parts of the teaching itself.

18:20. *Jesus answered him: I have spoken openly to the world; I have always taught in synagogues and in the Temple, where all Jews come together; I have said nothing secretly...*

By the world, the Lord understands all those who listened to him. For he had, from the very start, addressed himself to everyone, and his teaching was a general one, meant for all and accessible to all who wanted to listen to him. It was presented in such a way that no exclusiveness could be found in it. But what Jesus cannot tell his judges is that the only ones affected by his teaching were those in whom the stirrings of love already existed. He cannot show them that the absence of love blocks off all access to his teaching. The high priest would never understand that; he sees in the teaching only a system of thought that speaks to reason: reason accepts it if it shows itself to be sufficiently convincing and rejects it if it turns out to be too weakly argued. That a teaching might, with respect to its persuasiveness, depend upon something other than understanding would seem to him an offense against every principle of human knowledge.

The Lord has *taught in synagogues and in the Temple, where all Jews come together.* He has spoken where the Jews are accustomed to widening their knowledge, in the place that is designated for that and is accessible to all. *Secretly* he has *said nothing:* everything was presented to everyone. He has proclaimed no esoteric teaching. He has not taught in one way to a certain group of men and in a different way to another. He has not expounded partial truths to the world in order to reserve the entire truth for a select circle. In all his words, he has presented the whole truth and always attempted to reach everyone with it. His talks to the people were marked by just as little of accommodation or concession as those to the disciples. Behind his speeches there is no other truth that has to be uncovered. Everyone who wishes—that is, everyone who loves—can find the truth in each of his words. If the high priest had been present at the sermon, he could have gained enlightenment about the whole spirit of the new teaching.

Although the Lord has said nothing secretly, although in Catholicism there is no secret teaching behind the one openly taught, everything in this teaching is still extremely secret. Although nothing is concealed, much remains hidden to an understanding without love; what such an understanding sees as limited shows itself only through love in its true unlimitedness. What understanding is able to hear it finds acceptable; but if love is added, all the bounds of truth are shifted outward. The innermost secret of the Catholic, the secret of the always-more, cannot be tied down by mere understanding. When the Lord states that he has said nothing secretly, he thereby leaves what the high priest has grasped— the unity of his teaching and his disciples—with a real meaning. It is just that the high priest does not understand that meaning. The secret of the Lord lies precisely in the fact that understanding and love, teaching and life, become a unity in him. He has no other secret. Catholics are accused of projecting a lot of things as "secrets" into the word of God, but they really just interpret that in love. To the sense of love, all the secrets of the Incarnation—the secrets of the Holy Spirit, the Mother, the Lord himself and his love for man—become for the first time really deep and mysterious and thereby, too, infinitely gleanable. Everything that pertains to love is always mysterious; a love that were wholly penetrable by the understanding would no longer be love. And yet this secret of love is an open one and was proclaimed to all men.

18:21. *... Why do you ask me? Ask those who have heard me, what I said to them; they know what I said.*

Upon being arrested, the Lord had detached himself from his followers. Now he places himself, spiritually, in their midst: together with him, they form a communion. He can make reference to them. He sees them in unity with the Father, and himself as bound up with them through devotion to the Father. He sheds, so to speak, the signs of his chosenness. Earlier, there was talk that his teaching had need of men in order to be received. Here, this precept finds its application. The men of whom his teaching had need are actually present. With this reference, the Lord brings home to the high priest just how much the Faith forms a unity. At bottom, it makes no difference which of the faithful stands to account and defends the Faith of the unity.

To be sure, those who have listened to the Lord cannot answer in the way that he can. Their answer will have a personal and human coloring. It will be incomplete because, despite their life of faith, they know very little about the Faith. And what they know is distorted by their sins, encumbered by their prolonged ignorance. Thus this objective indifference regarding which person can answer stands in glaring contrast to the very great difference between the actual answer of the Lord and the answer of his disciples, for example, the answer of Peter or of the other disciple outside the court. And yet the answer of the disciples will later on have the advantage of being limited, rounded off, in a sense adapted to the human understanding of the hearers. Question and answer will unfold on a natural plane, and the extensional element inherent in all the Lord's answers—his openness, his thrust toward the Father, into the eternal, which he never introduces as anything but an incomprehensible perspective—will be absent. When the disciples answer, faith and lack of faith will come up against each other within a much smaller setting, which does not mean that the Lord's grace will not accompany those answers. They will be infinitely narrower than the answer of the Lord, but nevertheless clearer and more readily categorizable for those lacking faith.

Now, the high priest is not merely to question the faithful in general, but about *what I said to them.* The disciples will be able—after a fashion—to recount some of the things that they have heard from the Lord. And what they recount will not be wrong. And nevertheless the judge will understand it wrongly. In the life of the faithful, there is a whole sphere of the supernatural in the grace that becomes perceptible and communicable only to those who themselves have faith or are at least seeking it. Not those who act as judges. The high priest could see the faithful only as the accused. He would concern himself only with dry registration of the facts, and by no means with the deeper, the supernatural motives. An interpretation of the statements given, a tracing back of things to their causes, to the Spirit, to something imponderable, is not to be expected. In the records that are drawn up there is no place for love. Love, however, is the only bond that holds the Lord's teaching together and, in so doing, also explains it. The sphere of the supernatural, which does not exist for the judge because he has no sense for it nor access to it, is a function of love: the love of the Father, the love of the Son and the love of men for them. And the key to this entire sphere is, again, nothing but love. We seek this sphere perhaps out of something groping, formless, unselfconscious—but surely out of love. All the mysteries of Christianity have their living center in this zone of intimacy between God and man; and only he who participates in this life of love can understand something about it. Catholicism is a perpetual commission between the Lord and the Christian, an unfathomable livingness, even if in some points—in the confession of faith, in the sacraments, for example—it appears rigidified in forms. The believer will never be able to explain this life to the judge.

They know what I said. A characteristic saying of the Lord because it can be understood simply, yet contains the opening into the ever-greater. Thus they *know;* they will be able to present the high priest with the Christian answer, with what the Lord has said and what corresponds to the judge's capacity to understand. The disciples' answer could suffice in order to convince him of the correctness of the Lord's teaching. It would be able somehow to lay out the cornerstones of his teaching. But it would not contain something essential: the element of growing unendingness that allows every word of the Lord's, including this plain answer to his judge, to become an answer to the eternal Father. The Father, too, knows and has heard what he has said to his disciples. In every word of the Son's, he has recognized his own word in its infinite truth. This truth is also true on the natural plane, but for the believer it signifies more: the pure expression of love between Father and Son, the unity between them in the Holy Spirit, into which the faithful are drawn, so much so that, when the Lord replies to Annas, *They know what I said,* he simultaneously invites the Father to recognize in the teaching he proclaims the whole of his love, which draws men to itself in such a way that the word is able to come alive in them in its infinite sense.

18:22. *When he had said this, one of the officers standing by struck Jesus with his hand, saying: Is that how you answer the high priest?*

The Lord had spoken, at one and the same time, to the unbelieving Annas, the believing disciples and the loving Father. And the only answer that he receives comes from an unbelieving officer. He receives it not through words, but through being struck in the face. The officer thereby demonstrates that he not only has no idea of the grace of faith but also lacks receptivity to the word of faith. He was unable to attach any meaning to this word, he lacked any access to it. The language with which he replies, for its part, is a language to which the Lord has no access. To be sure, during the cleansing of the Temple, he too had struck out with blows. He had to speak the only language that was understood there; it was absolutely necessary that he carry out his commission, and since every door was barred to love, he had to gain entry by force. Now, by contrast, the language of sin speaks to him, the language that he does not understand. He is treated as if he deserved, because of his word, nothing other than blows. Unbelief does not even give the judge a chance to pronounce a verdict; it punishes before it even understands, indeed, in order to deprive itself of the possibility of understanding, in order not to run the risk of having to understand, in order not to feel the slightest desire to guess at the Lord's teaching from afar. It is pure unbelief, pure sin, that defends itself, in its way, against everything that calls its rule into question. It is the most direct answer that sin can give to the most concrete utterance of love.

The officer accompanies his action with words that simultaneously express his contempt for the Lord and his obsequiousness toward the high priest. He serves the one who pays him through a precisely defined and agreed sort of work. If Annas had evidenced the slightest interest in the Lord's teaching, then the officer's reply would have been adapted accordingly. Thus is the law of sin: unbelief gives birth to unbelief, sin calls not merely for new but for stronger sin. There is in sin a certain exaggeratedness. Perhaps the officer is, in himself, no worse than Annas. But he regards his office not as service to an objective cause but as service to particular men whose views he brings to expression. Since the view now in question is unbelief, he serves unbelief and regards his service as a kind of amplification. Not only because, as an officer, he can avail himself of rougher methods, but in order to make things easier—so that the judge can find before him not only someone accused but also someone previously convicted. He sharpens the positions of both the Lord and the judge. He places the Lord in the light of an accused person defending himself, whereas in fact the Lord only adapts to the passivity of his commission and defends himself with the sole weapon available to him through his relationship to the Father: with love.

18:23. *Jesus answered him: If I have spoken wrongly, bear witness to the wrong; but if I have spoken rightly, why do you strike me?*

Jesus raises the question of whether he has answered rightly or wrongly. The answer that he expects to this question is that of unbelief. His concern is to hear this answer. In that way, he would like to force the one who struck him to take a position. He would like to hear what unbelief can find wrong in his answer. Unbelief would then have to defend the wrong, justify its action, and this would give the Lord an opportunity to catch hold. When giving its justification, unbelief would have to use words and expressions that would, in turn, require a response from the Lord. Unbelief would have to expose itself, reveal a weak point, not just—as in striking a blow—cover itself up. And thus a conversation would arise. Perhaps the officer would be forced to admit that the Lord had spoken nothing wrongly. The radiantly Christian thing that he said was audible only to God. But what unbelief was capable of hearing was at least this: that it was a right answer. If the one who had struck the blow were freed of his obsequiousness, he would be more open to this outward truth. He would have to justify his unbelief from a new standpoint and thereby display his ignorance. His turning away from part of his sin would contain the possibility of a turning toward the Lord. Thus the Lord would like to bring him into the position of a penitent. He does not yet demand remorse of him, since this is first mediated by the Lord through his suffering. What he can demand now is the recognition of sin.

18:24. *Annas then sent him bound to Caiaphas, the high priest.*

The Lord is still bound. But, since being shackled, his situation has worsened and become more acute—he was struck in the face, and no one stood by him. Through the personal sin of the officer, his shackling has now, as it were, acquired a personal note. It becomes clear that he will take the Cross upon himself not just for sin and sinners in general, but for the individual sin and the individual sinner. It is this individual that binds him more firmly. And thus the individual, too, becomes more firmly bound; he is obligated to concern himself personally with the Lord's bonds. The more it is shown that the Lord suffers for the individual, the more the individual's responsibility for the Lord's being more bound comes to the fore.

And the more that men take part in the judging of the Lord, the more it can also be seen that the Lord's commission regarding the individual becomes more personal. It is as if the Lord had previously concerned himself mainly with mankind or with the representatives of mankind or with some group of men, so that the Cross appeared as the bearing of a nameless totality of sins. Only now can it be seen how the individual sin renders his fate more difficult. Thus we, too, must not rest content with a general, summary confession of sin, as though our sins were only a fleeting impulse within the sum total of the sins of the world. We are obligated to view them individually, to repent, to confess and also to give them over to the Lord individually. We must realize that it is precisely through the individual sin that we make the path of his suffering more difficult. Even sins that we committed earlier, perhaps without knowing that we personally offended the Lord through them, we should give over to his suffering in this way. Even if we would like to withhold such sins from him, they belong to him as Redeemer, and we must surrender them up to him. Whoever turns toward the Lord and is converted from his previous way of living possesses nothing of his own anymore, not even the sins he has committed. There is a dimension to the Lord's suffering that corresponds to precisely these sins, and the convert must take in the entire, the undivided response of the Lord. Catholic love of the Lord is so universal that it lays claim to everything in us, even to what seems to have been most our own. The person confessing must, however, explicitly know that his sin (like the officer's blow to the face) increases the Lord's suffering. Otherwise, he could not allow the Lord to give him a personal response to his sin. And the Lord wants to respond in love, personally. Therefore confession must never remain merely schematic. No sinner must make confession as if everyone committed similar sins, as if he were just one number in an infinite sum. He must not clothe his sins in abstract, concealing formulas, he must bare himself personally, in order to hear the personal word of love that enwraps him in redeeming grace.

18:25. *Now Simon Peter was standing and warming himself. They said to him: Are you not also one of his disciples? He denied it and said: I am not.*

Peter is occupied with looking after his bodily well-being. Amidst this activity the question is put to him. It finds him unprepared, in a state of lowly everydayness, but not in unbelief. He answers with a No, as if neither the question nor belief were of any concern to him. He answers as if he were not a representative of the Church but an uninvolved bystander, who is not interested in the Lord and, above all, not willing to do the slightest thing for the Lord. And yet he knows what the truth is, what belief means to him, how much, therefore, he would be obligated, in belief, above and beyond his own person. At the first opportunity that presents itself to him, he denies him, and in fact while warming himself, as if he saw in the question nothing but a disturbance of his momentary comfort.

The Lord is now like someone who collects all the sins that he comes across; he ties them into a bundle. He endures both the blow of the officer, the unbeliever, and the blow of Peter, the believer. Both of these sin in accordance with their personal incapacity and lack of understanding: the one from a distance, the other from a closeness; the one evades any encounter, the other denies him whom he has long since encountered; the one has not yet experienced anything of supernatural love, the other, as much as a man can experience. Thus both together embody two extremes, they form a framework into which the sins of all the others can be fitted: the officer's not wanting to know and Peter's knowing denial embrace all the possibilities of sinning against the Lord, against his love, his Spirit, his mission, against belonging to the Lord. Both affect him where he is most sensitive; both strike him, both bind him more strongly to suffering. The officer inflicts bodily harm upon the Lord, while Peter warms himself and, denying the Lord, pursues his own comfort. Both of them do not trouble themselves about the meaning of the bodily, which ought to be an experience of the spiritual.

18:26–27a. *One of the servants of the high priest, a kinsman of the man whose ear Peter had cut off, asked: Did I not see you in the garden with him? Peter again denied it; . . .*

This time the question becomes more precise: Peter has been seen with the Lord. If he denies it yet again, he does so against all the evidence. He has been seen, and he has been given to understand this in an unmistakable way. His having denied it twice has not proved convincing, and thus the range of possible ways out for Peter grows continually narrower. In having to answer a third time, he is caught in a blind alley. Now he is even reminded that he was present in the garden, that he had taken part in the Lord's walks and conversations.

How many memories might have been able to rise up in him. But once again, he denies it. He places himself outside of grace's sphere of influence in order not to be touched by it. He attempts to tear everything out of his heart that reminds him of the Lord's grace.

He does this as the disciple who has personally experienced the Lord's love. But did he really know what it means to be loved by the Lord? He had allowed that love to come to him, had somehow esteemed it, had even enjoyed a sense of well-being in it. And now, when an opportunity of relinquishing it presents itself, he willingly seizes that chance. It is almost as if he feels that this love had kept him under guardianship, that it had restricted him and hindered him in his personal freedom, that the paths he trod in the company of the Lord had not been his own paths. It was all right with him when the love of the Lord expended itself on him; expending himself in the love of the Lord, however, he does not want to do. Now, at the mention of the garden, it seems to him that he had felt, even if unadmittedly, a little out of place in the Lord's company. He would like to be himself again. He shakes off the cloak of love—with the same feelings as those of a priest who has lived wholly enwrapped in the love of the Lord, and who now denies him and seeks to escape from that love.

But Peter still has his office. He has it as a promise about which he knows only that it will grow in him. In this office, too, he feels uncomfortable. This Church is something so vague, so incomprehensible! She is still so far away! There will be time later on to fill the office. Peter surely knows, in his heart of hearts, that the Lord and the Church form a unity. And the Lord is endangered, so his Church must also be. But just as he does not stand by the Lord, so, too, he does not stand by his ecclesiastical office. He abandons them both at the same time. His earlier love strikes him as a kind of sentimental attachment, his denial is a cold calculation of the understanding. Both belong together; both are expressions of the essential lack of love. In both cases, Peter has not understood that the love and the office are not his affairs, but those of the Lord.

He freely places himself outside of grace. He denies grace, even though he is acquainted with it. He pronounces this No in his own name, even though his own name no longer belongs to him but is surety for the Church. He should have no right of disposal over this name and over the Church; he ought not to fling Christianity, like an inert mass, back and forth, now away from and now toward the Lord as he deems fit. He ought to be the representative of the Church as commissioned by the Lord. He should be the disciple who enlists support for the Lord. As commissioned by the Lord, he ought to be his closest and most immediate companion. Three times he has been inundated with grace: as man, as disciple and as representative of the Church. Three times he has disowned the Lord; he denies the grace in these three kinds of being.

And yet the denying Peter stands within the greater love of the Lord. He shakes it off, yet is inundated anew, again and again, by that greater love. He distances himself from the Cross and is only drawn more deeply into the Cross. He is trapped in the love of the Lord — and that is perhaps not the least thing that embitters him. He has faith, and within faith he denies faith. Faith has placed him in an impossible position; he defends himself against this tooth and nail. He perceives the fiasco of the Lord and, as inseparable from that, the fiasco of the Church. Not the Lord alone, but also the Church, stands rejected, stands separated from the mass of the people. But what use is all the love of the Lord if it causes Peter to lose the friendship of the people? How is he to be able to found a Church when faced with rejectedness? He feels that too much is being asked of him, that he is not adequate to his office, to his mission, to himself. As long as he had not encountered the Lord, his life was simple and viewable as a whole; now any such view has been lost because he has been one of the delegates and the larger view has passed to the Lord. As long as the Lord was free, Peter was able to look up to him in admiration, and something of his magnificence streamed over onto him, the disciple. He felt himself elevated; he almost saw himself more as the companion of the Lord than as his servant. Now the Master, whom he had recognized as the Son of God, the Liberator, is bound, dragged unresistingly before the court, struck in the face by an underling. All of his magnificence collapses into itself. He has nothing more with which he might be able to impress Peter. And so the latter's new faith, which was based on the Lord's magnificence, wanes and falls away. The faith of Peter and the freedom of the Lord belonged together as result and condition. Now it seems to Peter that his faith has been a mistake. It is impossible that the Free One could be unfree, impossible that the Son of God could be bound. Thus he is quick to divest himself of his faith and his commission. He longs to return to his normal former life, he would like to submerge himself in the ignorant mass of the people, to shake off all that which he now feels to be only shackles.

Peter is the symbol of weakness thrown back on its own resources. Having scarcely just been left alone, he already falls. In him, the Lord sees how great the measure of his suffering will be, since even his loyal followers know no loyalty. In him, he sees how the Church will look when she forgets the Lord. And in turn: she would remain as foolish and vulnerable if the Lord were not to keep rescuing her anew from her confusion.

18:27b *... and at once the cock crowed.*

In all these events a prophecy of the Lord is fulfilled. Peter is reminded of this—first, of the prophecy itself. His faith receives a new impetus, the faith that he had forgotten in denying the Lord. It seemed to him that faith and the Lord were two quite different things; it was not clear to him how much his turning away from the Lord was simultaneously a denial of his faith. He had, to be sure, a consciousness of betrayal; in his eyes, he had disowned a man, a friend, perhaps a leader. But not God, not his faith. And suddenly, as the cock crows, as the Lord's prophecy is fulfilled, he sees that the Lord and his faith are one. That the Lord was not only the bestower of that faith, but also its living centerpoint. That the power of the faith is substantially rooted in the person of the Lord. He has therefore not only denied a man but also an objective concern—the concern of his life, his faith. And that he has denied his faith he notices only when his faith receives new sustenance and comes alive again. It is as if, at that moment, the love of the Lord streams over him anew, and he also now realizes that that faith and love are one and that their unity lies in the Lord. And thus, too, that he has betrayed his office, since others stand behind him, those who were to believe through him, believers whom he ought to have represented and whom he has left in the lurch by his betrayal. What he had so far not really understood, what was in him as if latently, he now becomes clearly conscious of: his faith is no longer a personal matter, it is inseparable from the faith of others. He, Peter, is obligated to believe for others as well; he belongs not only to the Lord but just as much to the communion; thus he has turned his back not only on the Lord, but just as much on the communion. He understands that he is not at all an individual anymore, but the man of a universality in the Lord, bound and obligated in both directions. His oneness in the Lord will never again give him the opportunity of living as an individual. He is someone who no longer has any private rights. What he does, what he says, what he commands is of interest not only to him—and perhaps to him least of all—but to the Lord and to the communion. In that all these things surface and become indubitably clear at this moment, the crowing of the cock contains the grounding of the infallibility of the popes. Here the decision is made, here Peter is sacrificed for once and for all. Henceforth, betrayal will be prevented at the decisive juncture; through the Lord, Peter will be supported when he is in danger of falling away, his deficiencies will be made good before they can take effect. In the meantime, he possesses only the promise of his office, he has still not been finally installed; that can occur only after he has really understood what he is outside of the office, as a person: the relapsing sinner. But even as such, he already stands at the point of intersection between the Lord and the Church, there where he is nothing more than the Lord's spokesman to the Church and the Church's spokesman to the Lord. Now, however, he stands at this point as a betrayer: so that it might become obvious how much the Church as a whole is drawn into the suffering of the Lord, how much she has need, as a whole, of suffering, how she can hardly stand next to this suffering and remain uninvolved. And precisely through this betrayal at her summit, she is now in fact so drawn in that she can later emerge as purified and infallible at her summit. If Peter did not know what he did in his act of betrayal, then he needed to become aware, through remorse, of what he had done so as to know from then on that he lives solely from the Lord's grace. With the blow by the officer, it became clear that the Lord suffers for every individual. With the blow by Peter, the Catholic becomes clear: that he suffers in the individual for the Church as a whole. The officer, as an unbeliever, has no mission, and thus he is left only with his personal sin. Peter is the representative of the Church, as is every believing Christian along with him. The more the Church is a part of an individual's role, the broader are the potential consequences of his behavior. Peter no longer has access to a private life.

THE QUESTIONING BY PILATE

18:28. *Then they led Jesus from the house of Caiaphas to the praetorium. It was early morning. They themselves did not enter the praetorium, so that they might not be defiled, but might eat the Passover.*

The Jews accompany the Lord on every step of the path marked out for him. In so doing, they become participants in his Passion even though they have absolutely no knowledge of the essence of his suffering nor of how deeply each person walking this path becomes obligated to the Lord. Without knowing it, they are thus doing two things: in their unbelief, they do what they find right in human terms and—each individual personally as well as all of them together—deliver the Lord over. Through their unbelief, they bring about the Cross of the Lord and fulfill the measure of his suffering. And in making full the measure of their sin, they secure for themselves redemption. It is as if they have been struck by blindness: they stand directly before the greatest thing that God does for them, yet are all the while completely unsuspecting. What comes to pass is the opposite of what they want, and this is the miracle of grace. They are led by grace to precisely the place where they do not want to go at any price: to redemption, which is brought about through the Cross. In doing everything that is in their power to harm the Lord, they save themselves in the Lord. They lead him to judgment in their blind sense of justice, and they thereby fulfill the justice of God, which becomes for them grace.

They lead him to the praetorium. They will not try him themselves, but the steps they take lead him to judgment. They are the precursors of his judgment. And the Lord allows himself to be led, for his hour has come. Had it not come, he would, as before, stay out of their way. Now he follows after them, step by step, and every step leads him more deeply into suffering. With every step, it keeps mounting up. Every person whom he meets and who, as a sinner, is against him is someone for whom he will suffer. Every action that is not faith is an action that he takes upon himself. When he was taken prisoner, he saw his coming suffering as a sum total and affirmed it as a whole. Now its content becomes more and more differentiated, he has to run up against every individual sin, take it upon himself. At first the burden was a formless one; now he begins to feel the effect of every individual sin, its special weight, its qualitatively unique effect. And now, precisely as individual and different, the sins begin to mount up to infinity. They encircle him more and more, they press in toward him, they are the only reality, while the Father becomes constantly more distant and pallid.

It was early morning, the dawning of a new day. This day will have long hours and minutes, and each of them will increase the suffering, will bring sin nearer and make God more distant. For the crowd, it is just one day among others; they have their plans for today and for them life goes on after his death, their thoughts are on the coming festival. For the Lord, this early morning is the dawning of the inevitable. They find themselves with all of their projects for this day and for the following days. He finds himself with nothing other than this day. He will plan the course of no further day, he will have no further time to make use of. Even his day is already an arranged, a passive day. His day will be whatever sin makes of it. For him, there is no more time to organize, but only the time of suffering: his hour has come.

They themselves did not enter the praetorium, so that they might not be defiled. They keep the law; they know how to distinguish right from wrong. What happens meanwhile to the Lord is a matter of sheer indifference to them. They think about their own festival, but do not think about his. In their eyes, they remain pure, and by that they distance themselves yet again from him. That he becomes impure they do not consider, that does not matter to them. At this specified time, they have set their minds upon celebrating their Passover. His Passover and his suffering are without time, but through this timeless time he returns to the Father. They see their Passover in exact detail; he sees nothing more because he has also given this sight back to the Father. They eat the Paschal meal; he is slaughtered as the Paschal Lamb.

18:29. *So Pilate went out to them and said: What accusation do you bring against this man?*

Pilate, who holds the office of judge and thus stands above the Jews, goes out to them and asks about the substance of their accusation. By so doing, he almost forestalls the movement for the accusing and bringing of the Lord before the judge, in that he comes forth to meet those involved. He takes this action so that the Jews will not need to break their law. Implicit in this is both a confirmation and a forestalling of their law. He confirms it insofar as it is good: they ought not to defile themselves. He forestalls it insofar as it is bad, insofar as they falsely accuse the Lord in the name of their law. He checks the course of their intended prosecution and asks about its justification. He occupies a kind of neutral position in which he respects the Old Law and takes no steps against its representatives, but also wants to allow the new law and its representatives their due.

But the Lord stands bound before him. As such, he is, so to speak, in a state of suspension, on a thin edge between the Old Law, which is administered by unjust people, and a sort of law that apparently has yet to be broadly institutionalized. In this situation, he is bound by his affirmation to the Father, which has perhaps never been so strongly at one with the affirmation of the Mother as at this precise moment. Is not her situation the same? The Lord as poised between the just Old Law which is, however, unjustly administered and a new one which is intimated by Pilate's question and concerning which nothing is yet known of what it will bring. The Mother in her affirmation as poised between the earthly law of motherhood, which is, however, not applied in an earthly sense, but seems open and suspended in anticipation, and a new law that she does not yet know and cannot comprehend. The Lord as bound by his affirmation to the Father, which arose from complete love and is now drawn into the passivity of suffering. It becomes constantly more burdensome, constantly more difficult to say Yes. The Mother as bound to the pregnancy in which she is at the mercy of an ongoing fate; bound up in her flesh, passive like every pregnant woman, with an openness to the mystery that she does not grasp but that she has nevertheless accepted. The Lord, too, as bound in body, passive as every person in fetters is passive, and yet, in this situation, forsaking his suffering as a merely natural catastrophe in order to place himself knowingly and personally at the disposal of every personal sin. The Mother, for her

43

part, in her pregnancy, forsaking the natural course of conception, the knowledge of the human father, in order to allow herself to be isolated personally within the extraordinary. Both forgo the anonymity of the universally human. The Mother takes upon herself the exceptionality of this uniquely divine chosenness: she conceives *this* Son; and this Son, yet again, takes upon himself the quite exceptional thing that he owes to his Mother: the uniquely human. In this having been singled out, which isolates and binds them both, they both become ready for the Passion. On the edge of this affirmation, however, each and every Christian affirmation ultimately stands: bound between the Old Law, which in one way or another is perverted or suspended, and the incomprehensible, which breaks into it and calls it into question; bound in the spirit toward God and in the body toward the world; more precisely: bound between the affirmation of the Mother toward life and the affirmation of the Son, before Pilate, toward death. The Mother says Yes to life, to God, with everything that is to come and that she does not know. And the Son gives over to God his coming death along with everything incomprehensible that accompanies it. Both give themselves over together to a respectively characteristic destiny into which they become tied. The Mother will give birth, the Son will die, both entrusting God with everything that gives evidence of the happening as with everything comprehensible and calculable about it.

18:30. *They answered him: If this man were not an evildoer, we would not have handed him over.*

The Jews justify themselves in their answer. They answer Pilate's objective question in a highly subjective way. They want to vindicate themselves and their deed, and, in fact, to do so under the assumption that the Lord's guilt is proven by their very act of delivering him up. What they cannot understand about him amounts, for them, to his having been convicted of guilt already. It produces in them a sense of discomfort, and they make a leap from this to talk of proven guilt. The unease that they feel is the gap between the Old and the New Covenant, but they do not want to admit to that unease; they project it upon the Lord, as guilt, and thus distance themselves as much from the Old as from the New Covenant. They withdraw to a place that is outside of any law and is located only within themselves. They barricade themselves in and reject everything that they have not brought with them to the precise place where they stand. They render themselves inaccessible not only to the Lord—they have been that to him for long—but also to the Old Law, which had its sense of justice, and to Pilate, who wants to act as mediator. They have arrived at a place where nothing but one's own ego can still thrive. They fence themselves off from all objectivity; they posit themselves as at once both cause and effect; they assume that the outer is the same as the inner, whether when accepting or resisting. They commit themselves voluntarily to their own prison, they disengage themselves from everything around them, even from themselves, their inner objectivity. This, too, is incarcerated. They spurn not only general, universally binding truth, but also inner, personal truth. Thus they end up outside of any kind of truth.

They are not unrelated to the denying Peter. Both he and they deny all that went before in order to close themselves wholly to it. Peter claims not to know the Lord. The Jews want nothing more to do with him. Peter is asked whether he is one of Christ's disciples, and he would have had the opportunity to reply with something positive. The Jews are asked what they can say by way of accusation, and they would also have had the opportunity to describe the happening and its context objectively. Both, however, are so caught up in themselves that, at the time, they want nothing other than an end to their relations with the Lord, and must consequently set up their own ego as the universally valid.

The answer given by the Jews emphasizes not only the Lord's guilt but also their knowledge of his guilt. It is not possible that they would hand over anyone who is not an evildoer. They can distinguish precisely between good and evil, between those who are to be condemned and those who are not. They grant to themselves this sort of instinct for justice. Their decision has been taken, there is nothing more to be said about it. Whatever Pilate might decide, their standpoint is unalterable. Pilate ought to realize that. He should not confuse them with such as are not sure of their case. They have their certainty, and in fact in the only correct place: in themselves.

18:31. *Pilate said to them: Take him yourselves and judge him by your own law. The Jews said to him: It is not lawful for us to put any man to death.*

Pilate gives the Lord back before having received him. He wants to have nothing to do with the matter. He does not want to handle precisely this case. He sees in the Lord not only the man, but also the teaching; and he would like to give the teaching back untouched. Not only as a judge does he not want to bear responsibility in relation to the Lord, but also as a man he does not want to be disquieted by the teaching. He sees no other means of achieving this than those of giving back, pushing aside, adjourning without passing judgment. In this, Pilate is a symbol of most people, whether unbelievers or believers. At a decisive moment, they all affect a cool indifference, a wait-and-see attitude. Unbelief discerns in the new teaching something dangerous, which could damage it because it could cause certain firmly fixed assumptions to totter. That would be unpleasant. Everything is all right the way it is; anything new is unwanted and will be rejected so that indifference can abide in its quietude. Weak faith pushes the new teaching aside in order not to have to transform itself into strong faith. For it, too, the Lord is all right the way he is; it, too, desires above all not to be shaken in its equanimity. Regarding everything that presents itself, it wants to make the decision itself, and does so by passing the decision back to the Lord and waiting. This faith will not withhold itself fully from the sacramental life of the Church; it will receive baptism and the last rites, and in the intervening time do what is most necessary to stay protected. For it knows its weakness and needs its supports; it loves to have the variations in the mood of life played out within a steadfast framework. But from this no surprises are wanted. One has done enough when one has demonstrated a certain abiding good will for the institutions of the Church. But every time that a sudden decision is required, things are adjourned. One is neither for nor against. Risking a decision would perhaps require more than one is, for the time being, willing to give. Everything should take its course within the legal framework. Thus Pilate makes the suggestion: *Judge him by your own law.*

The Jews, however, reply: *It is not lawful for us to put any man to death.* They, too, want to stay within their law. What they say shows this. At the same time, they accuse the Lord of having placed himself outside of their law. He must die because, according to his own words, he has come to expand their law, to give it new life, to break it open. But he must also die because they themselves, as personalities, want no part of him. The standpoint that they adopt is supported from both these sides at once: from the law and from their personal judgment. It cannot be said that they distort the law here; but they are thankful that it can be adapted to suit their personal will. They keep the law, but they fill its shell with an alien spirit. The spirit of the law is Christ, but they do not want to free that spirit from the shell. They have correctly recognized one thing: the spirit of the Lord and the mere shell of the Old Law are not compatible with each other. The Lord does not adapt himself to the mere shell; he always offers his whole truth. In each instance, it is clear in his word that his truth is greater in the Father than in his word, because although his word is no doubt there to be understood and accepted by men, it embodies at the same time the will of the Father, which is so great that it cannot be taken in other than by man's giving up his own standpoint and entering wholly into God's word. If man hears an earthly word, then he is the hearer and the one who takes in; if he hears God's word, then he is taken in by God's Word, assuming that he surrenders himself to it. He lives in the Word; he dies in himself in order to live in the Word. This is the thing that the Jews want to avoid at any cost.

18:32. *This was to fulfill the word which Jesus had spoken to show by what death he was to die.*

He had foretold that he would die a violent death at the hands of man. But that is possible only if the Gentiles kill him, since it is forbidden the Jews to kill. The prophecy must be fulfilled, and indeed, for the sake of the Father. It is the greatest pain that one could inflict on the Father: the killing of the Son; but in dying, the Son shows such love for the Father that it outweighs even that pain. It is almost as if the Son, in his journey through the world, provokes an infinite intensification of the ignominy that can be heaped upon the Father just to demonstrate how suprainfinite his love for the Father is: it outweighs even the greatest ignominy. Where the ignominy that the world heaps upon God reaches its peak, there, too, the love of the Son for the Father—and, with that, the Father's glorification—reaches its perfection. Where the Father in his pain is affected most sensitively, there the Son takes every pain away from him. After men have killed the Son, the Father has become richer in love; for his created realm is restored to him through the greater love of the Son.

The prophecy must also be fulfilled for its own sake, because the word of the Son is the word of the Father. It is an ultimate form of obedience on behalf of the Son to allow himself to be killed in order that this word of prophecy, as the Father's word, might not be thwarted. At the same time, it is an acknowledgment of the entire Old Covenant, which is the word of the Father: in this way, the old and the new word, the word of the Father and the word of the Son, are made to coincide. Both words are one and the same Word, which was in the beginning with God. It had been conclusively demonstrated to men that it was the voice of God that had spoken in the Old as in the New Covenant. An equation is made manifest: On the one side, God, who, in his bosom, carries the Son in himself, the law and the promise of the Son; on the other side, God as distinct from the incarnated Son, the New Covenant, and the Son who, as dwelling in the world, fulfills the promise. The two sides are in balance.

18:33. *Pilate entered the praetorium again and called Jesus, and said to him: Are you the King of the Jews?*

Pilate has to make a preliminary decision and must thus concern himself with Jesus. He begins with a question. The question seeks an answer. The question signifies some progress in Pilate's behavior insofar as he now reconciles himself to what cannot be altered. At the same time, it is a regress because he involves himself with Jesus as with a mere "case" that he has to look into. Before that, he refused so as not to have to take part in the matter. Now he involves himself by deciding to assess the matter only as a case, that is, not to take any internal part in it.

He begins, not with any part of the teaching, but thrusts immediately into the center: *Are you the King of the Jews?* At the moment when the Lord is being handed over and completely denied by the Jews, Pilate nevertheless asks him if he rules over them. He is aware that, if Jesus were really their king, his relationship with God would be a very close one. Only someone who came from God could be King of the Jews. With this question, Pilate meets the Lord halfway. He gives him the opportunity for a centrally relevant answer. Within his question, two other questions really lie hidden: Is this man an imposter or not? and: Could God really have become man? Has God finally revealed himself in a living, immediately present form? In this one question, Pilate has addressed Christ as man and the Christian teaching as revelation. In his question, there is the same dualism that also expresses itself in his attitude: to reserve his personal opinion and nevertheless to perform his official duty. What is official in him will pass a judgment; what is living will stand to one side. Regarding the Lord, he moves toward the concrete by conjoining him as a living man with his office as Messiah and fulfiller of God's word. Regarding himself, he moves toward the abstract by distinguishing himself as a living man from his office as judge. He does two things at once so that he can somehow back away from the demands of both. He thinks that he is adding while in truth he is subtracting. He grasps for unity and wants to evade it. He judges by withdrawing himself from judgment. He questions the Lord by tying him down on both sides and slipping his own head out of the noose.

18:34. Jesus answered: Do you say this of your own accord, or did others say it to you about me?

Jesus answers Pilate's equivocally intended question with a two-fold question which, however, is completely unequivocal. With this question, he wants to give Pilate the opportunity to take a clear position. *Do you say this of your own accord* means: Do you have a presentiment of grace? Does Pilate intuit, although he has not previously known the Lord, something unique in him? Does he notice that he is greater than all the men he has previously encountered, that he could be a king? *Or did others say it to you about me?* Is Pilate relying only on public opinion, whether in the sense of dismissal: he cannot be a king, or in the sense of admiration: he would have what it takes to be a king? Seen from the outside, there is nothing in Pilate's question to indicate whether a personally-held position is behind it or whether it is just a repetition of what everyone else says.

These two possibilities, which are so close to one another, the Lord would like to see precisely separated.

The Lord's question goes out to all Christians who have been somehow affected by grace, and presage, intuit, know certain things simply because they live in closeness to the Lord. These should and must differ from the others who know about the realities of grace only by hearsay, who take up and pass on what is Christian only as accepted opinion, and pass it on in such a way that one never knows exactly whether what they say is their own or someone else's. If it is their own, it is living faith; they would then possess the will to devotion. If it is someone else's, they would possess only a qualified faith without the will to devotion. The question goes out to each one: Have you opened yourself to grace or only to hearsay? If someone really believes, then he has unlocked himself to grace as a power that immediately becomes stronger in the soul than one's own ego. If he does not really believe, then he is attempting to keep his belief in reserve; however, it dries up instantly because it is not rooted in the living soul. Belief has a right of asylum in man; if it is not taken in, it must waste away. It wants to be taken in as one who immediately possesses all rights in the soul and makes use of them because it wants to lead the whole soul to God. That is what that the Lord is asking Pilate.

18:35. *Pilate answered: Am I a Jew? Your own nation and the chief priests have handed you over to me; what have you done?*

Am I a Jew? means here: Do you regard me as capable of sensing your grace? Do you believe that you can be anything other than an average man in my eyes? If you were King of the Jews, then I would have to assume that others had chosen you to be king or that you have set yourself up over them. The possibility that I might be receptive to your teaching does not exist. In making this rejection, Pilate sees something that the Jews have perhaps never seen: that the Lord's teaching, if it were correct, would have to imply an expanding of the Old Covenant. He sees stages. He sees that Judaism could contain within itself the possibility of further development through a New Covenant. He sees the whole objectively. But he does not himself belong to the Jews and is therefore relieved of any obligation to come to terms with the Lord as the representative of the new or expanded faith.

In order to make clear at once that although he recognizes this possibility he does not believe in it, he adds: *Your own nation and the chief priests have handed you over to me:* those, namely, who would have to stand by you do not want anything to do with you. It follows that they have not set you up as their king. You are given no recognition by them. The chief priests, who know the law, disown you; the people, who stand behind you, hand you over as well. *What have you done?* There must be some reason for their handing you over; you must have angered them if they reject you so sharply and conclusively. The answer that Pilate expects is a reference to some evident and defined act that could be an appropriate object of legal judgment. An act that could be dealt with in terms of the judicial legal system. In reality, he knows that no such act is involved here, that much more is at issue than some limited deed, namely, an attitude of mind, or even more, a claim that could only be corroborated in the Lord: that he is the Son of God. He knows that it is not a matter of external and worldly things, but that, instead, everything culminates in this astounding statement. With his question, he attempts to back away from that fact. He does not want to be drawn into these Jewish concerns; he wants to be no disciple, to examine no didactic sayings and to advance no opposing teaching. He desires some clear deed. This he could analyze, judge and, if necessary, condemn. Then he would be spared the need for any inner deliberation.

18:36. *Jesus answered: My Kingdom is not of this world; if my Kingdom were of this world, my servants would fight, that I might not be handed over to the Jews; but my Kingdom is not now of the world.*

So the Lord has a kingdom. He stands by that. It is his Father's Kingdom, the Kingdom of love. To those who do not believe, who do not love, this Kingdom is fully closed. Only through love, which contains in itself belief, is its gate thrown open. His Kingdom encloses the whole of love, the whole of faith, and is itself enclosed by the Father. It is a Kingdom in the Father, a Kingdom without borders because the borders of the Kingdom and the borders of the Father reach out together into the same unendingness. And yet it is a

Kingdom with a definite form; for it is the Kingdom of the Son within the Father. He, the Son, knows it. He sees his Kingdom as a whole, which remains unseeable as such to all others. He alone can, in the Father, survey and encompass it. But even if no one else sees it as a whole, anyone who possesses love can nevertheless find the way to it. He is taken into the Kingdom in such a way as to become himself a part of the Kingdom, not just as one that has a function in the Kingdom but as a part of the Kingdom itself, which is love. Love, if it is to be living, must be lived out; it cannot just hover above men and outside of them. It must, if it is to be love, dwell within them. In the Kingdom of love, love is the power; and it would be powerless if it found none to embody it. When, however, it has found such, then they are not the carriers of power, not the cratophors, not the representatives of love; they do not resolve love into themselves but, vice versa, love resolves them into itself.

This Kingdom is in God, in heaven, in eternity. *It is not of this world.* It is, however, the Kingdom of the Son, because the Son brings with him into this Kingdom the gift of the world, the world as redeemed by him. No sinner can enter this Kingdom, but only the beloved, who live in love and at the same time are lovers who keep love alive. It is the Kingdom of the Son because the Son has founded it through his love in the Father. The Father had created this earthly world; but it was not his own world, it was not heaven. It fell away into sin. Then came the Son who, through his love, was to give the Father's world back to him, not just as it was before, as the old earthly world — rather, he brought it back to him as a new world. As a world of love, which he transferred from the world into heaven, into the Father. The love that he gave to the world, and through which he turned creatures into millions of lovers, was his own love, which came from heaven and now, in the world and with the world, returns to heaven. The Son possesses, as it were, a twofold love and devotedness: one, when he devoted himself in eternity to the Father and made himself available for the world's redemption, and in which, as it were, he remains silent about the fact that the other love, which he will bring back to the Father from the world, will once again be his, the Son's, love. In this devotedness to the world, he has filled all beings with his love of the Father and thus brings them home together with his own love. In his remaining silent lies the ultimate mystery of the love that suppresses nothing but does not state everything, because not everything needs to be stated and because all love wants to surprise through unsuspected love. In love, there always remains a residuum that is not articulated, precisely because love gives itself wholly. It does not say everything: what it attempts, what it suffers, what it strives for; it conceals its pains in order to present the beloved with nothing but the peaks, the fruits and joys of love. The Cross of the Lord, too, is one of his secrets; he takes it wholly upon himself in order to transmit only the fruits of it to God and men.

Whoever lives in love lives in the Kingdom of the Lord, even if he lives on this earth. To those who do not have love, his Kingdom remains concealed, even if they see its eternal contours. They do not understand how Christians are able to live on earth as if they paid no heed to the laws of this world. Their faith, their prayer and penance are incomprehensible to them. They see in it a strange quirk which they judge no differently from those other eccentricities of men that they ultimately tolerate in a good-natured or smiling way. They have no idea of the Kingdom of the Lord in which Christians live. For only in faith do those gain entry to the Kingdom, even though they live in this world which is not the Kingdom of the Lord. And even to them, the largest part of their life in this Kingdom remains concealed. If a Christian prays in church before the tabernacle, he knows in faith that the Lord is present. He places himself with his concerns before the Lord. He prays to him or contemplates one of his mysteries. He believes that he knows what he is doing. But what he does is nevertheless not of this world; he does not comprehend what happens. He is like a blind man taking a stroll in the sun; he assumes that the landscape around him is wonderful; he supposes this on the basis of a mysterious feeling. He has no reason to doubt the truth of what people tell him; he even feels the warming sunshine. But he sees nothing. He only believes. This is the position of the believer in the midst of the Kingdom. He has no right to want to rescue himself by forsaking this world for the next; for the time being, it is his mission to live in this world, where love does not rule, and to allow the love of the Kingdom to shine into this world without love. If he fulfills that mission, then he will receive the grace that something more of the Lord's Kingdom will exist in this world. And while it increases in this world, it is not the case that it decreases in the other world; rather, it increases in the other world to the same extent that it increases in this world. For the love beyond bears fruit in the love here, and through this the love here opens itself to the love beyond.

My Kingdom is not of this world. But the Kingdom of Christ must *live* in order to exist. Otherwise, it would no longer be a kingdom. The Kingdom in heaven can increase only if it receives augmentation from this world: the Christians on earth must let the seeds of the love of the Lord sprout in themselves and fructify the Kingdom in heaven. Every love is movement and fruitfulness because the love between Father and Son is movement and fruitfulness. The Son comes into the world as a consequence of his movement of love toward the Father and in order, precisely through this movement of coming, to render it fruitful in the world. He sows the seeds of love in it and thereby occasions the blossoming of the Father's Kingdom of love in the world. He carries this world over into the beyond; he effects the blossoming of the world into his Kingdom. He does this by bringing himself and the love of the Father with him from the beyond into this world; for his Kingdom is always there where he and love are. He thus takes down the barriers between this world and the beyond; his Kingdom is everywhere except in sin. Only there where sin and unbelief rule in the world, where he and his love are not accepted, is his Kingdom still not established. The grace that the Lord brings with him is similar to the fruitfulness of the male that can impregnate; but he does not become fruitful in the full sense until his seed is received, carried, and brought to birth. Similarly, the Kingdom of the Lord and his fruitfulness need to become fruitful in the world that receives him and is thus transformed into his Kingdom.

If my Kingdom were of this world, then it would thereby be characterized as having boundaries that were visible to everyone, that could be perceived by the senses and the mind. It would then be a kingdom according to a human plan; in its conception and in its execution, it would be a human work. Its architects and lawgivers would be men, there would exist in it a human court of justice, and that court would perhaps choose, approve or tolerate the Lord as the King of this

Kingdom. Such a kingdom is intrinsically unthinkable. It would dissolve itself on the first day of its existence, because a divine work cannot possibly be founded and directed by men. Thus he does not develop the thought any further, but says only: then *my servants would fight, that I might not be handed over to the Jews.* There would then have been a human system of justice to which he would have had to turn to allow himself to be defended by it. He would, perhaps, have had something like a bodyguard, and it would have done what a body-guard usually does in such circumstances. But he has no such servants because his Kingdom is no worldly one. He gives evidence of the fact that he has no earthly kingdom; he makes no claim to worldly rights, he is not recognized by the world as a king, but is instead handed over as a villain. And yet he has servants. He has a following. But it has not followed him. It consists of a group of men who in part are not present and in part, if they are present, take no steps to defend him or, if they attempt something, do something misguided which he does not support. The unity between the King and his followers consists in the fact that the latter *allow* him to be handed over. That they do nothing to safeguard him. In the eyes of the world, the Lord's disciples distinguish themselves in no way from other men; and yet they are stamped with something that, even in the minds of the others, separates them off from the world; they are the followers of Christ. By going with the Lord, they showed that he was a power for them, that they granted him a right over their lives; to that extent one could allow them to pass as servants of the Lord. But at the moment when their service ought to manifest itself, they draw back. The first of the functions that one would expect of them they do not fulfill. They do not fulfill them because they belong to the Kingdom of their Lord, which is not of this world. And their significance as servants who have already begun their service does not at all lie, for the time being, on this earth. What they have to accomplish here they will do, for the most part, only when the Lord's stay on earth will be ended, when he will have returned entirely to his Kingdom. Then Peter will be his representative, precisely he who now fails him and denies him; and the others—who now, at the decisive moment, are not to be seen and about whom, in human terms, no one actually has more than a quite vague image—will then become pillars of the

Kingdom. In the meantime, the bond between the Lord and the servants consists in the fact that he is handed over, enters into solitude, and that his servants do not prevent that fate but allow it to occur. With the statement about his servants, the Lord closes himself off, in a sense, from the happenings in the world: his servants do not fight for him and he is handed over to the Jews, irrevocably. His suffering has begun. He will endure it in order to bring his Kingdom— characterized as it is by nothing visible, by nothing other than his being handed over, indeed, consisting of nothing else in this world— back into the Kingdom of the Father.

But my Kingdom is not now of the world. It is not *now* of the world because men separate the now off from eternity. This now has a human ring, it is spoken of with reference to men. For the Lord, the now, the hour that is coming, is always included in eternity. Men, by contrast, want to separate their now off from eternity, to structure it themselves. To this reckoning of time by men, who take their time from themselves and charge it to themselves, the Kingdom does not belong. It persists from eternity into eternity. It is not of the world because it is from above, because it contradicts in every respect what we expect, hope for and desire from a kingdom that is supposed to unite us. We seek our own in everything, the Lord seeks his own in nothing. In everything, we are intent upon our advantage, whereas he only loves his Kingdom, only fructifies it, only unites it. As long as we act outside of faith, we constantly disunite, whereas his Kingdom constantly strives toward unity, indeed, is unity itself. Our world is a multiplicity in sin; we know what is mine and what is yours. He knows only that which is his Father's, and he wishes to unite what is his and what is ours by bringing them into this. In love, he brings everything to a unity of possession, and thus he also produces the unity of every individual being by allowing it to blossom (not to wither) into the unity of God. And because he knows only that which is the Father's, he knows him in himself and himself in him; his knowing is unity in love, and he strives to draw all of us into this relationship of the Father to the Son. The Father and he are the united ones; we are the solitary ones, and we remain isolated as long as we contradict love. Our contradiction consists in the fact that we set conditions and attempt to bring our self-will and our sin along with us when we pretend to know him. But sin sunders, while love unites. As long as we do not relinquish our sin, love cannot reach us. We split it apart before we get to the point of apprehending the unity. And thus, as long as we are sinners, our world remains the world of the I, whereas his world is the world of the you; his Kingdom is the Kingdom of the Father, and his entire power the power of love. The contradiction in us consists in the fact that we speak against him, against him as the Son but just as much against him in us, against his life in us, there where he has already drawn near to us. We attempt to play the flesh off against the spirit and the Son against the Father. And if he tells us that his Kingdom is not of this world, we fail to hear the voice of unity, but rather, hear as if God were against man, heaven against earth, the beyond against this world, the spirit against the flesh. Or if we desire a unity of both, then we think that *we* ourselves would have to reconcile heaven and earth, that we could project our earth into heaven, that we should effect the resolving of faith into reason. We set ourselves against any unity that simply takes us up into unity. We would have to believe and to love in order to build the bridge of unity, in order to allow it to be built by God, in order to allow God and heaven to become stronger than man and earth. But we are afraid of nothing so much as of this unity. Thus we always construct our "syntheses" as "antitheses" of our kingdom to his Kingdom. We fail to complete the transition from death to life. We see death, which we strive against, as an end. For here below, everything strives toward death. As long as one sees everything from here below, one can only speak of death as a boundary "beyond" which, perhaps, something else begins. The Lord, by contrast, who sees everything from above, discerns in everything the signs of incipient entry into his Kingdom, the first approaches to eternity. We are bolted but not really locked; if we were locked, then this would mean that we had let ourselves be closed up within the Trinity and that God would thus have become the real unity for us. We would be in the Kingdom of unity, and the Kingdom of unity would be in us. If our entire being were to live in the attitude of prayer, then we would close ourselves off to external things and open ourselves up inwardly to God. We would fold our hands, but spread our arms and spirit out toward God. We would shut ourselves off to sin and open ourselves to the remorse of God, which — since what speaks in remorse is more God than the ego — we are given to hear by him. We would forgo our own voice and allow it to become a response to the voice of the Lord. Our prayer would no longer be a presenting of conditions and thus a rejection, but rather, a pure acceptance of God's unconditionality, a silent allowing oneself to be drawn into the Word that is spoken by God. We would no longer prattle on endlessly in order to gain admittance into his stillness. That would be the Kingdom of prayer, the prayer of the Kingdom. But we are still always busy with acting, while the Lord is waiting, and our deeds and actions express the fact that we do not want his love. His love, by contrast, is the waiting; he persists lovingly, for however long, until he has us all. We do one thing or another so that, in our view, something might get done, while he simply remains the one he is. Waiting is a part of his essence and is a characteristic of his Kingdom. By being always involved in acting, we are the rejection, while he remains the persisting acceptance. We are the temporal, because we act with a view to this or that now which we are yet never able to hold fast; he is the eternal, which endures because it is. And yet, in our busyness, we are the calm of death. Our deed is so limited and so trivial that, in the eyes of God (who sees us as we ought to be), it is as nothing. We do what he does not want to see, and do not do what he could see, the good. Our deed is thus dead, done in death. The Lord, by contrast, is the anxiety of life, that anxiety which comes over us when, with his life, he draws near in order to raise us out of our death; the restlessness that shatters our death calm, an anxiety and a restlessness that we do not want to accept and that he himself, therefore, must bear in our place, takes with him into his Cross in order to spare us from that, too, and to transform the deathly in it into the highest life.

We still continue to strive against him and cannot enter into his Kingdom, which is the Kingdom of the Father. We would have to turn ourselves around. We look downward: at the earth, at death, at the end. We ought to look upward, to the origin, which is with God, which is God himself. His Kingdom begins there where the kingdom of our ego ends, where love begins. Love, however, is he, and he will lead our end over into his beginning, into the Kingdom that is not of this world.

18:37. *Pilate said to him: So you are a king? Jesus answered: You say that I am a king. For this I was born, and for this I have come into the world, to bear witness to the truth. Everyone who is of the truth hears my voice.*

Pilate has understood that, even though the Kingdom of the Lord is not of this world, he still possesses a kingdom. In what his Kingdom consists, of course, he does not comprehend; but his question shows nevertheless that it originates from a kind of insight. It is the insight of unbelief, which is not bereft of insight, the expression of an intellectual sense of justice without love. Outside of love and faith, one can see much that is objectively correct, do much that is definitely morally "good". But all this insight and action remain caught up inside the world and the ego. Pilate has comprehended something and intended something. But this something has no weight and no validity in the Lord's Kingdom because it is not a something of love. Pilate has seen that Jesus is a king and that he comprehends nothing of his Kingdom. But he has no need even to acquaint himself with this Kingdom. He does not feel obliged to open himself up to the truth of the Kingdom. He has no curiosity. He does not want to become drawn into something that he cannot view in its entirety. He wants to go only his own way. Therefore, he also asks no further questions about the nature of the Kingdom.

Jesus answered: You say that I am a king. The words of Pilate thus contain the truth; but he does not see it. His words are greater than his intention and his understanding. If his words were in love, then they would contain the complete truth. The words of the Lord do not cease to be living once they have been uttered; they are fruitful, and in their fruitfulness is so much love that no end is contained in them. Pilate's words, by contrast, are dead as soon as they have passed his lips. The Lord, as a man, speaks living words; unbelief can speak nothing other than dead words, for every word that has life contains the word of Christ. *I am a king.* Of what, he does not say, for his Kingdom cannot be described. Pilate, who has arrived at the dry insight that the Lord is a king, is inclined to imagine a definite tract of land, with a definite power, a definite number of subjects and surveyable boundaries. But the Lord gives no kind of definition of his Kingdom, since every region is ultimately part of his Kingdom (for all regions belong to the Father), and since the power is the omnipotence of the Father and the number of subjects is the same as the number of men, who all belong to the Father. He has said earlier that his Kingdom is not *now* of the world, because the now is something temporal. But his Kingdom is in eternity and can wait until every temporal now has run its course, until every temporal obstruction has ceased and he can lead the world back into the unity of the Father. The prayer, the power and the number have no boundaries; the Son rules in every place where the Father is, who has handed over all power to him; he rules over every where and every when in the space and time of the Father, that is, in all eternity; and his subjects are all those created by the Father, that is, men in eternity.

For this I was born. Namely, in order to be King. He is King through his birth, because he is born out of love and love is the ground of his birth. That he is born is the realization of a promise of love. Love is so much the substance of his life, already in his birth, in his development, that he can never be named without love's being thought and imagined at the same time. He is here as both the birth of love and the King of love. Pilate has imagined to himself a kingdom over which Christ could rule. But while he rules over his Kingdom, his Kingdom also rules him (because he is ruled by love). His whole Kingdom is love in eternity, and love existed already in eternity; it was realized in the relationship of the Trinity. Now, however, it is clarified and expanded by the world's being drawn into this love. Thus love, which existed already, is born once again. And this birth of love is love in a double sense: it is this as birth out of God because the birth derives from the redemptive decision by Father and Son, and it is this as birth out of the Mother, who, in her word of affirmation, simultaneously affirms the Son and the love of God. She sees in God a livingness of love such as to enable this love to bring the Son in the Mother to the world.

As one face of the Son is turned toward God and the other toward the world, so he is supported in the world by the love of God and the love of the Mother. Without being thus supported through love, his earthly life would be impossible. That the love of the Father supports him we understand in faith. However, that the Mother supports him in love, that he has to be supported by the love of a human being—this is something that we do not think of. And yet: that, at his birth, he received a response from the world to his question of love for love—this was the precondition for his birth. To his question, the Mother answers with Yes. She says Yes to the love of the Father and of the Son. She has this opportunity: to say Yes, an opportunity that is grace and that, when it is realized, draws the Mother out of herself and into love and grace and the efficacy of love and grace. Through grace, she is brought passively into the relationship, but this relatedness transforms itself at once into an active effectiveness within love. Thus, through her love, she is not uninvolved in the crowning of her Son as King. The first one who is illuminated by her love is her Son. And he receives this honor from the Mother who has become Queen of Heaven through his birth.

He is born as the Son of the Mother; of a Mother who gives birth in extremest poverty in a stable because the entire Kingdom of her Son is of heaven and unfolds from within heaven, including the events of his birth and his kingship. The Mother, who is Queen by virtue of her word of affirmation, keeps the whole of her majesty on deposit with the Father until the moment when she fully enters heaven, because she aligns herself with the Kingdom of the Son, which is not of this world, yet she accompanies him in this world and supports him in his mission like a quite ordinary woman. She lives simultaneously in heaven and on earth, but in a different way than does the Son, because she does not at all need to allow her heavenly life on earth to come to the fore. Her proper activity, her apostolate in the world, is essentially prayer. She wins, to all appearances, no converts; she carries out her work in concealment, in heaven. But she also makes no claims on her heavenly existence and majesty, she leads, alongside her concealed earthly life, no second, heavenly life of glory; she has deposited her majesty with God to such an extent that she wants to make herself available for her Son's work only as a veiled handmaid. And in that, she effaces herself totally.

For the Son, being born and being King are the same. For the Mother, giving birth and being Queen are the same. The Son, however, has *come into the world, to bear witness to the truth.* The truth, which is the Father. This truth had been hidden and forgotten by men. As soon as they found themselves no longer in the Father, they had forgotten the Father and his truth. Sin hindered them from seeking the truth there and finding it. Hence, there was only one possibility of making them accessible again to the Father: to take away sin. This the Son could do in no way other than through bearing witness to the Father, who is the truth, and this witness, in order to maintain any force, also had to be given conclusive form. It had to exhibit the same character as the life of the Lord itself. Just as his life was lived with a view toward God and toward men, so his testimony had to manifest the correctness of the proclaimed truth in both those directions. With that, truth takes on a double face: the Father is love and men should be drawn into this love. The Son must prove to the Father that men love him, and he does that by becoming a man and loving the Father from within the world to the greatest possible extreme. On the other hand, he must prove to men that God loves them, and he, who is God, does that by showing them his love. This double proof is furnished by the Son in his life on earth and, most lastingly, on the Cross. Here, he takes the sins of men upon himself and thus effects their redemption, and he proves his love to the Father to the extent of dying in abandonment. By this he also shows that love and sacrifice belong together, that love is prepared to make any sacrifice, and that this sacrifice of love consists in obedience, in which, therefore, is the Kingdom of Christ. For only a king can obey so consummately. Anyone who is not king can obey only to a certain degree, in terms of a limited task, because he does not possess unlimited power. To obey completely and unlimitedly is possible only for one who surveys the entirety of obedience, serves the whole in all his deeds, possesses the highest power and can thus obligate and surrender himself without limitation. It is the obedience of the Son that, as man, he treads the path set out for him by the Father as far as to the end of love, with an act of sacrifice in which love no longer recognizes itself.

Everyone who is of the truth hears my voice. Anyone who finds himself in the Lord's proximity can hear him with his bodily ears. All those who stood around him — the disciples, the Jews and the people — have heard something of his words and attached some meaning or other to what they heard. But the closer they were to faith, the more they have perceived of the divine sense of his words; they acquired a sense and a taste for the always-more. The Lord makes use of many a word and a human voice in order to speak inwardly to the soul, to the spirit, to the whole man. Each time, he offers everything, but men never take in the fullness of the content of his words. At best, they strive to do so. To take in everything means to live in love, indeed, to be love wholly. That will not be attainable until the next life, where the Lord will fulfill all that has been promised. For the time being, men translate the words of the Lord into the finite. In themselves, they have no limits, but they acquire such if one perceives or reads them apart from the fullness of faith and adapts them to the structure of one's own personality. In heaven, because heaven is the Kingdom of love, these words all have their unlimited, infinite sense. As long as we are in this world, we strive, despite everything, again and again, toward finitude. We do not want to believe in the Ever-Greater of God until we first have a firm, secure concept that is adapted to our finitude. When, however, we come to live *in truth,* namely, in eternity, all of our concepts will be totally surpassed by the truth and reality of God and his love. Everything will then be widened so much that we will scarcely understand any longer how that which, here below, we called our love of the Lord has anything to do with true love. Everything here below remains tied to our body, to our finitude and sensory nature; even our love of God is limited by that. For us, love of God is one form of love among others, comparable to the love that we feel for earthly and finite things. In heaven, by contrast, the body will be a pure tool of the soul, a reminder of the fact that God has created us, but no longer a hindrance to perfect love.

We hear the voice of the Lord, too, when we first begin to have faith. As a divine voice, it responds in us through grace at the moment when we attempt to give it a meaning. As soon as we have the slightest share in the truth that is love, this voice does not go totally unheeded in us, no matter what form question and answer may take. The Lord's question, as such, is already an answer if the hearer is *of the truth,* that is, of love and grace; it brings its answer with it, contains it burningly within itself. It brings its "reaction" with it as soon as the living word of the Lord (which is ultimately he himself) touches the grace in us and mixes with it. The word of the Lord is always both question and answer at once: as an answer to the question of truth in us and as containing our answer in its question and answer.

The Lord says that to Pilate, who wants to understand objectively but is not in love. Pilate thus fails to hear the word because he is not in truth. The meaning of the word is not accessible to Pilate. At most, he can ascertain that he can gather nothing from these words. What is positive in them is closed to him. He is also symbolic of those neutral persons who are not positively prevented from hearing by any other faith. But because they are merely "neutral", the word also says nothing to them. They see everything only from the outside, they apprehend nothing in what is heard. They could do that only if they were in truth, that is, in love.

18:38. *Pilate said to him: What is truth? After he had said this, he went out to the Jews again and told them: I find no crime in him.*

More significant than his renewed questioning is the fact that Pilate expects no answer to it. He would also not even be able to understand it because he has no faith. He can put the question; but in uttering it, he himself does not know what he is saying. He knows that the concept of truth can be set apart negatively from some things, he knows of many things that are not truth. From certain fragments of argumentation, from mutually consistent questions and answers, the pieces of something positive are visible to him. But somehow the totality becomes lost, and all he knows of the path ahead is that it eludes him. He sees that the Lord's truth and his own do not coincide.

The Lord, who is beginning his suffering, who starts to become no longer of this world while the truth of the Father appears in a constantly more alien light, now lives increasingly in his own truth, which is immediate. He is in worsening suffering and in growing alienation from the will and essence of the Father. He becomes locked up within himself. Truth, however, must always be unlocked and open. It must be able to be communicated. The truth of the Lord, by contrast, now consists in the fact that his truth becomes more and more inaccessible, more and more concealed. If he now wanted to speak of the truth that is simultaneously love, he would have to develop the love from the direction of renunciation, from there where it has seemingly lost everything radiant and affirmative in order to appear as nothing anymore but sacrifice. What most people look for in love is only joy and pleasure. Whoever has only a sensual experience of love that is tied to the body, whoever calls love only that which flows toward him and which he receives, cannot be made to understand that love can be pure renunciation, that what the Lord now takes upon himself is the renunciation of love itself, the renunciation of every enrichment, that the truth of love can inhere in this, that this highest love and truth consists now in the discarding of all signs of grace and love. If someone were to look only at what becomes visible, namely, that a man is dragged toward death who is himself in spiritual darkness, it would have to seem to him true madness that precisely in this occurrence truth should inhere, and in fact, the summation of all truth, the meaning of the world. If he does not see what went before and what comes after this, if he is caught up completely in this moment, then in no case will he understand even the slightest aspect of it. He will have to interpret the world as pure incomprehensibility. And the Lord finds himself in precisely that situation, wholly locked up within the darkness of his renunciation. Pilate's question, which requires no answer, he is also not at all able to answer; for what is now truth, his truth and thus truth absolutely, has no way out, no opening to the outside.

The disciples, whom the Lord had called at the beginning and to whom he had transmitted an image of love during the years that they were together, could intuit something of this love, even of the incomprehensible love between him and the Father. Together with the Lord, they have walked the path toward his suffering as toward an incomprehensible destiny; and thus there now remains to them, amidst the darkness of being excluded, a ray of light: the memory of what has been, a knowledge that there was once love and that, from its standpoint, there was a view into what is now something incomprehensible. For Pilate, who has never believed, that is not the case. For him, there is no relationship at all between the truth that he knows and the truth of the Lord. The disciples are like those Christians who, in the midst of a catastrophe, can begin to pray because, perhaps, they learned how to pray at some stage of their youth. Pilate has never learned this; he cannot turn toward the truth because he does not know what truth is. Whoever has once prayed, and, in so doing, was in truth, has a germ of truth in himself that is indestructible, a light that, no matter how small, no matter how forgotten, is inextinguishable. Prayer belongs to truth.

After he had said this, he went out to the Jews again. He does not invite them in because he knows that they are not permitted to enter his house. His lawlessness does not mislead him into offending against their laws. These also do not permit him to pronounce the Lord guilty. He *told them: I find no crime in him.* The laws of the Jews, which Pilate honors, are obviously contrary to the truth of the Lord. Pilate, who stands outside of both laws, has examined both in his objective way. He has found nothing in the Lord that would necessitate a condemnation, and in fact, neither according to the laws of the Jews—which he considers in his objective, detached manner—nor according to his own views. He gets no further than this. Since he does not listen to the Lord, he can also find nothing positive about him. He does not feel himself repulsed, but just as little attracted, won over. He remains outside of the truth of the Lord. He informs the Jews of the results of his inquiries, calmly and untouched. And yet his matter-of-factness is not objective. He has encountered the Lord, who is the truth, but he has perceived nothing of this truth. He remains encapsulated in himself. Thus, his apparent objectivity is, in truth, only a closed attitude to the truth. If one wishes to reach the truth, there is no possibility of deliberating "objectively" with the Lord. One cannot remain at the level of external observation, as, for instance, when admiring a church as a work of art while not allowing oneself to be affected in the least by its spirit and its inner purpose. The indifference of Pilate is the opposite of indifference in God.

18:39. *But you have a custom that I should release one man for you at the Passover; will you have me release for you the King of the Jews?*

Pilate shows consideration for their customs by offering them the release of Jesus. And in fact, release without any judgment. If it were possible to resolve the whole case in this way, then both parties, Pilate and the Jews, would be relieved of responsibility. Every one could interpret the release in the way that seemed best to him. For Pilate, this would be the most desirable outcome: he suspects that any further grappling with the truth of the Lord would not remain without consequences for him; he feels that his equilibrium is under threat. To endorse the Lord and his teaching would have unforeseeable consequences; to reject them would require a thorough investigation. This investigation, for its part, would demand that Pilate examine himself; he would have to surrender his indifference and, with that, a strong position; he could possibly be forced to recognize the supremacy of the truth of the Lord. Perhaps also concealed in Pilate's offer is the hope that, through the release, the case might clarify itself; the coming days could clear up many a thing that now seems confused. Thus he puts things off by refusing to take a position and, beneath an appearance of objectivity and magnanimity, desperately defends his own interests.

And yet he speaks of Jesus as the *King of the Jews.* He adopts this title. Here, he does not know what he is doing. That a surrendering of himself is inherent in this. He does not know it, just as others to come after him will also, time and again, fail to know it. But one can never adopt something from the Lord without thereby surrendering something of one's own. It is as if Pilate takes out a kind of small, nonbinding loan from the Lord. The Lord, however, tolerates no loans. He gives, and does not take back. Pilate does not notice that something in him has shattered, that his voice now has a different sound. He is no longer the self-satisfied Roman; something of the Lord has attached itself to him, and he will never again be rid of it. He has stood alongside the King of the Jews. No matter where one opens the door just a little, he finds room enough there to gain entry and to establish himself. To the Jews, it may have sounded like mockery when Pilate spoke of the King of the Jews. With respect to the Lord, it was not meant to be mocking.

18:40. *They cried out again: Not this man, but Barabbas! Now Barabbas was a robber.*

Although the Jews have not discussed the possibility of a release with one another beforehand, they all nevertheless share the same opinion immediately; *not this man, but Barabbas.* Barabbas is someone with a clear, full-blown sin. And they love full-blown sins. They have not themselves committed them, these sins for which one is publicly branded and punished. They have a Pharasaical aversion to them which they loudly proclaim. Yet they are nevertheless attracted by them: just as the Lord loves the ever-greater of love, so they love the ever-greater of sin. The sin of their neighbor, which is of the same magnitude as their own sin, is of little interest to them—at most, to the extent that they would like to know what the other experienced and felt when committing it that they themselves perhaps have not experienced and felt. The sin, however, that towers above them appears interesting to them by virtue of its mere dimensions. One can make use of it, if only as the occasion for gossip or indignation or as a cautionary example. The "guilt" of the Lord, by contrast, contains for them something unadmitted, something incomprehensible which irritates them. They would like to get their hands on a solution, and they see in the fact that the Lord provides no solution a usurpation of their spirit, a demand upon them. This they cannot bear. Since they have no love, they do not want to be reminded of love. Since they have no vision, they do not want anyone else to have it. Since they do not want to surrender themselves, they must immediately make something objectionable out of everything that the Lord says and does. They want to be sufficient unto themselves, and they see that the Lord is not sufficient unto himself. He lives in the Father, and is spent lavishly by the Father just as he himself spends lavishly of the Father. He is like that because he is love, their opponent. They feel themselves threatened by love; they know that, if they became obedient, all their self-satisfaction would collapse into nothingness. They are that which is barren, withered, run aground, rigidified into law. Therefore, they cannot tolerate it that love should come, like a whirlwind, to thaw out the ice in hearts.

Now Barabbas was a robber. Just what his offense was is unimportant. He has, in any case, sinned out of lack of love for the sake of some personal advantage. He risked imprisonment and death in order to secure that advantage for himself. The Lord, by contrast, chose death from the very beginning, out of love for the Father, because he knows no advantage for himself except the one: the Father and love of him.

THE DEATH SENTENCE

19:1. *Then Pilate took Jesus and scourged him.*

Pilate now does his official duty. He himself steps into the background and allows the justice of the human court to take its course. The Lord is scourged. He experiences in his body what pain is, and he is humiliated in his soul by those who strike him. His loneliness becomes complete. Lonely is not only he who is alone, but also he who is abandoned; and the Lord is more than abandoned: he is an outcast, he is despised as this lone individual and must endure in silence, and even no longer comprehendingly, all that is done to him. For he is already totally enclosed within the Father's commission of suffering; he is no longer able to compare that which men do to him and that which he himself wants to do; he can only patiently endure. Also, he does not suffer bodily in order to be able to say to himself, in spirit, that he is making a voluntary sacrifice, for he has voluntarily deprived himself of the ability to see his sacrifice. If a man scourges himself, then he has the consolation of being able to offer that sacrifice to God. The scourging of the Lord, by contrast, is without any consolation because he now can see nothing useful at all in his sacrifice. The divinity in him has veiled itself over to such an extent that he suffers entirely in his humanity. He is now that which unbelieving theology regards him as: the pure, innocent man. He is like a child that is being mistreated and cannot at all imagine why that is happening to him. He sees only the yawning contradiction between the evilness of his tormentors and his consciousness of being innocent. Much less still does he think of reward or success. He bears the sacrifice just as God gives it to him: without consolation. A Christian should never speculate, regarding any sacrifice that he makes, on its gravity, limits or merits. He should make the sacrifice without wanting to experience the consolation of its being accepted.

Although the scourging is merely the start of the suffering to come, it nevertheless contains in itself the complete sacrifice. It is suffering in disconsolation, in hopelessness, in utter perversion of order. The Son wanted to divert the humiliation away from the Father, and now he is derided and the Father is derided in him. He wanted to take the sins of the world upon himself, wanted to be the subject upon whom they were unburdened. And now he is nothing but the object upon which they are discharged. The power of sight is left to him insofar as he sees how the Father has to suffer through him (since the sins that vent themselves on him are intended to be vented against God); it is taken from him insofar as he does not see what he spares the Father and how his sacrifice is the compensation for the humiliation brought upon him.

He is maltreated at the level of his body, which is a body like that of every created being. He sustains on it the blows of all those who have sinned in their bodies. He carries the marks of sin in itself. He collects in his body the traces of all bodily sins. He atones in flesh for the flesh. Linked to the scourging of the Lord is everything in the Christian life that means mortification of the flesh, physical penance and overcoming the body, fasting and chastisement, but also binding in the sense of the monastic life in general. Because the Lord allows his body to be bound and scourged for us, we, too, do not refuse binding and penance. We can make our body available for such penance, whereas our spirit, which always belongs to the Lord and which we no longer have any right to renounce, cannot be offered in the same freely-willed way. One can probably know what no longer disposing over one's body would mean; but what no longer disposing over one's spirit would mean cannot be known in advance by anyone, and thus also cannot be disposed over.

The scourging of the Lord is humiliating. It is a desecration. The daily asceticism of the Christian—which is only a shadow, a hint of emulation—has also, in its persistency, something humiliating about it. It is embarrassing and seemingly petty. It goes into particulars and is made up of a multitude of unpleasant and contemptible things. It separates us, so to speak, from the greatness and magnanimity of God. And yet it is in his separation from the Father, in his painful and disgraceful solitude, that the Lord opens for us the way to the Father.

19:2. *And the soldiers plaited a crown of thorns, and put it on his head, and arrayed him in a purple robe; . . .*

The meanest of things that exist is chosen to crown him with, but the meanest that also wounds the most painfully. He is crowned in such a way that the appearance of honoring him contains the expression of utter contempt and the will to torment him. They accord him this sign of superiority in order to mock him as being inferior. Those, however, who thus crown him do not know what they do, because they cannot survey the distance whose extremes they thereby mark out: between the highest of the high and the lowest of the low. He is sensible of both: the pain of the crown that constricts his head and inflicts bleeding wounds, and the infinite contradiction that inheres in this crowning. He has come in order to love, to love in a way in which men have never before been loved, and he should have been entitled to the crown of love. If love could be conceived at all as hierarchical, he would be permitted to lay claim to this crown. Precisely being crowned in love by the lowest of men could have amounted to fulfilment for him. And now this crowning turns into a symbol of his absolute failure. Everything that could have been done to him out of love occurs in the contrary direction, in evilness and baseness and sin. Adequate here is this alone: that they, the wholly lowly, come to him with the lowliest in order to crown him, the real King, with that which they have. But this proper framework is filled out to its edges with a perverted content. The pain that the Lord experiences in this crowning is above all the pain of the complete failure of his mission. He has accomplished nothing with his love. His humility is vain humiliation. He longed for no fame; he wanted only love. Now, however, he is made to see what he is and what he has achieved. He wanted to establish the Kingdom of the Father on earth, but earth crowns him with nothing but contempt and disgrace. Every single thorn jabs him in a small way, and the large jab of hate goes right to his heart. He has brought the great Yes of God, but he receives for an answer a thousandfold petty No, which amasses itself into one great No. This contradiction rends his soul, just as the wounds on his brow rend his head. To the splendor and magnanimity of the divine offer answers the wretchedness and cowardice of the human refusal. They have but one aim: to make him suffer, him, who had but one aim: to spare them suffering. He, the peerless, is crowned by these anonyms who are nameless because they are utterly base.

Then the *purple robe* is draped around his beaten body; around his pain-racked body, which bears the sensible marks of his scourging, the heavy robe is draped, enclothing, covering, concealing, allowing to be forgotten and almost effacing everything. A new contradiction opens up: between the martyred body and the pomp of the robe that covers it. And this enclothing is intended as a new mockery. The robe has covered the abused body, but thereby only intensified the abuse. This robe the Lord has left behind for us. He gives it to us so that we might be enclothed in it when we are derided and beaten for his sake, because no one should see or suspect the wounds from the outside. To be enclothed in this robe of the Lord means to be covered by the robe of his love.

Between the body and the robe lies faith. The robe was forced upon the Lord. The tormentors no longer wanted to see the results of their work; that was so as to be able the better to mock him. The Church, too, should wear this robe; it is the uniform of the Lord. The tortured body of Christianity should conceal itself beneath the purple robe; both, however, are linked through faith. The Lord's word of affirmation is deposited with the Father; but, precisely because he deposits it for himself, he presents it to us in his stead: between Passion and representation. Because the sinner has vented his sins upon the body of the Lord in order then to cover that body mockingly with the concealing robe, the Lord can drape the robe of his service around us sinners after our soul has been rent by penitence. Out of the robe that sin gives to him the Lord derives the robe that presents us with his grace; the gown of sin becomes the pure gown of the Lord. Thus the Lord creates an intimacy between us and him within the common robe of being Christian. It is a gown that clothes, before the eyes of the world, that which the Lord sees in us: our sin, our failure, our conflicts in penitence, our shame, our suffering with him. To the eyes of the world, we are nothing other than a more or less colorless member of the community.

The robe of the Lord is also the robe of virginity. It clothes the scourged body, the body that has renounced love. This renunciation has to be clothed. The torturers, who do not understand the mystery, cover it over. They do not even want to know about it. In this enclothed figure belongs the mystery of the Lord, and that is how he gives it back to the Father. The first to wear this veil is his Mother. The entire mystery of her life—the infinite renunciation that inheres in her word of affirmation and rends her soul—is concealed beneath the veil of the Virgin. Son and Mother each lose their body: the Son in the pains of the Passion, the Mother in the blind devotion of her word of affirmation; both lose it in the same enclothement, which gives the sacrifice back to God and withholds it from the eyes of the world.

While the Lord's head is crowned with thorns, his body is draped with the purple robe. The head of the Lord is with God, his body is among men. The head is crowned with a crown of divinity that ultimately belongs to the Father. The head is spirit; the head is origin and bestower of faith, love and hope in their complete fulfilment. The head is every kind of service to the Father, every agreement made between Father and Son. On the example of this head, the sinners must make visible what redemption of the world is. On it, the crowners reveal their measureless guilt; on it, they allow to become clear how much the head is separated from sin. On it must become visible the yawning chaos that lies between sin that kills and love that makes living. Here, all those things appear in the brightest light, which will afterward be reconciled through the sacrifice of the Cross and accepted in love. The body is emblematic of what dwells among us, of what we, too, should be: the brother among brothers, the human appearance of God on earth. It, too, is scorned and mocked. Both are rejected: the head-Father that came to bring the Kingdom, and the body-Brother that came to redeem through his sacrifice. By acting as they do, they once again allow the sacrifice itself to arise in all its compelling magnitude. Only now does the hideousness of sin become clear with utmost palpability. Earlier, one might have been inclined to find excuses for it: as lack of knowledge, as weakness and frailty. Only now does it become clear what sin is, absolute sin, which needs absolute love if it is to be redeemed.

The Lord manifests in himself the nature of the Father and that of the pure man. He brings to the world the message of the Father and the example of the sinless life. Men react with scorn to both. They mock the head in the revealing ignominy of the crown; they mock the body in the enclothing ignominy of the robe. The Lord retains the crown for himself, but forms the robe into the grace of ecclesiastical life. The robe becomes the form of the Church herself: the enclothing institution and representation beneath which the recipients should become the body of Christ, of which he is the head by virtue of being crowned by the Father. But men recognize neither head nor body; they deny the head, and they are averse not only to seeing the body but, even more so, to being it. Thus the Lord, in his suffering, must be both: head and body. And only after his lonely suffering in head and body will there be participation for the Church as body in the Lord as head. And because he now suffers both alone—the suffering of head and body—so in the future, too, he will suffer, as her head, the suffering of the body of the Church; over and over, he will take upon himself yet again the sins and errors of the Church and bear all the Church's burdens. From all directions, the Christian suffering of the Church and of mankind falls in its entirety upon him; he takes it upon himself in ultimate pain and allows himself to be covered by the robe, thereby denying the Church and mankind the ability to see and survey his suffering while, at the same time, drawing them, without sight, into the mystery of the suffering. He alone knows what is beneath the robe, and he takes it into his suffering body.

19:3. . . . *they came up to him, saying: Hail, King of the Jews! and struck him with their hands.*

In mockery, they gave him the title that corresponds to his crowning. For them, this form of address is nothing but ridicule; for the Lord, however, it lays bare the seriousness of things unattained. In the mirror of this title, he casts a look back over his life and sees what has not been achieved. Thus they affect him much more grievously with this scorn than they suspect. They attempt to affect him, but they think that their scorn wounds him only because it gives him a title that is not rightly his: *King of the Jews.* He, however, knows that he has come in order to be King. *King of the Jews* would imply a limitation of his claim to rule but would at least be a phrase indicating work attained and completed. He was sent to the Jews, and he would have wanted to bring them back to the Father as converts. In the light of that unattained aim he sees all the other things that have not been achieved. He was not even able to bring home the Jews! He is well aware that he came in order to redeem mankind; but, in this night of the Passion, he does not want to see how much his work is the supplementation of everything deficient, the constant surrendering up of his own substance. Because he no longer sees himself with the Father, he also no longer sees the supplemental role that he has taken upon himself for every individual thing and is precisely now discharging through his suffering. In the eyes of the Father, nothing better can be done than what he is now doing: surrendering himself up for all and thereby also finding himself again in all. In the eyes of the Son, by contrast, it all seems like a complete failure, because he can no longer hold his self-surrender in view but is caught up in its very process, sensing only the loss of himself but no longer its meaning and results. This form of surrender, which recalls the eucharistic form, is precisely what the Father had hoped for from him, and he wishes for nothing more ardently than to find the surrendered Son again in all creatures.

And [they] struck him with their hands. They underline the spiritual suffering that they inflict on him with a bodily one in order to make things quite clear. Every sin does that. And just as men inflict them upon him, so the Lord accepts the sufferings for redemption: by comprising in himself the unity of spiritual and bodily pain. He redeems the sinners not by looking at some general, theoretical level of sin, but by looking at the concrete sins that they have committed, in spirit and in body. The servants who both mock and beat him thereby bind spirit and body so inseparably together that the two can now only be redeemed together.

The Son redeems the sinner by replacing and rounding out all that he lacks before God. He gives him that on the basis of which he is purified and recognized by the Father, and he is recognized on the basis of the Son's living in him. This livingness of the Son in every one of the redeemed is the thing that the Son now no longer sees. It is, at the same time, the thing in man which, above and beyond his works, makes faith necessary to his justification. If Christianity consisted only in works—for example, mercifulness, keeping the commandments, consecration of self—then man would redeem himself and the Father would not recognize the Son in him. If he is to be able to do that, if the Son is really to live in man, if he is truly to be the substance of that which justifies man before the Father, then above and beyond the works faith must be alive in man: faith in justification through the Son, in the grace of the Son, in the Son himself in man. In the end, faith is that in man which is of the Son. In order to implant this in man, he gives himself over into the night of no longer seeing.

19:4. *Pilate went out again, and said to them: See, I am bringing him out to you, that you may know that I find no crime in him.*

Pilate repeats what he has already done once before. But in the meantime he has had the Lord scourged and exposed him to the vengeance and cruelty of the servants. So everything has proceeded much further. Pilate, who proclaimed the Lord's innocence, has meanwhile become guilty; he has tortured the Lord in a way permitted only for punishment of the guilty. And the Lord himself is more deeply involved in suffering than before. Everything has become more inexorable, more unavoidable. The Passion proceeds apace; the possibility of a freely-willed action becomes ever more remote for the Lord; his powerlessness, his weakness and abandonment rise to the fore. As well, the Father has stronger proofs of the Son's love, he feels himself, so to speak, strengthened by the Son's weakness; everything that he foresaw is unfolding in the flesh before his eyes. Everything promised is truth. Everything is drawn into the Passion and made a part of it.

Since the power of sight has been taken from the Son, his *obedience* begins to become blind obedience, an obedience that is not understood by those who are not involved in it. His body, which he had always consecrated and surrendered to the Father in *purity,* is no longer a thing that he possesses; he feels it as nothing more now than pain. Divested in this way, he is utter *poverty,* to the extent that even his entire spiritual and bodily renunciation is concealed beneath the robe that does not belong to him. In the three forms of poverty, chastity and obedience, he is now nothing but the Father's instrument for the redemption of the world. He comprises in himself every possible sort of renunciation, he is the expression of renunciation itself, and is thus dearer to the Father than ever. For the Son has deposited with the Father all that he possessed, including even all his love. In himself, he is now nothing but someone surrendered over, who does not want to know what is to befall him. The only knowledge that he allows to affect him is this: the horror will assume the form that is necessary for the accomplishment of the work of the Father.

Pilate finds *no crime in him.* He is right. But he sees merely this negative side because he would be able to see the positive only through the faith that he does not have. Thus the one who finds no crime in him is nevertheless numbered among those who deliver him up. All who do not have faith and love are numbered among these.

19:5. *So Jesus came out, wearing the crown of thorns and the purple robe. Pilate said to them: Behold the man!*

The Lord comes out before the people, attired in the signs of his nonfulfilled kingship. In this nonfulfilment of his rule, his entire mission is contained. For if it had been fulfilled on earth, it would have been limited in space and time and thus would not be his mission. Like any human leader, he would have ruled over a part of the earth; he would have converted those whom he met, created a certain renown for himself through his speeches and been able to die in peace after his beneficent activities. All of that, however, would have had nothing to do with redemption. So, in all areas, he only made starts, only sowed beginnings, and the new law that he brought was only adopted by a few and only conditionally. On some hearts, he engraved the sign of the divine Always-More, the sign of what is unfulfillable in this world. For what he wants is the whole, he is supposed to bring an undivided mankind back into eternity for the Father. What happens in this world is only a preparation. Were he to perfect men here below, then they would be completed, they would meet death as closed beings. But they must, on the contrary, be burst apart in order to arrive at death as open beings. All of life must become a continually new movement of man toward God. To be Christian means this: to close nothing off as completed, but to open oneself up into the always-more of the Son's love for the Father. And if he is there for us as the one who brings us the always-more of faith, love and hope, then it is the Father who remains for him as the Always-More in love. As the nonfulfilled—and thus, for the world, the contemptible—he is displayed to all. In himself, he wants never to be fulfilled, but only to live in the ever-greater fullness of the Father. And thus he is presented to the world.

Behold the man! Thus Pilate presents him. As the one in whom he found no crime but also as the one already burdened with the punishment of the guilty, as one scourged and crowned with thorns. In the eyes of Pilate, he will surely have some sort of guilt to atone for. He is, after all, a man, and no man is without guilt. Thus Pilate can justify chastising him a bit in order to pacify the Jews. Are not men all of one and the same stock? And now he presents him: as this man, who has suffered what any other would also have been able to suffer. And he does not know what he is saying. He does not know that he is referring to *the* man, the archetype of man, man as God has always conceived of him. And to the pure man, who, through his excessive suffering, has atoned for what he perhaps could have committed to such an extent that nothing more of his guilt can be seen, but only the naked, bare, pure man who stands here before God and the world. This *pure* man is now the Lord, who has deposited his divinity with God and whose magnificence is so fully concealed and withdrawn from him that he now wants to know nothing more of it. And not only in his own eyes is he now wholly the man, but also in the eyes of the Father. So naked and pure is this man that he no longer possesses even his destiny, but has left it in God's hands and goes denuded into the darkest night of suffering. Even all inner participation—the conscious bearing, the mastering of the suffering, that is, the most inward, most subjective part of the suffering—he has committed to the Father; the whole of the suffering is in the Father's sole possession. The Father is the unlimited master of the suffering, the Son is only the one who carries it out, who surrenders himself up. In this, too, he is the complete, the pure man, man as he ought to be, man in God, given over to his keeping in utmost submission and surrender, compliant with everything that God makes out of him. If God deprives a sinner of something, perhaps only for the purpose of allowing him to suffer and bestowing upon him the blessing of suffering, then the sinner usually gets over it by consoling himself with some other good thing that remains to him. He turns away from the suffering and toward something consoling in order not to feel the loss. For the Lord, there is no consolation in his suffering because he dedicates himself wholly to what the Father wants and bestows upon him: the suffering.

19:6. When the chief priests and the officers saw him, they cried out: Crucify him, crucify him! Pilate said to them: Take him yourselves and crucify him, for I find no crime in him.

For the first time, the anger and hate in the Jews consolidates into a fanatical mass demonstration. It suffices that they catch sight of the Lord in these trappings—with all the signs of someone abandoned, fully changed as compared with his earlier self—for their vague hatred to break out in savagery. They are itching to continue on the established path: the comparison between the Lord formerly and the Lord now demands, in their minds, a pressing-on in the direction of crucifixion. He is wretched, and on this wretchedness they feed their rage. His impotence affords them an unexpected opportunity for intensified sin. He is contemptible, and they may vent all their contempt on him without being punished. They no longer need to hold themselves back. The collapse of his dignity is for them the occasion for the collapse of their façade. But behind this pitiful smallness of their disposition is clearly visible the large sin that unveils itself at this moment. The image of love suffering arouses in them their basest sin and causes them to rebel against love. They, the individuals, feel themselves being called, but they desperately block their ears and flee into the screaming collectivity in order to hide themselves in it. Into the absolute refusal of love, into the gloomy hate that has looked directly into the eye of the light of love and hates the light because it is light. In the middle of the Passion, things come for a moment to a standstill, and men have the opportunity to observe their work up to that point. They could now open themselves to love, they could take part in what has already been suffered. They could wipe away and make good what the Lord has gone through by offering themselves to him now in love. Like two men who are quarreling and suddenly realize that the whole dispute is senseless, they could propose peace to him. They would have an opportunity to turn from haters into lovers. But too late! They are no longer interested in reconciliation. Thus only one solution remains to them: *Crucify him!* His death alone will deliver them from his hated presence, from the unanswered question that inheres in him. They have long since chosen the means of death, secretly, in their hearts. Now the demand surges to the fore, insistent, raging and succinct. To this demand, the Lord opposes only his silence, which is inwardly already a searching in night for the God who withdraws himself.

When we seek after God in one or another of life's situations, we would like to receive an answer at once so that we can govern our behavior by it. The Lord's situation, however, is hopeless. He begins now to search for God without hoping for a specific answer. His search is an absolute one, the search of pure man, an offer to the Father to do his will: namely, to search amidst suffering without any hope. At the moment when men pass the death sentence on him, he can no longer discuss things with them; he can now be but inward devotedness to the Father who has vanished. Also, he can no longer communicate this devotedness nor manifest it externally. He can do nothing more than maintain silence directed toward the Father. Everything else would be too loud. It would, through the tragic masquerade into which the Lord has been forced, become a theatrical gesture that would look like forcing and tempting men. Only the Lord's silence now reflects his complete freedom, which he possesses in the Father, to suffer for the world.

Take him yourselves and crucify him. Up to the last, Pilate has thought that he should play the role of judge. Now he discovers that the Jews have long since made their decision independently of him and that his words die away unheard. He is no longer in the position of being able to judge freely. Thus he would now like to hand the Lord over to the chief priests so that they might carry out judgment of him themselves. He tries to combine this handing over with a shifting of responsibility: *for I find no crime in him.* In so doing, he evidences his powerlessness before the Lord. He has nothing that would support a condemnation. He spares himself having to prove the innocence of the Lord and to defend him accordingly.

19:7. *The Jews answered him: We have a law, and by that law he ought to die, because he has made himself the Son of God.*

The Jews are happy to assume responsibility for his death. They will not remain guilty of lacking the proof of his guilt that Pilate cannot provide. They appeal once again to their law, and find, on the basis of this law, that he must die. For him, there is only this death sentence, *because he has made himself the Son of God,* because he has therefore claimed to be the promise itself. The Jews have become so accustomed to giving the Old Covenant a final meaning that they do not regard as even worth discussing whether the hour of transition to the New Covenant could perhaps have arrived, whether that which the Lord has proclaimed to them is valid, and whether the miracles, some of which they have seen with their own eyes and about which they have surely heard enough, are not really divine signs. They seek all their truth in that which they have hermetically sealed and which has thereby become meaningless: in the law and in themselves. The law was meaningful as a preparation for the New Covenant; it came to its close at the moment when it was broken through by the Lord in the direction of the Father. And they themselves were meaningful as long as they lived within the expected promise, as long as their whole existence was to them a preparation for the coming fulfilment. But their life is doomed to death, has become meaningless, at the moment when the law is broken through and they refuse to participate in the new life that is demanded of them. Both openings ought to have coincided: the opening of faith, living from the opening of the Son in the Father. The Son, too, was once closed up in the Father and locked shut; but at the moment when he stepped forth he fulfilled the demand that God has made of men. Father and Son are the first who fulfill that which they demand. They broke open the closedness of divinity when the Son appeared and the Holy Spirit descended upon him. And this breaking open of the Trinity occurred in order, through the resultant opening, to draw in everything, to bring home everything that can be brought home: the entire world.

He has made himself the Son of God. For the Jews, the highest thing is seen as respect for God that keeps its distance. One can perhaps describe oneself as a child of God; to claim that one is his Son can only be blasphemy. They may well perceive God as all-powerful, but also in a sense as powerless, insofar as they do not think him, who can do everything, capable of this one thing: of having a Son. What the

Lord states about himself can be interpreted only as pure arrogance. They are not interested in the possibility of a divine-human unity in the Lord; since he speaks to them as a man, they think that they have the right to judge him from a purely human standpoint. For them, the divine character of his nature, which shines forth through the human one, can only be an expression of his presumptuousness. They know God. He created the world. He is the highest that there is. If God were to have a son, which is impossible, then it would be even more impossible that he should allow him to descend into the ordinariness of lowly human nature. He would, in fact, have to forbid his doing so.

And yet God created men in his own image; but they did not have the humility to appropriate the divine in themselves. They were intended to strive toward the divine, but since they did not do so, the Son of God strove toward the human. They ought to have striven, in grace, all the way to eternal life, but now the Son strives all the way to temporal death. Both movements are in God, both are willed by God. But our movement in God toward God came to a standstill through sin; it would have been interrupted forever if the Son had not moved toward us. Through his movement, he gives our movement back to us. The Jews abandoned their movement because God seemed too high and too distant to them. The Son overcame, and annihilated in himself, the whole of the distance between heaven and earth: as true man, he is at the same time the likeness of the Father in God. By appearing to us and stating that he is the Son, he brought us the supreme gift: direct access to God. He shows us the distance that has been overcome in him. He comes from above and thereby evidences himself as the Son of God: whoever loves him loves God. But he comes also as brother and neighbor, and whoever loves his neighbor loves him. Thus, in the unity of love, the whole of the distance between God and man has dropped away. Previously one saw, above all, how the Son leads men to the Father: he rounds them out, he presents them to the Father as his brethren. Now, his converse movement also becomes clear: how he introduces the Father to men, how he brings God nearer to them. That, however, in the eyes of the Jews, is the real sin: to bring God nearer. Only a distant God can be the true one. The Lord sees the life of men as death because they do not have the Father in them; in their eyes, however, he must suffer death because he claims that he has the Father in him.

19:8. *When Pilate heard these words, he was the more afraid; . . .*

Pilate recognizes that the path taken will lead to the death of the Lord. Thus his previous discomfort becomes a growing anxiety. He is not afraid of God, and also not of the Lord; what fills him with anxiety is the obvious injustice of these proceedings. It is his sense of justice that lies at the root of this anxiety. Included in it, he also feels anxiety about himself: about the unease that will overcome him because he has condemned an innocent man, about his bad conscience, about the impossibility of being able, from now on, to regard his judicial justice as the measure of all things. He is at the point of failing. Although he cannot be touched by the divinity of the Lord, he still assesses him correctly in a negative sense: he is, humanly speaking, not guilty. But what are human affairs coming to if human law is in such a state that a fanatical clique can break it, and in fact openly, before the judge? If, within the law, the inhuman can be demanded and attained? The world order is shaken, and together with it the soul of Pilate.

19:9. *. . . he entered the praetorium again and said to Jesus: Where are you from? But Jesus gave no answer.*

Outside, the Jews are screaming, and inside, the Lord is alone. As Pilate goes once again from outside to inside, he becomes more clearly conscious of the distance between both worlds. Outside, the raging mob, hate and darkness; inside, the silent divinity of the Lord. So Pilate attempts to obtain one last piece of evidence for a judgment, and asks the Lord about his place of origin. His question is more urgent than the previous ones, because he would also like to allay his anxiety. He would be almost relieved if he could now find something in the Lord that he could condemn. It would be less bitter to confess to the Jews that he had belatedly arrived at their view than to have to surrender him up as guiltless to their rage. Pilate knows that he will never again be rid of this anxiety. It is an anxiety to which nothing can be opposed and with which no rational argument can deal. But the question comes too late; the Lord no longer answers.

He has already stated so often from where he has come, he has made reference to the Father in constantly new phrasings. Pilate has missed his chance; the Lord disdains to allow faith to grow from *this* anxiety, which stems entirely from self-righteousness. Pilate knows no humility, no seeking, no prayer; otherwise, the Lord would have answered at once. This being too late applies to each of us. We all continually put things off. We set conditions, we haggle, we save up our devotion until we no longer have any alternative, until, without any magnanimity, we are simply forced by external factors. By then, however, the Lord could react to our question, too, with silence.

What ultimately gives no answer to Pilate's anxiety is the anxiety in the Lord himself. Not anxiety about what is to come. Rather, anxiety about what is already there. Anxiety as an expression of the entire situation. Anxiety as balance. At an end is the free activity, the active apostolate. Now it is time for enduring sin, its darkness, its shrinking back from the light, its anxiety. Including the anxiety of Pilate. It is not a converting answer that can help Pilate now. Rather, the Lord takes his anxiety upon himself, allows it to take possession of his divine-human soul. This anxiety of the Lord is directed not toward some future thing but toward the present. If anxiety is directed toward something to come, for example, an approaching, unavoidable catastrophe, then all of the person's attention concentrates itself upon that event, magnifying it in his mind beyond all measure. And yet it is anxiety about some future thing, and there perhaps still remains the possibility of averting it, of escaping it. Anxiety about something absolutely present precludes any hope of flight. That is the suffering of the Lord, the Christian anxiety. It is not precipitated by anything tangible. It is not concentrated upon anything. It is utterly formless. On the Cross, this anxiety will, in a way, be more understandable: the Lord will find himself overtaxed to the last degree in soul and body, will be wholly an end, wholly an emptiness. Now, it is more a matter of taking anxiety upon himself, of consciously entering into anxiety. As if he were saying to God: Give me still more anxiety, for I cannot bear the anxiety I now have. As if all paths within anxiety led only more deeply into anxiety. In this anxiety, the Lord gives no answer, because his whole answer is that of anxiety in anxiety.

19:10. *Pilate therefore said to him: You will not speak to me? Do you not know that I have power to release you, and power to crucify you?*

Pilate cannot understand why the Lord, who is, after all, under his power, gives him no answer. He is accustomed to having his prisoners give willing answers precisely to him, since they know that everything depends on his favorable disposition. He has the impression that the Lord is not aware of his power. Still more: he has the feeling that his power and the power of the Lord are two wholly different, incommensurable quantities. In his incomprehensible anxiety—incomprehensible for him because it is strange to him, because it estranges him from his innermost self—he becomes in a way clear-sighted. He sees that the Lord, too, has power over something powerful that is beyond him, that he has no access to at all. He tries, in sober terms, to outline the situation to the Lord and to explain the greatness of the worldly power to him. He knows no more impressive way to express this power than to point to the contrast between being released and being condemned to crucifixion. For Pilate, the distance between these two seems most enormous. For the Lord, it is, at this moment, but a tiny distance, not even able to be considered. He is at the mercy not of the power of Pilate but of the Passion in God. Human things no longer touch him; whether he is released or whether he is crucified cannot alter the fact that he is abandoned to the ultimate darkness. He is locked into the Passion, he is at the point of giving back to the Father the highest thing that a man possesses, his life, and, through his death, of leading the lives of all sinners toward eternal life. He is caught up in this event to such a degree that his release or his crucifixion are but empty words to him. At this moment, he knows only one thing, which fills him completely: anxiety in the suffering that has already begun. Pilate directs his words to someone who has already disposed of his life, who, as a man, is already no longer reachable by words because only one thing is more alive in him than ever before: his word of affirmation to the Father, which now takes the form of anxiety. For him, all of Pilate's power is the absolute sign of the powerlessness of the sinner. Translated into his own anxiety, it is an intensification of this anxiety through which he comprehends sinners more deeply.

19:11. *Jesus answered him: You would have no power over me unless it had been given you from above; therefore he who delivered me to you has the greater sin.*

The Lord answers now, without concerning himself about further aspects of his destiny. His destiny is in God and not in men. But he tells Pilate that his power comes from above. And in fact, the power of Pilate originates from above in two respects. First, from the nature of justice, which requires laws and also needs those who serve the law. And then, too, insofar as the Lord is destined to be condemned by none other than him. This does not at all mean that God desires judicial murder in order that his will might be fulfilled. Rather, Pilate has been installed here as judge and invested with judicial power by God, and this power entrusted to him by God would, in principle, enable him to pass a correct judgment. In his conversations with the Lord, he has glimpsed again and again the opportunity for a true judgment; grace stood before him and was so close that he could have grasped it. It is not God who forces him to make a wrong judgment; he has shut himself off from grace himself because his own sense of justice and his dry letter of the law appear more important to him than God. God leaves him with a free choice; he is not the prisoner of divine power but of his own power, which prevents him from choosing the good in freedom. By rejecting the power that God offers him, the power to be powerful in God, the power of grace, which should have allowed him to become a free instrument of God's plans, he becomes the prisoner of his own power and must serve God as a slave in his captivity. God does not lead his Son to him in order to have him sentenced by him, but in order to have him judged by the court of man, and it is for man to decide how he will judge the Son of God. It is up to man to recognize the Lord and open himself to grace or to reject him and close himself off to grace. In both cases, the power of God will emerge victorious over the power of man: in the one case, together with it; in the other, in opposition to it.

Therefore he who delivered me to you has the greater sin. The Lord is not without understanding for the confused situation of his judge. He recognizes degrees of guilt. Judas, who handed him over, possessed a quite different knowledge of grace. He sinned within grace against grace. Pilate attempts to extricate himself from his dilemma within his own power—he has previously known no other. Judas has seen and experienced everything: the Lord's miracles, his words, his love. And still he betrayed him, handed him over, abandoned him, sold him. Pilate is confined within the stifling little world of human thought. Judas would have been free to refuse betrayal through a simple No; Pilate would have had to set himself against the course of events with expenditure of the greatest force, with the courage of his entire personality, in order to stop its unfolding. The Lord's judgment here is the opposite of the judgment of some Christians, who often have more hate and contempt for the complacency of not giving committed support than for true betrayal.

19:12. *Upon this Pilate sought to release him, but the Jews cried out: If you release this man, you are not Caesar's friend; every one who makes himself a king sets himself against Caesar.*

Pilate senses that everything is developing more and more quickly counter to his will. So he now thinks only of one thing: to extricate himself. He sees no other way to do this than to release the Lord. Only by doing that will he be able to rid himself of the pressure that he is under. Up to now, he has had nothing else above him but the law, which he knew and by which he governed his actions. Now something new and completely incomprehensible threatens to open up above him that would carry him away with it into unknown adventures. The anxiety in him becomes a signal that his innermost self is now involved, that part of him which he does not otherwise talk about. Everything has begun to totter, he himself, the Lord, the Jews; all norms are taken from him, he can no longer see the situation as a whole. Thus he clings to releasing the Lord as if to a last straw. But his weakness shows itself only too clearly, and the Jews find it easy to break in here and take the field with stronger arguments.

Their new reasonings are inescapable. They are taken from Pilate's own closest sphere. As an official of Caesar's, he ought to look after Caesar's interests, to interpret the law in Caesar's sense. If the Lord declares that he is a king, then that claim implies rebellion against Caesar. Anyone who supports it makes himself guilty of the same outrage. The Jews pull the whole trial out of the private sphere, where it had previously been unfolding, and turn it into the "major issue" of an insult to Caesar; they put a public, and indeed world-historical, complexion on the accusation and the judgment, and Pilate is now to regard himself as a subordinate agent within the powerful branchwork of Caesar's legal structure. They want to affect Pilate in the most personal way by appealing to the impersonal in him. At the same time, they render him exposed: where justice would be expected—so they say to him—he shows a clemency that could betray his most secret intentions, that could allow his wrongdoing to appear no less great than the wrongdoing of the accused.

19:13. *When Pilate heard these words, he brought Jesus out and sat down on the judgment seat at a place called the Pavement, and in Hebrew, Gabbatha.*
Pilate brings the Lord out. He brings both of them, himself and Jesus, together under the law of the Jews: he will leave the judgment up to them. So once again the Lord steps forth, not of his own free will, but as led. He steps forth before a public that he no longer chooses, to which his relation is no longer that of a free man. He stands before it as someone accused, as someone handed over, in the end, as someone abandoned. The judge will lend him no further support.

The Lord stands in the midst of men, and each one participates in his fate. Each is attracted or repulsed by him, reacts with sympathy or disgust to him. No one can take a neutral stance toward him. The Jews have rejected him. Pilate has long wavered; now, at the moment when the Lord no longer allows him to be indifferent, he aligns himself with the Jews. At the trial, only the Jews and Pilate are to play a part. The others who have also encountered the Lord, who in one way or another have stood by him, suggestedly, tentatively, seekingly or already affirmingly—all of them are present in no way other than as included in the Lord. At this trial, they are no longer in attendance. They are, so to speak, covered by the Lord, and need not be present. The only one who has spoken the complete word of affirmation, the Mother, now lives wholly within the complete anxiety of the Son. John, through his love of the Lord and even more through the Lord's love of him, is a participant in the Lord's inner suffering. Peter, by contrast, is exempted from anxiety because he holds the office. The rest stand on their own at all levels between unease and feelinglessness. But they are all in the Lord. The Lord suffers the greatest anxiety about Peter, because Peter, insofar as he represents the Church, is exempted from anxiety. Insofar as the Church is the Bride, she does not know the masculine anxiety of the Bridegroom. The Lord takes her anxiety wholly upon himself. Because the Lord fulfills the totality of engagement, the Church does not now need to fulfill it as such. The Lord now takes all those who are his with him, insofar as they form the Church, without asking them first. His anxiety is the engagement for all. But he also contains within him the forms of ecclesiastical life: Martha and Mary and all the others. Everything that he has set up in visible form, that is *existent* and representative, has its engagement in him. An individual Carmelite woman can share in the Lord's anxiety by receiving the grace of participation; Carmel as such, as an institution, is wholly exempted from this anxiety, since the Lord has taken the totality of engagement upon himself. By contrast, every individual who believes, who grows, who permits the Lord to carry out in him what he demands of him: love of his neighbor—that individual participates in his anxiety. It is the anxiety of suffering, which can assume any form, a fruitful anxiety because it is the anxiety of redemption. In every form, however, this anxiety implies dim-sightedness: no one sees it as a whole, no one understands it, no one knows what it is for and where it leads. In everyone dwells the anxious question: What for? All know that something has been sown in them that apparently fails to flower. Everywhere, Christians suffer under the futility of Christianity. That is the unity of the anxiety. Peter, by contrast, busies himself in the meantime with his administration. He has no idea what it means to be the Rock. But he is busy with the Lord and with himself: with his denial and with the grace of the Lord; he attempts to put his affairs in order. And that is already, without his realizing it, the laying of the foundation stone of the administration of the Church. He and all the others are represented here, at the trial, solely through the Lord.

Thus are present here the Lord—seemingly alone but with many in him—Pilate and the Jews. The trial will be contested between the spurners, the waverer and the Lord. The Lord remains silent. He does not judge. He does not defend himself, because he stands precisely where he has to stand: in the place where he represents the sinners of the world. Opposed to him stands sin: the Jews, who, along with Judas, embody grievous sin; and Pilate, who has already heard the assessment of his guilt from the Lord—it is less grievous than that of the Jews. The judgment is pronounced by Pilate—by moderate sin, which, through its lack of committed support, fails to prevent the trial. Ultimately judged are the grievous sins, which even feel themselves justified by the offense committed.

19:14. *Now it was the day of Preparation of the Passover; it was about the sixth hour. He said to the Jews: Behold your King!*

The Passover feast is nearing, and if the Jews want to celebrate it, the judgment must be made quickly. Not only inwardly does everything press in the direction of the Cross. Outwardly, too, space and time become more and more constricted.

Behold your King! Pilate makes use of the term that was so often attacked by the Jews. He does so in an ambiguous sense. He gives the Lord the title that he deserves. He does not say anything against the Lord. It is almost as if he wants to honor him. On the other hand, however, he provokes the Jews by giving their accusation back to them in a compressed form. By presenting himself as the superior one in relation to both sides, he only exhibits more glaringly the wavering aspect of his own position. He does not want to take sides against the Lord. But just as little is he able and willing to act against the Jews. In the state of anxiety in which he finds himself, nothing would be dearer to him than peace and quiet. In the state of anxiety, by contrast, in which the Lord finds himself, there is nothing that would be dearer to him than anxiety. As dark as it is, he knows one thing: he must suffer it through. He does not enjoy it, it is terrible for him, but he knows that he must remain in it. Its inescapability is really inescapable. Its necessity is really necessary. Anxiety is now the way in which he has God. The growing anxiety within him, although connected with an apparent slipping away of God, is nevertheless a gaining in God. This he knows.

What he will now be deprived of, what he has long ago surrendered, namely, his life as a man on earth, is precious to him. He does not throw it away like something contemptible or even just something indifferent. He had looked forward to being allowed to exist not only as the eternal Son of God but also as a creature of the Father. The Father formed his human soul and his human body; he gave them to him—as to every man—as a personal gift. Thus, on earth, the Son had lived from thankfulness to the Father, not only because he was permitted to come to the world in order to sacrifice himself but even just because he was permitted to receive the Father's gift of existing as a man. Now he must painfully separate himself from that gift. It was perhaps an act of renunciation for him to become man and to deposit his magnificence with the Father. But it is also a sacrifice for him to take leave of this human form, especially since the ability to see his return to God and to eternal life, and, more importantly, to see his Resurrection, has been denied to him. Also, the following anxiety now arises within him: that, as a man, he will be nailed to the Cross. In the full strength of his years, he is on the way toward death, as a man who has obviously still not fulfilled his mission, who could perhaps still accomplish it, but does not have the consolation of being permitted to start over again. He sees how utterly hopeless things are regarding the fulfilment of his mission in this world. His increasing anxiety takes this form, too. Pilate's words no longer affect him. Neither through the fullness that they might possibly have nor through the emptiness that they have in reality. His fate continues, closed in upon itself, to take its course.

19:15. *They cried out: Away with him, away with him, crucify him! Pilate said to them: Shall I crucify your King? The chief priests answered: We have no king but Caesar.*

The Jews can no longer stand the sight of the Lord. They know of no new reason through which to justify their feelings, so they just scream: *Away!* The real reason is this: that complete purity stands in complete weakness before their sin. This purity is weak because purity deprived of the sight of God can only be weak. A purity that was based solely on morality, that was its own end, that possessed no rootedness in the world of faith, would have no reason to become weak if God withdrew from it. Moral purity of this sort is an inwardly closed quantity that is left in the hands of the individual: it can refrain at any time from certain matters or acts that it assesses as impure, and it can largely determine for itself how long it wishes to apply the chosen standard. Such purity has no roots in God; it is therefore lacking in true strength and is, in truth, sheer weakness. Ethical purity does not become strong until it is a product of faith, until it is rooted in God and in love. If the Lord's purity were only virtuousness, only that which the Jews know and see, then it would really be weakness: it would be that which they now see manifested in him. They do not, however, see how much his purity is rooted in God and has its strength there. It is precisely what is weakness in him, externally, that is his strength. Seen from the standpoint of unbelief, his purity is foolish, naïve and therefore contemptible. It has nothing of the heroic splendor of earthly virtue about it. Therefore nothing in his purity attracts the Jews, it only provokes them. His purity is like a language that they do not know; they can only find it irritating. Virtue in God and virtue on the basis of mere morality are things that do not coincide. Virtue in God is the life of faith and love; if someone within that life falls into sin, then he does not thereby lose his roots in God, and God will, in one way or another, draw him back again to him. By contrast, virtue that is grounded in itself, that is its own end and rests solely upon moral laws, is, should it fall, completely shattered and no longer reparable. Since it does not have its wholeness in and with God, it can no longer regain the wholeness that it supposedly had in itself. Thus incompatible things stand in opposition here, and the virtue of this world has no other response to the virtue of God than the cry: *Away, away!*

The Jews can no longer stand the sight of the Lord. In that sight are contained, disparately, a question and an answer. The question comes from the Lord, who is not understandable by them and presents himself that way to them. Through the quality of incomprehensibility that attaches to him, they feel a challenge to concern themselves with him. Yet they want to avoid precisely that at all costs; he is now a closed case for them. On a wholly different level, he is for them an answer. When they go through their laws, when they engage in their reflections, they do so with a view to the great promise. They know that, if not in them, then in the word of God, something is still to come. The Messiah has not yet appeared. And there is always the theoretical possibility that God's promised one could be identical with the one who stands bound before them. Or that he could at least possess a key to God, an approach or a transition to the great promise. Then it would be an answer. But if that were so, then they would have to change themselves. Then they would need to have in themselves the possibility of a question, the substance of a question. But they do not have that, because the substance of the answer has nothing to do with their substance. And they do not want to change themselves. Their sin and the purity of the Lord do not even form an antithesis; they nowhere touch upon one another. The two are not concept and counter-concept. The God that they serve and the God that the Lord brings are completely alien to each other. They would not have the slightest idea where to start in order to bring about a concordance. Thus they see only the one solution: *Away, away with him!*

Every morality that is an end in itself, and excludes faith, crucifies the Lord. And every opening within a closed morality that is an end in itself is nothing but a further securing of its closedness; every surrender that serves to further being an end in itself is only that much firmer a closure.

Crucify him! The chief priests demand his death. Whatever they do not understand must be done away with unconditionally. Whatever they cannot answer is not allowed to question. Whatever attacks the god who dwells in me is already, on principle, deserving of death. For my god, who dwells in me, fits me so well, is tailored so perfectly to my measure, that I do not tolerate the slightest alteration. My god brooks no comparisons that do not lie in me, no alien standards, nothing but himself. If my god had sent the Messiah, then I would have recognized him immediately. I know my god so well, I have invested him with so much of my nature, that I recognize him in all of his forms. If he who stands before me were really the Son of God, then I would recognize him as such without fail: he would have the qualities that my god has in me. Since, however, he cannot prove his identity, he must die a shameful death; he is a fraud who, moreover, has played his part badly because he did not even take the trouble to establish a link to me. If he were the son of the god that I know, then I would have recognized myself in him as in a mirror. But this one I do not know.

Pilate said to them: Shall I crucify your King? Pilate still characterizes him as King, and places the title of king side by side with the Cross. It is as if his stand in favor of the Lord were strengthening. Precisely because he has no access to the inner world of the Lord, because he cannot mirror himself in the Lord, cannot convert belief into unbelief— precisely because of that he becomes aware, as if by premonition, that something solemn and truthful stands before him here. What awakens in him is the opposite of the Jewish outlook. He does not require the God whom he could perhaps worship to enable him to perceive himself in him, to be an extension of himself. Precisely this he does not do. The Jews lack belief because they think they recognize themselves in God; Pilate lacks belief because he cannot recognize himself in God. The Christian, however, believes not because he perceives himself in God but because the Lord recognizes himself in him.

Implicit in what Pilate says is a kind of recommendation of the Lord to the Jews. To be sure, he would still like to be rid of the responsibility, and attempts to transfer it to the Jews. However, he no longer does so from pure egotism, but because he has somehow been touched by the greatness of the Lord. Basically, he would be thankful if the Jews, too, would acknowledge this greatness which he senses, and if they could make use of the Lord within their sphere. Then the solution would appear fully satisfactory to him, and he himself would be saved, not only in his official capacity but also in his moral personhood.

The chief priests answered: We have no king but Caesar. By saying this, they seem to recognize the law of the Romans as entirely their own. They do so in order to reject the Lord all the more thoroughly. They take the opportunity for this explanation all the more gladly because they expect to turn it to a twofold purpose. Firstly, to make an impression on Pilate. The more favorably disposed he becomes toward them, the more receptive he will be to their wishes. Also, their declaration of contrition will serve to commend them in higher places as well. But secondly—and this is, at the moment, perhaps the decisive thing—they will thereby get rid of the Lord altogether. They are so fed up with finding themselves confronted by him that any means for bringing the matter to an end is acceptable to them.

All the legal arguments have not sufficed to dispose of the Lord. With the Lord, there is no mere process of disputation: every answer to a question put by the Lord, and every question put to him, if it is to have validity and enable a living exchange, must spring from a commitment in the person. It is like the situation regarding proof of the existence of God: one can undermine everything negative with argumentation until one reaches the point where one sees that there is no longer anything opposing the possibility of what is in question. But moving from there to positive belief is a leap: the leap of inner yielding, of opening, of surrendering. A renouncing of the presumptuousness of one's own reason. Something childlike. A beginning of trust, and that means a beginning of love. Belief always contains this element of renouncing oneself so that God might be given room. Thus, at some time or other, one must also give way to the Lord, let go of what is one's own in order to accept what is his. Nobody arrives at belief by means of mere discussion, although belief can be quite well defended by reason. But Christianity is richer than all reason, so rich that it cannot be captured in any arguments. The Jews exclude this eternal amplitude. Since they know only reason and its expediency, they have no room for the Lord and belief in him.

19:16–17a. *Then he handed him over to them to be crucified. So they took Jesus and led him away.*

Pilate gives in utterly. Through the Jews' pledge of allegiance to Caesar, he is strengthened in his subjective consciousness of office. He bends to the will of the Jews, who, through their declaration, have underlined his power. In his anxiety, his insecurity and weakness, he feels obliged to give them, as those who now recognize the lawful power, some part in his authority. In the end, he is happy not to have to concern himself any longer with the Lord. What he was able to ascertain, in his detached objectivity, he acted upon. Had he gone any further, he would have fallen into dependency upon the Lord. Were he to open himself to belief, then he would also have to pass his judgment in belief. He could not both recognize the Lord as his inner authority and take legal action against him externally. Recognizing him, he would have to come to his defense in quite a different way.

That would, of course, lie within his power. He would then move personally into the Lord's sphere of influence. But under no circumstances does he want to forgo his personal rights. And it seems to him that acceptance of Christian faith is definitely bound up with that kind of renunciation. If he should begin to believe, then for a time he could probably still exercise his own authority to state what is clear to him, what he can believe, to what extent he can agree. He could still pass judgment. But then, at some time or other, he would have to hand judgmental authority over to the Lord, and from that point on, the Lord would determine what is to be done. Such a handing over seems too hard for him. Thus his position is similar to that of the Jews before him. The only difference is that the Jews reject in hate, while Pilate rejects in good will. He is one of the catholicizers who never want to draw the ultimate conclusion so that they will not have to surrender themselves. Therefore, he hands the Lord over, in order to be rid of him personally and thus to be able to retain his benevolent attitude. His benevolence will then be bound up with a certain regret: he will feel sorry, but will feel sorry without any obligation.

The *Jews* have attained what they wanted. Their state of mind is quite different from that of Pilate. They are exultant. They have won Pilate over by their declaration of allegiance, and they will bring the Lord to the Cross. From then on, they will once again be able to live undisturbed, in accordance with their old law. Those of them who would have been inclined, on the basis of the unknown power of God, to regard the relationship to the law as expandable are now glad to be able to brush that temptation aside. The whole matter has turned out to have been a hoax, and the old cycle is closed again, more strongly than ever. They do not yet know that the previous state of affairs will never reestablish itself because they themselves are no longer the same. The Lord has conveyed the living question of God to them, and they have rejected it. They will return no more to the law of God. They are in disobedience; at the point when God offered them his Son's love, they interposed their own interests and thereby turned their backs on God.

The *Lord* is left with his anxiety and his love. With a love of God and men that remains unvaryingly living, but is more and more deprived of nearness to the Father, so that it enters wholly into the restlessness of the anxiety and increases that anxiety. It becomes itself anxiously incomprehensible to him. His perception of men is clearer than ever: he sees their sins inescapably before him. But what he had done previously in his life—blot out their sins through his living love in order to bring them to the Father—he can no longer do, because the Father himself is receding from him. Thus he must take these sins up into his anxiety as well. The anxiety is now intensified through the love of the Father and through the sins of men; the two, which are related as water to fire, coalesce here in a unity of anxiety. The Father's love for him and his love for the Father radiate back to him in the form of anxiety: the Father bestows his love on him in the form of anxiety, and his love for the Father who has vanished causes him anxiety. Likewise, his love for men, too, radiates back to him as anxiety because it is not accepted by them. There is no longer any possibility at all of escaping this abyss of anxiety; every glance that he could direct away from anxiety would have to be a glance toward the Father or toward the sinner, and that would occasion an increase in anxiety. Within himself, there is increasing weakness, because anxiety fills him to such an extent that it saps all of the strength he had possessed. It is an ever-intensifying anxiety; he moves toward it, moves into it; he perceives that he had seen the Father more clearly, and sin less sharply, yesterday or an hour ago than he does now, and that the Father is vanishing while sin is burgeoning. He is caught up in this progression, and an end is not in sight. Once, the plan for redemption, which he had conceived together with the Father, was clear to him. Now, all clarity recedes from him, he becomes more and more helplessly subject, and he understands less and less why that is so. This anxiety of pure helpless subjectedness, in which the word of affirmation that he uttered in eternity emerges, so to speak, in its naked essence, is the same anxiety as that of the Mother when she began to carry him, the anxiety of being helplessly subject to God and to this Child in her: day by day it becomes more alien to her; she experiences it as the form of her destiny, which was precipitated by her word of affirmation but is more incomprehensible to her than ever. For if the Mother could comprehend her affirmation, she would have no part in coredemption. No one who directs his own affairs can coredeem, but only someone who has relinquished that direction to God. For redemption, even if it is effected by the Son and coeffected by the Mother, has its ultimate ground in the all-directing God.

The *Father* sees all of the Son's anxiety. He has to allow the Son to suffer in his loneliness. The Son's anxiety affects him, but, in order to let the anxiety become complete, he must wholly withdraw himself. The more the Son's anxiety intensifies, the more the Father deprives him of vision so that the Son might have the opportunity to prove completely his complete love. By doing that, the Father accommodates the Son; he knows that the Son wants to make a complete sacrifice of complete love. In order that this sacrifice might attain its fullness, any sort of alleviation that the Father could grant must be omitted. The Father does not thereby exclude himself from the Son's anxiety. He has complete participation in that anxiety, the only thing being that this participation must not become sensible to the Son. And the whole of the night into which the Son more and more deeply sinks is the night that is condoned and imposed by the Father, the Father's night. The Father does not allow his light to shine into the Son's darkness because the whole of the darkness now stands open for the world's sin. If light were in it, then the world's sin would not be in it; but the world's sin must enter into God's darkness in order to be redeemed there. The Son is passive in this darkness: he has relinquished his light. The Father is active in it: he actively prevents his light from shining into the Son's darkness. In order that the Son's darkness might not be affected by his light, the Father, too, conceals himself in darkness, so as to be sure that no ray of his light will now reach the Son. The Son moves into the darkness of weakness because he has deposited all his strength with the Father: the Father, however, needs all his strength—his own and that deposited with him by the Son—in order to bear this darkness and to refrain from cutting short the Son's suffering.

The *Holy Spirit* takes part in this happening between Father and Son. He noticeably increases the weakness of the Son by depriving him more and more of any possibility of support; by contrast, he strengthens, so to speak, the Father by keeping the plan for redemption before his eyes. Regarding the relationship between Father and Son, it is his task to render their sympathetic involvement both complete and impossible. Any sympathetic impulses that could lead to contact from one to the other he absorbs into himself and, precisely by doing that, becomes the witness to complete darkness. When Father and Son are once again united, he will once again become nothing but light, and will be able to remind them that the darkness had existed. This function as witness will enable Father and Son to see how great their love and their sacrifices were. Just as the Holy Spirit bears witness, through his being, to the fruitfulness of the eternal love and unity between Father and Son, so he now gives testimony to the fact that their love could reach as far as to the point of total alienation, of total mutual renunciation.

So they took Jesus and led him away. It looks as if men are now the ones who decide, who seize control and have mastery over the Lord and his truth. They are the active force, and he is surrendered weakness. Nothing more of his truth seeks outward expression. There is nothing that touches men; between them and the Lord there is no longer any sort of exchange. They have achieved what they wanted, and he, too, has achieved that: he is now in the condition for the sake of which he has come into the world. They apparently have mastery not only over him but over his truth, which has no more opportunity to proclaim itself. He is now just one thing: bound obedience; and to men it appears as if his teaching of love and hope has suffered utter collapse. His teaching does not even give him the strength to die as a hero, just as it had also not had enough strength to be effective in words. Thus it has not lent him any unexpected, supernatural power and will be of no consequence in his death. In their eyes, a faith must be defensible, and they were entitled to assume that the Lord would derive visible strength from his teaching. After all, even a false faith has the power, subjectively, to give its adherents the possibility of an honorable death, just as it had sufficient power to transmit itself to other men. And now, to their astonishment, they see that the Lord is no longer capable of instructing them, that he no longer even makes an attempt to convert them to his teaching or simply to avow something publicly that might have some connection with his earlier preaching. Above all, he had always preached love, and now he is someone who neither receives love anymore nor is in a position to speak of it or radiate it. Indeed, he himself no longer seems able to live out of love, since, in his extreme weakness, it is as if all love has been lost to him. They fail to see that precisely this condition is the condition of perfect love, because the Son was capable of transferring the whole of his love to the Father in such a way that he approaches death as dispossessed of all perceptible love. To the extent, then, that love ceases for the Lord, interest in the new teaching ceases for the Jews. There is nothing more left that might be debated here, that might be able to engage their minds. What is still to come now is nothing more than the speedy conclusion of this disagreeable episode. The Lord, however, suffers in all the areas in which suffering is possible. Everywhere that love was previously alive in him there is now just suffering, longing, complete incomprehension and incapacity, complete night. One would like to think that, in this night, in which he lives through the highpoint of his mission, he at least enjoys the satisfaction of continuing to stand in the service of the Father, exactly there where the Father wants to have him and where he wanted to place himself out of love for the Father. Although he may feel himself abandoned by the Father and by men, as well as by what was most particularly his—namely, of course, love—he could still rest in the knowledge that it is all his mission. Or that it will all pass and that he will afterward be with the Father again. Or that, as a result of this horrible night, men will be redeemed. But these consoling perspectives are fully closed to him, because he himself has wished to suffer completely, to possess nothing more that is not unconditional, absolute suffering.

In this condition, he allows himself to be led away. He does it in the same spirit in which he allowed everything to be taken from him. He has *given* everything to the Father, and this action now appears as the Father's having *taken* everything from him. That he gave it away voluntarily, he no longer wants to see. That he is being led away, will have no place other than that allotted to him by his enemies, intensifies in him the feeling of utter forlornness, of final destitution. Not even the place where he is belongs to him anymore.

THE CRUCIFIXION

19:17b. *. . . and he went out, bearing his own cross, to the place called the Place of a Skull, which is called in Hebrew, Golgotha.*

To the eye, it is only a cross of wood that he bears, too heavy, too large for him. So heavy that his strength is not capable of bearing it, that the disparity between being able to bear it and having to bear it becomes gapingly visible. But what he in truth bears is far less this visible wooden cross than all of what he was willing, through his mission, to take upon himself. It is everything that he has to give. Therefore it contains every offense that each of God's creatures commits against him throughout all time. It is so much that it can not at all be listed in specific detail, so much that it has no name even when taken in general. It is what had already been committed as sin, and already done to the Lord, at the time of his birth, as well as what will still be undertaken against the Father and him until the end of the world. It is not only every conceivable sin, it is every glance that averts itself from the Father, every word that is not a word of love, everything that constantly divides us from the Father. The Son takes all of that up into his Cross and makes things right through his love. If, however, love were noticeably alive in him, then he would, so to speak, transform every sin directly into love, almost automatically, mechanically, continuously, without being touched by it in his innermost self. His own love would be so great that he would experience neither sin nor its expiation as a particularly heavy burden. Since, however, he has deposited the whole of his love with the Father, the major as well as the apparently minor and slightest sins affect him, in every instance, most deeply. He has lost the protection of love, is left unprotectedly exposed to sin, not just *once* to *one* sin but, as if in an eternity of suffering, to every sin.

The visible cross indicates in its form the movement of the Son: the vertical beam points toward heaven, toward the Father. But the movement of the beam breaks off, and the Son looks out from the cross upon the earth. The horizontal beam points broadly outward, encompassing, like the Eucharist, all mankind, the entire world. And it, too, is broken off, and the Son does not see its continuation. He bears his cross without sensing its directions, its intentions and effects; he sees only what is limited and broken off, and feels the burden. This burden is the burden of our sins, which, as such, is simply too much for him, already at the physical level of bearing sin, and even more so at the mental. Physically, he is endowed with the strength of a man, and the material cross is too heavy for that strength. But since he suffers mentally, too, not as God but as a man, and since only this strength of a man is available to him as a man, he is actually bearing more than he can bear. When he made his agreement with the Father to bear the sins of the whole world, his divine love was then available to him in its total fullness. And now, at the moment when he would need it most urgently in order to fulfill his work, it is as if he were deprived of it. Thus the disparity becomes complete: he bears the burden of God and must bear it with the soul of a man, a soul that has lost the vision of God. The excessiveness of demand on him could be taken no further. He does not want to suffer exaltedly, like a God, but *humbly*, as a man would suffer. Yet, from the side of his divinity, the absolute vision of sin remains to him, and this is totally superhuman. It is as if, as God, he had promised to drink the oceans dry, which would, for God, have been something easy. But now, as man, he must carry out what he promised; God takes him seriously, and thus nothing remains to him but the impossible deed and the infinite suffering that goes with it.

19:18. *There they crucified him, and with him two others, one on either side, and Jesus between them.*

It is the *there* that has been chosen for his death: in the present by men, and from eternity by the Father. It is the Place of the Skull, where lie the remains of many. The Lord knows this place, and thus he looks out upon death before his death. And yet this death now has a face quite different from the one he had imagined. The death for which he came into the world, and which is the sacrifice that he wanted to make for the Father, is now nothing more than harshness and emptiness. He came in order to fulfill faith, love and hope; he came with the fullness of the truth that originally had its place between him and the Father, that drew its being from their mutual love. But now he is experiencing increasing abandonment, and his loneliness is so great that there is no longer any place in him for the light and consolation of that truth. A new fullness wells up within him now that forces everything else out: the fullness of man's sins. And he feels every individual sin just as if it were his own. He no longer differentiates between mine and yours. And the sins are not alleviated by remorse, not accompanied by hope for the Father's pardon nor by the love that he, the Lord, shows for the sinners. He wants to bear, and has to bear, the sacrifice in darkness. His capacity to take sin up into himself is so great that he now knows nothing in himself but incapacity, an incapacity to take hold of anything that would not be sin. And insofar as these sins are all the opposite of self-surrendering love, he suffers most from this lack, this being deprived of all divine life.

And as the Lord observes the preparations that are being made for his death, sin, too, overtakes him more and more. The sinners that surround him here sin against him. They manifest the essence of sin quite markedly: they are directly intent upon killing him. For the Lord, sin now takes on a wholly new aspect. Previously, he saw it as a force in the world that he wanted to counter with his love. He saw the original sin in which men are born, the sins of habitude, of contagion through other sinners, the ignorance of the Father, the powerlessness of men. All this he wanted to abolish: to show them the Father, to turn everything to the good with his forgiving love, to accompany them all through their lives from confession to confession, from absolution to absolution. But now he has given his lived-out love back to the Father. Formerly, when he had run up against sin and it had threatened to become too difficult, the Holy Spirit had always rekindled in him the courage for love, as if the Spirit could not tolerate his appearing weak before the Father. For to possess, as God, a human nature required no little assistance: he was supposed not only, as God, to be man, but also, as man, to be God; he was not only allowed to humble himself, but also had always to elevate himself, and between humbling and elevating there was no fixed mean, but rather a constant movement, for which, to be sure, his divine spirit was strong enough, but for which his flesh would have been inadequate had it not received constantly new invigoration from the Holy Spirit. Without that invigoration, he could perhaps have become so weary that even the Father would perhaps have been no longer able to accept the mission because it went too far beyond the powers of a man. Therefore the Holy Spirit supported the Son's humbling as well as his elevation to his divine-human office. Up to now, through the work of the Holy Spirit, things never came to the point at which the sacrifice would have become too difficult. It was he who provided the necessary help and strength, mediating between heaven and earth to such an extent that the sacrifice never appeared meaningless. Finally, however, in order to bring the sacrifice to its absolute level, even the Holy Spirit concealed himself along with the Father. He is, to be sure, with the Father in that he hinders him, as it were, from going to the Son, and he is also with the Son, but in such a way that he weakens him and withdraws from him his helpful contributions. It is as if he is now an *expression of the Word:* the Word is the Son, and he, the Third Person in God, is the successor to the Son who, as such, has taken over obligations: obligations of the Son and obligations to the Son which he now upholds with the Father. He is their agreement become objectified. The Son, deprived of any experienced love and filled with the world's sin, now submits himself to the justice of the Father. He goes to judgment. He is now the man who has burdened himself with all sins although he himself is without guilt. The Father could now pass judgment accordingly. He could acquit the Son, which would correspond to pure justice. That, however, is prevented by the Holy Spirit, who knows the Father's intention to accept in full the entire sacrifice of the Son's love and thus, too, his representativeness of sinners. Not only the sacrifice of life but also that of love must be heeded by the Father, and in the love—given up and given away—that the Son has forgone, his affiliation with all the sinners of the world.

Thus the Son is, above all else, dispossessed. In place of the belief that he brings, there is night; in place of hope, hopelessness; in place of love, pure deprivation of love through the sin that fills everything in him. He no longer knows as he knew before, when he came into the world and all his knowledge was a luminous knowledge of love, a mystery of love. The sacrifice and the knowledge of it were both generated wholly out of love, in love both were living and transparent. Now, when access to love is blocked, so, too, is access to understanding. The Lord looks no longer toward God but straight into sin and its hopelessness. If a priest hears confession and recognizes the gravity of the sins that he allows himself to be confronted with, he nevertheless also possesses faith in the forgiveness of the Lord. He can refer the sinner to the Lord's grace, he can open the way from sin to redemption. The Lord, however, does not now take any cognizance of redemption. He can be compared with a priest to whom the sins of the whole world have been confessed and who is so overwhelmed by their immeasurable mass, so weighed down, that he does not know, in his helplessness, where to find the strength for absolution. And the Lord is not allowed, for now, to know that he bears the hopelessness of all sins so that he will be able, later on, to remit all sins. Would it not be better that all sin should remain hidden and unaware of itself than that, as now, it should be so hideously exposed with no one being able to do anything about it? In this suffering are also included and embodied all false "confessions" and disclosures of sin that are hopeless because they have no knowledge of absolution. They are included because, in an excess of love, the Lord has taken even *their* hopelessness upon himself. This excess is the relinquishing of love itself. The love that the Son has now deposited with the Father is the treasure upon which the priest draws when he grants absolution. Throughout the sinner's whole *life,* from confession to confession, he is continually redeemed anew through this love that the Son has deposited with the Father, through this mystery of the reciprocal life of love between Father and Son. When he *dies,* then he is conclusively redeemed into heaven through the singular event of the death of the Lord on the Cross.

And with him two others, one on either side, and Jesus between them. The two robbers are common criminals who both, by virtue of being present, are granted participation in the proffered grace of the Lord's death. One of them is turned toward him, the other faces away from him. The one turned toward him receives the promise, the one facing away does not receive it. Both were accused, convicted and found deserving of death according to human judgment. The first one, who really is a criminal, will pass directly from this just human trial to entry into paradise. About the fate of the other one we know nothing, except that he was granted the grace of being allowed to die at the Lord's side and in the same way as the Lord. Perhaps for him, too, where earthly morality comes to an end, that end will become the beginning of a grace that allows his forfeit life to flow out into eternal life.

The three who are crucified seem to be interrelated in an ascending way: at the bottom, the one who faces away; in the middle, the one granted grace; and at the top, the Lord. But that is not the case, for the robbers are crucified *one on either side,* while the Lord hangs *in the middle.* For him, the distance to the right is just as long, and just as short, as that to the left. All three together, however, become the archetype of Christian death—the two robbers in spite of their sin, the Lord by taking all sin upon himself. There is something deserving of respect about the robbers' death: we see in it the proper relationship between guilt and sin. The Lord's death, by contrast, remains incomprehensible; in it there appears a cruel and almost ridiculous contrariety. In life, he had promised the highest, and this is how it ends! For the disciples as for the outsiders, there is almost something insulting about being presented with such a spectacle. In our eyes, the straightforward sin of the robbers is somehow closer to us, more familiar, more human; their death is a part of the world order, they themselves belong to us. The death of the Lord is something strange; he has nothing to do with our world, he seems to be a sheer eccentricity, and something like contempt and malicious pleasure enters into our view: it is what he pretty well deserves. Something of that sentiment will be transferred to every Christian death, particularly the deaths of those who perish for their belief. They, too, incur the odium of a certain ridiculousness. As long as anyone does not stand livingly within the Faith, does not attempt to die to himself in order to allow the Lord to live in him, then for him Christianity will never quite lose a tinge of embarrassment; he will claim his reserved judgment of Christian "extremism" as a human right and regard as a healthy instinct his almost unconscious resistance to any confusion with "fanaticism". This banishment of the Christian from the normal, natural world is suffered by the Lord when he perishes between the two robbers.

The Lord's suffering in the middle position also signifies a certain mediocrity. There can be those whom the death of the robbers does not leave without admiration: they feel themselves touched by the earthly tragedy, by the relationship between wrongdoing and atonement; they love this kind of greatness that includes sin within it. In the death of the Lord, which contains no sin, they find nothing to attract them. It strikes them as colorless. Now, the Lord could also have chosen an exalted form of death in order to satisfy our passion for grandeur. He did not do so. He covered his greatness beneath the cloak of a slightly contemptible ordinariness that, at the same time, also has an estranging effect. Henceforth, then, when assessing someone's lot in life, we may no longer judge by the standards of human greatness, or perhaps also human tragedy; for it may well be that, in the banality of a commonplace fate, the greatness of the Lord has ensconced itself.

The robbers who are crucified with the Lord, and who are allowed to participate, as the first and directly, in his death, are completely strange, unknown men who played no part in the whole prior course of events. It is by no means the closest associates of the Lord, not John and not Peter, who share his destiny. Again and again, the Lord draws that which is most alien into his death. And the Church has no right to withhold admittance to her and her sacraments from those on their deathbeds who, like the robbers, were seemingly remote from the Faith, had perhaps adhered to it only externally or after several attempts had turned away from it again. Even such as they, at the hour of their death, can be granted the grace of conversion, be suddenly drawn, while receiving the last sacraments, into the center of the mystery of the Lord's death. And the Lord lends the robbers support, as they die, by dying their human deaths with them divinely. One of them he redeems immediately and visibly, the other he allows to go the way of the sinner who remains unseeing, with nothing more being known of him than that the Lord died for him, too.

19:19. *Pilate also wrote a title and put it on the cross; it read: Jesus of Nazareth, the King of the Jews.*

Pilate comes back once again to the fact that Jesus is the King of the Jews. Now he even records this truth in writing. He knows that it is too late and that his inscription will not change anything. But he knows equally well that, in his innermost self, he finds no reasons for opposing this title, and furthermore, even feels convinced that there must be something true in it. He has the typical attitudes of the catholicizing outsider. He is ready to recognize the truth of the Church, but he does not have the strength to accept the consequences. Since that causes him increasing discomfort, he attempts to satisfy a certain sense of justice and to buy his way out through that. It was not out of scorn that he inscribed the title but from a feeling of growing respect. And what he wrote is not objectively false. If Christianity were a philosophy, a system, then Pilate would already be a Christian. He would have recognized, quite objectively, the existence of a truth. But because Christianity is a confession, requiring belief and hence devotion to something infinite that one cannot comprehend, Pilate is still a long way from being a Christian, despite his recognition. For he does not want to commit himself to devotion. Again and again, one will meet with this attitude, outside the Church, on the part of men who remain outside because they wished to have things their own way to the very end, because they do not want to accept that which distinguishes Christianity, to the very end, from a world view, namely, living love. They shrink back more from the consequences than from devotion itself. They resemble those women who, as long as they are in their fruitful years, never commit themselves to marriage. They would perhaps have been prepared to devote themselves, but the consequences—a child—are unwelcome to them. This is the situation from the beginning of Christianity onward, because it must be established with full clarity right from the start that what is involved here is something living, which makes demands and even lives from constantly demanding. Not only is the Lord the Ever-Greater, but because he is that he also demands from us the always-more. The more that he reveals himself, so much the more must he also draw things into his greatness.

The inscription is placed where it can be seen. Two things stand side by side in the document: that he comes from Nazareth—the human—and that he is the King of the Jews—the divine. Pilate puts the two side by side, as the apparent contradiction in the being of this crucified man, and leaves the riddle of this contradiction open above his death.

19:20. *Many of the Jews read this title, for the place where Jesus was crucified was near the city; and it was written in Hebrew, in Latin and in Greek.*

Many of the Jews read the inscription, and in fact Pilate has written it primarily for the sake of the Jews. Once again, he brings the whole conflict before their eyes, and they are to be forced to take a position regarding it. As they file past the Cross individually, man by man, and catch sight of the inscription, they are to be confronted once again, individually, with the consequence of their own verdict and are to draw their conclusion from that. Previously, they had passed judgment as a multitude. Now, they come individually or in small groups, and have a chance to reflect on that and to discuss it with one another. Inherent in this new opportunity that is offered to them would be the possibility of conversion of the individuals. Only as an individual can one become a Christian. Even if entire tribes or groups are converted, what is involved, if the conversion is authentic, can still only be a sum total of individual conversions. Each one is questioned as a person and each must answer. To be sure, the Lord will die for all, but in the sense that he dies for each individual. And thus his question, too, is always directed to the individual. And no one can excuse himself because of the belief or unbelief of the great multitude. He himself is questioned. Pilate knows that—as applied to others; only as applied to himself does he not know it. He would like to have others disquieted by the personal character of Christianity. For himself, however, he has rejected and resolved the question of the Lord.

The inscription is written in three languages: Hebrew, Latin and Greek. Hebrew is the sacred language, the language of the law. Latin is the administrative language, which imparts the stamp of state officialism. Greek is the language of all, the colloquial language that everyone must understand even if he might not know the others. And through these three languages, the Jewish readers are to be affected in a threefold way: by the Father, by the Son and by the Holy Spirit. For all three Persons are included under this title: *King of the Jews.* From time immemorial, the Jews were the chosen people, chosen by the Father to receive the promise. They are the guardians of the law of the Father. In order to keep his promise, he has sent them the Son, who came to fulfill the law. The Holy Spirit continually mediates this promise and fulfilment by mediating, during the Son's sojourn on earth, the living life between him and men as well as between him and God. Through the Hebrew words, the Father is signified, who stands at the origin of the people's being chosen; through the Greek, the Son, who speaks the language of mankind, who addresses himself to all, to all who are sinners, to Jews, Romans and Greeks; through the Latin, the Holy Spirit, who regularly links up with the official in order to implement it through his Spirit. He imparts to this officiary language—which only makes impersonal statements and has no intimate effective power—his personal, divine meaning, which he brings with him from heaven and which gives it explosive and simultaneously universal force.

Many Jews understand all three languages; they read the inscription in all three and are wounded by each in a new way. Through the Hebrew, they feel themselves personally affected in their tribal consciousness. The Latin—given that they have subjected themselves to Rome yet have not been subjected inwardly—sounds like an official accusation directed especially at them: they wanted to have their own king, and it seems as if *they* bore the whole insurrection on their conscience, and an attempt were being made to strike at them by punishing their king. The Greek affects them because they give the impression of forming a separate clique within mankind; that sets them apart, but even though they are in truth set apart, they still do not like to have their attention called to the fact. Wherever, then, they are vulnerable, this inscription affects them.

19:21. *The chief priests of the Jews then said to Pilate: Do not write, "The King of the Jews", but "This man said, I am King of the Jews."*

In order to emphasize their subservience once again, the Jews send their chief priests to petition Pilate. They would like to blunt the point of something they regard as an indictment of them: it should be expressly observed that they by no means endorse what is asserted in the inscription. It is no longer the mass of the people that comes forward, but a deputation, so that their attempt to dissociate them-selves might bear an official stamp. The blame, on the other hand, must fall back upon the Lord: *This man said, I am King of the Jews.* They take exception to the content of that claim. And their very taking exception seems to them to contain proof of the falsity of the claim. Thus they show that they remain unchanged, those who they were from the beginning; that their language, their judgment can never detach itself from the truth. And above all, that the kingship of the Lord can only have an earthly content. For them, kingship means either being king by virtue of birth or being chosen as king. Any-thing else would be usurpation. That God himself, before whom they wish to bow down, sends a king whose power actually rests with God, who derives his rights and obligations directly from God — this they are incapable of recognizing, since, for themselves, they derive rights and obligations solely from the letter and not directly from God. Under the New Covenant, by contrast, it is only through love that the law and the letter are interpreted, and thus through the Lord, or more precisely (because love never signifies stagnation), through the Lord's love for men and through his love for the Father. The Jews can expect only a kingdom of the letter. That God could lower himself to creating a Kingdom of love, in which the law would be something quite secondary, goes beyond their understanding. What they want is law, tables of thou-shalt-nots, power and security.

And yet Christians must guard against making the Lord's King-dom of love into a new Jewish kingdom. This love of the Lord, which is a true but spiritual power, must not in any way be materi-ally isolated, as, for example, in a separate worship of his heart. If one did not see that his heart is wholly bound up with the aforemen-tioned movement of love toward the Father and toward men, and that its livingness exists only within that context, then one would be forced to isolate it more and more, to dress it up more and more in sentimental words, and ultimately to turn this symbol of the living Kingdom into a dead object of devotion. It is also possible, out of sheer enthusiasm for a "Kingdom of Christ", to move farther and farther away from the living King and to end by exalting nothing more than the King's scepter. In the Church, too, it is possible to allow what is living to become ritualistically petrified.

It is common to both Jews and rigidified Christians that they do not themselves want to be drawn into the true service of the King. The dangerous torrent of the Lord's love, which they extol, must not sweep *them* along with it. They trivialize his Kingdom into an innocuous matter that ultimately has nothing to do with them. If the Lord had revealed himself as the earthly king of the Jews, then they would have been aware of it and would, for better or worse, have had to adapt to this honor that God had shown them and place themselves at his service. They would simply have deferred to the power of the king. They would not have been at all free to resist it. And if *we* were to receive so many shows of grace from the Lord that we were, so to speak, sensually overpowered from outside ourselves, if every breath that we drew were to contain perceptible love for the Lord, then we, too, would be forced to serve him, even if we did not wish to. But God does not want service of that kind. We have our freedom to decide, and God offers us faith and love. As long as we, like the Jews, seek all proofs of genuineness within ourselves, we cannot take up God's proposal. But there is a bridge between experience and faith: we have to love one another. Love of one's neighbor is the key to love of the Lord. The only thing is that it must be genuine love of one's neighbor—not merely external, material dedication, but rather true inner devotion, spiritual assistance and a sincere offering of ourselves. If it is this, then love of our neighbor will lead us without fail to love of God; between the two there exists a kind of osmosis, because Christ is at once both God and man, and there is nowhere in him any point at which separation could take hold. He is simultaneously both exaltedness and humiliation. Accordingly, when the Jews reject his kingship, and thus his exaltedness, they also reject his sacrifice. They demand his sacrifice as an atonement for *his* sins, and they fail to notice that it is the atonement for theirs. Because they measure every man—and thus the Lord as well—by their own standards, which means against themselves, they project into him everything that they think and do. They can analyze themselves into a very complicated table of values and then judge the entire world by that; nevertheless, they measure everything against themselves. They see, for example, that they are well-meaning. Anyone more well-meaning than they would be stupid, and anyone much less, carping. They themselves are at the midpoint of the scale. They produce every criterion out of themselves. Thus they necessarily reject the kingship of Christ.

The kingship and the heart of the Lord are both unmeasurable, because they are both inherent in the Lord's love for God and the world. As long as we measure them by our standards, we have not understood them, for we possess no such standards. The last thing in us is love, which has its standard in the unique love between Father and Son.

19:22. *Pilate answered: What I have written I have written.*

Pilate does not allow himself to be influenced. What he has written he wrote in a more or less official capacity, and he does not allow his official actions to be dictated by the Jews. On the other hand, he sees more and more clearly that the Lord cannot be guilty of anything, and that the blame for his death must therefore lie elsewhere. It is too late now to undertake inquiries into this; Pilate is also not in any mood for undertaking such inquiries, since they could not be carried out solely in an official capacity, but would require the participation, in fact the surrender, of his own personality. Becoming involved with the Lord has wide repercussions; one never reaches an end with the Lord, but rather, something unknown gets progressively drawn into the matter. Thus, he sees something of the always-more, although he does not see its source in the Father. All that he can do in this situation is to stand by what he has inscribed. He is not himself clear about just what he thinks of its contents; but he has proclaimed it, in the three languages of his office, to the prosecution and to the general public. What has happened has been passed on to the whole world. It is not only those who were direct witnesses of the occurrence who will have to come to terms with it. Through Pilate, the death of the Lord becomes a part of history. He forces everyone who learns of the Lord's actions to come to terms with his kingship.

19:23. *When the soldiers had crucified Jesus they took his garments and made four parts, one for each soldier; also his tunic. But the tunic was without seam, woven from top to bottom; . . .*

The Lord's garments are the soldiers' booty. They distribute this booty justly, according to a justice based on their own experience. They are a rough lot, and their justice is a regulating of mutual lust for booty. Anyone who took more than he deserved would have to expect to be punished by the others. This justice has nothing to do with morality and law. They have earned their booty by nailing the Lord to the Cross. What they felt as they did so, what became of their sense of justice during that time, is not stated. All that is important to them is the reward for their deed, the distribution of the booty. They divide among themselves everything that the Lord possessed by way of earthly goods. And that everything is his garments, which had served to protect his body. Thus, although he had walked this earth for more than thirty years, he possessed nothing more by way of earthly things than what he required for the present moment. And now even that little is taken from him, so that he is naked when brought to the Cross.

Among the garments is the Lord's tunic, which is seamless and consists of one single fabric. This tunic, which he wore, is the symbol of his life. His life, too, is seamless from start to finish: he came from God into the finitude of this life, he was born, he lived and died, but his beginning and his end lie in the infinitude of the Father. His whole personal being is that which was given to him by the Father: it stems from the one substance of the Father, and there is nothing in his personhood that manifests any quality and nature other than, in each particular case, precisely and solely the divine, the fatherly sort of being. So much so that even his earthly appearance, his earthly life, the countenance that he turns toward us, express nothing other, can speak to us of nothing other, than his vision of the Father. And if his being is embodied in this tunic, which becomes the possession of the soldiers, then that occurs so that those who attempt to participate in his being and his love should begin to understand the seamlessness, the endlessness of his substance, and therefore also his gift. In the individual Christian, too, the Christian substance is seamless. Regarding this or that Christian—for example, some saint—we believe that we can identify individual actions and deeds, can see beginnings, developments and endings. But we never know what was already present in him when we begin to determine just when some given thing was begun and what its effects have been. All Christian life is seamless because it is participation in the seamless unity of Father and Son. Not only in God are love and devotion unending; in the world, too, they cannot be chopped up into pieces: the love of all who love is so internally cohesive that no one can know where it begins and ends. A lover loves because others, because ultimately perhaps all others, love along with him, share this love with him, make this love possible in him. Whatever comes to pass in Christian love and grace participates in the being of the Lord, and thus has neither beginning nor end insofar as the love comes from above, out of the oneness of eternity.

We do not know who received the tunic. It vanishes, it is dispersed, it is given away namelessly, it is lost to view, and thus it fulfills its purpose as a memento, as a relic of the Lord. And just as the Lord's tunic fulfills and unfolds its meaning also as a symbol, so everything that comes into contact with the saints expands, within the embodying—and therefore also grace-embodying—symbol, into the essential. That is the reason for the existence of all relics: in order to lead us from corporeal things to the seamless, unending grace of the Lord. Even if a relic should one day restore a sick person to health or otherwise effect the granting of some request, the grace received is never, therefore, a limited one. Every such granting is always but an occasion for the widening of faith and love, which are, in themselves, unlimited: just as the Lord's tunic refers directly to the seamless unity of the Lord with the Father, or as the whole earthly countenance of the Lord reveals his eternal vision of God. Any finitization of the grace that inheres in the relics would be mere superstition, not Christian faith. Superstition is death, while seamless Christian faith is life.

The Lord knows quite well what he is doing when he leaves his garments and his tunic behind to be divided up. He could have allowed this legacy, too, to become lost to history, just as so many of his words and deeds have died away in the world unused and unrecorded. He gives this earthly legacy over to men in the full knowledge that the relics will not become a stimulus to life for everyone, but rather, for some, will be an inducement to death, to superstition. Just as he permits the cults of his kingship and his heart even though they can be misused, so here, too, he has no fear of the possible consequences. For along with his garments and tunic goes his living grace, which is capable, again and again, of awakening the life of faith wherever death exists. In his Church, it will be no different: she, who appears so dead, is nevertheless life, because she is in his power and because he can always awaken her to new love and devotion. Everything which, in the eyes of the faithful, may appear withered, aberrant and benumbed can nevertheless be all right in its secret essence, because the Church, too, must take account of the lowliness of things human. In everything material, there can inhere a secret livingness, and it is not potential misuse that is the most pitiable thing about the Church, but always, rather, the ecclesiastical arrogance that imagines itself to be above such misuse. It is up to true Christians to demonstrate constantly anew the true meaning of all symbols, relics and signs of the Church, to bestow upon them anew the meaning that always inhered in them and was always a true Christian life.

The sacraments, as signs and symbols, possess in themselves a spiritual force; but we usually attend only to the grace that they contain and not to the sign. The relics and the sacramentals also possess, if in a different way, a spiritual grace in their symbolism, and here we attend most often more to the sign than to the grace. The sacraments derive so much from above that we almost ignore their worldly side; the sacramentals, so much from below that we do not understand them spiritually enough. But the great that comes from above and the small that rises from below meet precisely at that midpoint where the two faces of the Lord—the one turned toward the Father and the one turned toward the world—are one. *From top to bottom,* the Lord's tunic is seamless, from heaven to earth, from God to sinner.

19:24–25a. . . . *so they said to one another: Let us not tear it, but cast lots for it to see whose it shall be. This was to fulfill the Scripture: They parted my garments among them, and for my clothing they cast lots. So the soldiers did this.*

The soldiers do not dare to tear the seamless tunic. They know that it must remain whole. The decision is to be made by casting lots.

The fall of the lot is something that does not lie within their justice; it is a power that they do not themselves determine, but one that they are happy to abide by. As much of their booty as is divisible they distribute according to the law of their justice; what is indivisible they bring under a special law whose rules they themselves do not know. They blindly trust a power that cannot be defined by them, namely, chance. Thus they show that they need something in their lives—and ultimately make use of it as well—that is no longer decided by them themselves. They acknowledge the existence of something that remains indeterminable by them. It does not play a large role in their lives, yet it crops up occasionally, and in this instance it increases the pleasure that they take in their little distribution. It imparts to their reward a touch of the unexpected, of suspense. He who wins the tunic is "lucky". The draw was kind to him. The others feel no envy, for they have, after all, agreed to the game. But in truth, they do all these things because *Scripture must be fulfilled.* Chance, from the viewpoint of God, is the fulfilment of a prophecy. By conceding a place to chance, the soldiers bring themselves directly under the power of the Old Law. Through their need for the unexpected, something foretold is lawfully fulfilled: that the Lord's garments would be divided up among themselves by his persecutors *and that lots* would be cast for his clothing. So the *soldiers did this:* they began to leave open a sphere in their lives that is not controlled by their human justice, and the possibility existed that this sphere could be one of grace, that God could make use of this sphere in order to fulfill a prophecy and thus also to draw them into the sphere of grace.

19:25b. *But standing by the cross of Jesus were his mother, and his mother's sister, Mary the wife of Clopas, and Mary Magdalen.*

By the Cross of the Lord stand three women. The first is his Mother, who has accompanied him from his birth to his death, who accompanied him even before his birth in that she had consented to him, and who will continue to accompany him until his Ascension—who was always his because she had participated all along in his being. Through her word of affirmation, she received his substance into herself, but her being was already marked from all time by her

Son's substance. She was not only the Mother for her Son, she was the Mother in the whole determination of her being through the Son, even before she had agreed to the motherhood through her word of affirmation. The preparation for her motherhood was already motherhood. In that, she fulfills the destination of woman: she is the Mother as such, the Mother of all, the Mother for all. The essence of her motherhood is what allows her to say Yes to the angel's question, just as the affirmation of a nun, when taking her vows, is the consequence of her affirmation upon entrance. Mary embodies, beneath the Cross, the Mother as such.

Next to her stands the second one: the wife of Clopas, who embodies any woman in particular. But this representative of any woman at all is distinguished by the fact that she is connected with the Mother of the Lord, that she thus has some idea of the relationship between the Mother and the Son. She is present in that capacity, and embodies the Catholic woman in general. She has been selected to stand beneath the Cross, and it is actually almost a coincidence that she has a name. Just as Mary is Mother, so she is woman.

Finally, as the third one, there is present the sinner. Her presence is just as clearly required as that of the two others. She is one of those for whom the Lord had set out on his earthly path and whom he has converted while on that path. Woman, as having been redeemed from her grievous sin.

At the Cross, these three women fulfill their role of suffering, of love and of gratitude. Each one of them, each with her characteristic quality, stands there again and again wherever there is suffering in the name of the Lord. Together they fulfill, again and again, that which is needed in order to give the Cross the resonance that God had envisaged for it. It is impossible to imagine the Cross without them. They all suffer: the Mother, because she is losing her Son; the wife of Clopas, because she fulfills the meaning of her existence in this suffering; and the Magdalen must sense that the Lord is atoning for her sin after having freed her of it. Together, they circumscribe the possible modes of womanly suffering by simply standing there and suffering, each in, and according to, the measure conferred by God.

They stand *by the Cross.* They are that which, outside the Cross, is now living. They do not stand next to it, like that false kingship, that false heart, stood next to the truth. At the same time, therefore, they stand in the Cross. The Mother stood there from the very start, when, through her fulfilling word of affirmation, she codetermined the possibility of the Son's word of affirmation, while her own word of affirmation was determined through the infinite reciprocal word of affirmation of Father and Son. She embodies everything that *makes possible* the mission, and therefore also the suffering, of the Son. Mary Magdalen, by contrast, embodies the *fulfilment* of the mission. She is the one redeemed from her sins: the fruit of the Cross who, as such, is present at the suffering for her sin. The third is the anonymous, the common woman, whose role appears rather dim, with only her presence attesting to the fact that her task is essential. All three women live on after the Cross. Because they live and suffer in the Cross they remain alive: thus they fulfill their mission, and that mission is everlasting. Mary does this as the wholly pure one, the vessel of the Holy Spirit, providing accompaniment and assistance in every case of human suffering, and always emerging, amid its purification, as the already purified purity. Radiant and mild, there appears in her motherliness, whose greatness sustains itself throughout the suffering, all that she has cosuffered in the suffering of her Son. But the second, nameless woman also fulfills her mission when she comes to the grace of the suffering and stands between the purest one and the sinner. She is distinguished by no special holiness, her calling is not special participation in the Passion; she only demonstrates the possibility that someone can stand by the Lord in his hour of death, wordlessly, wholly veiled in the unobtrusive. That this woman is present is characteristic of the pure, groundless, overflowing grace of the Lord. Magdalen, who was permitted to receive the Lord's grace, now fulfills the office of her gratitude and penance by coenduring something of the suffering of the Cross.

Thus stand opposite one another the purest one and the sinner. But the Lord cares not only about the purest one who accompanies him and about the sinner whom he has cleansed of most grievous sin; he cares no less about Mary the wife of Clopas; and if his suffering is a suffering for all, then those who stand in the anonymous middle should not forget that they, too, have stood beneath the Cross, that one need be neither exceptionally pure nor exceptionally sinful in order to be looked upon in a special way by the Lord at the Cross. Neither from our viewpoint nor from the Lord's do exceptional purity or exceptional sinfulness signify prejudgment to blessedness. Christianity is not a religion of extremes. Not even a religion of special identifying marks. Not only what is articulated, prominent and organized forms the Church, but also what is unknown, anonymous and seemingly ordinary. And everything extreme that in fact exists, and also ought to exist, must possess something of the humility of the middle.

19:26. *When Jesus saw his mother, and the disciple whom he loved standing near, he said to his mother: Woman, behold, your son!*

In one glance, Jesus sees his Mother and the beloved disciple. And it is basically to both that he appeals by just addressing the Mother. For his words are never directed exclusively at a single individual. If he says something to someone, then it is always meant for another as well. When he says to his Mother, *Woman, behold, your son!* John is already included in those words. The Lord addresses his Mother in the hour that, for her, is the hardest. She is not unprepared for this hour, but the hour does not therefore weigh any less heavily upon her. For it is now that she gives her beloved Son back to God. She does this in darkness. While the Son loses his contact with God, the Mother, too, loses sight of his path. A sacrifice that is performed in full view would not be a Christian sacrifice. If a man renounces some lower good for the sake of some higher one that he knows and has in view, then that is no sacrifice but only a choice between two goods, one of which appears more important than the other. But if he renounces some good that he loves in order that God might receive what he desires, then that implies a true sacrifice, because he does not know what form God will give to that which he offers him. The sacrifice lies in surrendering the ability to hold this in view. So it is here, too: in making their sacrifice, Mother and Son lose it from view together. All human justification for the sacrifice, say, in the form of hope, is deposited with God.

But at once, the Lord still gives the Mother a human consolation. In departing from her, he leaves behind to her his beloved John. To him he bequeaths his sonship. He does this because the Mother is so much a mother that she cannot cease being a mother for even a moment. So little can she lose this particular quality, which she always possessed, that, when the Son departs from her, he must give her the disciple to take his place. She could perhaps see something cruel in this: that the divine and uniquely beloved Son should give her this replacement consisting of some selected man. But through the replacement, the meaning of the sacrifice is fulfilled. The Mother, whose task it is to be a mother, cannot be left without a child. For her maternal mission is a divine mission and is eternal. That the Lord leaves John to her illustrates his personal love for the man John and equally his love for the disciple John. The first, insofar as he presents John with the gift of his Mother, and his Mother with that of John; the second, insofar as the love of the Lord is alive in the disciple, and the Lord, in presenting the Mother with John, thereby presents her with his own love in the disciple. In him, the Mother will recognize the love that the Son had for the disciple as well as the love of the Son that is alive, as love, in the disciple. For the love that the Lord has for one of his own never stops merely at that: it is the most communicable thing that exists, and it also only remains living if it is passed on to others. The essence of the Lord's love of a man lies in this lavish expenditure, and is thus lavish expendability: if one receives it, then one is forced to expend it in turn. And in fact, the man who receives it should never pass on only whatever of it he cannot hold, whatever is too much for him; for *that* excess flows out and back of its own accord. Rather, he should pass on precisely that which he can hold, that which enters into him. In the love of the Lord, as opposed to human love, there inheres no jealousy and exclusiveness at all. Between man and woman, everything must be exchanged in strict privacy, in shelteredness and protectedness. It belongs to the essence of this love that it remains, in its intimacy, exclusive. The love of the Lord is no less personal, but in it everything is open, and the only response that the Lord expects from us to his love is this: that we do not lock that love away in ourselves. If a wife were to show to an admirer those same forms of love that she had received and learned from her husband, those that he had, as it were, personally devised and presented to her, then the husband would be affected by this infidelity in a particularly painful way. Nothing like this can be found in the love of the Lord: it is precisely what is most personal in his love that must be passed on to others, precisely what is most intimate that he is not jealous of. This element of having to pass the love on can signify the *sacrifice* that the Lord demands of our love, just as the love that he shows for the Mother, when presenting her with John, is a fruit of the Mother's sacrifice. In the Christian sphere, love and sacrifice have a direct relationship to each other, one so living that it can nowhere be broken without entailing the death of the love and the sacrifice. Both live in the Lord *from each other,* in an inseparable unity. No one who has sacrificed everything for the Lord can, on the basis of that sacrifice, ask to be rewarded with the Lord's love, as if love and sacrifice were related to one another as plus and minus, as if one went into the other as in a mathematical calculation. The reward of the sacrificial love of the Lord is at once another sacrificial love.

Thus the Lord chooses the one whom he loves in order to give him to the Mother. He does this so as to make her sacrifice bearable. He separates himself from her in love by leaving love, as surety, behind for her. At the same time, however, John embodies in himself all Christians, and ultimately, in fact, all men. He is first of all the exponent of the Lord, then of the disciples, then of the Church and finally of mankind; so that the motherhood of Mary, which initially seemed limited to the Son, thereby acquires its primary character as motherhood in general. Through her actual word of affirmation, she became the Mother of the one Son. But that motherhood expands again, in accordance with its origin, into motherhood as such. She will lack the Son; that is her sacrifice. But in his place he has given her, in John, all of mankind for a son. Thus, out of her motherhood of mere readiness, there arises an effective real motherhood in relation to the whole of humanity. This transition is conditioned, from the side of the Son, through the grace of the Cross, which puts mankind in the place of the one Son; and, from the side of the Mother, through the fact that, with her word of affirmation—between her potentially general motherhood at the beginning and her actually general motherhood at the end—she had conceived and given birth to the real Son of the Father. It is not inconsequential for the Mother that she has given birth to precisely *this* Son, who is the son as such: the grace of this sonship has a retroactive effect on the grace of her motherhood: it opens and broadens it, as does every grace, but precisely in the sense of her motherhood. On the other side, the Son has fulfilled the Father's commission as Son of the Mother: he has brought men back to God and redeemed them. The grace of his redemptive work, the grace of his being the Redeemer, is the grace that retroactively affects the Mother: a grace through which all men become his brothers and thereby also his Mother's sons. Thus she was, at the beginning, the potential Mother, just as he was the potential Redeemer: both, in their own way, possessed Redemption as a commission. In fulfilling his commission, the Son, in his grace, presents the Mother with the same fulfilment of commission, thereby installing her as the Mother of all men. He does this when, as her only Son, he dies and vanishes, thus bringing to an end her motherhood of one; and as he now reenters the infinite light of the Divinity, he returns to her the Christian motherhood that was fulfilled through him. Now, she is Mother in the comprehensive, the catholic sense.

This motherhood of Mary is *virginal*. It is so because her motherhood, like her virginity, is enclosed in her relationship with the divine Son. And her universal motherhood is no second, new relationship alongside that with the Son. Thus, within the Church, every virginity has a divine, fruitful character only when it is an expression of love of the Lord and devotion to the Lord, in which the woman gives up her self in order to leave leadership and control to the Lord. A virginity that maintained itself solely out of fear of bodily surrender—even if it pretended to be love of purity—would necessarily be sterile. Conversely, however, fruitful Christian motherhood is also virginal because it receives what is ultimate not from the husband but from God, does not stop at the finitude of a human relationship and fruitfulness but lives as joy in a self-sacrificing devotedness. Thus, through the *one* Son, Mary is turned in the direction of all. Were her motherhood not virginal, then she would have had a limited number of physical children. It is only as virginal that her motherhood can be universal. Through this, she is granted participation in the grace of the Eucharist, in which the only Son of the Father bestows himself endlessly. Just as the eternal and unique devotion between Father and Son flows out into the temporal and unbounded devotion of the Eucharist, so the unique virginal relation between Mother and Son flows out into the endless bestowal of her spiritual motherhood.

It must also not be overlooked here that the Lord speaks these words, in which he leaves John to the Mother, precisely from the Cross, at the moment when the Father is already concealed. In this situation, he presents mankind to the Mother who, for her part, is deprived of the sight of God, but will nevertheless fulfill her task as Mother of all within that regained sight, just as the Son, too, will survey from within that sight the fulfilled sacrifice of redemption. Once again, their destinies are reflected in one another. That she is his physical Mother he knows even in his darkness. And he gives to her, as her physical Son to his physical Mother, his human brother John. All of this unfolds—since the sight of God is closed off—within human bounds; but precisely for that reason, it all has an infinite, divine meaning. It is the Lord's legacy to the world at the moment when he departs from the world, a mysterious, closed testament that will be opened in the grace of vision and reveal its divine aspect.

For his part, the Son can now deposit nothing more with the Father because everything already lies with the Father. And yet he must, since he is still alive, continue to sow. The sprouting of this seed is guaranteed by the Holy Spirit, who accepts it as a legacy in order, once the Son returns to the Father, to present it to the Father as the seed of the Son. When he does that, he fulfills his office with respect to the Mother, who is his vessel: through him, she becomes anew the Mother of all men. At the beginning, when the Son was to become man, everything was ready: the Son was ready to come into the world, the Father was ready to send him, the Mother was ready to conceive him. Lacking was only the act, the triggering, the igniting spark. That role was assumed by the Holy Spirit. And the Mother, out of love for the Father, conceived the Son in this Holy Spirit, whom, as it were, she did not know, and who was, for her, the unknown in God. And yet in all this the Spirit was not an impersonal function, but acted in a supremely sovereign way, as the Third Person in God. Under commission from the Father, he effected the conceiving of the Son in the Mother. For this conceiving he remains grateful to the Mother, and he now shows her his gratitude by allowing her to be his vessel eternally and installing her in eternal motherhood because of it.

19:27. Then he said to the disciple: Behold, your mother! And from that hour the disciple took her to his own home.

Now the Lord also gives the beloved Mother to the beloved disciple. It is an act of consummate love, and thus an act that knows no end, that is immediately brought into the sphere of the infinite. He shares his Mother with John, he gives her to him for a Mother. She is henceforth to be the one whom John recognizes as his Mother.

That, too, is a mystery of virginity. The virginal Lord gives the virginal Mother to the virginal disciple. The act of love that the Lord performs here, and that will have no end in this world, draws its substance from the beyond, from the realm of all that is boundless. Virginity is fully and utterly a mystery of the beyond. In this world, nothing of it becomes visible but the renunciation and the privation, yet its deficiency in this world is participation in the fullness of the beyond: participation in the mystery of fruitfulness of the Divine Persons. Nothing is more fruitful than the relationship between Father and Son: each of their deeds is implicit with an unconditional fruit. The whole of the Son's fruitfulness in this world stems from his relationship with the Father and *is,* at the same time, a revelation of the relationship itself. That is why the Son must be virginal. If he were not, then there would be moments at which he would reveal and mirror himself rather than the Father. That, however, is quite impossible. His fruitfulness is completely bound up with the Father beyond. But both the Mother and the disciple John participate in this fruitfulness of the Lord.

The virginal Lord made the beloved disciple so similar to himself that he wanted to make him his closest relative. He initiated him into his mysteries. It was needful that he learn, within the bounds of the human, to give lavishly of himself, just as the Lord, as Son of God, gives lavishly of himself. The Lord possessed the full vision of the Father; John, as much vision as the Lord communicated to him. The Lord, then, was completely virginal, and he wished that John, too, whom he saw as his friend and servant, should live from him just as he lived from the Father, virginally.

The whole of the life of the Lord had not only not known sin, but also drawn nourishment from the positive purity of the free look toward the Father. Therefore, he wished to find in John a similar purity and freedom of spiritual look, in and through him, toward the Father. From the very beginning, John had to give up all claim to living for the moment, and he fulfilled and fructified his life, his joy, his love with eternal values bestowed upon him by the Lord.

The Lord is engaged in his most fruitful deed: in the suffering of unseeing surrender to the Father. In and through it, he brings men back to the Father as redeemed. This suffering, too, does not have its roots in this world and does not exhaust itself in a merely human Passion. It is rooted in the beyond of the Father, and radiates, in turn, out into eternal life. Before the Son enters the ultimate suffering, his wordless dying, he reverts one more time to his earthly work, giving it eternal delineation. Out of the men who surround him, he must form something that will outlast his death and take fruitful effect where he will no longer be visibly present. From the depths of the mystery of his Incarnation, he brings to light one last fruitfulness, which will no longer be tied to any number. He gives the beloved disciple to his Mother, not as his friend but as a son. And just as little as the Mother had conceived the Son by a man will John be a son to her in the physical sense. He will be a son in the Spirit, because his sonship has its beginning where the whole mystery of the virginity of the Mother, as of the Son, lies hidden. From the Lord, John has learned to love him now and always with a view to the love of the Father, that is, not to stop at the beloved Lord, but to love through and beyond him to the source of love in the Father. Here, for the Christian, lies a mystery of the virginity that becomes, in an almost secondary way, a mystery of his own personality, because the whole draws its substance, its effect, its persistence and development into eternity, from the Son. A man who wishes to serve the Son wholly, who wishes to sacrifice his whole life to him so that he might make free use of it, cannot direct his glance toward the Lord by way of some created being; he must look straight toward him, without any intermediate link. If someone has to care for a family, then this stands, in a sense, between him and the Lord; he must look at the Lord through the family members. For him, his personal relationship to his relatives, in its finitude and limitedness, becomes the way to the Lord. The virgin, by contrast, is immediate to the Lord, and his relationship to his neighbor is one of commission and mission from within that immediacy. Inherent in immediacy to the Lord is immediate participation in his fruitfulness in the Spirit. A strange thing about bodily fruitfulness is that, in itself, it is prodigious to an almost infinite degree, but that, out of the enormous multitude of its potentialities, only an insignificantly small number actually come to development. It is as if the bodily element, the limitedness of matter, hindered the development of all its potentialities. In the virginal, otherworldly fruitfulness of the Lord, these limitations fall away; his fruits are, in truth, vast beyond measure. In the bodily act, there is an offering up of infinite possibilities, but in such a way as to be limited to a single human being; through this, too, the fruitfulness is narrowed. In offering oneself up to the Lord, who is God, this limitation, too, falls away, because the Lord offers himself up unendingly to the unending Father, thereby allowing the fruitfulness of the virginal to become limitless. Bodily fruitfulness is always a loss if one considers the potentialities that are offered up in it. Spiritual fruitfulness in the Lord and in his Mother is always a surplus. It is always richer than one could have expected because it always lives from the grace of the Cross. Whoever sires or bears a child in body can look upon his fruit, but one thing still remains hidden from him when he does: the relationship of his child to the Lord. One looks upon its finitude but not its infinitude, which consists in its relationship to God. In spiritual fruitfulness, the whole is inherent from the start in infinity, and thus nothing can be viewed in totality. God can perhaps show the virginal person something of spiritual fatherhood or motherhood, but he who is thus favored will immediately give the whole mystery back to God as the only Father. No one who knows about grace will presume to describe himself as the spiritual father of another Christian. In bodily fruitfulness, the parents are aware of their fruitfulness, whereas the children have to learn whose children they are from their parents. In spiritual parenthood, by contrast, the children usually know better than the parents themselves to whom they owe their lives. All earthly fruitfulness requires overseeing the fruit. Fruitfulness in the Lord, by contrast, requires giving up all claim to overseeing one's own life. It is precisely through ceding to the Lord supervision over everything of one's own that the infinite fruitfulness of virginity becomes possible. Earthly fruitfulness contains within itself certain earthly cares that impede having the Lord as our only care; that the individual members of the family really do look toward God is not implicit in entry into marriage, but remains a constant concern. By contrast, the community of those who are virginal in the Lord, the monastic community, does not have this concern, for it is part of its essence that all who, through their position in life, have consecrated themselves exclusively to the Lord are exclusively turned toward the Lord, or at least ought to be on the basis of their social position.

The Jews perhaps imagined that the Messiah would leave bodily children behind on earth and allocate to each of them an office in his Church. One son might perhaps have formed the beginning of the hierarchy, others might have embodied certain qualities of the Church, and others might have founded ecclesiastical bodies and orders. Then this Messiah would have had to possess a spouse who would have stood at his side in some way, and his mother would have been situated, in relation to these children, back in the earlier generation. A human family line would have been started. A present-day representative of the hierarchy would look back to an ancestral father who was the son of the Messiah, whose mother was an Israelite. Thus everything would exhaust itself in a hierarchical succession, and the view toward God would no longer be free. Because, however, the Lord requires above all that our looking toward God be immediate, he therefore breaks off the earthly succession. On the one hand, he installs the disciples, whom he has brought forth spiritually, in his own place; on the other hand, he does not leave the Mother, who has given birth to him, behind him, but places her next to him like a bride, so as to make her the spiritual Mother of his children. Thus the Christian who looks back upon the apostles looks at once upon the Lord and the Mother and, through and beyond both, directly upon the Father. That this is possible is a mystery of the virginity.

The proof of the fact that virginity is fruitful lies in the way that the Lord deals with the Mother here. Her virginity was a mystery bestowed upon her that, since his birth, he had guarded and, so to speak, left untouched. On the Cross, he reaches back to this possession, and breaks open the closed circle between him and his Mother in order to give entry to a third person, John. He brings him into this mystery and, along with him, all the others whom he represents and who will follow after him. In so doing, he expands the virginity and motherhood of his Mother into a mystery of infinite fruitfulness.

In his words on the Cross, the Lord exercises control over the Mother as well as over the disciple. He does not ask them in the way that, at the beginning, he had asked the Mother and sought the agreement of the disciples to being his successors. He now exercises control over them because, through their virginity in him, they are already his own, and therefore stand at his disposal. Virginity in the Lord is always grounded in *obedience*, which is itself grounded in love. Hence, true virginity does not exist until it acquires the form of obligation and obedience. At just which point in the existence of a human being the form of life becomes one of virginity—in childhood, in the years of maturity, or still later—that would be indeterminable if the decisive factor were solely the bodily one. But postponed or obstructed marriages do not amount to Christian virginity. In this matter, only voluntary binding to the Lord is decisive: the spiritual promise and, more fully still, the *taking of vows*. For such binding, one needs to be suitable. Anyone whom chastity were to render so distraught, so preoccupied with his natural drives that this concern, rather than any positive binding to the Lord, became the main content of his life, would not be suited for virginity as his position in life. For virginity is primarily a spiritual status. It consists not only in sexual continence, but also tolerates no human substitute, whether inside or outside of the sexual sphere. It is an expression of the purity of the Lord and his Mother. It has its beginning at a specific point, but expands itself from there until it encompasses the whole of purity. It is the binding to this purity.

The Lord exercises control over the virginal. He does so, however, by depriving himself of his Mother and his disciple. He does this in an act of *poverty*, indeed, in a condition of extremest poverty, for which the distribution of his garments was an expression. If, then, he demands of the virginal a renunciation of earthly love, a poverty of earthly love, he thereby only draws them into his own mystery.

Hence, the Cross is the unity of the three vows and, at the same time, the sign of fruitfulness as such. For all this has issued solely from, and is justified solely through, the Cross. In it lies the unity of renunciation and fruitfulness. In Christianity, renunciation never occurs for its own sake; rather, the Lord allows every renunciation to flow on into the mystery of his Cross and thus into the mystery of fruitfulness. We give what is ours over to him, but we know that he takes it up into what is his. Out of our saying No to some earthly good he makes a saying Yes to his truth. The unity of the two—the earthly No and the heavenly Yes—is his Cross.

And from that hour the disciple took her to his own home. This is a new beginning. The start of a life together in virginity, with a profusion of new commissions that become only slowly visible, that are as yet hardly anticipated, but that begin to spring up everywhere. A beginning to which one can revert again and again, because here lies the archetype of the new fruitfulness. It is the first time that man and woman are active together in this new life of fruitfulness. The Mother's life with Joseph was a life that had to assume the form of communality for the sake of protecting the Lord. Her life with John, by contrast, assumes the form of communality in order to offer protection to followers in the calling of John as in that of the Mother: a living, ongoing protection that finds its realization in the common earthly life of those two, but that already has its effects in the beyond and allows them to shine down on earth from there.

It is not the virginal disciple alone nor the virginal Mother alone who embodies, for the future of the Church, the form of virginal life. Instead, at the beginning of this way of life stands a virginal couple. That is a mystery of the absolute love of the Lord. He loved both of them so much that, upon his departure, he designated them as founders of a new lineage: that of his priests and monastic people. Bringing the two together is also a fruit of the quite human love of the Lord for both. Out of the purest earthly love, he allows them to participate in his love for the Father. God, who conceived of the creatures and brought them into being, has permitted his Son to assume the form of one of these creatures; he has also presented him with a new love, the love that would live in each of his creatures if sin had not hindered it. And since the Son is God, he cannot otherwise receive this love than by integrating it into his love for the Father. He cannot otherwise accept earthly, creaturely love than by allowing it to be fructified, to grow and to flourish within his love for the Father, from which his divine love for men also stems. By force of this human love as integrated into divine love, the Lord brings the Mother and the disciple together, and their life in common will be the first realization on earth of this love that lives in God. It will be this in so pure and perfect a sense that it will not exhaust itself in itself, but will become, out of the vast surplus that it contains in its purity, the prototype and primal source for all who, following after, will live in the same form of love.

Mary and John live together virginally not as man and wife, but as mother and son (which is also in keeping with their respective ages). Their virginal love for one another is certainly not character-ized by self-denial or struggle against natural drives, but by their common love of the Lord, their common look toward the Lord. Virginity by no means consists primarily in negative resistance or mortification, but in a positive blossoming of the possibilities of love such as are contained in the Lord and characterized by his interfusing of human love with divine love of the Father. God created men as male and female, and commanded them to multiply in love. Not for the sake of that multiplication, however, would the Lord have needed to come into the world, but rather, so that men might grow in love itself; for they had forgotten, through sin, that multiplication should also always mean a growing in God. Therefore, the Lord had to direct them primarily toward growth in love, in order to establish a counterbalance to mere multiplication in sin so that pure growth in God might be allowed to become clear.

The virginal, who are no stronger than other men in human terms, receive their strength from the Lord, and in fact, continually, through the vital power of the Eucharist. In his earthly appearance, the Lord was a human manifestation of love that stemmed from divine love; in the Eucharist, however, his appearance is simul-taneously a product of his divine and his human love. And the mystery of the Eucharist is a mystery of virginity. Therefore even the priest who participates in this mystery becomes so drawn into it that having virginal status suggests itself for him. How could he who participates in the eucharistic generation of the Lord be, at the same time, a cause of the generation of earthly children! His relationship with the Lord in Holy Mass resembles that of strictest monogamy. And all the more so given that his relation to the Lord is also illumined through the Mother, who virginally generated the virginal Son. She stands imperceptibly behind the priest when he utters the words of consecration. The sacrifice that the priest offers therefore implies something of the Mother's sacrifice. It is no bloody, mutilating sacrifice, but a veiled, joyful sacrifice, wholly offered up to the love of the Father for the Son.

Virginity in the Church is ultimately a proof of the truth of the Lord's love. Observed from a distance, it could seem as if the Lord had been no true man at all, as if he did not really know human life at all because he did not know marriage. But the fact that, down through the ages, innumerable people have chosen virginity as a way of life, and indeed, out of love of the Lord, shows that it is a real possibility for humans to forgo marriage out of love of God, rather than weakness or inability to cope with life, and that this possibility can stem solely from an original grace of the Lord and his love itself. And virginity is not something inhuman, not something eccentric or humorless, no spiritualized life in contempt of the flesh. Rather, the sacrificer is so weak that he has nothing better to offer as a sacrifice than this small thing, which bears no relation to the Lord's sacrifice. Virginity is an almost humorous attempt (so great is the disproportion!) to walk in the footsteps of the Lord.

A virginal man forgoes the power of fathering children, the power over a wife. A virginal woman, by contrast, forgoes primarily not a husband, but a family. In what the *Lord* forgoes, both of these are inherent: renunciation of a wife and a family for the sake of life in the Father. The *Mother,* by contrast, has forgone a husband; but for that she received, in commission, a family: the domestic as a symbol of the larger, spiritual family, Christianity. That is the mission that supplements her contemplation. For a man's word of affirmation issues primarily in the sphere of action, which, as a priest, he also in a sense oversees. The Mother's word of affirmation, and thus that of a woman in general, issues in openness to any and every possible directive from God; it is the affirmation of pure listening, of contemplation. Out of this virginal affirmation, God creates fruitfulness and, with that, motherhood. That is why the Mother, who forgoes an earthly family, receives in turn precisely the maternal as her allocated commission, and every virginity that follows her will be used by God for purposes of divine fruitfulness.

Male and female virginity arise out of the Cross. There, the Lord initiates those closest to him into his innermost mysteries of life. And as little as his suffering is exhausted in himself, but continues to be borne by those who are his, so little is the mystery of virginity exhausted in himself, but becomes fruitful in the Church. Both mysteries—suffering and virginity—show themselves yet again to be one: in their origin as in their unfolding. Both have meaning only in the Lord. Suffering in itself, apart from looking toward the Lord, is desperation; continence in itself, apart from looking toward the Lord, is sterility. Both, conjoined to looking toward the Lord, are the highest fruitfulness, which is initiated through the communality between the Mother and John in the love of the Lord.

19:28. *After this Jesus, knowing that all was now finished, said (to fulfill the Scripture): I thirst.*

The Lord knows that all is now finished. His life is finished, what will succeed it is also finished. In the course of his sojourn on earth, he has put in place everything out of which the later Church will arise in the many-sidedness of her life; he has entrusted his disciples and all those who believe in him with their special task. And after he has then given his Mother to his favorite disciple, nothing further remains for him but to suffer; he can devote himself exclusively to suffering, plunge for once and for all into suffering. He has no more arrangements to make; he has done, out of love, all that the Father, in love, could expect of him; so now he need only give the waning amount of love that yet remains with him fully back to the Father, until the degree of his suffering is completed in fullness.

Thus he says, (*to fulfill the Scripture*): I thirst. This thirst, which possesses him totally, is the thirst for love. His bodily thirst, brought on by his pains, is only a meager one if measured by the thirst in his soul for possession of the Father. Everywhere that he otherwise experienced love there is now emptiness and longing. Just as someone who thirsts bodily and can find no water suffers beyond proportion because the great, all-pervasive discomfort of the thirst takes hold of him totally, so the Lord, in his thirsting soul, suffers beyond proportion because he has been deprived of his only wellspring, the Father. Even the hope of ever seeing the Father again has been taken from him. And the more that he convinces himself of the unrelenting severity of the separation, the more that the Father's love is concealed from his love so that Father's commission might be fulfilled, then the more immeasurably his thirst increases. In his isolation lies the centerpoint of his suffering, for separation from God is for him something absolutely impossible. Many have been crucified before him and after him, but none of them has experienced abandonment by the Father. And many have been abandoned by God, but none who has known eternally the eternal love of the Father. To be divested of a love that one has never experienced is not hard; but to be separated from a love from which one has lived since eternity, one which constitutes the entire substance of one's own being—that is lethal. When lovers find themselves facing separation, they attempt, before that separation, to give each other as many proofs of love, pledges and keepsakes as possible; yet, during their separation, all these mementos have a doubly painful effect: they are an occasion for feeling what is absent more bitterly. Similarly, everything now reminds the Son of the lost Father. And at the same time, the Son had wanted to give the Father the highest proof of love, and had therefore intentionally designed the Cross in such a way as to involve the highest degree of abandonment, a pain that would have to shatter him were he not himself God. He also did not want to become accustomed by degrees to loss of the love; the separation was to be an absolute and sudden one, with no softening or adjusting. The Father knows, therefore, how seriously the Son takes this offering up of his life; and he foresees that his fatherly love will afterward be permitted to shine boundlessly around the Son because his gratitude to the Son will be boundless, as matches the boundlessness of the suffering. The Father has begotten the Son, and the Son owes his life to the Father; but from now on the Father, too, will owe life to the Son, he will owe that to the Son and redeemed creation as well. He will owe to the Son a new, living relation of love to his creatures. Everything that the Son has set in place—the Church, the consecrated life under vows and participation in the life of the Son—all this is an enrichment of heaven, an adornment of the Father's realm, softening every boundary between heaven and earth. All this magnificence the Father owes to the Son.

That place within the Son where he possesses a dual countenance—one turned toward the Father and one toward the world—that place which is most characteristic of the Son, does not become *empty,* but remains in existence. No longer, it is true, in him himself, for he will return once again wholly to God, but in those whom he has put in that place in his stead. There, the Lord—who is now left only with suffering and no longer possesses the sight of heaven—has installed, from within his suffering, the Mother and John. It is the place where they can no longer refuse anything, the place that is offered to all of us, and where we are *secure* in the Lord's *keeping.* It is the place of vocation, the place where, above and beyond all our inferiority, we can no longer do anything but fulfill his will, because his love is predominant within us. The place where we no longer weigh what it is that we want to give him, but are unconditionally *prepossessed* by his thirst.

In him, however, this thirst is an increasing darkness. He finds himself on his journey back, deprived of his divine light and of the light of the Father, caught up in the darkness of sin. His own purity is forced by sin into uttermost darkness. If he were a sinner, then he would somehow understand this burden of darkness; he would, so to speak, recognize his sin in it. He would also recognize the sin of others by his own. Even if the punishment were unjust and excessive, it would not remain totally alien to him, since he would know that he deserved punishment. Hence, the darkness would, in a sense, be familiar to him. The Lord, however, is the sinless one, and thus the darkness of sin is something wholly alien to him. Through the darkness of sin, he is thrust completely into darkness. For him, it is not something his own, something that he is at home with, but something radically alien. For him, it is a darkness that repels its very self. If God's love were only to shine into this darkness, then the Lord would see where he stands and what he is doing; he could recognize the alienness of sin and bear it more easily. And if the Son were to look upon sinners in the light of his divine love, then he would see them as already redeemed and could love them as such. Both these things are now impossible. Hence, he is left with nothing but darkness and thirst, which increase to an infinite degree.

19:29. A bowl full of vinegar stood there; so they put a sponge full of the vinegar on hyssop and held it to his mouth.

They do what their office requires. They carry out this act as well, which is part of the procedures for death by crucifixion. It is not a personal act, they perform it almost automatically. The worst—the death sentence, the rage of the Jews, the denial by the disciples—is over. What is now still to occur is only the playing out of destiny. What they do cannot alleviate the Lord's thirst. This thirst is unquenchable, for its object is God, is love; it is an expression of ultimate abandonment. To all appearances, there is no more room in the Lord for anything but abandonment and suffering, and, through the sins that he takes upon himself, his capacity for feeling himself abandoned and for suffering increases more and more until his death.

19:30. When Jesus had received the vinegar, he said: It is finished; and he bowed his head and gave up his spirit.

The Lord receives what is offered to him, experiencing no alleviation from it, but only the last possible degree of increase to his suffering. Now the end has been reached: *It is finished.* His powers are expended, he is emptied to the point that his head drops; the fullness out of which he gives us faith, love and hope has been taken from him so utterly that there is now room in him only for sin, which fills him to the very brim. What he had, he has given to the Father, so as to be able to take from men all that they possess: the full measure of sin. The offense that all those sins had caused to the Father can no longer be found in the Father: the Son suffers for sin in such a way that the Father will no longer have to suffer because of it. From now on, the Son will block and take into himself such offenses, thus shielding the Father from what was intended for him. As much of sin as comes toward the Father is transformed by the Son and then, as his love, given over to the Father. In that way, he brings the love of the world back to the Father.

For all future time, however, the Father wishes to be manifest in the world in no way other than in the Son's love. He presents him with the world that the Son has brought back and presented to him. Thus, too, it has been accomplished that the Father is now actually revealed to the world in the Son, which means that the meaning of all the Son's work has also been fulfilled. Because the Son has borne the whole of sin, the Father desires that the Son should now also represent the complete love of God in the world.

And so *he bowed his head.* He lets it drop toward the world and the sinners that surround him. His glance no longer searches for the Father, it is now directed solely at sinners. The last thing that he takes with him from this world is the sight of sinners, those whom he had come to redeem.

Since everything has been finished in this abandonment, for the Son as well as the Father, *he gives up his spirit.* In so doing, he does not recognize how his completed mission is taken up into the Father's love. He hands its completion over to the Father without being able to see what has been achieved. He may well see that his mission is finished, but he does not see that it was finished in love and has been taken up into the Father's love, since all of his love is still on deposit with the Father.

19:31. *Since it was the day of Preparation, in order to prevent the bodies from remaining on the cross on the Sabbath (for that Sabbath was a high day), the Jews asked Pilate that their legs might be broken, and that they might be taken away.*

With the death of the Lord, the Cross becomes a closed matter for the Jews. They turn at once to the approaching festival, and make their preparations for it. They do not ask how things stand regarding the correctness of their verdict; they do not bother themselves about the fate of the witnesses, and they bother about the bodies only in order to have them removed so as not to disturb the festival. So they press to have the legs of the crucified broken. Their cold objectivity is not changed by the death of the Lord. No question remains with them that might require an answer. Thus they show once again how distant they were from the mystery of the Lord, how little access they had to his teaching.

The least that the Lord expects of those who have once encountered him is that they continue to concern themselves with him, and in fact, not just through solitary brooding, but in a kind of discussion with him, in a kind of inclination and openness toward him, even if this does not yet occur in belief. The interest of the Jews, however, is directed solely toward having the Lord be as dead as possible.

19:32–33. *So the soldiers came and broke the legs of the first, and of the other who had been crucified with him; but when they came to Jesus and saw that he was already dead, they did not break his legs.*

The soldiers continue to act in terms of their commission, mechanically. But they act, unconsciously, under commission of prophecy as well. They, who are basically uninvolved spiritually, see the difference between the death of the robbers and the death of the Lord. They realize at first sight that the Lord is completely dead. The slight uncertainty that comes over an onlooker at the sight of those who have just died is not possible at the sight of the Lord. He is clearly dead. The other two are probably so as well, and yet the soldiers break their legs. The Jews are completely cut off from any belief. The soldiers, to be sure, are not believers, but they have a strange certainty in relation to the Lord. In his death, they see a special quality, something so compelling that any proof is idle. These men are not rich in spirit, but they have been present and can draw distinctions. Implicit in their view is the mysterious fact that everyone who has once had something to do with the Lord has thereby been made receptive to a certain something that does not lie in him. In everyone who has even just genuinely heard of the Lord lies something that calls for an answer. This is the gift for causing disquiet that the Father gave him to take with him when he sent him into the world: in relation to the Son, no one can remain indifferent. In relation to nothing in the world—no founder of religion, no world view, no philosophy—does that apply. It is the privilege of the Lord.

19:34. *But one of the soldiers pierced his side with a spear, and at once there came out blood and water.*

The Lord dispenses even after he is already dead, he gives forth the last of what his body still contains. This, his last, is still there after he has already suffered to the end, and is brought out by someone who has no idea of the infinite fruitfulness of this last. What the Lord no longer bestows in suffering is as fruitful as his suffering was. The blood is fruitful and the water is fruitful. Both flow out separately and can be distinguished, both conceal in themselves their own mystery. It is a mystery because it issues forth from the mystery of the heart of the Lord. The sacraments of water and blood, baptism and the Eucharist, have already been established; but the Christian fruitfulness of these mysteries, their outflowing life and their over-flow of grace, originates only in the mystery of the wound in his side. As sacraments, both are separate; therefore the water and blood flow out separately. But they have a common origin: it is the wounded body of the Lord. This common element grounds the fact that the sacraments, too, not only stand alongside one another but exist within one another: blood also has a part in baptism, water also has a part in the Eucharist. Whoever has received baptism is referred further to the Eucharist, just as the Eucharist contains in itself the grace of baptism. The life of the sacraments is so constituted that they all unfold within one another. All the sacraments are signs of the Lord's grace; only confirmation occupies a special position because it confers the Holy Spirit. But baptism and confirmation, for their part, belong together. And thus God's Third Person is drawn here into the mystery of the Incarnation; the Spirit is integrated, as it were, into the ecclesiastical order. Of course, baptism of the Lord himself was an act of the Holy Spirit, for at that baptism the Spirit descended. Here, however, through the wound in his side, baptism is once again confirmed by the Lord, it is taken up into his suffering, given the stamp of his humanity; and so now, conversely, confirmation, too, which belongs to baptism as its supplement, becomes a twofold effect of the Second and Third Persons. In this as well, the intertwined life of the sacraments is manifest. By the blood, which is still living after the death of the Lord, the livingness of the blood in the Eucharist is symbolized. The Eucharist is *really* flesh and blood: the blood that flows from the wound is like proof of this become visible. The first persons who see it, the soldiers, feel no thirst for the Eucharist. But the Eucharist is offered to all, even to those who are not touched by it. Receiving it, of course, is permitted only to those who believe. For his part, the Lord can do nothing other than exert his influence and pour himself out upon all men without distinction, whether they believe or not. Differentiating between those who accept and those who do not is accomplished not by the Lord, but by men.

The wound in his side is also a symbol of the apostolate. All the way up to his death, the Lord is pure communication of himself. Even in his death, he knows no death, no end; out of his death there flows forth grace. His death is so living that, even in death, he is still communicable, and what he gives is so constituted that it does not stop at its recipient, but transforms itself in him at once into a wellspring for his neighbor. The Lord is Eucharist, which means infinite distribution and communication. Every received Host is itself, in turn, Eucharist: everyone who has taken Communion should bear visibly on his person that distinguishing something which the soldiers saw on the body of Christ. He bears in himself the wordless apostolate, the outflowing of love as such, which simply communicates itself. But this fruitfulness stems solely from the original mystery of the Lord, and can never be communicated apart from communication of something of the mystery itself. It belongs to the mysterious essence of Christian fruitfulness that it is always passed on *as* a mystery. Therefore, within the Catholic sphere, there is so much talk of mystery in every instructional context. The mystery being spoken of here, however, is the mystery of love. Hence, it is also passed on to others only through love. Christian truth can be disclosed to a seeker only through his sensing, in the self of the one who is explaining it, something of this mystery, either as direct human love or, if the instructor is a priest, at least in the form of love of his office, and in that, of the Lord.

The mystery is exposed through the *wound* that opens his side and affords a view into the mystery of the Lord's human body. Were it not the Lord himself who provides this introduction into his mystery, one would be tempted to think of desecration. But he does it himself; not only is he naked before us, but even rent open. He is poorer than he ever has been, since not even his dead body belongs to him anymore; he exposes it. This, too, belongs to the mystery of fruitfulness—that he himself wishes to hold no more mystery for us. He allows himself to bear more than he can to expose his mystery, yet precisely this leads from one mystery into another, indeed, is itself the greatest mystery. Every mystery that he communicates gives birth to a new one: that is his fruitfulness; but all these mysteries are ones of love and therefore of self-surrender.

That the Lord reveals his mystery to us precisely through his wound is, once again, a special kind of exposure. If we were to grasp nothing else of his mysteries, then the sight of his wound would at least make humanly understandable to us the sort of mystery to which the wound is the gateway. Perhaps the average Christian comprehends but little of the depth of the mysteries of baptism and the Eucharist. But he understands the Lord's wound, and can trustingly embrace in that all that he has not understood.

Thus the mystery of the wound itself is also part of what is bestowed. Just as the Lord allows the grace of the sacraments to flow forth in fullness, so there is ultimately no mystery of the Lord's suffering in which he does not allow those who are his to share in some way or other. Even the Lord's wounds live on in his Church; here, too, they are and remain the gateway to grace and to the mysteries and to the innermost source of love.

Insofar as the wound in his side is the entrance to the mysteries, it contains, in relation to the other wounds—of the head, of the back, of the hands and feet—a quite special mystery. All the other wounds were inflicted upon the living body of the Lord; they entered into his suffering and formed a living part of it. By contrast, the wound in his side, of which John speaks, rends open the dead Lord. Its mystery is a mystery turned toward the beyond, toward Holy Saturday: here, everything that signifies otherworldly redemption flows forth. Through this wound, the Lord, precisely as a dead man, is the one exposed; no longer just the bestower, but the bestowed. Through it, he is what is poured out, the offered sacrifice, and this mystery is a mystery of the beyond. On the Cross, his suffering was caused by *withdrawal* of love, and indeed, a continuous, lasting and ever-increasing withdrawal. Although the Lord had surrendered and deposited everything from the very start, more and more, up to the end, was nevertheless taken from him. After his death, he is in the condition of *being withdrawn*. During his suffering on the Cross, the love that he had deposited was still at his disposal. He could have reached out for it. He could have interrupted his suffering in order to take his love back again. Now, however, when nothing more *is being* withdrawn, since it has already been withdrawn—for the Lord is dead, in the condition of being dead—he can decide nothing more. Being able to decide has itself been withdrawn from him. Holy Saturday is the experience of actually being dead, the pure emptiness. Holy Saturday is more a gift from the Father to the Son than from the Son to the Father. For in this mystery, the Son lives no longer in the darkness of sin, of the world, of mankind, but he is granted that look into the darkness which the Father had previously reserved to himself. The Father allows him to see this darkness in death, he communicates it to the dead Son. For the Son, being dead is no merely external characteristic, but a condition that he suffers under for our sake (and without ceasing to be Eternal Life). Being dead is, above all, the extinction of every sort of striving, wishing to have, hoping for, bringing to realization. And since the Lord wants to become acquainted with pre-Christian death, every striving toward heaven is now also broken off within this experience. Not the notion of heaven itself, but the connection with it, the path that leads toward it. When a sinner in this world thinks of heaven, then that occurs in hope. He knows that heaven means fulfilment, even if he cannot picture this to himself. The Lord, who has come down from heaven, did not know longing during his life on earth. He possessed the vision of heaven, and for him his earthly path was like a part of that heaven: the part in which he now had an opportunity to demonstrate his love to the Father. When the sinful man on earth "earns" his heaven, as the German saying goes, this means above all that his sins are redeemed again and again by the Lord, who earns heaven for him through his path on earth. And on that path, the Lord constantly saw this one possibility, which he also realized: to give increasingly the highest proof of his love to the Father, increasingly, as long as his path on earth continued, and increasingly, when, having been taken up into heaven again, he redeemed all creatures. In his death on Holy Saturday, by contrast, he no longer sees heaven as his place and as the place into which he redeems sinners. Initiated into the darkness of the Father, he sees heaven as that which he wishes for the Father. For his wishes are always included in the wishes of the Father. To wish anything for himself would not accord with his being dead.

A fruit of redemption that the Son has deposited with the Father on Holy Saturday is Purgatory. It has its origin in the Cross. The Father makes use of the fruit of the Cross in order to temper divine justice, which held the sinners captive, with new mercifulness. From the Cross, hope is brought down to the netherworld; from the Cross, a fire unleashed in which justice and mercifulness are intermixed. Through the Lord's arrival there, the powers of the netherworld, of death and of evil, are driven, as it were, into the backmost recesses of hell, and the devil's chain is made shorter. Purgatory arises as if under the Lord's striding feet; he brings comfort to this place of hopelessness, fire to this place of iciness, mercifulness to this place of justice. Up to now, it was something reserved to the Father, comparable to that "tree of knowledge" that no one was allowed to touch. It was also the only mystery that the Father had not already given over to the Son who became man, for he had entrusted the entire world to him, except for the darkness of death. Now he also initiates him, through direct experience, into this mystery, and the Son's penetration into this region transforms it: he breaks down the gates of the netherworld and discloses to those who are there the entrance to heaven.

And in yet another sense, his journey into the netherworld is the journey of a victor. Like a triumphant field marshal, he musters the defeated troops and the spoils of victory: the fettered powers of evil and conquered sin. He gazes from there where he is upon bare sin, the sin of the world as washed away from redeemed men, not actually become more personal but formless and unbounded, whose removal from sinners was the work of his Cross. But in order to look this enemy in the eye in all of his naked fiendishness, he must be in darkness. Not as the living one of Easter, but as the dead one of Holy Saturday must he accomplish this journey. Not in the light of victory does he now want to observe sin, but in the darkness that characterizes it in itself. Were he to see it in the light of redemption, then he would see the Father. But in death he does not look into eternal life. He also does not actually look upon Purgatory, but rather, Purgatory is the consequence of his trip through hell. He looks directly into the final mystery of the Father who created the world: the mystery that the devil was left with the power to seduce mankind.

This mystery of the Father lies hidden in this darkness. God would have had the power to let his light shine forth everywhere, not even to allow evil to arise, or simply to suppress it. That he did not do so is one of the most impenetrable things about him. Men should be free; they were not created as finished beings, they should grow toward God of their own accord. God wished to give his heaven only to grown-up sons. In this area of freedom lies the darkness of God and the possibility of sin. But even the darkness of God was a mystery of love.

19:35. *He who saw it has borne witness—his testimony is true, and he knows that he tells the truth—that you also may believe.*

The disciple who was allowed to look into these mysteries gives testimony to the fact. He knows, however, that the truth he speaks is full of mysteries, and can thus only be believed. No matter how much John may have participated in the life of the Lord, how much he may have grasped of baptism and the Eucharist—at the instant when he glimpses the opening in his side, he understands that all the things so far lived through and experienced were only small beginnings, now burst open into the ever-greater of those mysteries of the beyond that are revealed in the darkness of the wound. These beginnings are no doubt discernible to human eyes, and they bind the one who sees them to the always-more of having to understand and participate. But he who glimpses the love of the Lord knows, at the same time, that it will eternally transcend everything that he has experienced and can ever comprehend. John experiences that in a new, previously hidden sense. He knows now that the love of the Lord is alive not only there where he perceptibly communicates it, but also there where it is imperceptibly effective, and that every instance of the efficacy of his love contains further new efficacy. In baptism, it does not exhaust itself in the personal gift of grace, and in the Eucharist, it is not limited to the one who receives it. The opened-up side proves that the communications of the Lord can never, and in no way, fall victim to death, that they are always—more so than ever amid death—consummate life, because they are love. This is the truth that John's testimony holds.

And he knows that he tells the truth—*that you also may believe*. It is not because he has spoken and given testimony that he knows that he is in the truth, but he knows that he tells the truth—*that you also may believe*. Thus he knows, for the first time, that proven, sensibly perceived truths not only have to be true in themselves, but that they can also be true in quite another sense, that the meaning of their truth is grounded at quite another point: in the necessity of belief by those who accept the testimony. And thus, in a sense, that belief is less a consequence of truth than truth a necessity of belief. This transposition becomes clear from within love. For the true truth is love. The knowledge that is under discussion here is not a general knowledge, but rather the knowledge of John, who lives in love, and it had to be given expression in precisely that situation. Love has its basis in itself; it is its own justification and meaning, and whoever lives in love searches for no reason other than love. Behind love there is no further basis. Whoever obeys God solely out of awe must, at least inwardly, ask for a reason for what God has commanded, even if, outwardly, he obeys without saying a word. Whoever obeys God out of love, however, does not question inwardly, but performs out of love the work of love, which contains in itself the truth. When one wishes to give children a surprise, one tells them to close their eyes and open their mouths, and if they are guileless, and know not fear but only love, they will obey. Thus here, at the Cross, love closes its eyes in order to receive the truth blindly. What John saw and experienced beneath the Cross has given him the complete love that desires nothing any longer but pure belief.

19:36. *For these things took place that the Scripture might be fulfilled: Not a bone of him shall be broken.*

Even after the death of the Lord, the Scripture is fulfilled. Not only up to the Cross does the Son's path lie at the disposal of the Father's love, but also that which he later suffers without control, and his path through hell are included in his commission. But inherent in this commission as well is the requirement that all of the Father's Old Testament must be fulfilled. The Son wishes, of course, to carry out completely the Father's mission, to give him new proofs of his love constantly, and to create, in all those proofs, ever-new starting points for belief among men. Every instance of fulfilment of Scripture can become, however, for some person who is seeking the way to God, a starting point for belief. In accordance with the infinite diversity of men, God also bestows countless paths to belief. Belief is indivisible, but the ways to it are infinite. Holy Saturday is a proof of the love of the Father for the Son, but everything that happens to the Son's body during his journey through hell also contains such proofs. God does not wish that opportunities for belief should come to a standstill during the hours until the Resurrection; rather, the way for belief, which means for the Son's love, should remain open everywhere. Even the deceased Son, who no longer has things at his disposal, should be able to continue carrying out his commission, which remains unbroken even in death.

19:37. *And again another Scripture says: They shall look on him whom they have pierced.*

A second prophecy was fulfilled by the soldier who cut open the Lord's side: it pertains not only to the body of him whom they have pierced, but to him in general. More is implicit in these words than the mere looking upon a lifeless, pierced body. It is a looking that leads on to something further: from the inflicted wound up past the body that suffered it and on to the one whose body it is. This looking upon him is like a condensed summary of the course of Christian vision in general. It constantly leads on to something further, it leads through and beyond things, it shows the ever-greater of the Lord and of God. It shows a wound, it shows a body, but through and beyond that, the body of the Son of Man, who is God. And no one sees him as clearly as his Mother and the disciple who loved him.

In the context of this looking, John stands as a new son alongside the Mother, as a complete brother to the Lord, representative of all who are drawn into the same mystery, all priests and monastics and all who are virginal. Through the piercing of the Lord's side, he has gained special insight into the origin of baptism and the Eucharist. He has ceased to be an individual personality in order, from now on, to be only a servant of the love of the New Covenant.

Mary stands there as the Mother of all men, as the Mother of

Sorrows, who is pierced even in love and receives, through that piercing, the consummate fruitfulness of her motherhood. She gains a new relation to the Son, who leads her new children to her by allowing her to participate in his suffering. Her wound is simultaneously public and hidden: hidden because only the Son knows of it, and public because all men harvest the fruits of her suffering. This fruitfulness of her suffering amongst men allows her, for her part, to lead men to the Son. She steps out of her role of pure contemplation; she also steps forth from her position behind the Son, in order to be placed in a new position within the apostolate. From now on, she stands next to the Son, turned facing toward him, fully revealed in her woundedness before him, just as he who makes confession is revealed before his father confessor; and this is the attitude in which the Son receives her and, together with her, all whom she brings to him. The Lord, too, has a new source of fruitfulness in the Mother's suffering, since now, out of gratitude for her accompaniment in suffering, he grants her participation in all the mysteries of his own fruitfulness. Just as the Father, out of love, shows the Son his ultimate darkness and, in that, his consummate love, so the Son secures for the Mother, through her participation in his wound, associatedness in the dispensed fruitfulness.

John stands in a twofold relation to this. On the one hand, he is the son of this Mother. On the other hand, he is, from now on, the custodian of the mystery of love even with respect to her, and to that extent the Mother is open and transparent to him, too, so that he has her fruitfulness at his disposal. It is the fruitfulness of opening up, of showing, that John can draw upon. This complete openness of the Mother is a mystery of her purity. In young girls, it is often a sign of the most unspoilt purity when they quite unabashedly mention or recount many things about which women otherwise modestly avoid speaking. The Mother is purer than any young girl ever was; she possesses a naïveté, an ingenuousness in saying what she thinks, that is the opposite of any offense against modesty, namely, an unmistakable sign of her complete virginity. She makes no secret of her purity; she allows John to share in all that she has. Every word that she speaks, every movement that she makes, is disclosure and surrender of her self. She exists in that state at which true confession aims. A mortal sinner, when making confession, will confess above all his full-fledged sins; he will hardly find it in him to divulge all the rest that is more characteristic of the general state of being sinful, his deficiency of love. Anyone who is concerned to open himself more fully when making confession will try to expose this habitual state as well. The purer a person is, the more he will attempt, in his confession, to show and uncover himself in his entirety. Beyond all sin, the Mother stands in absolute openness facing John, who possesses both love and office. This relationship of disclosure to each other is a grace that has flowed from the open wound in the Lord's side. The Mother and John live permanently in this state, which we attain, at best, only for brief moments: at the moment of absolution. It is the spirit of virginity as it lives on in the Church among those who are called to this state: in the monastery, in the seminary, in the occurrence of the virginal within the world. All who are thus called live within a mission, and in fact, as those who open themselves in service to this mission and are therefore disclosed to one another within that mission. This is also the reason that confession is made to a *priest*. John sees the Lord's opened side, he sees his most hidden mystery, something which he did not at all desire to see, yet whose sight he nevertheless finds fulfilling. From within his looking here, he is initiated into looking into men: from looking into the opened side of the Lord to looking into the opened soul of the sinner. That is the office of love. This looking remains a mystery, because every look into a soul is, in itself, already a mystery and a kind of miracle, and this applies even more to looking at what God alone sees in the soul. Therefore confession takes place in secret, under the seal of confession. The office of the Mother and the disciple remains, then, not merely a fruit of the Cross, but is always referred back anew to the wound, and thus to the wounding, by the fact that the openness of virginity and the seeing of confessed sin remain always dependent upon the wound seen in the Lord's side.

19:38. *After this, Joseph of Arimathea, who was a disciple of Jesus, but secretly for fear of the Jews, asked Pilate that he might take away the body of Jesus, and Pilate gave him leave. So he came and took away his body.*

Joseph of Arimathea is a disciple in secret. The Lord has allowed him to be so. He has demanded no public acknowledgment from him, and expected no apostolic activity of him. He has permitted him to live his faith in secret. Already at the beginning of the Church, then, he made this exception, as it was dangerous for all the disciples to be openly associated with the Lord. John would not have been able, out of love, to do anything other than acknowledge his allegiance to him; Peter has denied him, but he ought not to have done so, for he was already installed in office. Of the others, too, we know that they had to stand with him, that their life of faith could never have unfolded within a purely private sphere. Joseph is the exception permitted by the Lord during his lifetime. Perhaps the Lord regarded the difficulties that public acknowledgment would expose this one to as too great, or his belief as still too weak to bear up under such testings. But this instance of keeping one's faith secret was envisaged for only a limited period. Thus there can, indeed, be faith without any external mission; the mission can lie hidden for a long time only in contemplation, but it never remains devoid of action to the very end. At some time or another, even the most inward contemplation will have to be tested externally. If only because of the sacraments, belief within the Church cannot be kept secret indefinitely. But also, the community of the faithful demands that anyone belonging to the Church should pray and be active within her in a visible and open way. Only for a short time and for important reasons can anyone forsake this duty. Even when no external apostolate is demanded, every Christian is required to acknowledge his membership of the Church in due course. Thus Joseph remained, indeed, under cover for fear of the Jews, but only so as to be able to act within his commission at the appropriate moment. For the Lord's body would not have been handed over to one of the apostles.

And Pilate gave him leave. He is still disturbed about not having been able to oppose the death of the Lord. It was never his intention to block the Lord's mission through directives issued by him. He permitted the crucifixion because he lacked the courage to offer any resistance to it. Therefore he now permits the body to be taken down from the Cross. Since Joseph is not known to be a disciple of the Lord, the Jews also have nothing against the body's being handed over to a stranger.

So he came and took away his body. The Lord's body is at the disposal of others. After he has given, out of his opened side, the last that his body contained, the body itself is now left to the believers. Inherent in this is the beginning of the worship of relics. What in life was a vessel of holiness is left by God himself to the veneration and piety of the faithful. Pilate and the Jews have no objections to this. Pilate perhaps suspects that Joseph is a believer, that the Lord's body is of much concern to him, but since this relates to the private sphere of a belief foreign to him, he has no reason to take exception. He cannot share this veneration because he himself does not believe, because for him the body of the Lord is without effect. Were he to believe, then he would know that what is objectively hallowed retains its relation to God.

Relics should be a pointing toward God. In those objects deriving from the Lord and the saints that we possess, we should rediscover his livingness. Because something was part of the Lord's actual living, it remains an occasion for giving the Son back to the Father livingly, in faith, love and hope. The danger is great that the owner of the relic will see in it a kind of static possession that he relates to himself and closes up within himself, whereas the relic really ought to open *him* toward God. All property within the Church is subject to this law. All objects that remind us of God and grace, all things that have spiritual value, have meaning only if they are continually given back to God and regarded as merely gifts on loan from God. Wealth is always a danger for the Church. A poor man sets no great store by his possessions, he gives them back to God more easily than does the rich man. The more a man possesses, the more he closes himself in with his wealth. The Church ought to love and esteem poverty today just as it did in earliest times. A poor communion with an ill-provided church feels itself slighted, yet is basically to be envied. At the beginning and end of his life, the Lord possessed nothing, and during his life he was as poor as the poorest of men. And in this poverty he accomplished his mission. He founded a Church, but built no churches. He did not even beg for his Church, but committed it trustingly to the grace of God. Property can be a means to something else in the Church, but never an end in itself.

19:39–40. *Nicodemus also, who had at first come to him by night, came bringing a mixture of myrrh and aloes about a hundred pounds' weight. They took the body of Jesus, and bound it in linen cloths with the spices, as is the burial custom of the Jews.*

At first, Nicodemus had come at night, so as not to attract any attention while yet being able to experience the sensational event himself. In the meantime, the grace of the Lord has led him to faith. He relinquished wanting to have the last word in relation to God, and left that to the Lord. Now he comes in order to perform the last rites for the Lord. But he is still a Jew, and thus he wants to embalm him in accordance with the burial customs of the Jews. No more than the disciples prior to Easter has he grasped that, in Christianity, the essential thing is no longer the body but the soul, and that the life of the soul no more comes to an end than does the life of the Christian teaching. The soul is everlasting; what happens to the body makes little difference. But although the Lord had referred again and again to eternal life, to life in the love of the Father, that is still a mystery to all his disciples. They cannot at all conceive of the meaning of a soul that lives on in God. Their new belief extends as far as to the human manifestation of Christ; what lies behind that remains, for the time being, almost wholly closed to them. Their belief is a patchwork: they see the Old Covenant, its having been burst open, and its partial continuation; they see the Lord with his new message and his widening of the number of individual believers. But they do not grasp the role of the Lord in these two expansive movements. Comprehension of the unity of these parts is not given to them until the Resurrection. On the one hand, things look like a breaking-open of heaven: God, who bestows his love upon them in the Lord. On the other hand, things look like a breaking-open of the ego: they themselves are opened in love to the Lord and to their neighbor. But they cannot bring these two sorts of breaking-open into synthesis; they do not see that the two paths are basically just one: the path of the Lord's love toward the Father. They see a beginning movement of God toward the world, and a beginning movement of the ego toward God. But that the Lord, positioned in the middle, combines both paths, lives them perfectly and makes them possible for us—this they cannot now see. The central piece, which brings everything together, is still missing. It will not be put in place until the Son returns to the Father. The unity is produced by the unity of his path, from the Father to the world, and our path, through him to the Father. It is now only the day of preparation, everything is held in readiness, is being prepared. It is still not possible to subordinate the external to the inner, the incidental to the significant. So Christian love still exercises itself in the forms of the old Jewish burial custom. It does so in expectation of something that it does not itself know. For the moment, this veneration is the right kind, since the body of the Lord is still dead. On the other hand, faith and love are alive in it, and the forms in which these are expressed remain of secondary importance. The Lord does not expect that antiquated customs should be broken down where that is not necessary. Once his body has become living, he will himself develop the new forms of worship out of the old ones.

The body of the Lord is bound. Every possibility of movement is denied him. He is shackled not only by death, but by cloth bindings as well. No one has even the faintest thought of the possibility that a dead body could ever move itself again. This process of immobilization, which began already with the Crucifixion, is now completed. Those who bind him do not think of his Spirit, which is stronger than his body and has the power to cast off all fetters. Even if angels were to help him to break free of his bonds, then that would still occur only because his Spirit holds power over them. The Lord becomes bound through the sins of the faithful; but when he arises from the dead, he also breaks free of our sins. Joseph and Nicodemus, to be sure, act in no way sinfully, but as those who are doing more than they realize and who carry out a symbolic activity. A man stricken by very great pains has an involuntary, almost unconscious urge to pass them on to others, to see others suffer, too. Whoever suffers, in his soul, as an unbeliever will prefer to seek the company of those who share in his suffering, whether because they have gone through the same thing themselves or because they are susceptible to compassion. By contrast, whoever suffers as a believer will first instinctively give his suffering over to God and deposit it in the mystery of the suffering, unknown to him, of the Son. Thus our sins, too, bind the Lord bodily once again, thereby showing our blame for the Lord's bodily death. And what we knew of our sins was only this external, bodily side. That the soul of Christ had to suffer so much through our sins was something we never suspected, it was a mystery between the Father and him. This depth of sin is first disclosed to us through the completion of the Lord's suffering. We could not bind the soul of the Lord; it bound itself in freedom and in the love of the Father; it was more the Father than we who bound it for the sake of redemption.

The last way, then, that men treat the Lord, this side of death, is to bind him once again. Only on the other side will there be the binding and loosing that the Lord will bestow after he has loosed in general. Following that great loosing, there will no longer be any binding other than one performed with a view to loosing. The present binding, on Holy Saturday, already points ahead to redemption, but those doing the binding are not aware of this. What they do has its limits in the body of the Lord. After the Resurrection, there will be no further possibility of stopping at this body. A meditation on Christ's suffering that aimed to stop at his body, that saw only the pains, the wounds and the hopelessness but not the larger context of love between Father and Son, would not be a Christian meditation on the suffering.

19:41. *Now in the place where he was crucified there was a garden, and in the garden a new tomb where no one had ever been laid.*

When the Lord was alive, the disciples had spent much time together with him in the garden. A garden is a protected place, a place of rest, of detachment, of shelter, of contemplation, of peace. The original paradise had also been a garden. Now they take the dead Lord into the sort of garden that he loved. But they do not know where his soul abides in the meanwhile—in the opposite of a garden, in the opposite of paradise, in that contemplation which is the darkest of all: in contemplation of Sheol. The mystery of Holy Saturday is essentially contemplation. It is the looking at darkness in darkness.

Prayer is that which man offers to God. Contemplation is that which God shows to man. On Holy Saturday, the Father allows the Son to experience the most intimate thing that he possesses: his darkness, which was otherwise always concealed by the light, like something about which no one speaks, like the ultimate personal mystery into which one initiates no other man. Now, however, the Father discloses this mystery to the Son by allowing the mystery itself, instead of him, to speak to him. God *shows* him his mystery; but in showing him his *mystery,* he does not show himself. Often, the greatest nearness and intimacy exists between people not when they speak or associate with each other, but when they are turned away from each other. One can want to show the other something so secret and hidden that he can do this only in his own absence, can point toward it only when turned away, perhaps only in writing, but in any case only indirectly. And this revelation of the mystery requires, at the same time, absolute trust in the love of the other, who accepts it as a mystery (perhaps even as one not understood) in the same measure that it is communicated as a mystery. Everything happens in this silence, which is deeper than any words. Thus the Father shows the Son his mystery in darkness, as darkness, and the Son will contemplate it in darkness and allow it to remain as darkness. He does so because he sees the Father as greater than himself, because, in the eyes of the Son, the Father is the Ever-Greater that he does not now even want to equal. Although the Son has accomplished everything, although he has given everything back to the Father that he received from him, although he has brought his entire creation back to him by going so far as to look upon every single sinner with the eyes of love and redeeming him and, in his love, leading him back to the Father, he will still never infer from his awareness of having fulfilled his mission some right for *himself,* and demand of the Father: "Father, give up your mystery of justice! Destroy the darkness now!" That is not the way that the love of the Son overcomes the justice of the Father. He will never turn his devotion into a means of extortion. Precisely in having brought the Father's creation to perfection through redemption, the Son is more convinced than ever of the Father's greatness and love, and he therefore accepts the mystery of darkness just as the Father offers it to him: in the turning away of the Father himself. He comes home with an attitude of reserve that makes no demands, that acknowledges the Father and desires only what the Father gives him.

They laid him in *a new tomb.* It was not possible to lay him in an old one; he could, it is true, be crucified together with others; he could tread the path of his life on earth together with others, but the path that he now takes is unique and unprecedented. It is a virginal path, never previously trodden. He opens it for the first time through his death. His body, too, must be symbolic of this new path and life, for his body was also a part of his complete sacrifice. And to the mystery of the Resurrection there can ultimately be but *one* witness: God. God, who receives back the Son he sent forth and accompanies him anew. For this it is necessary that the Son be alone. Thus things accord with the initial agreement, when Father and Son were alone in the Holy Spirit. Only in the full loneliness of love can they encounter each other again. The mystery of the Resurrection is wholly and utterly a mystery of eternal life. Only after it has been accomplished are we once again admitted, in order to worship it and participate in it.

God sent his Son down from heaven. But in order to bring him home, to receive him to himself again, God comes down, so to speak, from heaven to earth. He honors his Son on earth through the Resurrection; at this festive occasion, he makes his entry into his new creation. In a sense, entry to earth was barred to the Father through sin, because everything was turned away from him. The Son has turned the face of creation back toward him again. Thus the Father, for his part, who had to turn away from sin, can now turn back toward the world again. The Son departed from a God who was turned away from creation. On Holy Saturday, at the end of the mission, before God turns back once again to the world, he turns away from the Son in love, in order to allow him to share in his mystery. God's initial turning away from the world occurred in anger, his final turning away from the Son occurs in love, and in the Resurrection the Father will be turned in love toward both the Son and the world. When two people really love each other, then either of them can do what he pleases, whether the most disconcerting of things, the most incomprehensible to all—for the lovers it will be all right and will never cast doubt on their love. Thus, too, the Son is not disconcerted by the turning away of the Father; he knows that the Father is doing the right thing, and their love does not suffer because of it. The turning toward is not a recantation of the turning away, as if the Father and Son first had to come closer to each other again after a period of estrangement; for both, their love shines only that much more brightly in the darkness.

Holy Saturday is a mystery of the passage of the incarnated Son into the darkness of the Ever-Greater Father. During the occurrence of this passage, the Son's attitude is a fully trusting one. So it must be when children are introduced into the mystery of the parents. Often, after such an introduction, an initial period of estrangement follows, for instance, of a girl from her father, who now appears distant and incomprehensible to her. The mystery is dark, it arises at precisely that point where there seemed to be nothing but clear love. But if the introduction takes place wholly in love, and if all the circumstances are favorable, then an estrangement need not occur at all.

For a husband and wife, there is, on the wedding night, a darkness before the full self-surrender, a blind feeling one's way toward the unknown mystery, an abandonment of oneself to this unknown thing. After the consummation, however, some kind of disappointment and estrangement usually sets in again; for the husband, because his desire is satiated; for the wife, perhaps, because she had imagined that things would be different, had hoped to be taken in some other way, or even just because something seemingly unending shows its limitedness. In the mystery of Holy Saturday, things are the other way around. Father and Son are given to one another from eternity, and in this mutual surrender there was no mystery. Now, by contrast, the Son contemplates the mystery of the Father, who shows not himself, but his mystery. Since this instance of surrender occurs within their consummate mutual surrender from eternity, no sort of disappointment can attach to it, for every estrangement is in some sense a looking back upon itself, a measuring itself against itself. If married love were as perfect as a human love can be in God, there would be neither an occasion for estrangement nor the possibility of estrangement in seeing and experiencing the dark mystery of one's partner.

What the dead Son sees on Holy Saturday is the opposite of paradise and, at the same time, the complete lack of any form of erotic love. He sees here what God had to create as a counterbalance to paradise. Man and woman were put into paradise in order to give themselves to one another and to be fruitful in that mutual surrender.

If sin had not come into the picture, this mystery would have remained one of beauty in God. Sin, however, alienated it more and more from God and, through that, also alienated the couple more and more from each other. It allowed darkness to seep more and more into this mystery. Without sin, there would have been nothing impure surrounding the mystery of sex, nor would there have been any sort of anxiety or shyness in children regarding this mystery. All estrangement is a consequence and expression of sin. In pure death, there is nothing but pure estrangement, the external opposite of paradisal devotedness. Erotic love was devised by the Creator; it contained everything that should incline and guide creatures toward devoted surrender, the whole course and development of the movement of love, the whole plan of the creature's behavior, which is aimed at making his surrender acceptable and accepted, and indeed, not as sacrifice but in pleasure. But all that was abused and undermined by sin. Outwardly, it still looks like love, but seen from within, it is selfishness. From the viewpoint of death, the same acts that appear as love in the world are divested of their erotic trumpery and appear naked in their cold egoism. Sin diverts the course of erotic love, which should move from the ego by way of the other to God, in order to lead him back through the other to the ego.

Thus the world of death was God's necessary response to sin. For here, sin attains to its truth, which would otherwise nowhere have become evident, to a truth such as God's justice demands. Into this darkness, the Father leads the Son. At the same time, however, he thereby divulges to him the mystery of his justice. It is the Son's first real encounter with this netherworld. God has given two responses to sin: the netherworld and the Son. The netherworld as the necessary consequence of sin, the Son as the free willingness to atone for sin. Now, the two encounter each other. This encounter is no demonic mystery but a Christian one, a mystery of love. For it has its origin in the Father's love: out of love, he gives his mystery over to the Son, and his Son over to death. Everything remains a mystery of communion between Father and Son. But also a mystery of darkness, since, in the netherworld, the Son experiences the estrangement of sin. Yet the darkness of sin remains enclasped in the darkness of love.

19:42. *So because of the Jewish day of Preparation, as the tomb was close at hand, they laid Jesus there.*

They act under a dual commission: one set by the festival that is drawing near and presses for quick resolution of the matter, and one from God, who has made provision for this near, empty tomb from eternity. To the Jews, the festival alone is significant; for them, everything that was connected with Jesus has been concluded, and the disquiet that he caused in them has abated. They have achieved what they wanted, they have seen his dead body and they know that he has been buried. Now they can devote themselves to the festival.

THE DISCIPLES AT THE TOMB

20:1. *Now on the first day of the week Mary Magdalen came to the tomb early, while it was still dark, and saw that the stone had been taken away from the tomb.*

Mary Magdalen keeps faith in her heart. In her womanly way, out of a desire for the nearness of the Lord, she concerns herself with his tomb. He is the one who took away her sin; him she has lost. She directs her life away from herself and her sin, and toward him. Other believers, who were not such openly condemned sinners, have perhaps undergone this unique Christian transition less fully and unmistakably than she. Through her conversion, Mary has been freed from herself to such an extent that she is now nothing more than room for love.

She had sinned from perverted love; the true love has set her free, a love that aroused feelings of remorse in her which, in turn, blossomed fruitfully into love. The deeds of Mary, who cares for the Lord's tomb, are not empty proofs of her love, but living, fruitful actions. In an exemplary way, she has learned that Christian remorse is something wholly different from sterile regret about what one has done. The meaning of Christian remorse lies totally and exclusively in redeemed love. A remorse that continually circles around the sin committed, that feeds on sorrowfulness about that sin, is fully un-Christian. Remorse in love of the Lord is there solely to ensure completion of one's turning away from sin and to make room for love and service to the Lord. Every grievous sin that the Lord pardons *must* bring about the birth of love in the soul: the beginning of a readiness to take on the Lord's mission. So *penance,* too, is a form of love that grows out of remorse. We must not see and understand the penance of the "Magdalens" in the Church as anything other than an act of grateful love, and thus of joy. No matter which form it may assume—that of prayer or fast or vigil or works—it must, if it is to be Christian penance, occur in love and be fruitful in love.

Mary begins her work early in the morning, *while it was still dark.* That is an allusion to the penitent nature of her work. But love motivates her to this penance, this coming to see whether the tomb is in an orderly condition. She has a right to the Lord. She even has a right to be concerned about his body, for he has redeemed her from bodily sin and made her his bride. Here she embodies, within the Church as Bride, the archetype of bride once again at the individual level. As such, she has her duties to the Bridegroom. She possesses the watchfulness of the bride. She knows what she has been redeemed from and what the Lord has protected her from ever since. Thus, too, she is constantly prepared to make sacrifices, more so than others, and it is no coincidence that she is the first to appear at the tomb. *And she saw that the stone had been taken away from the tomb.*

20:2. *So she ran, and went to Simon Peter and the other disciple, the one whom Jesus loved, and said to them: They have taken the Lord out of the tomb, and we do not know where they have laid him.*

She hurries to the two disciples whom she can reach most quickly: the one who represents the office of the Church and the one who embodies love. She wants to communicate with them. In their conversing they form, as a group, the newly established Church. The Lord and the Mother are missing. But the Lord is the Bridegroom, and the Mother has her place with the Bridegroom. The group of three, by contrast, embodies the earthly Church, illumined from beyond, that the Lord has established during his sojourn on earth. There is the office, which still does not grasp its own scope and that was deeply entangled in denial: it is sure and unsure at the same time. *Peter* knows that his office lies in the hands of the Lord, and that he nevertheless has to administer it. He senses the breach between the inflexibility of his commission, which cannot be parcelled out, and the weakness and pliability of his own person. Nothing about Peter is more obvious than this split, and he would have to lead a miserable double life were not the Lord to meet powerfully the demands of that something in him whose demands he himself, between his inadequacy and the office that surpasses him, is not capable of meeting. The Lord is the sole connecting link in him between office and personality. In the Lord alone can he effect the synthesis. For Peter, life in the Lord signifies the resting point of his being; without this center, he could only swing back and forth and waver like someone utterly distraught, could only keep seeking himself without ever finding himself. The Lord, however, through his grace, lifts him out of his unfruitful restlessness in order to give fruitful form to what remains unclosably open in him between the absoluteness of his office and the limitedness of his personality.

Mary Magdalen embodies, within this new Church, the communion, which is active in gratefulness. She, too, has her sole center in the Lord. She, too, would be tossed restlessly back and forth between her sin and her devotion without the Lord. The Lord forms what she does into fruitful activity in gratefulness. She has drawn her life and energy from the love, the charity, of the Lord, and her charitable actions can be nothing other than a shining out into the Church of the experienced charity of the Lord.

John, the beloved who loves, the neighbor to the Lord, embodies here the neighbor in general: the nearest neighbor. He is the archetype of all friendship with the Lord. But Christian friendship always has a eucharistic character. The Lord loves John and is loved by him. But he expects that the friendly love he shows for the disciple will be passed on by him, in the same sense, to all his neighbors. The command of the Lord to love one's neighbors bears the stamp of his own love, which was love for every man as his neighbor. No one is more distant from the Lord than others; no one is loved secondarily or more weakly. This is what John embodies as an exemplary type. Did he not exist, then men would regard the crucified love of the Lord as something general and abstract that touches them personally in only a minor way. However, the Lord's human, close and friendly love for John shows that mankind is not just incidentally drawn into the Lord's love for the Father, but that every individual is singled out and attracted by it. That it is a matter of a personal, living interchange, which loses nothing of its livingness when one partakes of it, but only increases fruitfully through use—from one neighbor to the other—in the eucharistic sense that is uniquely characteristic of the Lord's love. John appears here as the human bearer of this divine love, and the indwelling of the Lord in him is what turns Johannine love into Christian love. In Peter, the Lord was the axis, the zenith; in Magdalen, he was the turning from sin toward God and the fruitfulness of life; John needs neither peace nor remorse, he lives totally in love, and in him the Lord is the livingness of love for one's neighbor. Through the gift of his love that the Lord has bestowed upon him, John's love is no longer a merely human one, but Catholic love in God, an already heavenly love, which is no longer tied to the person of John, no longer serves his human purposes, a love that has been made serviceable to the Lord himself, one that remains the same whether the Lord is alive or dead, whether he is resurrected or in heaven, one that draws its sustenance from the divine love of the Lord, one that has been lifted above itself and has its source in the Lord himself. John carries with him, wherever he might be, this divine thing that is pure love, not as in a vessel that contains it, but like a wellspring that issues forth together with the Lord. He forms, within the Church, the human communication of love under commission from the Lord.

These three elements, then, are to be found in the Church: first the framework, the office, the organization. Then the movement away from the ego and toward God according to the tenor of the ecclesiastical framework. Finally, the movement down from the Lord and back toward the Lord, from the bestowed love of the Lord to bestowal of his love along with him, in the way that the Lord himself comes from the Father and goes to the Father. We ought not to ask how John, who is, after all, just a limited man, can reflect the totality of the Lord's love. For one thing, the Lord did not bestow his love in a measure proportionate to the disciple, and if he gave him an individual mission, he did not do so in accordance with the disciple's human imperfection. Although the mission is a particular one, distinct from all others, it still cannot be called limited because it is intended to help dispense the Lord's infinite love. The measure of the love and the measure of the mission do not, in fact, coincide, but they complement one another, and indeed, in John, they do this so fully that he becomes, for the Church, an archetype of all missions. Using him as an example, the Lord wants to show his Church that, from the very start, he has summoned her to an all-embracing task and wished to form her into a Bride worthy of the Bridegroom. The imperceptible mission of any man is always proportional to the love, even if the perceptible mission appears minutely small and unimportant. A perfect love can remain completely hidden within the Church, but it will nevertheless be perfectly effective. John stands, at the beginning of the Church, as the one who embodies the correspondence between love and mission.

Peter, who sinned when he was conscious of his officiary function, Mary Magdalen, who sinned before she had encountered the Lord, and John, who sees his whole life summed up in the Lord's love, embody together the form of love, faith and duty that the Lord imparts to the New Covenant. Everything that occurs afterward, in the Church and in the living love of the Lord, takes place within the demands that were set for these three. All three paths, different though they be, nevertheless manifest but *one* direction: the direction that the Lord gave to them by leading them, through him, to the Father. Within this direction, which determines everything and carries everything away with it, it is no longer possible to have a total view of the earthly direction of a Christian life. No one knows what is cause and what is effect: whether, for example, a period of martyrdom in the Church is a cause or an effect of greater love in the world. No one knows which is prior: the sin of the unfaithful or the suffering of the faithful, the guilt of the Church or her penance. All these questions become idle at the point where the three life directions of Peter, Magdalen and John merge into the one direction of the life of the Lord, which he communicates to his Church. Peter encounters the Lord, is installed in his office and falls into sin. Magdalen emerges from sin, encounters the Lord and becomes a saint. Both these things happen within the Church, in ways that are visible only to God, that issue from him and lead back to him. The one certainty is this: God desires that we should be led to him through the Son and that the area in which the path is to be found should be the area that he established as the Catholic Church.

So, then, Mary hurries to the two disciples with what she has to report. She is a plain and simple woman; she thinks in a commonsensical way. Her love for the Lord, which is a living love, demands no miracles. It is enough for her to be able to be active in the love of the Lord. She does not think of demanding anything extraordinary. She is quite prepared, of course, to accept any miracle that stems from the Lord. But she does not primarily think in terms of miracles. If the Lord's body is no longer there, then she concludes that someone has taken it away. And she does not know *where they have laid him.* She has not gone looking for it herself. Her initial task is none other than to report the matter. This mission is necessary because the Church is a communion in the Lord, because the fact that the Lord is missing cannot be kept private, but rather, the responsible members of the Church must deal with the matter in the right way. These members are order and love; it is the duty of both together to find the Lord. In love, the Lord is common to all, but his missions remain individually distributed. Mary's mission is completed with her report of the matter; the mission of the others begins at the point where hers ends. And by properly fulfilling her mission, Mary has made it easier, indeed, made it possible at all, for the others to fulfill their mission.

20:3. *Peter then came out with the other disciple, and they went toward the tomb.*

Immediately and without hesitation, the two disciples begin to fulfill their mission. They live in grace, and it is grace in them that accepts their commissions in order to carry them out at once. Grace is fruitfulness as such. Everything that man does in order to arrive at grace already takes place in grace. It is the primary thing; not only the goal but the beginning as well. It makes use of human means in order to arrive at itself; man does not make use of himself in order to arrive at grace. Thus grace effects its own increase with the help of man. Grace issues its commissions without man's having to trouble much about it. Within the commission of grace, man must also make his plans independently, consider and evaluate the means of carrying them out so as to arrive at proposed goals. But everything is only the carrying out of a command. He will carry it out as cleverly and as well as he can. And yet: if the work is done in grace, it cannot but come to a good and fruitful end. For the two disciples, the words of Mary Magdalen embody the conveying of the commission. They do not take long to reflect on the matter but simply obey, in accordance with the way that grace mediates simple obedience.

20:4. *They both ran together, but the other disciple outran Peter and reached the tomb first; . . .*

Both run, both as fast as they can, but in the Church love always runs faster than office. It perceives what is commissioned more quickly, it always engages itself unstintingly. Office, even when functioning at its greatest speed, can never catch up with love. Office has to look after everyone, has to take everyone with it if possible, show consideration for everyone, proceed as uniformly as possible. It cannot go to the Lord with only those who run ahead fastest; it has to concern itself with the whole of the flock entrusted to it, with all the slow and halfhearted. Love consists in giving lavishly; it is nothing but giving lavishly, and in that it is the quickest. It gives of itself without stopping to think; it desires the attainable and the unattainable, because it desires everything. Office has to weigh things up, and also look back at what has been achieved, in order to do better when taking further steps. Love is personal, it has no worries other than itself. Office is impersonal, and must take account of the order and state of things. But love is no crazed fool that runs senselessly. For *both,* after all, run *together.* It stays in touch with office, within reachable distance from office. But it is still the one that leads office along behind it. Office is clumsier, because it has to remain calm and collected; love, by contrast, has nothing to lose because it has already lost itself and lives on extravagance.

As Peter runs, he thinks about things. He reflects, he conjectures, he gives himself over to contemplation. John, by contrast, who will be the first to arrive, will be the second to know contemplation; at the tomb, he will begin to look. Contemplation is something that comes from God; office, in the course of its activities, attempts to stay close to God. Love, by contrast, always comes from God and therefore always has the possibility of acting immediately. It not only gives lavishly of itself, but has this excess in itself that enables it to do so immediately because so much has been given lavishly to it.

20:5. . . . *and stooping to look in, he saw the linen clothes lying there, but he did not go in.*

John, who is the first to arrive at the tomb, immediately takes a look, and, once he has seen, needs no further proofs. He possesses the certainty that love gives, love in God. Vision and love are so much a unity that one cannot make them independent of each other. We cannot ask whether vision is a criterion for love or vice versa. Each is precondition, cause and effect to the other. For at bottom they are one. In this lies the distinction between love and infatuation. Infatuation makes one blind; it wants to see the beloved object in the way that it wants to see it, and the image that arises as a result has little in common with the true image of that object. It is only the correlative to all the longings of the infatuated person. He projects into it everything that remains unattainable to him while still seeming desirable. Ultimately, it is only the ideal image of himself. Love, on the other hand, loves the beloved just as he is, and tries to adapt itself to him. It does not, like infatuation, start with itself, but rather with reality as it is. It does not gloss over the shortcomings of the beloved, but views them in the light of the Lord and reflects on what it can do for the beloved, in the Lord, so as to bring him closer to God. For love is a gift of the Lord; all gifts of the Lord, however, lead to the Father. Hence, every love between human beings also leads to the Father. In its grace, the love of the Lord rounds imperfect man out to what he ought to be before the Father and in the Father, and the Lord permits those who love to share in the vision of this image. Out of the narrow vision of man as he is, he grants to those who love the heavenly vision of what man ought to be and, through grace, will be. Just as John sees the linen cloths lying on the ground, and out of this vision, which is almost nothing, immediately has the whole vision of the living love of the Lord, so the lover glimpses, through the narrow external appearance of the beloved in the grace of the Lord, his original image in the Father. That this original image exists is the work of the supplementary grace of the Lord. Only in love is this vision possible. The lover cannot communicate it to anyone who does not love, for the latter will be blind to it. And anyone who does not share John's love will not believe his vision of the vitality of love out of the linen cloths lying there. Such a person would come up with hundreds of other possible explanations for the phenomenon. At the very least, he would require lengthy processes of argument in order to exclude alternative interpretations. Whoever does not have love loses a lot of time. He will run more slowly, understand more slowly. He demands assurances, proofs, periods of probation. Love, by contrast, sees and understands at first glance: this is right in God — even if the meaning of this reaction is not yet transparent to it.

But he did not go in. Because the vision of love is enough for him. Whatever else there might be to see is no concern of his. The Lord is, indeed, not there. His commission was the vision, and with that it has been carried out. Even in lavishly bestowed love there is an order, a governance. It avoids the superfluous. It goes precisely to the point of fulfilling its commission, and no further. For the love that John must prove concerns the Lord, and it is proven as soon as he has grasped the Lord's love out of the cloths that lie there. That is *discretion* in love. The disciple stands there so lovingly and devotedly that the Lord can call and summon him at any time. He does not push himself forward. He does not question the beloved at every minute about what he can do for him and whether he has any particular wish. . . . With indiscreet questions like that, he would really be calling attention more to his own love than thinking of the beloved. It is not one and the same thing if a man prays simply in order to worship the Lord or if he does so in order to remind him that he is still there and awaits his favor. True love holds itself in readiness for the moment when it is needed. John lays his head on the Lord's breast at the moment when the Lord has need of him. Now he knows that the Lord, whose livingness he has recognized, will summon him at the proper time if he needs him. Love never wishes to attract attention to itself.

20:6–7. *Then Simon Peter came, following him, and went into the tomb; he saw the linen cloths lying, and the napkin, which had been on his head, not lying with the linen cloths but rolled up in a place by itself.*

Peter, following after, sees at first exactly the same thing as John: the empty tomb and the linen cloths. But he goes further. For office must inquire into things; it has need of certainty in a supernatural sense. It must objectively possess and be able to deliver the evidence, regardless of whether understanding is subjectively present or not. Objective proof is necessary for objective proclamation. Even if Peter were, for his own part, already certain, he would have to subordinate his personal judgment to general, objective and official certainty. Every possibility of enthusiastic self-indulgence must be excluded, the way in from the outside must be solidly and reliably structured. John's vision cannot be seen and judged at all by someone who does not love. Therefore, another vision is required, namely, official vision. But Peter's inquiring, too, must take place in love. For the Lord loves his Church, he loves office; he knows that office is capable of bringing about many things that love alone could not bring about. Love always presupposes a capacity for love; it must, in order to fulfill itself, chance upon such capacities. Office can, and should, reach even those who arrive at possession of love in an only secondary way, through following along after. Love can grasp much that is fleeting, while office is forced to build on the permanent. It must keep to the path of moderation, and must therefore often avoid the smallest byways of love. Hence, open conflicts may well arise between office and love even though both are in the right. Each must meet the demands of its basic presuppositions. In so doing, love will always have to suffer, whether its suffering comes from the Church or directly from the Lord. Its office will be to suffer; whereas office does not suffer. Office must, because of its catholicity, undergo but minor fluctuations. Its certainty is different in kind from the certainty of love, which, as such, does not know the certainty of office.

John is the first at the tomb: he sees, he believes, he knows. After him comes Peter: he sees, he inquires, he believes. His inquiry is indifferent regarding what concerns John. This inquiry must be made for the sake of those who have strayed, those who are nonbelievers. For love, it would not be necessary. And it is not only what Peter now inquires into that he must render serviceable to his ecclesiastical milieu, but also, in a new and different sense, John's love. For the *lover* must subordinate himself to the Church. *Love* itself can be integrated into no framework other than itself. Thus, for example, a saint will much more prefer not to be canonized; but out of love for the Church, which is based on love for the Lord, he will acquiesce in this ecclesiastical procedure and subordinate himself to its decision. His love for God does not thereby become standardized, it remains untouched by the canonization; the lover, however, is rendered serviceable to love by being utilized as a tool within love as a whole. Through ecclesiastical office, the instrumentality of love can acquire greater efficacy while the love is not thereby affected. In true love, an instinct is alive that wishes to be tested and assigned its place by the Church in order that its lavish self-bestowal might occur more in the sense of Christian love, namely, to the benefit of all. Such love would even accept being condemned by the Church and expelled if that were to entail a greater service to love, if the Church's love were to become more radiant through this sacrifice. Office can require it to renounce its insights, but never its love itself. Love does not need classification; it is part of its passion to be classified in such a way as to arrive at its truest activity.

While Peter inquires into what John has already recognized in love, the latter's love does not remain unfruitful. But its fruitfulness is deposited in the meantime with God, who makes use of it as he wishes. It will be given over by God to the Church for general administration at the moment when the Church has finished her inquiry and arrived at the truth. The situation is not, however, one in which there is tension between God and the Church, with the Church having no share in the temporarily deposited love. Both of the two, Peter and John, are in God and, at the same time, in the Church; during the inquiry, neither does John cease to be in the Church nor Peter cease to be in God. But God and the Church are not the same; they are related to each other like soul and body in their living, mutual connectedness, and while Peter stands at the center of the body of the Church, John has to live in love with God—both in the places that have been marked out for them. God is free and has no obligation to delay the revelations of his love until the Church has reached her decision; hence, John's love has no obligation to interrupt the life of love during the period of the Church's inquiry. He and his love exist, after all, within the Church. He exists within her to such an extent that, even if the Church's decision should prove erroneously negative, he would not separate himself from the Church. He would have to bow to her decision while nevertheless not giving up the opening toward God. He would have to deposit his truth, in love, wholly and utterly with the love and truth of God, and await the final decision from God. Were a command to come from God, but also an opposing command from the Church, then, caught between the two, he would have to keep trying to obtain permission from the Church to embark on the path commanded by God, but to obey the Church in all matters falling within her authority in the meantime. Subjecting oneself to God is a work of love; in the Church, deferring what is personal for the sake of the communion at large is equally a work of love. If these two works are in contradiction, then God holds the fruitfulness of this love, which has seemingly become futile, in trust for the individual, who can no longer act, and for the Church, whose mistakes, after all, never signify damnation for the faithful. From this love, the earthly Church will derive benefit in her heavenly center.

He saw the linen cloths lying, and the napkin, which had been on his head, not lying with the linen cloths but rolled up in a place by itself. That the napkin is rolled up is a sign of order. In his investigation, Peter must rely on this sign. On one side, he sees the cloths that have been thrown there, something which John had seen by himself: disorder. He sees something that John had not seen, namely, order, which allows him to set about deliberating with his human understanding, excluding possibilities and coming to a conclusion: what has occurred is quite right, it is logical and makes sense. The linen cloths had been wrapped around the Lord's body; they are left in a heap. The napkin had covered his head; it has been carefully rolled up. In this, Peter recognizes a differentiation, a valuing and esteeming of the head which is inappropriate for the body. This confirms once again that everything happened as it should have. Through the removal of the cloths, however, both the body and the head—the spirit—of the Lord have been set free. Thus there are also positive indications of an occurrence that makes sense, and not merely the negative exclusion of impossible hypotheses.

The inquiry by Peter leads to the same result as the vision of John. The latter received, from the almost negative impression of the disordered cloths, a positive vision. Peter had to bring together the positive and the negative impressions and compare them. John has, in grace, transformed the negative into something positive; Peter was able, in grace, to eliminate the negative through the positive.

20:8. *Then the other disciple, who reached the tomb first, also went in, and he saw and believed.*

Now John, too, enters the tomb, sees what Peter had seen, grasps what Peter had grasped and believes. But he had already believed before that. Before that, he believed within God's revelation. Now he believes anew, in another way, in the ecclesiastical sense, on the basis of the proofs that the Church shows to him. His personal belief takes on a new cast within the Church's teaching. For the Church, his belief is now more valid than it was before. Outward conversion can be situated between these two points in time: the transition from being seized by the grace of faith to being received into the Church. During this period, the expectant one hopes to find that the personal insight bestowed upon him by God is also reflected in the views of the Church. Only once this confirmation from the side of the Church has ensued will he also be able to pass on to others his knowledge of what pertains to the Lord. Only in the Church will he receive the sacraments and, along with them, the ecclesiastical mission to proclaim the Faith. The period of waiting during Peter's inquiry can also be the novitiate or postulancy of a candidate for admission to a religious order, and the ensuing belief, the confirmation of his divine calling through the Church or the order. Should the order reject a novice who had, in truth, been called by God—should, in general, anyone direct a person toward some path other than the one chosen by God—then that person would have to realize that his life will, to be sure, assume the form of a sacrifice for his own and the Church's sin, but that, precisely because of this, it will not be deprived of fruitfulness. At the Church's point of origin, however, the Lord has placed the ideal case, in which Peter's inquiry coincides with John's love; the ideal case, which remains worth striving toward for all who come after, because it allows no kind of guilt to become evident, but only mutual love.

In the background to these events, however, stands Mary, who was given to John as a Mother and who discloses herself to him as does a penitent to his father confessor. Her belief is not tested. Only John's belief is tested, and she will believe what John believes. Through him, the man and priest, she stands as woman in the Church. Her belief is linked to the belief of revelation, since both form the unity of virginity. But John's belief of revelation, for its part, forms a unity with the ecclesiastical belief of Peter. In this respect, John is the middle figure in whom Mary and Peter are united. He is that because he embodies love. To be sure, Mary did not wait for John in order to believe; her belief is immediate. And yet it becomes living step by step with that of John. But because she is the Mother, the Church cannot test and decide regarding the substance of her belief, other than in the sense that the Mother already knows. Her belief is in the same position as the infallibility of the Church. It was at the same time, at the Cross, that the Mother and the Church became the Bride of Christ.

The Holy Spirit is at the disposal of Peter and the Church as the Bride of Christ, but in such a way that he must also always be summoned by her. The Bride of Christ is, in her relation to the Spirit, always the one who makes requests. That she possesses the attribute of infallibility does not relieve her of the duty of prayer to the Spirit. What already *exists* must, so to speak, also become permanent. Thus, in marriage, there are fixed relationships between man and wife; but, for the husband, possessing the wife does not preclude the necessity of tender courtship; otherwise, their love would ossify. With Mary, the situation was different when she became the Bride of the Holy Spirit: she did not have to request, but rather, to assent. The Church, by contrast, must request, and in this request and its granting she finds a guideline to the truth. Herein lies, for her, her control over herself. There are, in the Church, times when she stands farther from Christ, and times when she stands nearer to him again. For her herself, just how she stands in relation to him can scarcely be clearly seen. By contrast, her relation to the Holy Spirit is, in a way, testable by her, namely, from within the relationship of requesting and granting. Here, she has to recognize that the will that guides her is not her own will; she must perceive, within the light that shows the way, a difference between the light of the Holy Spirit and that of her own insight. And only to the extent that she constantly perceives this difference does she know that she finds herself at one with the Lord. Here, however, it is by no means permitted that she posit a difference between the view of the Holy Spirit and her own view.[1] The foundation for this relation between the Church and

---

[1] She might, for example, initially examine, in the "pure objectivity" of the Holy Spirit, some matter or person that she would find uncomfortable or detestable from a purely human standpoint, thereby leaving out of consideration her own human-Christian love. If, however, she is charged with the examination by God, then she will receive for that purpose a sufficient measure of human-

the Holy Spirit was laid by Peter's inquiry at the tomb, that is, at a moment when the Lord and the Father were unreachable. Precisely at such a moment, however, the Holy Spirit is reachable: he takes over the functions of God. Here, once again, the officiary role of the Holy Spirit becomes clear in its unity with ecclesiastical office.

The Holy Spirit's relation to John is a different one. John has not made inquiries, and yet he believes. Peter is tied to earth; John is tied to heaven. He embodies the same Church, but as the Church of love, of the beyond, which has no need of inquiries. His love is rooted in God to such an extent that the Holy Spirit *cannot* be absent from it. That he is in love means at once that he is also in the Holy Spirit. The official Church is in the Spirit insofar as she repeatedly assures herself of the Spirit, repeatedly examines her position, repeatedly pleads anew for the Spirit. The loving Church, by contrast, does not first need to call down the Spirit in order to know that she is in God; for in love, the proper nearness and the proper distance are already established. John knows, in an elementary way, that he is loved and himself loves. He does not need to ask questions in order to keep assuring himself of love. For him, the Spirit is a support for trusting in God and the Lord. The Father and Son are now unreachable for John, too, but he does not even think of reaching them. Peter inquires in order to be prepared at the given moment. John is already prepared, he is nothing other than that. Peter has acquired an office that he did not himself wish for. Thus the Spirit must constantly watch over that office; he who holds it must constantly obtain new guidelines from the Holy Spirit, and keep monitoring whether what has been done was also really done in the Spirit. John has no need for that, because love from the Spirit is common to Christians, and a relationship of agreement and trust exists. He possesses the prerequisite for his commission before

---

Christian goodwill to carry out the examination in a unity of love that combines, within Christ's love, both the Church's human love and the Holy Spirit's divine love. And the human love, which the Church might allow to hold sway in this examination, would be for her a certain sign that she was examining within the Holy Spirit.

it is issued. The commission is always the fulfilment of his own inclination: to love.

The Mother stood at the service of the Holy Spirit. She became his Bride, and had thus already accomplished what he expected of her: she concurred with him and became through him the Mother of the Lord. Thus the Spirit would be obligated to support her whenever she had need of him. He could not deny himself to her after she had not denied herself to him. Through the grace of the Motherhood that God allotted to her, she was elevated to the height of the Spirit. If the Child lived in her womb, then the Spirit, too, has lived in her; but from one in whom he lives he does not withdraw anymore, not even after the birth of the Child. That he lives in her is shown by the fact that, from being the Mother of the One, she became the Mother of all; and the Son was able to install her as the Mother of all because he knew that the Spirit lives in her.

Thus the Holy Spirit is omnipresent in the Church: in the office, in love and in the Mother he is, in the most differing forms, the same. He is the one, then, who binds the Church into a unity. Unity is his function. Not only do Peter and John, on the one hand, and John and the Mother, on the other, form a unity, but the office, too, is unthinkable apart from the Mother. For, in the Church, the Mother herself has a function for the Church, an office, and in fact, a primary one: God had required her in order to found the new Church. And when the Bridegroom appears, the Bride must also have a Mother: he gives her his own bodily Mother, in the Holy Spirit, to be her Mother. Thus the Mother stands both between and above Peter and John: she has an office and she has love; her love is her office.

20:9. . . . *for as yet they did not know the Scripture, that he must rise from the dead.*

The faith of the apostles is still limited. The Lord's life among them had opened them to concrete truths; they were expanded in many directions and became capable of absorbing more. But now that they have been deprived of the security that the visible presence of the Lord had awakened in them, they are unable, of themselves, to allow the above-and-beyond, the always-more, the greater revelation to take place in them. They remain available for service without themselves being capable of grasping this availability for service. To be sure, they have grasped that what has happened to the Lord is *right*. But they are far removed from being able to draw the ultimate, the Christian, conclusion from this. Once the moment has come for them to accept what they now dare not comprehend, belief in the Resurrection of the Lord will—since their readiness is a living one—take possession of them effortlessly.

The one who is best able to wait is *Peter*. Being able to wait belongs to office, which never has any interest in a rush of events. It has the attribute of inertia. Love, by contrast, which lives in a continual above-and-beyond, expects everything: *John*, too, still knows nothing of the Resurrection, but as soon as he has experienced it, he will not be astounded, for it will be the fulfilment of his expectation. True love does not calculate, does not assure itself of what is to come, but it always expects. In so doing, it desires nothing for itself, but it contains belief and hope in itself. It is not insatiability, which always wants more proofs, gifts, revelations; on the contrary, the smallest proof in love is large. What it seeks is not constant, boundless increase, but rather, the vitality of ever new, forth-flowing love. It is itself an open readiness that is also ready to round everything off. Regarding the Lord, of course, it does not, as with men, need to round anything off. But also in relation to him, love is so much a readiness that even the most unexpected falls within its expectation, even if the Lord again and again exceeds all expectations. Finally, the *Mother* lives in love and knows expectation. But not as the above-and-beyond; her hope is wholly included within her belief. She lives in her Son to such an extent that she participated, in the Spirit, in his Resurrection. She contains him within herself like a Mother; she knows about him, she is in touch with him, she has him in all her senses, in scent and in taste. Even if she does not, as a human being, know about the Resurrection, she nevertheless knows about it in the Spirit. She knows that this death is nothing final. John's love reaches out in expectation toward the Lord; the Mother's love both bestows itself and is enclosed within itself: the Child remains in her, even when the Son stands next to her. She simply knows.

The disciples know nothing of the Resurrection. And they perhaps do not know Scripture very precisely. That the Lord fulfills Scripture they have always understood in every instance when it was explained to them. But their ignorance does not diminish their readiness. Once the Resurrection has taken place, they will then discover that it has fulfilled Scripture. The Lord himself will also give this proof to the Church. To be sure, it is not part of Peter's office to test the Lord; still, in the inquiry that he has to make, he must keep to the proofs and guidelines that the Lord offers him, in this or that case, through fulfilment of Scripture. It is as if the Lord, through the course of his life, could be tied right back into Scripture: all his deeds and experiences are fulfilments of Scripture. These proofs, which he himself produces, remain binding for Peter. So it is that one makes inquiry in the Church: by measuring things against Scripture. The Lord exists within his Church to such an extent that he allows himself to be tested through Scripture. In this testing, it is by no means a matter of correspondence: the life of the Lord does not correspond to the old Scripture. Only in essential points do the two coincide, and these points are proof enough. This is to remain the case in the New Covenant as well. The Scripture of the New Covenant is also no source about the life of the Lord in the sense of a usual historical document. Here, too, only the essential points have been recorded. Spanning these are arches and bridges, and it is at such places that *tradition* begins its work: in these unfilled spaces it lives. That there can be tradition beside Scripture has its explanation in the vitality of love: tradition and love have in common the fact that they develop and grow. Everything must remain within the spirit of Scripture; but as soon as love is there, this spirit will be a living one. Prior to the appearance of the Lord, there was only Scripture; in the Old Covenant, there could not yet have been a divine tradition because love had not yet become man. At that time, only the letter was available as a canon of God's word. The Lord's love goes beyond the letter, but without denying it. Tradition, too, passes beyond Scripture, but has to allow its spirit to be aligned with the spirit of Scripture; it can never stand in contradiction to Scripture. It can be nothing but a development of what has already been laid down in Scripture, and love must be evident as the origin and goal of that development. Tradition must be defended for the sake of love, since everything in the Church must grow, develop and be living, just as love, the soul of the New Covenant, is itself living. If everything in Scripture were already explicitly present and developed, then no living life would be possible. The Church is Bride; everything about her is expectation and hope in love. She can be based in nothing that is final or concluded, in nothing that would be incapable of further growth. Otherwise, her love would no longer be living. Both of the two, Scripture and tradition, belong together, like the clearly marked boundaries of office and the continually new growth of love.

20:10. *Then the disciples went back to their homes.*

They have fulfilled their commission. They have seen, inquired and recognized as right. In this fulfilment, they have arrived at a resting point: they are allowed to go home. Office, which made its inquiry, is satisfied with the inquiry and does not look for further interpretations beyond what is suggested by the existing facts. It does not lose itself in empty speculations, and establishes no guidelines for future behavior. John returns home with an expanded love. His belief has received new reinforcement. Faith is never a good that one can allow to remain as it is in order to draw sustenance from it. It must be continually fructified anew through love.

MARY AT THE TOMB

20:11. *But Mary stood weeping outside the tomb, and as she wept, she stooped to look into the tomb;...*

Mary stands at the tomb and weeps. She is the woman who has experienced the kindness of the Lord, clung to it in order to be rid of her sin; and love brought it about that she was rid of it. She is conscious of her sin and weakness. The power to overcome them she received from the Lord. She has constant need of that power, not primarily in order to avoid slipping back into sin, for she abhors it, but because, in order to be able to live, she relies constantly on the protection and love of the Lord. Her weakness leans wholly on him, who lends it support. Few, perhaps, have comprehended the kindness of the Lord to such a degree: the greatness of his redeeming power, the brightness of his unifying love. But it is still more the magnificence of his human reality, as opposed to that of his divinity, that she senses. Otherwise, she would have grasped that this magnificence does not come to an end in death; and otherwise, she would not feel so urgent a need for his physical presence. What she weeps about most is that all the might of the Lord seems to have collapsed. In all who are near to her she sees only weakness. She had expected unprecedented consequences from the Lord, rolling onward like a wave: what had happened to her should also happen to others. Gladly would she have brought crowds of men to him, gladly would she have become the messenger of his grace. She possesses something like a measuring stick for estimating the size of her loss. She knows how great the abyss of her sin was, and how boundless the grace of the Lord that filled it: this relationship provides her with a measuring stick. Through it, she knows much more about the Lord than the most loving of wives can know about her husband. Her tears are simultaneously tears of sorrow and tears of gratitude. The Lord, who has redeemed her from her sin, has, after all, declared himself ready to bear the whole of her guilt. Standing beneath the Cross, she has experienced for herself something of his readiness. There, the Christian sense of penitence was awakened in her, in which sorrow for the Lord's suffering combines with joyful gratitude. Her destiny is determined by the convergence of these two concepts: redemption and suffering. For the Christian, joy and penitence are inseparably intertwined. Pain about one's own sin is at one with joy about having been redeemed; and this joy, in turn, is at one with pain about the Lord's suffering, which prompts one to share in bearing it. The gift of penitence to Mary is a gift from the Lord to the whole Church; a gift that can be handed on to others, that is grace and that therefore contains joy in itself. In this gift, Mary gives back to God something that was one of his gifts: sensual love. This renunciation is well-suited, in a special way, to penitence. In it, a gift is offered to God, in gratitude and joy, that is something good, but that one freely renounces out of love. In this renunciation, there is no element of inhibition or perversion, but simply an attempt at gratitude out of joyfulness of heart. It is an offering on the part of the whole body, in its natural, God-created form. Neither must the body be mutilated nor the relevant drive be artificially suppressed. Instead, this normal gift from God must be entrusted to God in its normal, unspoilt condition. Fasting out of penitence is all right as long as normal hunger persists and the person does not become sick; keeping vigil is penance as long as the normal need for sleep is preserved; physical chastisement is in order as long as the punishment inflicted on the body is one that does not essentially damage it. For we must not only give God's gifts back to him in an unspoilt condition, but must return them to him in such a state that they are capable of being used for further deeds and sacrifices. All penance remains symbolic. It must be constituted in a way that enables it to be continued or resumed. Should someone wish to mutilate a member of his body, then he would no longer be capable of using it to work for God. And he would be able to look back upon the mutilation as upon a completed act, which is never consistent with the purpose of Christian penance. This must always remain conscious of how completely inessential its work remains in comparison with that of the Lord. Penance is demanded earnestly and with absolute urgency, yet it always remains a scarcely noticeable first attempt, an almost-nothing, something inconsequential even to us—humorous, in fact—at which we can only smile. That which we sacrifice by implication is always pathetic and trifling, because here it is we ourselves who hold sway; and yet we should not overstep this boundary, but rather, attempt to remain within the bounds that allow our penance to appear unobtrusive. The Lord, who bestows all penitence, measures by other criteria—regarding both just what of it he accepts and just what penitential suffering he himself imposes. Here, man loses sight of things, and can even be drawn by the Lord into his own penance.

And as she wept, she stooped to look into the tomb. Mary weeps more for the Lord than for herself. Her tears guide her glance toward the tomb. It is a weeping that remains in the Lord, that thus, unknowingly, calls for grace. Grace is already inherent, imperceptibly, in the expectation of the one making penance, even if it often first manifests itself only in its effects. But we should not demand manifest grace as a reward for penitence; that would be bargaining, and not a sacrifice. In penitence, one relinquishes the right to control things. Therefore Mary looks into the *empty* grave. She turns her glance toward the place of the Lord, but that place is empty. So it should also be. That is what correct belief requires. Mary has trust, and pours it into the incomprehensible emptiness. She does the best that she can, for she cannot know of the Resurrection. Thus she goes to the place where the Lord was, where there is hope of perhaps finding him. She *seeks.* She looks, under commission from the Lord, into the emptiness. She is in *unseeingness.* Her sight has been taken from her by the Lord. But as she unseeingly looks, since this looking is hers by commission, she believes. Behind her, she has redemption from her sins and the experience of the Cross; in front of her, she has only the emptiness of the tomb. But she must not cling to what has been, must not look backward. Belief demands that she endure looking into the emptiness. By taking into herself the emptiness of the tomb, she unconsciously renders herself capable of taking on eternal life. Through the fact that she seeks the Lord there where he no longer is, she becomes capable of the ever-greater, the more-than-human, the divine. She takes the emptiness, the concludedness, into herself, along with the belief that transcends all that; therefore, what she sees is empty and no longer a tomb. It was empty before and is now empty again, and in the interval it had nevertheless contained in itself the whole of belief: Resurrection in some inconceivable, nondeterminable place. Resurrection is there where the Father and Son are. As long as I exist, as long as my self occupies space, resurrection is not possible. As long as the self fills up the emptiness of space, the emptiness in which resurrection occurs is not present. As long as I fill up empty space with my look, my being, my hope, my "good works", resurrection is not possible. Resurrection is the unhoped-for as such. We are not redeemed in order to look back and receive the Lord into ourselves, but rather, so that the Lord, from beyond, might look back at us and we vanish into him. We are no longer the ones that we were: in comparison with what we now are, what we had been is nothing but an empty tomb. We are no longer what we were, we are a part of the mission of the Lord. If the Lord has redeemed Mary, then what remains is not the old Mary, minus her sin, but a being that had so great a sin that it now has an equally great empty space for the Lord. This is the effect of absolution: that it does not simply take sin away, but turns the empty space left by sin into a magnificent place for the Lord in which the angels can appear. Those who had wanted to cast the first stone went away because they were aware of their sin. They departed because they had self-knowledge. If they had also had knowledge of the Lord, they would have stayed in order to participate in the grace of confession and to allow their emptiness to be taken up by the fullness of the Lord. They did not wish to look into the emptiness of the tomb. They wanted to have something pleasing to the eye. Who wants to look into an empty tomb? Who wants to make penance? All that is pointless, dry and empty — because in it, one everywhere runs up against the livingness of the Lord, which one does not see, does not understand, does not grasp, does not feel. And nevertheless: as soon as all prayer, all devotion and penitence, is taken into the empty tomb, it becomes living, because there, at last, room exists for what I am not and what I do not see: the emptiness beyond my self, at whose edge I stand, toward which I stoop, into which I look. Stand there like that: then everything else becomes superfluous. That is the life of Christians: to the others, a standing at the edge of emptiness, a wasted life. To us, the only meaning.

20:12. *. . . and she saw two angels in white, sitting where the body of Jesus had lain, one at the head and one at the feet.*

Two angels keep watch over the place where the Lord had lain. They are the angels whom he had taken with him on his journey through life, who had remained invisible, and who only now become perceptible to—and solely to—Mary Magdalen. They become so at the moment when Mary has given herself wholly over into the emptiness of the tomb. She is not astonished to see the angels, for they are a continuation of her look into the emptiness. Its immediate continuation as the look of eternal life, entrance to which the two angels symbolize. It is no vision, no product of her imagination; she really sees them, because they are really there. They were already there before, though not perceptibly, either for Peter or for John. Mary perceives them; for she must learn, in a special way, to comprehend the beyondness of the Lord. Still, the manifestation takes place not for her personally, but for the instruction of belief in general. Following the previous revelation of the Lord, belief might think that the division between this world and the beyond corresponds to that between earthly life and the life after death. There is, however, a nearing approach of heaven already in this world, and that is symbolized by the angels. They are like a neutral, pure embodiment of the beyond. It is possible to see heaven already from this side of death, although only through the look into emptiness. Mary has no longer belonged to herself for some time; she has become an entity of the Church, emptied and poured out. She no longer thinks of the necessity for her own waning and for the waxing of the Lord within her. She thinks only of the Lord; she grieves not in a personal sense, because *she* has lost the Lord, but in an apostolic sense: she grieves for the sake of those sinners from whom the Lord has been taken away. It is perhaps the first wholly apostolic instance of suffering. She suffers not because of some penance that she has imposed upon herself, and in her penitence there is no sort of backward look or sideways glance at herself. She suffers purely in the penance that the Lord has given her to suffer; within it, she no longer exists as a personal sinner. That is her emptiness, and that is why she can be granted sight of the angels.

Her seeing, as soon as it occurs, is quite clear and detailed. She sees *two angels in white.* She does not need to edge more closely toward them; she does not see ghosts, "white figures", that she interprets as angels. What she sees is completely clear from the start. Through her suffering, she is wholly free for the apostolate, and the angels that sit there belong to her apostolate. Angels are messengers, and she will become a messenger. Heavenly and earthly mission meet within her seeing.

Belief needs the hiatus of emptiness in order to arrive at seeing. As long as a person believes by referring everything back to himself, he cannot see. Seeing first begins when the reference back to oneself ends. Mary sees, of course, with her bodily eyes, but with eyes that have become ready, through looking into emptiness, to be struck by the light of the beyond.

One of the angels sits *at the head,* and one *at the feet, of where the body of Jesus had lain.* They delimit, so to speak, the earthly form of the Lord. They mark out his dimensions. His bodily mass can be expressed only through angels. Only from the direction of heaven can the space that he filled on earth be designated. They are, to be sure, dimensions on earth, but they were imparted to earth from heaven above. Just as the time of the Lord was no chronological time, but a time that stems from the Father and remains with the Father even on earth, so his space, too, stems not from the world, but from heaven. Thus, the angels embody the boundary between heaven and earth. They are signposts that point from the earthly toward the heavenly, erected there where sensory reality ends in order to make room for pure belief. Their special attribute is the always-more that is characteristic of the Lord. They are like an embodiment of his own Always-More. They are the above-and-beyond of Christian belief. There are few things that illustrate more palpably than these angels the movement of belief away from itself and up toward God. They merely designate the space that the Lord had filled; but they do so through a manifestation of heavenly nature and in a mission that is pure preparation for the taking up of the Son's mission. For a moment's duration, they reduce that mission to the size of the man, to the size of the sinner, who lies there in order then to make room immediately for the breadth of the Lord's belief in the man—upon whom one can perhaps some day look back, of whom, however, only that empty place is now visible which has the dimensions of the vanished self. It is not conceivable that the Lord's body could still lie there and the angels be visible at the same time. If the earthly body were still lying there, then Mary would see in it the expiatory sacrifice for her sins, thereby referring the Lord back to himself. Now, however, the reference is one from emptiness toward heaven. Wherever heaven appears, the earthly place must be made empty. Inasmuch as the signposts point from the empty tomb toward heaven, the Lord forgoes calling himself to mind once again as a bodily man, and inasmuch as he forgoes appearing in the flesh, the sinful self remains forgotten as well. In this lies a final relinquishment, a final divesting of the Lord. Nothing of him remains behind but his naked mission, embodied by the angels who indicate his pathway once more: the pathway from earth to heaven. Hence, the angels almost indicate the Father more than the Son: they indicate out of kenosis, out of the Son's self-annihilation into the fullness of the Father.

It is no accident that it is Mary, the sinner who has made confession, who sees this. The emptiness through which she arrived at her seeing has its counterpart in confession and the forgiveness of sins. If the Lord were still lying there bodily, the sinner would have to think that he lay there for her sake, in place of her, and sin would take on importance once again. Inasmuch as the Lord reveals himself to her in such a way that his bodily dimensions are merely suggested by an emptiness, he shows her that the dimensions of her sin, too, can now only be marked out by an emptiness, that her whole life now consists solely in a movement away from sin and up into heaven. When a sinner has made confession, then the two angels are what is essential, and no longer the empty place left by the vanished body. To the one who has made confession, heaven is shown in openness. There is no sort of persistence in remorse or in penitence; remorse and penitence find their measure in the movement of the soul toward heaven. Otherwise, sin would show itself more strongly than the grace of the Lord. This grace opens heaven up so widely and so *luminously* that all sin is overshone by its radiance.

20:13. They said to her: Woman, why are you weeping? She said to them; Because they have taken away my Lord, and I do not know where they have laid him.

The angels begin to speak. Hence, they are not mere appearances; their words are perceived by human ears. They thereby show that they are emissaries of God, that God gives them the possibility of letting themselves be heard. They are audible to pure belief, but by means of the senses. Not for nothing do they sit at the head and feet of the Lord: just as his head symbolizes his divinity with the Father, and his feet, his journey upon earth, so the angels mediate between heaven and earth, between belief and the senses. They stand on the finest of dividing lines, where the Lord also stands: one face turned toward the Father, the other toward men. But inasmuch as they stand there, they simultaneously bridge that line, because belief itself mediates between heaven and earth. In their appearing, they fulfill a purpose. They come as signposts and consolers, and their consolation is inherent in what they indicate. They show the empty place. But in Mary's mind, this place will, from then on, be inseparably bound up with the heavenly manifestation. And they console her by asking a question. All questions that come from the Church, from the angels, or from God are always consolations: they exert an opening effect on a soul closed up in sorrow. Whether the question is asked by God himself, by the angels or by the Church is unessential. It is always a question from the beyond, which redirects worldly life toward the beyond. Only belief can hear this question, and to hear it implies being seized, almost an act of violence. In listening, one is open toward the beyond, and this openness is filled by the voice of the beyond. The beyond takes possession, in a suddenly descending grace, which is like an embrace, or a kiss. The answer that man gives to this seizing question consists of his human answer plus something extra from the side of the one who presented him with the question. He answers with himself and, simultaneously, with a new substance. Through the appearance of the angels, Mary is changed in her very nature; she receives, as a result of what she has seen, more of the heavenly into her nature than she previously possessed, more of the substance of the beyond. Heavenly questions asked of believers always touch upon belief. In a question from God, an angel or the Church, there is always an implicit demand for an answer in belief. If a nonbeliever were to hear the voice of God, then this voice would, above all, give him the opportunity of entering into belief. Every call from the beyond comes about with a view to belief. The summoning question, however, is usually directed at what is immediate, what lies nearest to hand. It can, perhaps, demand the highest sort of effort. But it never demands a split. The split lies between lack of belief and belief. Even ecclesiastical obedience can, in certain circumstances, require making breaks. The immediate voice of God, by contrast, always stands in continuity with life.

Mary tells the reason for her sorrow: *They have taken away my Lord.* She needs him, for she loves him. He has freed her from sin, made her accessible to faith. He has opened her up as completely as possible, and she can no longer imagine a life without him. She wishes to serve him as long as she lives. She knows how much she needs his nearness; she has to live in the shadow of his grace. But she cannot imagine this grace apart from his physical presence. She is not prepared for a life in the grace of a Lord who has become unseeable. She needs this grace, however, less for herself than for the others: she lives in the hope of being allowed to transmit to others the grace of her confession and absolution. Such transmission is inconceivable to her without the sensible, living activity of the Lord. She does not even entertain that possibility. *And I do not know where they have laid him.* She is at a loss as to where she should begin her search for the Lord. She thinks that Christian seeking is a seeking in space. She would like to find traces, be given relevant information. She thinks that she is now left entirely to her own resources, and this thought is unbearable to her. She had left everything up to the Lord, and wants to take instructions from no one but him. But the Lord is not there; and so she is totally helpless. She still does not know that, if God requires us to seek, he also always provides clues—visible and invisible. She may well sense that she would have to turn somehow to the invisible Lord. Through the angels, she begins to establish a relation to the Lord in the beyond. But she still does not trust that she will ever find him. She is in a state of great loneliness and disconsolation. But the angels are a visible sign of the fact that there are ways out of this aloneness. They are the visible clue, the clear traces that lead to God. For every believer, even for one who sees no angels, there are always, in this life, traces leading to God that are visible in belief. Every believer will often be lonely. Mary was lonely at the Cross, and now she is so again. Yet Cross and loneliness are never an end, but always a transition, or rather, a transformation. Mary knew the bodily Lord. She was separated from him, and had to enter into the most bitter loneliness of her tears in order, through that, to become of the beyond herself, to become prepared for the other, spiritual form of the Lord. Only through this transformation is she made ready for her new mission, which is no longer to serve the salvation of her own soul, but to spread the message to others. Thus, in the midst of belief, Mary lives in aridity; in the midst of consolation, in disconsolation. It is an apostolic disconsolation. Her guilt has been pardoned, but her mission is still not clear. Hence, she does not know where the Lord is. Her disconsolation is no longer directed toward herself, but wholly toward her service; therefore, it is fruitful. It is the disconsolation experienced by everyone who is to be drawn into the always-more of the mission of the Lord.

20:14. *Saying this, she turned around and saw Jesus standing, but she did not know that it was Jesus.*

Mary's belief has come into contact with nothingness in the emptiness, has encountered there the angels that pointed toward heaven, and now turns away from that emptiness in order to pass into the fullness of the Lord that stands before it, but has not yet been recognized. All the stages of this path that Mary traverses here are possibilities of the Christian life. Through his own resources, man can only advance as far as to the emptiness of the tomb. To get from the empty tomb to the living Lord, he has to be led. It is reserved to God to determine the precise nature of this leading. Man can wish that his belief might become living at the empty tomb. That this should happen through a seeing of angels he cannot wish. Looking into emptiness is the active contemplation at which, in belief, he can arrive by his own efforts. Being led from belief to the Lord by the angels is passive contemplation; but in this, too, everything takes place quite simply and naturally. The angels speak a plain, comprehensible language that presupposes no great intelligence or high-flown ecstasy to be understood. God's arrangement that Mary should be consoled by angels and see the Lord is as simple as the whole gospel. Up until the emptiness of the tomb, she is the one who acts, who knows what she wants, who goes there because she wishes to. She is the one full of devotion. As soon as the angels appear, she is led; she is more the one who is taken than the one who gives of herself. The activity of prayer reaches as far as to the emptiness of the tomb, as far as to being emptied out and to disconsolation. Beyond this point, guidance from above begins. This guidance, characteristically, leads initially to seeking, and only through that seeking to finding. In this way, everything Pharisaical is precluded. Were Mary of a Pharisaical spirit, then she would rest satisfied with the emptiness of the tomb, astonished and gratified that she still believed despite that emptiness. She would want to go just as far as her comprehension reached. She would have the feeling that she had done everything that was in her power, for she had even endured looking into emptiness. But inasmuch as she is drawn into the movement of seeking, she can be taken out of emptiness and into the fullness that includes in itself an eternal, fulfilled seeking.

She saw Jesus standing, but she did not know that it was Jesus. That Jesus stands is in contradiction with the lying position designated by the angels. She was led to this contradiction by what the angels indicated. Mary, who does not foresee what is to come, who asks for no guarantees, lives solely in a state of obscure trustfulness. If she has traversed her path thus far with understanding, she is now ready to give herself over without comprehension to what is to come. It is even as if the Lord had taken her understanding from her. This is evident from the contrast: she supposes him to be lying and dead, and sees him standing and alive. Were she to regard what she sees with understanding, then she would know that he has been resurrected. But she looks in nonunderstanding. Insight into what has occurred is by no means poured into her. Her understanding lags behind her devotion. If belief and understanding were one, then all her sorrow, the whole process of her being guided, would be superfluous. But the Lord wants her guided belief, which is possible only when her understanding has been left behind. He wants blind devotion, not insight that keeps pace eternally. Otherwise, her belief would just suffice for her "self-salvation", her "self-perfection", but not for absolute service. Since, then, she is looking for a Jesus who is lying, she does not recognize him as standing. She seeks a certain image of the Lord that she has known in terms of her understanding, yet at the same time knows, in her belief, that the Lord is greater than her understanding depicts him to her as being. But now she fails to recognize him when he is greater. She is first able to recognize him when she is spoken to by him.

20:15. Jesus said to her: Woman, why are you weeping? Whom do you seek? Supposing him to be the gardener, she said to him: Sir, if you have carried him away, tell me where you have laid him, and I will take him away.

The Lord questions with the same words that the angels did: *Why are you weeping?* But his question immediately goes further: *Whom do you seek?* With that, he gives a clear indication of his superiority to the angels. To be sure, the angels know, too, that she is seeking the Lord. But what they are charged with asking does not go that far. Mary has made confession to the Lord. She gives him the right to see everything within her, to question, to bring things up for discussion. The priest's seal of confession is intended to effect absolute openness in the one making confession, a condition of lasting unconcealment beyond all social conventions. The Lord's second question takes the first one further. It does not look back to the state of sin that was recognized and is now over and done with. Every true question looks toward the future and has consolation as its goal. It should bring a soul closer to the Lord. A priest has the right to ask such a question. The question, of the kind that the Lord employs here and thereby bequeaths to his Church and his priests, is the most delicate and discreet thing that exists. It exposes nothing unnecessary, it has but the one purpose: to lead closer to him. The spirit of a priest when hearing confession, if he loves and believes, is at one with the Spirit of the Lord. If the priest is not in the Lord's love, then, of course, he can distort or misuse the Lord's question; but if he is in his love, then his question aims at nothing but making easier the search for the Lord.

The Lord helps Mary to search while he is already present. This is what he always does, including the case of confession. We will always have to seek him because he is the Ever-Greater; but our seeking will never be hopeless, because all true seeking takes place in his presence and the Lord will unfailingly grant it a finding—which, in turn, will at once be supplanted by a new, urgent seeking.

How much Mary still has need of seeking, even though she already knows the Lord, she demonstrates by taking him for the *gardener*. She surmises in him the possibility of help, but without knowing that he is help itself. The gardener would be the one who takes care of the tomb. He embodies the finite possibility of help. In fact, Mary is standing before infinite help, but she is so caught up in her seeking and sorrow that she does not recognize it. Only vaguely does she detect in this figure before her a readiness to help, and in the hope that the stranger perhaps holds the key to the whole mystery, she speaks to him: *Sir, if you have carried him away, tell me where you have laid him, and I will take him away.* What she wishes to have is the body of the Lord. It could perhaps impart a certain positive sense to her grieving love, transform her useless sorrow into useful caretaking. Thus, she still sees everything totally in terms of finitude. Only the debt of gratitude that she feels toward the Lord is not limited and bound by any death. In her loving belief, she is able to survive the Lord's death, but in a way that is still totally finite for her and does not yet manifest the infinite content of belief. And yet everything in her is ready to be expanded into the infinite. The readiness for the whole of belief is there, but only in pupation, like a butterfly in its cocoon. Its wings still need to grow. Also, Mary's attitude is very womanly. In her devotion, she resembles the wife who has not yet wholly belonged to her husband: she is ready for that, but she does not yet know what the husband will make of her devotion. She would like to have children; but the idea of actually having them is beyond her and seems improbable. So it is in Christian life: one offers oneself for something more; but if that something more is allocated, it turns out to be totally different than expected.

20:16. *Jesus said to her: Mary. She turned and said to him in Hebrew: Rabboni! (which means Teacher).*

Now the Lord speaks to her as her Lord. And she answers him and recognizes him by what he says. Inasmuch as the Lord calls her by name, he shows that he knows her, and opens up what was previously closed in her. She answers: *Teacher!* thereby showing that she is completely open to him, that the finite thought and finite love in her have really given way to infinite thought and infinite love.

Through the Lord's speaking to her, she is granted a part in a wholly new mystery. She becomes the first to be addressed by the Resurrected, the first to belong to him; the first whom he seals up in his love. This he does by speaking to her of his own accord. She is found before she herself finds, she is loved before she herself loves. That is the highest thing that can happen to a seeker: to be found. And implicit in it is an infinite obligation that one must continue seeking until one is found. It is also not by chance that the Lord, who has suffered for sinners, speaks first to the notorious sinner, thereby showing her that he knows her and recognizes her as his. It is to her, and not to Peter and John, that he pays this incomprehensible honor. Nor is it possible that Mary might become arrogant because of receiving this distinction; for the loving address of the Lord *posits* complete humility: at the moment when she is thus distinguished, she also knows that she receives the distinction as a former sinner. For it was not to reinforce those who love or to increase the dignity of office that the Lord took the Cross upon himself; rather, it was solely to redeem his Father's creatures from their sin. He died on the Cross for everyone, for the known and the unknown, the influential and the insignificant, for all the anonymous sins of the world. But now he shows to him who has been pardoned that the suffering was undergone for him personally. Mary, the individual, and not merely the member of some limitless crowd, is addressed by the Redeemer. She, the individual, was taken along by the Lord to the Cross as a matter of course, she was there before his eyes. Love and office are preliminary to the Cross. The efficacy of the sacrament of confession, however, originates in the Cross. And what the Lord does here resembles a sacramental absolution. Admittedly, Mary's sin has already been forgiven. But it is as if everything still remains in suspension. Only now, when redemption has been completed, when the Lord is in the process of instituting the sacrament of confession, does he allow Mary to participate—as the first to do so—in this new gift. Only now is she really made capable of finding the Lord and of comprehending, in a heavenly way, his always-being-more. Before entering the Church, one is perhaps interested, one accumulates various items of knowledge; but it is not until the Lord calls one by name that the soul is opened to the divinity of the Lord. Now, no sum total retains its validity, for any and every number is broken through. Thus the calling of Mary's name by the Lord also becomes a symbol of baptism.

For Mary, there is but one possible reply: *Teacher!* In this word is contained all the fullness of action and contemplation, of prayer and meditation, a consummate surrender to the Lord. It is also a reply that passes over much. She says nothing to him, she tells him nothing, she does not describe for him the suffering of her search. She sees nothing but him, exclusively him. It is the moment at which, for once, man really says Yes, really possesses largeness of heart, in the power of being called by the Lord. The moment at which one no longer weeps because one is searching, but weeps because the Lord is there. The point that no science of the soul can explain because it is really "God in me". The all-overpowering presence.

20:17. *Jesus said to her: Do not touch me, for I have not yet ascended to the Father; but go to my brethren and say to them, I am ascending to my Father and your Father, to my God and your God.*

At this moment, the Lord is untouchable. Mary has touched him before, and she will touch him again. But now it is as if he stands outside his mission. He has accomplished his suffering, but he has not yet returned to the Father. The Easter message, which he wants to bring to men from the Cross, is not his own message. It belongs to the Father, and he wants to have it blessed once again by the Father. He wants to go to the Father before he comes to men with the message purchased by his suffering. In his present state, he cannot number himself among men. He wants to come back to them as one who is just coming from heaven, as one who, after his suffering, brings with him all the consolation of the Father.

The touch that Mary desired was a touch of love and gratitude. She wanted to demonstrate to him, in a quite human way, her love at his reappearance and, in a quite womanly way, to reestablish the lost connection between one human being and another. The Lord has no objection to such a touch, but first he wants to be the one that he wants to be for us: the one who arrives as new and fresh from heaven. Were we to receive him entirely as the man he was, and to regard nothing as having intervened between his two states of being but his suffering, then this meeting could not take place in pure joyfulness. We would have to think constantly of the immeasurable suffering that he went through for our sake. But he is the one who has suffered in order to present a sacrifice of love to the Father; and by first presenting the Father with this sacrifice, he will come back to us showing the whole transfiguration that the Father will present him with in return. In relation to the Father, too, he wants to be the one who goes back to men only under the Father's commission. He does not want to have men receive his love before the Father does. First, he wishes to demonstrate his love to the Father, to thank the Father for what has been accomplished and to obtain the added mission from the Father. If he is to come back, then he will come back from the Father. The Father should not be able to think that he is establishing, of his own volition, his own kingdom among men.

And yet he appears, before he has been to the Father, to the sinner, Magdalen. At the Cross, she decisively represented sin, sin that has been pardoned and redeemed. In Mary, he sees his work as if in a mirror. She has repented before him and made confession to him; she has shown him what grace is able to do: that it is a path to God. To her, the sinner, he also owes his path through the Cross to the Father. Thus he says to her on Easter morning that this path has now been actually traversed. He draws her into the mystery of his return to the Father. He shows to her, she who has made confession, his ascent to God, which is inseparable from her own. It is a sign of supreme intimacy that the Lord shows himself to her before he ascends: she is to participate in this most inward of mysteries involving him and the Father. But this is in keeping with her commission. She is to gain insight into this necessary first renewal of contact by the Son with the Father, insight into the essence of the mission: that everything originates from the Father and returns again to the Father. Just as a person making confession needs to know that it is not the absolving priest who is the ultimate, but rather, God, and that no boundary line may therefore be drawn at the perceptible act of absolution, so now Mary needs to see, if she is to understand the mission, the return of the Son to the Father. Later on, she will be allowed to touch the Lord, when both are again integrated into the mission.

Thus the interim stop that the Lord makes on his journey to the Father is necessary from both sides. Neither should the Father believe that the Son has decided to stay among men, nor may men be allowed to believe that he has completed his work without the Father. This ascension by the Son is his Easter ascension, not his later ascension into heaven. It is an inseparable aspect of Easter day itself, an occurrence that is already over when, that evening, the apostles touch the Lord and eat and drink with him. He has risen again visibly as a man in order to rise again into the invisibility of God. The Father has awakened him, and the Son must now appear before the Father as the Resurrected, he must show the Father the effects of the work that the Father did in him: awakening him as the eternal Son who he always was, endowed with all the gifts of belief, with love, hope and eternal life, and simultaneously with his created human life, which is now at last the Father's perfected creation. This creation the Son must show to the Father. The Lord's Easter visit to the Father is his giving of thanks in the name of all creation, and it is similar to the giving of thanks after Holy Communion. Just as we receive the Lord and must surrender ourselves wholly to him because we live wholly in him and from him, so the Son, after his Resurrection, after having received the Father's life into himself, must turn wholly to the Father because he now lives wholly in him and from him. This is also the full vitalization, the full transfiguration of the Cross: the binding together of the horizontal and the vertical beams, the binding together of Father and world, and the perfecting of both creation and redemption.

With that, it is also the perfecting of love, a totally new form of love, and in fact, the grounding of Christian love: in the distancing of the "do not touch me", but at the same time in the infinite nearness and tenderness of the Lord's love, which shows itself to the sinner even before it has shown itself to the Father, and allows him a look into his ascent to the Father. Moreover, it is the quite simple, human love of the Lord, which does not "act like God" but rather, within belief, breaks down all divisions.

But go to my brethren and say to them, I am ascending. Mary, who has now been enriched with new knowledge, immediately receives a commission, an apostolic mission. Every gaining of new knowledge in the Lord is inseparably tied to a commission. Also, Mary is in the purity that she received through making confession. And the whole of the private scene between the Lord and Mary becomes open in the direction of the apostolate: it is used to further the mission. Everything that a loving person possesses is put to use, is expropriated for the service of the Lord. Mission is bestowed upon anyone who has made confession. Confession is not a balancing out between sin and grace; the superabundance of confessional grace shows itself in the fact that the fulfilling grace exceeds by far the deficiency needing to be filled: the place of sin is taken not only by pardon, but also by mission.

The message from the Lord is intended for his brethren, that is, for believers. Since they are believers, they, too, will at once hand the commission on to others. Hence, a commission given to believers by the Lord is always an infinite one, because it will be handed on to others by each who receives it. And the Lord's ascending path to the Father, into the infinity of the Father, runs parallel to the commission in belief: for this also runs, so to speak horizontally, into the infinite. And the apostolic, whose direction is expansion, has to keep spreading until all men find the path to the Father.

To my Father and your Father, to my God and your God. The Lord now stresses something that he has not previously stressed: that his Father is also our Father. He always was that, but we had ceased to be his children. Through our sin, he had become only a possible Father; and through his Cross, the Son made him our real Father once again. On the Cross, he provided the proof that we are the children of God. He cancelled out our sin, and thus brought it about that the Father can once again accept us as his children. To be sure, he had already spoken earlier of the fact that his Father was also our Father. But never had he done so with such liveliness as now. The way that he says it almost suggests that he is already now eucharistically present in each of us, that all distance has already been offset: the distance between our existence on earth and our being as children of heaven. The Son smoothed all that out and rounded things off, so that we may acknowledge our Father in the way that he acknowledges him, worship our God in the way that he worships his God. There is no question, no hindrance, no uncertainty anymore. In the eternal Son, we, as children of the house, have the right of access to our common Father. He is the door of heaven. There are no longer any causes for objection as regards the Father, as regards ascension to heaven together with the Son. The objection of sin exists no more. What the Lord requires is that we simply go along with him and acknowledge that his Father is our Father, his God our God. And anyone wishing to point not only to his past, but also his future sin as a cause for objection would be referred by the Lord to Magdalen: to confession and, with that, to the resurrection of the dead as the ultimate proof of his love. Far from wishing to establish a distance through his word, he wishes, on the contrary, to bring about a union, a synthesis: his God is one with our God. We should no longer look upon the Father other than through the eyes of the Son.

20:18. *Mary Magdalen went and said to the disciples: I have seen the Lord; and she told them that he had said these things to her.*

Mary goes off and carries out her commission. She does so in unity with the Lord. She embellishes nothing, she does not paint things other than as they were. But she indicates, by what she recounts, what grace has come to them all through the Cross. The disciples take it all in, each according to his capacity. About their understanding of it nothing further is known, because now only Mary's mission is significant. She becomes, in a comprehensive sense, an apostle. She, as a woman, is selected by the Lord to convey a report to the disciples, and thus also, the hierarchy. In the Church, then, there are direct communications from the Lord that have to be transmitted to the hierarchy. In this case, by a woman, a sinner who has been converted. And in fact, her message contains precisely that which the disciples feel to be the highest mystery of the Lord. Thus, there is this special commission of Magdalen's in the Church; it exists much less in penitence than in the apostolate, much less in her turning away from sin than in what the Lord has made of her. Mary does not speak of herself at all. She does not draw on her guilt and her remorse in order to give form to her message, to let it stand out more effectively. She draws exclusively on the Lord. When it is a matter of her commission, confession is out of place. Confession and conversion are a secret between her and the Lord which is of no concern to the disciples. Her message is not affected by her particular quality as a former sinner. Also, the listeners do not attend to the special nature of the messenger, but simply accept the message in belief. Only the *grace* of confession radiates from the one who has been sent: it is the Lord's infinite trust in the converted that becomes manifest in her.

THE EASTER OFFERING

20:19. *On the evening of that day, the first day of the week, the doors being shut where the disciples were, for fear of the Jews, Jesus came and stood among them and said to them: Peace be with you.*

The Lord enters a closed room to appear before a gathering of his disciples. Hence, the disciples, as a group, already form a kind of Church, in which they exercise their belief and which they keep closed to the Jews. Outwardly, they are afraid of the Jews, for these have superior might. They have taken the Lord away from them. Thus the doors are barred to the Jews, which means at the same time: closed off against unbelief. The disciples already constitute a community that is dependent on walling in what is extant, on imparting fixed, delineated form to the Faith and life within it. They are aware that much in these forms will change, that most relevant matters have only just been intimated, and that, regarding some things, they do not have even a vague anticipation of what will come. But they know just as well that whatever they already securely possess must be guarded and lovingly nurtured. It is a grace that they already know this, for it is a grace to be permitted to preserve what one already possesses in the Lord. To be sure, love is there in order to be bestowed, and belief, in order to be propagated. But that is only possible if it is preserved and secured against the world. Under this comes the safeguarding of action in contemplation, of the apostolate in prayer. The insight that one is not allowed to withdraw, but *must* remain. A Christian is not allowed to be merely a channel for belief; knowledge of belief must be constantly appropriated by him. The disciples already have a common inheritance to defend, and both the justification and the necessity for Peter's office already become visible at the center of love. The Jews, of whom they are afraid, are everything that stands outside the livingness of their ecclesiastical community. It is not only fear of external attack by unbelief, it is also fear that something could be obscured by the new, that they might have to accept something alien, that endangering compromises would have to be made. First, they must once have stood all together at the center before; in pursuit of their mission, they can move out toward the periphery.

The closed doors indicate, further, the Church's freedom in her restrictedness. One is in freedom as long as one finds oneself in community with the others behind closed doors. In the Lord, freedom and restriction form a unity. And it is precisely here that the Lord will appear: in his own, closed house. He knows this house and evidences his knowing through his appearing. The two are one: being gathered together in his name and his appearing because of this being gathered together. Further, the closed doors indicate openness in closeness. Whoever possesses a valuable treasure and locks himself away with it, does so out of fear of losing it. Whoever locks himself away with his belief also certainly does so in order to protect it, but even more, in order to be better able to present it to others. For both in the state of being locked away and in that of being parceled out to others, the Lord's treasure is fruitful: it is so in contemplation as in action. If the Church's intention were exhausted with the shutting of the doors, then everything would remain unfruitful. But in belief, one can regard no single way of handling things as final; nothing exists here that is not, at the same time, in process. Since no person can survey the full effective range of his own actions, neither can he resolve upon anything final in belief, because new mandates from God can always reopen everything closed. Therefore, man should also not undertake anything final in the context of penance, for he might wish to deny himself something that God may later need from him again. Man never has the whole truth at his disposal; a portion of it always remains with God. In all communication of truth, there is a kind of *reservatio mentalis*. The reserving, however, is not done by us, but by God. When arranging matters as we think best, we must always say: assuming that God does not arrange things otherwise. For man to make use of *reservatio mentalis* is all right provided that he reserves something not for his own advantage, but for God's advantage. In belief, the *reservatio* of truth occurs on the part of God, who perhaps holds it back for communication to us at a later time. In belief, there is a forgoing of complete understanding of truth, an *abdicatio* of truth, which is based on the recognition that everything we know and love has, in God, the form of the ever-greater. It is impossible for a created being to comprehend the dimensions of this ever-greater. But this forgoing does not apply in the case of dogma. Here, nothing is relativized. Dogma is the door that is closed against everything nonChristian outside of it. As directed toward the outside, the dogmas are rigid and uncompromising. We must regard the door that the Lord closes behind him as closed for as long as he does not instruct us to do otherwise. And he himself does not open the door anymore, but goes right through the closed door. For him, then, the rigid closedness does not exist, for him every truth is open. But for us, the closing must be regarded as final, as absolute. If we were able to add something to the Lord's truth through our own thought, then everything would be repeatedly called into question, including within the confines of the Church. Then, however, the door would no longer be the Lord, but rather, man and his truth. The Lord alone has the freedom to enter, from the outside to the inside, through the closed doors. What is closed for us is open for him. In heaven, there will no longer be any closed doors because there will also no longer be any unbelief. Dogmas are securings of belief against outside dangers, not closures for the sake of closure. Dogma has a basis of immovable truth, but it opens itself out from that basis into the unlimitedness of living, inexhaustible truth in God. Objectively, it has an absolute point of departure; but it is also always relative in each person who subjectively assimilates it, because here absolute truth is grasped only partially and imperfectly, and exists within an open movement of belief toward the Lord. The framework of dogmatic truth is unshakable, but within its confines, the infinite truth of the Lord moves in sovereign freedom. God's truth is infinite, and is therefore always just outlined and suggested in dogmatic precepts. The measure of dogmatic truth remains the Lord himself; and the Lord can always see everything differently, and infinitely more fully, than any particular believer can see it. Neither individual believers nor the Church as a whole have any authority to make changes in dogma; but they are also not allowed to do so, because it is the Lord alone who comprises the truth of dogma. From the way that the absolute and the relative are intertwined, we can see that whereas a man may regard himself personally as the greatest sinner, he nevertheless has no right to regard someone else as more guilty than himself. Another person could, perhaps, by citing different reasons, prove to him that he is wrong; and he, too, could, in a certain respect, be right. But in the end both would be wrong, because the Lord alone holds in his hand the measuring stick of sin. All human judgments must, in the end, yield before his exclusive judgment. Similarly, the Lord remains the master of dogma, whose entire depths, which men do not plumb, are his own depths, which he avails himself of in freedom.

In the interior of this closed house, then, the Lord appears. He comes into his property, to his congregation, to a meditation that belongs to him and that he fulfills. He comes just as he will come to all subsequent living meditations; but because the eyes of his disciples are still used to his human appearance, he comes to them as a visible man. In itself, the situation is no different from the later situation of the Church, when she is assembled in belief for Mass, preaching or prayer and the Lord appears, in belief, in her midst. Regardless of just how he may happen to appear, everything that occurs in belief occurs in his presence and through him. Here, he appears visibly because, for the sake of later believers, everything in the gospel occurs in sensible form. On the one hand, he comes for the believers themselves, for their own benefit, for their joy and for confirmation of their belief. However, he also comes in an apostolic sense, for succeeding times. If the disciples had seen the Lord only within their prayer, in a vision, then they would not have had the tangible proof of the Resurrection that they needed for their preaching. It corresponds to the stage of their belief and that of the Church that the Lord appears to them in precisely this way. He adapts himself to their simple, robust thinking and feeling; and later preaching will draw sustenance from the unequivocal, direct form of his self-revelation. The disciples' uncomplicated way of thinking will lead to their reaching that great mass of men who are no more educated and refined than they themselves are. For them, the spiritual return of the Lord must be as visible as the Cross and his earlier path through life.

And it is not only their eyes that participate in his manifestation, but all their senses. The senses that the apostles first possessed as creatures of God, and that were slowly transformed in proportion to the degree that they became disciples. Not one of their five senses is now still the same as it was when the Lord left them to begin his suffering. They do not themselves become conscious of this. During the period in which their belief was expanded, not only it was subject to transformation, but also the functioning of their senses. Not in such a way that they might have been able to notice how the scope of their sensory experiences was growing. For the expansion was already Christian, it already belonged to the Lord, and was thus inaccessible to their comprehension. They know only that they experience new things and, what is more, expect new things. If they had previously used their hands to gain knowledge of things tangible and near, it is as if, during the years of their companionship with the Lord, their hands had become capable of feeling things farther away, of taking hold of things more extended. It was like a lengthening of the range of their human reach, of their field of apprehension, a lengthening that did not, however, lie within them, but expressly outside of them, in the Lord. And in fact, as something potential. And yet, at the given moment, as something real and ready to hand—there, namely, where the Lord's commission begins. And when the Lord left them, and the possibility of his being seeable came to an end even for their believing eyes, it was as if the increased material possibility of increased sensory perception were put aside, as if something that had been commenced were interrupted. As if they had been steadily working toward a certain goal, and now suddenly that goal had disappeared from view. As if they had been schooled in a certain occupation, been taught the relevant knowledge and techniques, and were now suddenly thrown into a totally different line of work. But they have experienced so many instances of their failure to understand particular foreshadowings in the Lord's words before that they do not pause to reflect on this laying aside of their expanded sensory capacity. All that they have experienced previously seems distant and abstract to them, and yet they do not arrive at clear formulation of this, because along with their senses, their love, too, was expanded. And precisely their love retains its inchoate, expectant character, thereby impeding their reflection. Indeed, it even forces them to recognize what has occurred as having been prearranged in the Lord's mind so that they might, now that he has become invisible and transfigured, be ready to serve him in a new way.

Something that had been painstakingly commenced was abruptly broken off, and without connection to it, on the other side of a chasm, a new path begins. In this chasm, in this incomprehensible fissure, the whole of *Christian mysticism* has its origin. It is as if human readiness for love, which had set its sights on something definite, were no longer able to find its object. As if a man were called by another to come and help, and when he hurries to him, finds that there is nothing the other needs; or as if someone were to ask him for a helping hand, and as he is preparing to give it, it turns out to be superfluous; or as if someone were to request a kiss from him, and when he draws near, the other has vanished. If this sort of thing occurs repeatedly, and, as it were, becomes the rule, then he will either—if he does not love completely—lose patience and refuse to offer himself further or—if he has the love—begin to perceive that he stands before a wholly surpassing mystery. A chasm yawns before him, which love must blindly pass over. The mystical begins beyond this chasm. What mattered to the Lord was the readiness of his disciples. With respect to this, fulfilment is transcendent; it does not stand in a relation of logical succession to it. If the Lord now appears to the disciples, then he does so within a readiness that they have deposited with God. Just as the Cross was the end of the mission of the Son, so it signifies for the disciples the end of the heightening of their personal, sensory readiness. God sees this breaking off in its total context, man does not. The new that comes in fulfilment comes solely from the Lord; but he brings it forth in the readiness that is on deposit with him. That is a mystery which the disciples do not become aware of at all. They know only *that* a mystery exists in the Cross; what it exists as they do not know. The Lord has divested them of something essential and taken it away with him; they have no idea where, or why. It is possible that the Lord will bring what was taken away back to them in an embellished form, but also that he might make use of what was entrusted to him in some other way, for others. Doing the latter, of course, is also his right as soon as man really entrusts something to him. But precisely because their heightened senses—as complements of the heightened readiness in which they lived—have now been taken from them, they lack the sensory capacity which would enable them to assess their situation. Those senses no longer belong to them; they have been simply put on deposit, and in fact, with the result that they no longer take account of anything but their own possibilities. They have "written them off". They retain nothing but a recollection of them; a true recollection, in which belief, love and hope retain their place. Only when this chasm occurs, this breaking off of the senses, can the Lord appear. Just as his Resurrection emerges out of the great chasm of his death and his descent into hell, so any instance of his appearing to the heightened senses of Christians emerges like a resurrection out of a small, personal death.

But now the Lord appears to them in reality. They are still so occupied with the Lord's death and the report of his return that they have not yet gone back to their own concerns: to their Christian life before the Cross, to having too much asked of them, to their personal readiness. Even their apostolate has been, so to speak, paralyzed; through the disappearance of the Lord, it has lost its concrete relevance. On the basis of their lack of understanding, they see no possibility of proclaiming the message of the Resurrection: Who would ever believe them? In the midst of this situation, the Lord appears—in a place where the doors are shut. But this very state of being shut no longer makes any difference. He is no longer bound by the laws of our world and our souls. He is bound solely by his own will and the entirety of the readiness that we have deposited with God. Thus he appears in, and out of, a complete night of the senses and understanding. Here, it is essential that this night is always the *Lord's* night, and not one that belongs to men, since every appearance of the Lord takes place within the mystery of the deposited senses. This night belongs so much to the Lord that, subjectively seen, he can even anticipate it: he or his Mother or the saints, for example, can appear to children who are only subsequently granted subjective participation in the night. This is, to be sure, connected internally with the appearance: every appearance produces an infinite thirst, a night. Anyone who has veritably seen the Lord and knows it, also knows that he must veritably communicate him to others, and with that the night begins. For in the end, one *cannot* communicate him to others. There is an utter discrepancy between the description of one's own experience and the experience itself. The task can never really be fulfilled. Thus man lands in the unclosable chasm that characterizes the mystical. Because the Lord never bestows his appearing other than as something following directly on from his own night and his fall into hell, he also never confers it subjectively other than in some sort of connection with his night. This night remains wholly the night of the Lord, and cannot be made comprehensible by any technical means. It remains so to the end, and never becomes the night of the mystic who is drawn into it. It stems directly from the Cross.

Never, then, does fulfilment link up with where the thread was broken off before the Cross. Never do readiness and fulfilment come together in an unbroken way. It is always God who exercises control over the heightened senses of the disciples that have been deposited with him. He can, to be sure, give what was offered back to man in such a way that he actually fulfills it through visions or other mystical experiences; but he can just as well put what was offered to other uses, for example, by granting an appearance to someone else who, for one reason or another, requires it for his apostolate. For all mystical graces are catholic graces. They stem from a readiness of Christians that is unconditional and therefore ecclesiastical. They are conferred upon a particular individual, but perhaps on the basis of someone else's readiness and always for others to make use of. Their distribution lies solely in the hands of the Lord, as does their utilization. In apportioning them, God is doubly free: inasmuch as communication of them in general is a free gift of his grace, and inasmuch as distribution of them itself occurs, once again, solely at his discretion. With that, any human judgment about these graces and the persons who receive them loses its point. It is completely impossible to draw conclusions about the "state of perfection" of a soul from the noncommunication of mystical graces, or to set up levels and degrees within these graces that would be anything more than individual experiences.

On the one hand, the Lord appears to the actual senses of the apostles, and on the other, within their belief. That he appears to their actual senses means that his appearance is no mere vision. He is so visible to the disciples that they cannot but think that anyone standing next to them would have to see the Lord just as they do.

The senses that perceive his appearance are the normal senses, the senses of created beings, of sinners, and they recognize him by his earthly, creaturely features. That he appears to them in this way, rather than in a vision, has its basis in their commission to preach. Despite that, he never again appears other than in belief, that is, within senses that have been expanded and extended through belief. Here, it may be that the Lord finds the belief already in existence when he appears or brings it with him by virtue of his appearing. These senses have their basis in the earthly senses, but they stem from God; they derive their existence and growth from belief, and in fact, from the belief that the Lord turns to that purpose. They thereby acquire a new perceptive capacity which is tied, to be sure, to their earthly senses, but is made possible solely through grace in belief. It is to these senses, insofar as they are distinguished from the earthly senses, that the later visions of the mystics will be addressed, for example, the vision of the Lord that will be granted to Paul at Damascus. On Easter evening, the disciples see the Lord in belief with their normal, if admittedly expanded, senses; they therefore also see him as an object affecting the senses that are so constituted, although not as an earthly object on an equal plane with their senses, but as an object that manifests itself from above to their earthly senses here below. In his appearances, the Lord is not primarily a natural object, but an object that he himself offers in belief to belief. The cognition no longer consists in a synthesis between our senses and some object affecting them, but in our senses as expanded by belief and an object that is directly presented to those senses by the Lord. No matter what the thing seen or watched or touched may be, the nature of the perceived image is due exclusively to the Lord. In order to render these senses, which are lent to us by the Lord, ready for use, belief is required as an indispensable condition. Belief alone is decisive. Thus—since the Cross—these expanded senses and their use can remain wholly on deposit in belief and never reach the point of functional activation; a Christian life can be lived out just as well wholly within unseeing belief. Any attempt at human training of these senses is not only tactless, and for that reason alone proscribed, but also utterly ineffective. If a believer perhaps has a perception today of something that he did not see yesterday, he cannot therefore seek to intensify his belief so as to be able to see more clearly and distinctly tomorrow what still seems unclear to him today. Any sort of training aimed at experience of the beyond is wrong. Even the wish for such an intensification is wrong, because the occasioning of all these experiences always lies solely with the grace of the Lord. All men who believe livingly are, in principle, rendered capable of undergoing such experiences by the fact that their senses are deposited in the Lord with God, even if fulfilment of this potentiality is not attained by everyone on earth. Just as priests or nuns would be no less capable of siring or conceiving children than other people, yet engender none because they have renounced this function, so all believers possess these senses in principle, but whether they become fruitful remains up to the Lord. He alone decides on how they are used. What the Lord demands in all cases is belief and love. He expects each one who encounters him to lay everything at his feet, to place the course of his life at the disposal of divine choice. Whether marriage or celibacy, whether priesthood or laity, the decision is made by the Lord. Man can only offer himself. Similarly, the Lord decides on the use of the spiritual senses, on whether they are to be employed or not. This is the grace of graces: to be allowed to make oneself available, because the Lord makes himself available to us. It is only as a component within this all-embracing grace that the calling to mysticism exists.

Inasmuch as the Lord comes back to the apostles, he bestows upon them an infinite, a limitless gift that has no end as long as the world exists and that is presented to every individual believer. In his love, he recreates us so that we become capable of receiving him, and in fact, from the slightest stirrings in prayer all the way to the most manifest visions of transcendent things. Even the simplest prayer, the most spontaneous appeal to God, has its potential to become living only in this response of the Lord, in his reappearing to the disciples. Whoever says in belief, "Lord, be among us", stands in the grace of expanded sensory experience, which extends so far that it reaches even this prayer. The smallest act of real praying is a contacting of God. All the possibilities of belief, from complete unseeingness to complete vision, are unfolded here; they are all secondary in comparison with the primary fact that God is available to us in belief, that he comes to us, that he appears to us whether we see him or not. Hence, the whole question of mysticism flows back into the peace and stillness of Christian prayer.

Peace be with you. The peace that the Lord wishes his disciples applies to the whole communion. The Lord brings them the very peace that he wishes them. He is himself this peace, he is now only peace: the peace of God in his Son. Perfect peace in perfect love. One does not see that any difference remains between peace and love. And it is just as much peace in belief and peace in hope, a hope that is distinguished from the earlier one through the suffering of the Cross. It is no peace that puts an end to struggle and movement, but a pure beginning. This peace, which was purchased on the Cross, now allies itself with belief, love and hope as a fundamental conception in Christian life.

The Lord has the times of contemplation, of action and of passion behind him. Now comes the time of peace. Of a peace that is a result of all three of those modes of existence, a result and at the same time an expansion, because he includes all three in himself and because this all-embracing new mode in him will become a treasure for all who come after him and find themselves existing in one of the three modes. Previously, what we saw was always the reciprocal relationship between action and contemplation and their issuance in the Passion, the cyclical aspect of this relationship, and the distinctness of the three modes from each other. Now, after the Cross, when these three forms of the Son's conversation with his Father have been concluded, when he has gone through all the stages of his love for the Father, he possesses anew the peace of God as an expression of perfect and fulfilled love. It is no longer peace as it was described earlier, the incomprehensible peace of the Lord amidst the strife of the world, but the pure peace of fulfilment, one so pure that, as a treasure of the Lord and the Church, it is available to all, forming the common basis of all Christian social classes or life circumstances.

The Lord passes this peace on to the apostles and to all believers: as their accompaniment, as their substance and nourishment. It is necessary to the action, the contemplation, and the passion of all who follow him. Whoever is active must aim at peace, mediate toward peace. He who cannot mediate peace is incapable of action. Perhaps his action takes him through all the stages of restlessness; but its ultimate stage must be peace. This peace, which anyone who is active must mediate, must not be something alien to himself, regardless of whether his action be unperturbed or agitated. What he must ultimately mediate has to issue in this peace. In contemplation, one must possess peace. Without peace, no meditation is possible. In it, one must bring to the Lord his peace. Whoever cannot succeed in being at peace in contemplation is not suited to it. For it is the assimilation of the peace of the meditator to the peace of the Lord. The Passion, to be sure, contains in itself cessation of peace; but the sacrifice of peace must nevertheless be decided upon and accepted in peace. In order to enter into the Passion, one must already have known the peace of the Lord, have committed oneself into his peace, and in fact, into his Easterly peace after the Cross. The call to enter the peacelessness of the Passion is just as much a night of the Lord as are all mystical graces. No one can deliberately evoke it for himself, but also no one should reject it if he is called.

The words *with you* refer to a legacy. The disciples receive something that they have to administer and pass on to others. Insofar as they are priests, this peace abides with them only briefly, because it is at once presented again to others. So much does it exist in order to be passed on to others that the Lord, along with the priest, communicates it anew at every Mass in the *"Pax Domini sit semper vobiscum"*. This is communication of peace in the eucharistic sense. Without the restlessness of the period before the Cross, in the ultimate peacefulness of Easter. At the same time, it is a turning back into simple prayer to the Lord: the dispensing of the Our Father. We have prayed as he has taught us to pray; may, then, everything in us worship him, the Lord, who now surrenders himself eucharistically. But he anticipates the Church by dispensing his peace to her. This return into pure peace runs parallel to the return by all mysticism into pure belief and pure love. The Lord expects from us a quite simple human surrender; he himself demonstrates such *surrender* to us in just as simple a form. Before he surrenders himself, he takes us once more unto himself. He offers us his arm so that we might lean on him for support. He enwraps us once more within his mystery before he presents it to us. A man could have brought all of his everydayness along with him to

Mass; he observes himself, he can scarcely dare, as the one who he is, to step up to the table of the Lord. The Lord sweeps all this hesitation aside by giving us peace. It is like a smile of the Lord that bridges over all distinctions, an establishment of equality: "Everything is all right as it is, the rest we will accomplish together." It is the humility of the Lord that does not want to humiliate.

This peace of the Lord must be spread, it must pass like a kiss from one to another, unattenuated and regardless of whether its transmittal occurs in action, contemplation or passion. The kiss is the symbol of surrender and unquestioning peace: all restlessness, all torment is extinguished in it. The Resurrection is the most simple thing that there is. With his words, the Lord forestalls all pathos and opens the way for every form of simple surrender.

20:20. *When he had said this, he showed them his hands and his side. Then the disciples were glad when they saw the Lord.*

He shows them these as proof of his identity. They are to recognize him by these, even more than by his wishing them peace. He shows them not only his hands, which are visible, but also his side, which was covered. Symbolically, then, he shows them his outside and his inside, and on both, the effects and traces of his suffering. He thereby indicates what path he has traversed since the last time they saw one another. This path left signs behind on him, signs that were impressed not for him, but for them. Signs that do not last just for a moment but will characterize him permanently. He shows them these because they belong to him, because they have, through his love, a right to this sight, and not only to the sight but to the whole mystery. This mystery, which was apparently played out solely between him and the sinners that had to crucify him, was in fact already played out between the Father and him before he was sent into the world, but for their sake. For they are the ones for whom he suffered in the first place. They owe it to him to understand what he has done for them. But he also owes it to them to show them this; because it was thanks to them that he was allowed to accomplish the Father's mission. There are moments when he sees them as sinners as well as redeemed — those for whom he accepted his mission and those who help him to accomplish that mission. Even more: those in whom, at times, the mission was locked up.

First, he shows them his hands, the outside, and then his side, the inside. For them, he no longer holds any mystery at all in which they might not have a share, although the period between the moment of his death and his return to them remains veiled to them. But no matter what shape this period may have taken for him, he characterizes it by showing his wound marks. Their great mystery is locked up in the receiving of them and the displaying of them.

In the interval between this receiving and displaying lies a time reserved for God alone. It contains the *wordlessness* that extends from giving up the Spirit to receiving him anew in the Resurrection. In this pause between his dying as a man and his rising as a man, the unity and identity of Christ lies wholly in his divinity. Jesus the man died in abandonment by God; he deposited his divinity with God to such an extent that, in his death, he appeared to be nothing more than a pure man. And yet the one who died there was the God-Man. And of the God-Man, that which died was the man. So that henceforth the mystery of Holy Saturday between Father and Son is more a mystery of the *God*-Man than of the God-*Man*. For no man would be capable of bearing this mystery of the eternal Father. The Son, to whom the Father shows the darkness, is not only he who had deposited his divinity with the Father in order to be able to become man. He is also the Son who has deposited the man that he was with himself in order to endure the darkness in this state of final divestment of everything that was his own. Here, it is as if the Son is cut off not only from the Father and from men, but also from himself. Thus Holy Saturday is a day of wordlessness. It is this in a kind of correspondence to the prenatal period during which the Son was in the womb of the Mother. There, he was enfolded in her purity, and his nearness to the Mother took the form of sequestration and silence. Here, he is placed into the womb of the netherworld, which harbors all that is impure and dark, and once again this nearness to the Father's mystery takes the form of separatedness and wordlessness. And the Son must now seek the Father there where he is not. But he cannot seek him in consciousness, in the light of love; rather, it is as if he must seek him as a lover who has been robbed of his love would seek a beloved who is without love. The Father, who is calling his Son home to him, sends him, at the same time, in the opposite direction, to a place where he surely is not. This is the unfathomable mystery of Holy Saturday: because the Son cannot seek the Father in love, he has to seek him there where he is not. The Father is not merely, as was the case on the Cross, veiled and lost to view, but now the Son is forced to enter that which is the opposite of the Father, to go where only one thing is certain: the absence of the Father. This is the perfect element in the hidden, withdrawn love: namely, pure *obedience,* which, in its perfection, consists of seeking love there where it is not.

It is the most extreme demand that the Father and Son make on one another in love. If a man were sentenced to the most severe physical punishment, and his friend were to ask to be allowed to suffer it in his place, then while the punishment was being inflicted the sufferer would think of his friend who was suffering with him in the next room and suffering from not being able to suffer, and this support would be his consolation. But were he to learn that the one who has been spared had meanwhile run off and left him, that would be unbearable. To this unbearable situation, however, the Father forces himself in order to allow the Son to suffer his Passion through in full, in order to allow the innermost essence of the Son's love to manifest itself: pure obedience in the netherworld.

Were Holy Saturday to be missing from the Lord's redemptive work, his suffering would remain, in a way, comparable to the sufferings of other men. His death would remain, despite everything, a human death. In his descent on Holy Saturday, the eternal, divine dimension of his death shows itself. Much pertaining to the Cross can still be comprehended, but after it comes the pure mystery about which we comprehend only the incomprehensible. In order that men might at least sense that here is the locus of the incomprehensible, there is this hiatus between Holy Saturday and Easter, between the receiving of the wounds and the displaying of the wounds. This gap is also not closed by the displaying. The displaying does not follow directly from the receiving. In between lies the journey through darkness. The wound on his hand is indicative more of the outward events. By the wound in his side, the inner sphere is situated between the receiving and the displaying: the interval between no longer sustaining and not yet being able to display. It is the sphere of utter darkness. The outward aspect, in which the disciples participate, he shows them through his hand. They participate in it by comprehending full well *that* he was crucified. Much less do they comprehend (although it does not escape them entirely) *why* he was crucified: the inner meaning of the Cross, which the wound in his side embodies. What is directly connected with the Cross, and thus becomes visible in his hand wounds, signifies for them, in a way, a revelation. However, they are thereby drawn into its mysterious interior, which they are scarcely capable of comprehending but which is still not totally concealed from them, since the covered wound in his side is also shown to them. The Lord has expanded their belief in such a way that the outward events—his death and his Resurrection—have a place in it. This they comprehend, since he fulfilled what was promised and allowed them to participate in both: in his death and his Resurrection. The other mystery, the mystery of the wound in his side, they know for the time being only *as* a mystery. They sense in it the mystery of the intimacy between Father and Son, but without penetrating it. Through the Cross, the Lord has made the Kingdom of God accessible to them, and they must now already participate in its mysteries even if they do not understand them. They have been granted a look into eternal life, as if they already belonged to it, as if it already formed a part of their experience. Not so that they will learn to understand more quickly when they once arrive in heaven, but so that the joy, love and satisfaction of the Lord can be opened more widely and be fuller because of the gift offered to them. Not even this does he want to keep for himself, which is something that the disciples are unable to understand. Even when the listening friend is totally unmusical, the musical friend performs his most beautiful music for him in order to give him all that he has.

The disciples were glad when they saw the Lord. They are glad with a naïve joy at the Lord's presence among them. This joy is so simple because it allows everything incomprehensible to go unheeded. They see only their joy. What makes them so joyful is the fact that he is actually there, in reality. He has, to be sure, given them no time to enable his memory to fade in their minds, and yet his actual *presence* exceeds all their expectations. It is the presence of one whom they already know, but who brings with him, in his simple actuality, the whole fullness of his being, person, mystery and divinity. Perhaps they rejoice most of all about the wound in his side, about the exposure of that which they do not understand. They see in this a new bond with the Lord. When a lover returns to the beloved after years of separation, he may perhaps take from his pocket a small stone which he had once picked up, as if by chance, during one of their walks together. He does not show her a ring or a picture, but rather, this insignificant little object, and the beloved then knows that, for all those years, she was incomprehensibly enfolded within the mystery of his memories. Oneness between men is perhaps at its greatest when they participate together in something incomprehensible.

Here, the whole significance of the joy lies in the manifestation of the Lord. It is not their joy that moves him to come forward and show himself; rather, their joy inheres solely in his freely appearing. Previously, the body of the Lord was never something that was shown. It was only a form with which to serve God and men in love, a gift that the Father had given to him so that it might be surrendered up. Now, through sinners, this body has acquired new features that have, to a certain extent, dematerialized it. It is the something upon which sin has impressed its marks. It is like material that men have worked upon and regarding which, as a result, they have a right of possession. For himself, this body has, so to speak, been alienated; it belongs to him no longer. His body will now bear the marks of men, which, however, bring him so much the more back into the Father's love. Just as a husband should share in the birth pains of his wife by not leaving her alone at this time, so now men, too, should share, concretely and intimately, in the wounds of the Lord, who incurred them representatively for their sake (just as the wife suffers her pains, as it were, for both partners). And this sharing should be nothing self-contained, no detached "devotion" in itself, but something that develops within ongoing love. Something that draws one more deeply into the mystery of the opened side. The apostles rejoice at entering into this mystery. It is the joy of the Church over the magnificent incomprehensibility of the Bridegroom in her midst.

20:21. *Jesus said to them again: Peace be with you. As the Father has sent me, even so I send you.*

Once again he grants them peace, but this time as an introduction to something new. For now begins a totally fresh phase of their mission, one that cannot get under way other than in peace. The new peace that he now wishes them is founded between him and them; it is the peace that he has to transmit to them and that stems from his peace in the Father: the peace of unquestionability, of tranquillity, of evident certainty. The peace that always lies at the beginning of a calling. The Lord had summoned them long ago, one after the other, and selected them to tread his path with him; but previously it was a human, understandable path. Now he calls them to a new succession, because he will no longer visibly accompany them and because he brings them the gift of the Cross as the foundation and synopsis of the new. Within this new context, their own responsibility will play a much greater role; therefore, the relationship must be newly founded in peace. In restlessness, one could perhaps win converts, but only in tranquillity can one take over his mission. In restlessness, one can seek and find, but only in tranquillity can one follow after. There comes a moment when one must stand before the Lord in complete tranquillity in order to receive his instructions tranquilly. Outwardly, the scene appears confused enough: the disciples involved in a matter of action, simultaneously experiencing a vision of the Lord, who is bringing them the fruit of his Passion, who now has his mission behind him, whereas it is just getting under way for the disciples, and amidst their joy a thousand questions clamor to be voiced in them. What went before was only a prelude: the peace that he wished them before was the peace that they knew and that comes back to them when they recognize the long-known Lord. But in the meanwhile, his bond with God and with them has become a totally new one, his commission has been given a new direction, since he now finds himself existing, to a certain extent, both in them and in God. The Cross was not an episode that is left behind him, the Passion remains alive in him, and the whole of his previous work is more firmly rooted than ever in the Father and in them. All this seems like a new instance of demanding too much of them. But when the excitement of their joy reaches its high point, he does not even take the time to lead them gradually back to calmness; quite abruptly, without any transition, he wishes them peace. It is in peace that they are to hear what he has to say to them and receive their commission. A commission that was not accepted in peace would not be an accepted commission at all. No matter how pressing the circumstances may be, every apostolic commission must be effected in calmness, face to face with the Lord. No calling, no summoning by the Lord can be settled in restlessness, but only in his peace, no matter how much the spirits may have raged in one's soul beforehand.

As the Father has sent me, even so I send you. In the same sending. There are not two sorts of mission: one mission of the Son and, alongside it, another mission of the disciples and Christians. There is only the one mission, which stems from the Father and was accepted by the Son. In its origin and its acceptance, every further mission draws its life from the first one. The substance of the mission is always the movement from the Father to the world and then back to the Father. The Father is the origin and the completion of the mission. The Son grants to each who follows him participation in the same substance, in the same directedness and limitlessness of his eternal mission. In being concretely carried out, then, it exhibits the attributes of him who has to accomplish it, that is, the attributes of the sinner, who *attempts,* in the Lord's name, to do his will. But even when God has the intention of achieving something specific and finite through a certain mission, he nevertheless bestows, in each case, the *whole* mission, the mission of movement, of succession, and only within this larger gift the specific purpose. What is to be achieved remains, as it were, one point within the whole mission. Everyone who attempts to work in the name of the Son works for the whole of the Son's mission. With the help of his limited, constrained nature, and in conjunction with grace, man can achieve something definite in any particular case, something visible or invisible, but the commission itself is always the whole commission. For every commission is a proof of the indivisible love of the Lord and, at the same time, a promise of eternal life. Love and eternal life are an immediate whole and form, as such, the substance of the mission. Love is, so to speak, the material in the realm of the spiritual. Mission is movement. In themselves, to be sure, love and eternal life are also movement. But they are immanent movement. Mission, by contrast, is transcendent movement. And yet both movements are, in the end, one: the love that the Lord gives and in which he confers eternal life goes, as if by its own nature, to the Father and is also sent by the Son to the Father. For the Son confers precisely the same mission that the Father conferred upon him. What he bestows is of the same essence as what he possesses. The difference consists solely in how it is received. The Son received the mission in such a way that what was imparted and what was received were the same. He received just as much as the Father communicated to him. He is so much God, and so much at the disposal of the Father, that there is no difference between what he can apprehend and himself. We sinners, by contrast, receive only in part; we perhaps attempt to receive, but we allow much to be lost. And that which we do receive is received in the grace of the Son. An unbeliever who considered the two missions would perhaps see no basis for comparison. In the Lord, he would perhaps see a greater man, a founder of religion, and in us, his adherents. And so he would discover no point of contact between him and us. A believer, by contrast, would perhaps see, above all, the failure on our part, if he really objectively sees what we do. He would see the fruitless efforts of Christians. In order that the unity of the mission might endure nonetheless, the Lord rounds everything out. Through his love and the communication of his eternal life, he assimilates us to the mission. He also does not want us to reflect constantly on our limited possibilities: "If only I were less sinful, if I possessed more talents, better health. . . . " Rather, we simply ought to do what we can, without marking off how far we are getting. Since the Lord observes us through the eyes of eternal life, and not through the eyes of mission (not even of his mission), he can round things out, bring our mission into conformity with his. And although our fulfilment is not in the least his fulfilment, he nevertheless allows no imbalance to arise between his eternal life and the eternal life that he has bestowed upon us. Between him and us there is no "total solubility", but rather, a kind of osmosis. A doctor can prescribe medicines for his patient; yet perhaps the patient's health is not actually restored by these, but by what the physician as a person transmitted to him, something indefinable, which cannot at all be precisely evaluated. Similarly, the

Lord nourishes us not with the medicine of a grace that is separable from him, but with his own blood; and through this transfusion of eternal life, he rounds out our mission.

Just, then, as the Father has sent him, so he sends them. He, who participates in the life of the Father, in the essence of the Father, who as God oversees the mission, sends them as his representatives— they, whose belief is weak and tenuous, who have scarcely the barest inkling of the mission, who, above all, do not inherently possess this love that he has from the Father. And yet he risks giving them the mission. He sends them just as the Father has sent him, without wishing to demand that they constantly render account to him. He places trust in them. But although he regards them, in his love, as his brothers, he knows perfectly that, if he does not stand with them, if he does not perceptibly and continually support them with his love, then they are capable of nothing other than falling, than casting the mission aside. Still, he bestows it upon them. Other courses would have been available to him. He could have been able to remain in the world until everything had been resolved. He could also have saved them the struggle. But he does not do that. He sends them just as the Father has created them, as the creatures of the Father that they already were before his coming. The only new thing that he adds to this is what he was allowed to bring to them: his love of the Father. Hence, he does not remove the possibility of their falling. No temptation will be spared them. He merely adds something new: love, the proof of his love of the Father. He enriches them, in their knowledge and essence, with something that they did not at all know, that they did not at all ask for: with his love of the Father. And because this love, which wishes above all to glorify and honor the Father, is tender and considerate, he leaves creatures just as they are, giving them once again, after he has suffered for them, only the mystery of his love of the Father. He does the opposite of what men usually do: he does not make himself like men so as to be better able to love them. In his love, it is only to the Father that the Son adapts, and he adapts men to the Father by giving them what the Father already has: his love of the Father. He brings nothing in his gospel that diminishes or increases man's creaturely nature, but purely and simply his grace, that is, his love of the Father. He brings no earthly comforts, no

improved conditions for the world, and also no reduction of induce-
ments to sin, no progress in social and moral affairs. He leaves all that
untouched; he does not change the problems of mankind, but brings
only one thing: love. As a result, some things on earth will perhaps
seem even more difficult and unsolvable. That does not bother him.
He desires only one thing: the increase of love. Prior to his appearance,
life was perhaps quite bearable, satisfied in itself. Then he appeared
and brought to men the offer of his love. Everything was plunged
into disorder; simultaneously, fulfilment and renunciation became
pressing issues. Yet the Lord's life, too, was nothing but fulfilment
and renunciation, because it was mission. As a result of his love's
breaking into the world, our life breaks out of its little framework,
because it, too, is part of the mission. The Lord has tested for himself
just what it means to love God and yet to live.

20:22. *And when he had said this, he breathed on them, and said to them:*
Receive the Holy Spirit.

He has spoken to them of quite far-removed matters, of an untouchable love. And now he breathes on them, thereby bringing everything
into a tangible nearness that accords with the previous showing of his
wounds. He reminds them once again of the reality of his earthly existence; even more, he allows them to participate in it, since his breath
blows sensibly upon them. Something of his innermost being is transferred to them. It is a sign of nearness, of contact, a sign of absolute
physical intimacy. Something mysterious, which stems from his own
bodily essence, is transferred to them, conveying to them something
incomprehensible about that essence. He places them bodily at the center of his life. He communicates directly with them regarding his substance, regarding the personal mystery of his life. People sometimes
breathe on newborn babies in order to elicit signs of life from them;
but that is a slight, wholly external stimulus. Here, the Lord's breath
imparts the whole of his inner mystery. Contained in this breath is
the answer to every question that one could ask him about his life.

The Lord thereby signifies as well that, within his teaching, body,
life and spirit become a unity. That it would therefore be wrong to
want to be only spirit, just as it would be wrong to want to be only
body. The elements that go to make up life and that are based in the

corporeal are not to be counted as nothing. The stress on the bodily that occurs here can also, of course, suggest as complete as possible a deadening of it; still, it concedes rights to the body that are duties for the spirit. There is a kind of congruence between body and spirit that the Lord causes to arise by breathing on the disciples. It signifies that life within the Church would not be possible if both did not exist in unity alongside each other. In an extended sense, it signifies the connection between action and contemplation.

Above all, however, it is the divulgence of a mystery of his life, and the life that fills him is the *Holy Spirit*. By breathing on the disciples, he communicates to them the mystery of his life: the Holy Spirit. Breath cannot be forced into any definite structure. It cannot be passed on in any way but through another breath. And insofar as the sensible breath becomes a symbol of eternal, spiritual breath, it signifies here the delivering over to the Church of life, of something that never becomes tangible and never takes on definite form, something that, as the inapprehensible, emanates only from the Lord and is conferred on the Church. In all the sacraments, there is this sensible element, which serves as a bearer of the spiritual without the spiritual's thereby becoming entrapped in it. In baptism, there is the pouring of water and the act of being breathed upon by the priest. In the Eucharist, the host is the bearer of eternal life. In every case, the sensible is of significance, yet never in such a way as to come into contradiction with the opposing, and impossibly high, requirement to ignore and forget the corporeal. It is only in this incomprehensible tension between matter and spirit that indissoluble unity is effected in the Christian context. The Church never elevates herself above the material and into a realm of the purely spiritual; but everything material is nevertheless immediately burst open by its spiritual content. The material emblems are all pregnant with significance; but there is never any proportionality between them and the grace that they contain. Every host is the entire Body of Christ; but whereas every host, as such, is equivalent to all others, the Body of Christ is always unique. Hence, even in the nothingness of a breath, there is room for the unimaginable greatness of the Holy Spirit, the most incomprehensible thing that exists in God.

Receive the Holy Spirit. By breathing on them, the Lord gives his followers that which characterizes his intimate life, as Son, with the Father, the most profound aspect of their divine communion. He gives this to them as their property, he allocates it to them. That he can do so is a fruit of the Cross. Through the Cross, he was given the possibility of bequeathing his life in this new form: in the gift of the Spirit, who is invisible. The Spirit's pathway to men always runs through the Son. However, similarly to the way that he received him from the Father, the Son does not give them the Spirit on his own initiative. Just as he and the Father had determined from the very beginning: one purpose of his mission was to consist in transmitting the Holy Spirit undividedly out of the life of the Son. Thus it could seem as if the Holy Spirit in God were only passive, since his role is decided by the Father and Son. And yet the Spirit blows where he will, and his coming is his own, freest act. But just as the Son placed himself at the Father's disposal in order to take on the mission of redemption, so the Spirit accepted in love the mandate of allowing himself to be utilized by the love of the Father and Son for the purpose of fulfilling the redemptive task.

Inherent in the gift that the Lord presents to his disciples is an immediate bursting open and sheer exorbitant demand. The Lord has always demanded the utmost of the disciples. The Spirit demands even more than that. He demands, as it were, more than they possess. What was breathed on them appears as nothing; but the power that it contains and unleashes is infinite. The disciples are not asked whether they want to be swept up into this storm. The Lord places them quite directly in the midst of it. He cannot do other than transmit to them this Spirit who was, from the very beginning, implicit in his mission. He was enclosed in it without men's knowing what the Lord was ultimately aiming toward. He demanded certain things of them in order to make of those things something that they did not know. They were neither asked nor informed in advance. They offered themselves without foreknowledge. And now they see the overwhelming result: *Receive the Holy Spirit.* Even before this, they did not understand the succession; they knew that it was impossible to catch up with the Lord. But the Lord himself, whom they knew, still formed the framework. Now, abysses suddenly yawn before them: out of the Lord, an Other emerges, still less familiar to them, and they are supposed to, indeed, they cannot but, receive him. They had perhaps suspected that the love between the Father and Son was the key to all mysteries, and that they themselves are enclosed in his love. But when the mystery now opens itself to them, it does not correspond to their expectations. They regarded themselves as already having been overtaxed, but at the end of this overtaxing, their true overtaxing is just beginning. An infinite goal seemed to lie before them, toward which they were supposed to journey without any hope of arriving. But now, this infinity is expanded into a second, still far more infinite infinity. The Lord's love was somehow commensurable, tailored to human nature; but now the storm of incommensurable love is unleashed, which breaks upon men like a natural catastrophe. At this moment, when all shores are flooded and everything is tottering, the Lord immediately pushes ahead. He opens up a pathway. He at once makes clear that everything is just love by speaking of forgiveness of sins.

20:23. *If you forgive the sins of any, they are forgiven; if you retain the sins of any, they are retained.*

There is nothing that is so locked into the mystery of love as sin. Nothing that requires so much love in order to be understood or explained. What is most profound in the knowledge of sin lies in love, and initially, in fact, in the original love of the Father. Then in the love of the Son, and finally in the love of the Holy Spirit. Only when the love that comes from the Father and the Son reaches us through the Holy Spirit does sin acquire the character that it exhibits since redemption: the character of complete remoteness from love, of refusal and rejection of love, of opposition to love. Not until then does the negative come so strongly and exclusively to the fore that only love is capable of blotting it out again, that only the purest love, the solely pure love, divine love, can return it to the center of love again. And now the Lord gives sinners, assuming that they have experienced his love and thirst for his love, the opportunity to overcome sin. And, in fact, through love.

What the Lord institutes here has its counterpart in the Eucharist. In the host, the Lord spreads himself out to infinity. In confession, he sorts out those who belong to him according to how he sees them with the eyes of redemption. How they participate in his love, live from his love. How they possess his love in the vitality of the Holy Spirit. Up until the Cross, the Lord had foreshadowed confession in various contexts; but previously *he* himself was always the one who pardoned. He exposed the sin, then covered it up at once with his love, so that only the latter remained visible. Those who were present recognized that only his love was capable of accomplishing this miracle. And in a way, they grew accustomed to it. Since then, they know that the living, the concrete and present, love of the Lord is required for blotting out a sin. Because, in their eyes, he embodies perfect love, they know that it is impossible, without him, to pardon a sin and render it undone. It never occurred to them that they could participate in this miracle of pardoning. They well know, through the Our Father and through the example of the Lord, that they ought to pardon those who have done them wrong. That seems difficult enough to them. But now they are suddenly supposed to comprehend this new thing: that they ought to pardon sins which (as they see it) are no concern of theirs. To comprehend, therefore, that every sin is a concern of theirs. At the moment when they are sure that certain sins in no way concern them, they have to understand that their communion with the Lord has become so living, through ties not only of love but also of the Holy Spirit, that from now on there will no longer be any sin that does not concern them. They ought to suffer from every offense committed against the Lord. They should exist in so close a communion with their brother, the Lord, that nothing can be done to him which leaves them unaffected. And on the other hand, through the Lord's command, they live in so close a communion with their brethren, the sinners, that there is not one of all the sins committed in which they do not participate as sinners. Even if their participation is only in grace, insofar as it was grace that prevented them from committing precisely that sin. But that grace, which has come to them and not to the others, is not something that they have earned; hence, their not having committed the sins of the others is not something that they have earned. This leads to but one conclusion for them: the grace that was bestowed upon them must, insofar as things are in their hands, be made to benefit all sinners. Every grace applies to all. The grace of no longer thieving belongs to all thieves. Other thieves have refused it, but that is irrelevant to the one who has been converted through grace. He exists in communion with his brethren, his neighbors, the thieves, and is thus constrained to share in their sins—if not in the committing of them, then in the expunging of them.

On the basis of this twofold communion and solidarity of the disciples, both with the Lord and with sinners, the Lord installs them in the position of confession: the face of the sinner turned toward the Lord, the face of the Lord turned toward the sinner. It is conscious representativeness in two directions, and thus the same position which the Lord also occupies: one face turned toward the Father, the other toward the world. This is where a priest stands. And just as the Lord, in his love, rounds out the shortcomings of his brethren, so a priest, in furtherance of this rounding out, brings sinners before the Lord. He, too, does so in a mediatory way, by taking the sinner up into himself and presenting him, in himself, to the Lord. Correspondingly, the Lord lives in him through his office, and the priest mediates the Lord to the sinner. Only within the representativeness of the Lord in relation to God is such representativeness possible.

With that, the pardoning of sins becomes an institution in the Church. A sinner who wishes to reconcile himself with God cannot do so in any way that he chooses: he has to adhere to the ecclesiastical forms established by the Lord. A particular side of the ecclesiastical framework is formed by the absolution of sin, and both the sinner and the Church have to adhere to this. A sinner could be convinced that he must confess as the Church requires, but that the absolution would be, for him, solely a personal process between the Lord and him, which would take place, as if by chance, in this external form. But that would not correspond to the will of the Lord. The Lord does not desire that office, and the priest who has been installed in office as an administrator of his grace, should be overlooked. On the Cross, he achieved the whole of redemption, in this world and in the beyond, in the temporal and in the eternal. And the fact that eternal redemption already truly occurs in this world, that it is not something merely "eschatological", he demonstrates by placing its administration in the hands of his earthly Church. He effects a continuity between his activity and the activity of the Church. He pardons, then, when a priest pardons. He does not say that he will not also pardon others besides those who make confession. But if pardoning occurs through a priest, then it also occurs through the Lord. A priest absolves in the name of the Lord.

Thus the Church pardons, too, and also the priest. And in fact, if the Lord pardons personally, a priest cannot just pardon officially and impersonally. He must, on commission from the Lord, carry out his act of pardoning personally as well. This is evident in cases where the confessed sin has personally affected the priest: whether because it was aimed at him personally or because he felt himself, for some other reason, directly affected and repulsed by its sinfulness. But from here, the circle expands outward. Everything that offends the Lord also offends his priests. Everyone who comes to a priest in order to make confession has surely offended him. The more a person is a priest, the more deeply he will feel the sins and offenses committed against the Lord. As a priest, it cannot possibly be a matter of indifference to him whether a person has committed a greater or lesser number of sins. Not only in order to be able to correct and judge the sin must he know it, but just as much in order to be able to adjust his own pardoning to its particular nature. His pardon must be so constituted as to ensure that it covers the whole of the confessing person's sin. For this, the priest requires the Holy Spirit, for he cannot pardon by virtue of his human love; he must pardon in true knowledge, in knowledge of the sin as well as of the pardon. This knowledge stems, however, from the Holy Spirit. A priest who was not interested in the sin, and who granted absolution from it in a merely mechanical way, would not have administered his office in the sense intended by the Lord. He must love and pardon in oneness with the Lord. He would have to love in such a way as to be capable of pardoning, within himself and on commission from the Lord and ultimately on commission from God, both personally and out of love.

The origin of absolution is the Son's commission to overcome, through his love, the offense that sin has caused to God. The Son wants to fulfill this commission in relation to the Father. He also wants the Father to be able to pardon the offense when he beholds a love that is greater than the offense. In the greatness of this love, sin is simply to disappear. And the Son is the only one who possesses this love. Therefore, he surrenders himself up to the world. The result of this self-surrender is absolution through confession. To be sure, the Son has suffered uniquely and thereby proven his love. But that love goes on living; it is immortal, and propagates itself in confession. Confession is fructified by his Cross; but on the other hand, the love that the Son brings back to the Father is fructified by confession. He wishes, after all, to bring back to him not only his own love, but unreservedly, as enclosed within that, our love as well. Otherwise, the world's love would remain wholly external to his. He must accordingly give his love the form of human love, and implant it in human hearts so that it might sprout there. Thus, absolution has its origin in heaven, where the Son takes the shame of the world upon himself. From there, it runs through the Cross, where he atones for that shame; is next handed over to the priest, who sees and pardons sin together with him; and passes finally to the sinner himself, who must recognize it in confession. For the sinner understands that he himself, with all his remorse and good deeds, cannot undo his sin. His sole salvation is the love of the Lord, which the Lord makes available to him, but by means of an additional love. He does not want to communicate his divine love other than in the form, and in the container, of a human love. In a priest, however, this human love is no purely human impulse: he does not, for instance, pardon *because* he has sinned like the one making confession; he pardons because in him the Lord, and in the Lord the Father, pardons. His love can be so pure for the sole reason that it is not his, but rather, the Lord's love in him. With that, the circle is closed between love and office.

On the one hand, then, confession is something strict, something fixed within the sturdy framework of the Church, and on the other hand, the most splendid gift of the Lord's love, the pure and immediate fruit of the Cross. What the Lord presents to the sinner here is his own position before the Father, because he, the Lord, has freely taken over this position from the sinner. The Son stands in suffering, so to speak, like one making confession before the Father, from whom he pleads for absolution. And he expects from the Father the position of one who absolves. He wants not only that the Father should receive love from him, but still more, that the Father should be able to give him his love. For he wishes, after all, to bring men not to himself but to the Father, to disclose to them the Father's love. He is the mediator of this love, he has invested himself with the role of mediator, and thus he cannot do other than mediate himself anew, through the priest in confession, to the world. Herein lies the catholic. What is official appears as at one with love. The Lord founds the office because he wishes to allow as many as possible to participate in love: in its active dissemination as in its passive reception. He translates the entire work of mediation that he has accomplished into human terms. He wants all whom he loves to experience the love of God in the form of love of one's neighbor, and in fact, in both directions: as lover and as beloved.

Therefore, Christians must also pardon one another outside the official sphere, as laymen. In the first instance, they must do so simply as following on from confessional grace itself. For any sin that God has pardoned is blotted out, and no man has the right to regard it as still existent. He must endorse God's judgment by pardoning, too. If we did not have confession, of course, we would never know whether a sin has really been pardoned and done away with; through the Lord's grace, and *also* through the Church and her mediation, such closing off is possible. This implies, however, that it is through the existence of confession that pardoning in the Church becomes, in general and for the very first time, something that can assume *finality*, settlements to which one never returns. The duty to pardon anyone who has offended us even becomes, through his pardoning by God, a pressing one. If a sinner has confessed to some unkindness, and subsequently asks the offended person to pardon him, then he is free of his sin and has discharged his human obligation. Were the offended person to refuse to pardon him, then he, for his part, would be committing a sin.

Every instance of confession thus provides testimony to the Son's mission: it exhibits before God that mission's content, namely, that love outweighs the offense given to God by sinners. This happens by virtue of the integration of the Church into the Son's mission, since God desires to receive more love than offense not only from the Son but also, through the Church, from men. A priest is thus drawn into the ever-greater of the Son: he does not see the whole of what he does when he confers absolution. In the act of absolving, he is supposed, on the one hand, to pardon every confessed sin (whose gravity he can never appreciate) as one committed against himself, since he represents the Lord; he is to pardon, in the name of the Lord, the offense committed against the Lord. This representativeness must, on the other hand, extend to the act of receiving the sin. The priest must really accept, recognize and weigh the sin, in the name of the Lord, in order to be able to remit it. Hence, by virtue of his office, he participates, in both these directions, in the activity of the Lord that transcends him.

For that, he requires the Holy Spirit. In confirmation, the Holy Spirit is conferred for the purpose of personal apostleship. In consecration as a priest, he is received in an official sense. It is the Spirit who imparts to the work of the Son's love the character of a *judgment,* which it must necessarily have in the context of office. The priest's recognition of sin and his judgment of sin are the work of the Spirit. But this work of judgment is a function of love. The Holy Spirit was with the Father when the latter created the world, when he separated light from darkness, water from earth, so as to bring order out of chaos. This primal act of separating out, this primal instance of judgment, was already aimed at furtherance of the good. Then came redemption from sin, the work of the Son, which did not, however, invalidate the work of the Father with its form of separating out and judging. It is the Holy Spirit who, as it were, guarantees the continuity between creation and redemption, who prevents everything from dissolving into a formless chaos of love, into a merely abstract emotionality. He imparts to love its magnitude, its divinity, its enduring structure, the form of an order-creating judgment whose content is love. Thus, in turn, he stands in clear parallel to the Church: as the Spirit of office in the function of love.

But it is not only for the purpose of recognition of sin that a priest has need of the Holy Spirit. When the priest receives sin, he shows himself willing to bear something of its burden. He assumes this burden not subjectively and personally, but officially. The subjective bearing of it is at once objectified by the Holy Spirit. Within the sacrament, there is no subjective representativeness in suffering. Rather, the taking over of this by the Spirit is implicit in the office.

If you retain the sins of any, they are retained. Insofar as the Spirit mediates recognition and judgment here, he prevents the sinner's being pardoned for something that must not be pardoned, since pardoning it would only be harmful to him. Everything is pardoned that the sinner has committed, that he feels repentant about, and that is an obstacle to his being reunited with the Lord. What must not be pardoned is anything that would serve, through being absolved, as a hindrance to the sinner's conversion because he does not recognize, or takes too lightly, his guilt and his offense against God. One of the purposes of confession is to render men more receptive to the Lord's love. Judgment about the nature of the sin and about the receptiveness of the sinner to true love is left by the Lord to the priest, who possesses the Holy Spirit. The Spirit makes it possible for a priest to mediate love, as a truly Christian gift, by keeping its living point of origin constantly in view: the pact between Father and Son according to which, through redemption, love is to acquire complete predominance over sin. This *moreness* of love remains, in confession as well, the criterion for redeeming absolution. And the Holy Spirit keeps watch over this criterion. Herein lies the masculine aspect of confession, which is not without reason administered by males. Love is too great to be mere sentiment. This masculine greatness was already inherent in the mystery of forsakenness on the Cross; in the sacrament, however, not only the fruit but also the character of the Passion is bestowed, and something of this character is implicit in the possibility of retaining sin, in the judgment of love. The denied absolution is postponed, not denied for ever. It is denied for the sake of the greater glory of God, inasmuch as it provides an opportunity for true, more profound repentance, for a breakthrough of love. Every postponement finds its measure in eternal life, in the greater glory of God. Nothing in the Church has a short-term resolution; hence, there is also no short-term absolution. Everything is integrated into the one, supratemporal process of redemption. Everything earthly must be tied back again, retroactively, into the origin of absolution in the mission of the Son. The confessing Christian must recover his place at the focal point of the pact between Father and Son: to the place where confession has its origin, its outcome must finally return to him. It is from there that we are released into eternal life. The denial has no goal but to render the one who makes confession capable of existing once again wholly within this point of origin. It is never a measure taken by cold righteousness, but rather, one of a love that can pardon later in a better way than now. It is a warranty that the Holy Spirit provides for the Lord so that confession might not be misused and love might remain holy. Therefore, a priest who denies someone absolution must always leave that person with an insight into why he was not able to confer it. At the same time, he must draw him into the movement of love, make him ready for the absolution to come. Confession always issues in eternal life, and if the one making confession cannot receive absolution, he must at least be drawn into the movement toward life. Both he who was pardoned and he who was not pardoned must similarly realize that they must inevitably come to share in eternal life.

THOMAS

20:24. *Now Thomas, one of the twelve, called the Twin, was not with them when Jesus came.*

The apostles were not all present when the Lord appeared: Thomas was missing. Hence, he has still not received the Holy Spirit. He did not experience along with the others this inexplicable appearance of the Lord through closed doors. The impossibility of explaining the Lord's presence in natural terms placed those who experienced it in a kind of isolation, a separateness from the context of the everyday, profane world. In this common experience, their sensory processes (because of what was unfollowable in his appearance) were interrupted; they have stood together in the midst of a supernatural vision, they are like those who have engaged together in spiritual exercises. Spiritual exercises are always a withdrawal from everyday life in order, through this interruption, to establish more firmly the connection with supernatural life. For the apostles, these were, so to speak, priestly exercises, which commenced with their isolation by the closed doors, continued on with the sudden, inexplicable appearance of the Lord and whose conclusion was marked by final conferring of their official powers. This experience has now become for them a kind of key to their Christian life: they are the ones who were present when the Lord appeared. And they know that there is an indication for them in this about how they are to treat others, who have not seen the Lord in this way. For their own part, they do not attempt to probe into the mystery of his appearance, and in this discretion lies a sign of genuineness. The Lord himself put no particular stress on the fact that he appeared in a supernatural way; therefore, the disciples, too, do not persist with it. There could also be an indiscreet way of engaging in spiritual exercises—a subjective, psychological probing into the inner mysteries of the Lord, into the nature and manner of his appearing—in which one would be occupied more with oneself than with God.

Thomas has not shared in what the others experienced. They

were granted participation in supernatural life without further difficulties and problems. He remained excluded from this, and must take another, special and more difficult path. And yet we can assume that Thomas, in his belief and love for the Lord, was roughly the spiritual equal of the others. That he is singled out need not be explained by his character. Its reason can lie wholly in what God ordained.

20:25. *So the other disciples told him: We have seen the Lord. But he said to them: Unless I see in his hands the print of the nails, and place my finger in the mark of the nails, and place my hand in his side, I will not believe.*

The others tell him nothing more than that they have seen the Lord. For what they have apprehended through having done so separates them from Thomas. They have shared in a mystery that they cannot explain to him even though Thomas is one of them. The only thing that they may tell him is that they have seen the Lord, and Thomas can then share in their joy at seeing him again. Hence, they do not exclude him from their company because of their new experience, but seek instead to draw him into it. But everything that was connected with the encounter—their redemption, the Lord's words, his breathing on them, the reception of the Holy Spirit, their consecration, the instituting of confession in the Church—they withhold from him. They know instinctively that Thomas, because of his having been absent, cannot share in these mysteries, that he has not received the Spirit, that he still remains at the level preceding the suffering of the Cross. They have passed beyond the Cross solely by virtue of the Lord's reappearance. Thus, although they can tell about that appearance, they cannot report that they are transformed through having been consecrated. Previously, they all possessed their allocated duties within the human community. Now, they possess an ecclesiastical office that is uniform and that places them on a totally new level of mission. The Spirit that they have received has communicated to them something of the discretion that the Lord himself showed when he appeared, and this prevents them from telling Thomas more. Just as a friend who has married does not speak about the secrets of his marriage with a friend who has become engaged.

To what the others disclose, Thomas replies that he requires proofs if he is to believe. Previously, his belief was no different from that of the others. Now, it suddenly begins to distinguish itself both from his earlier belief and from the belief of the others. He wants proofs, and in fact, sensibly perceptible proofs. He begins by focusing on something that he least understands: the wounds of the Lord. At bottom, he knows nothing more about these wounds than that they exist. Normally, one would seek proof of identity in some intelligible statement, not in some distinctive mark that one has still never seen for oneself. And yet, straight from the center of his belief, Thomas demands the right thing. He is seeking what is most profoundly Christian in the Lord's suffering. Although he embodies the doubter, the Lord has endowed him, in the midst of his doubt, with a characteristic feature of supernatural love. He wants to examine—more than the Lord himself, more than his love for the Lord—the signs of the Christian Passion. In the visible signs of the suffering, he suspects that there is something quite fundamental, an essence that is concentrated there. In the midst of his unbelief, he is actually concerned about belief. He wants to confirm what is primary in the Passion. Despite his unbelief, he is so much a Christian that he does not want to find just any Lord and Master, but the only one, whom he was no longer able to apprehend on the Cross. Through examining the wounds, he wants to be overwhelmed by the evidence of the Ever-Greater. His doubt is perhaps petty; but it has the authentic aspect that, if proofs are to be required, then what is absolute in Christianity should be confirmed through those proofs. His previous experiences lead him to want to encounter the one who comes in the highest thing that he knows. He owes it to himself and to the Lord to seek the latter precisely in his suffering. That which the Lord had shown first of his own accord, namely, his visible and his covered wounds—this is what Thomas presses toward.

He demands proof through his eyes, through his finger and through his whole hand. He does not rest content with one sense nor with one wound. He wants to observe and touch both the covered and the visible wounds. He does not say that he will not believe, but that he wants to inquire in order to believe, to inquire with all the means that are available to him, to inquire in such a way that one mode of inquiry is supplemented by another. He is perhaps aware that his demand lacks a certain scope, that it is very much related to his own senses. That this inquiry will not afford him the radiant, comprehensive view that belief has of the Lord's Resurrection and that shines forth from the words of the others. He wants to advance, one step at a time, along a short but sure stretch. With his doubts, which he is prepared to abandon, he initiates a new way of approaching the Lord: a deductive, methodical, rational form, as it were, of contemplating the life of the Lord, and a like way of approaching complete belief. He would perhaps be grateful if belief in the Lord's return were to come to him in as overflowing and living a form as it had to the others. But since that has not happened, he lives in a state of doubt, which he thinks he can cast off only by proceeding methodically. His belief will slowly grow, basing itself as it does—more strongly than is the case with the others—on his own intellect and its activity. Whereas the Lord retrieved the others by appearing to them, he himself must make his way to the Lord step by step.

Inasmuch as he makes his demands, he begins to expect the Lord, and prepares himself for seeing him. He depicts to himself what he will see, what he will do, how he will use his individual senses. He bequeaths to us the example of daily methodical contemplation as an active attempt to draw nearer to the Lord. Even someone who possessed radiant belief would nevertheless have to traverse this path in contemplation. For even radiant belief must adhere to the fact of revelation and accustom itself to this. Thomas bequeaths to the Church the sober pathway of contemplation. Anyone who has fallen away from the center of true, self-evident belief can, by his own devices, make his way back to that center only through such a step-by-step approach. Along this arduous path, radiant belief can, as if in reward for his efforts, suddenly be restored to him. For anyone who has grown disconsolate and is plagued by doubts, nothing remains but to inquire with all the means that are still available to him, with his very own enduring senses. There is perhaps something presumptuous in Thomas' trusting his own senses more than the Lord's pure gift of grace. Conversely, however, he nevertheless also places his senses at the Lord's disposal. Moreover, the testimony of the disciples will take on more persuasiveness if it is corroborated by Thomas' sense-based inquiry. They have all seen the miracle, but one of them procures tangible proofs of it that will be more effective for unbelievers. Finally, Thomas' examination, inasmuch as it begins with the wounds, concerns itself immediately with the mystery of the suffering, and thereby shows contemplation to be a fruit of the Cross. It begins with the visible, demonstrable traces of the suffering, in order to let itself be led directly on from these into the inwardness of the suffering and to the very core of the Person of the Lord. Mary of Bethany was introduced to contemplation by the Lord himself. For the doubter, the basis for contemplation first comes about when the Lord *is* Christian experience itself, so that our deficiency of experience can be supported entirely by him.

But Thomas lacks two things: vision of the Lord and total love of his neighbor. If he loved his brethren in the full, Christian sense, then he would believe them. If someone possesses this love, if he opens his spirit to it, then he does not need to see the Lord himself, but can believe through those who represent and proclaim him. Were Thomas a real Christian, whether it was he or someone else who had seen the Lord would be a matter of indifference to him. He would then know that the manifestations of the Lord always belong to everyone. But also the disciples who had seen, if they had possessed complete love, would necessarily have been able to convince Thomas. In the love that existed on both sides, it would have been possible to overcome his doubts. Thomas would then have been entitled to inquire, in love, into his belief; and the others would, in love, have allowed him this.

The others had been granted sight of the Lord's wounds without asking. They received into themselves the image of his wounds without prior desire to do so. The Lord had desired that they should see. Thomas, by contrast, himself desires to have the same vision. He will, in fact, be granted sight of the same wounds that the others saw; but he will see them in another way, because he will see them as a doubter and as one who demands to do so. The others have made their examination against their own will, they have given their eyes over to this examination because the Lord wanted it so. Thomas offers his eyes on his own initiative. For the others, who desired nothing, examination through one sense was enough because they already possessed the gift of belief. Thomas demands, as a supplement to sight and as its corroboration, to touch the wounds as well.

Indeed, he raises the level of his demand even further by requiring to place his hand in the covered side. He demands full exposure of the Lord's concealed wound. He desires to be admitted to the Lord's intimacy.

Here, Thomas goes too far. In all his self-revelations, the Lord is the one who takes the lead. It is reprehensible to want to experience and sense everything oneself. Not only what he places at the disposal of all, but also his concealed aspects, which he perhaps does not want to show to everyone. Possibly, the Lord might have wanted to reveal to the apostle his side wound as well. But had he not done so, it would have been because he thought that the others' belief should be enough for him. And the Lord might, perhaps, have wanted to grant him a slight touch, as with a finger, in order to initiate him into the mystery of his intimacy. So it is an added indiscretion of the disciple to want, as it were, to enter into the mystery of God with his entire hand. The belief that Thomas seeks is right there next to him: in his brethren. And since the Lord has consecrated them as priests, he has also given them the power to eliminate any obstacles in men that lie between them and God, not merely through absolution from sins, but also through formation of belief. And inasmuch as the Lord's disciples actually find their way to doubters, they demonstrate that the Lord is always prepared to take this path. Which of the two paths he chooses—whether through the disciples or through directly appearing—remains open.

If Thomas cannot examine, he will not believe. He thus leaves the Lord's grace no possible way of arousing his belief other than by going through with the examination. When he first began to believe, he had, to be sure, placed his knowledge at the Lord's disposal, but with conditions. The Lord is to stand constantly by his side, and to nurture his belief with continually new experiences. Then he will remain faithful. The vitality of both his belief and his love depends on a condition set by him. This condition seems to him not to have been wholly fulfilled through the Cross and the death of the Lord; so from that, he infers the right to make the continued existence—or better, the reawakening—of his belief dependent upon a new condition. He exercises control over his belief. Thus he does not allow the Lord to be in control. But whoever desires to love the Lord and to believe in him is left with just one alternative: that *his* love is the substance of our love, that *his* knowledge is the essence of our belief. If this offer has once been made, then it can only have been made once and for all, and the whole right of initiative has been transferred to the Lord. If man wishes to exercise control over his love of the Lord, then he sets up an accounting process between himself and God, and that is the death of love. But if he has comprehended that he can himself be the Lord's love, the vessel of his love, then he will lose all interest in accounting. That was the Lord's Easter gift to the disciples: that they were allowed to be his love, to participate in his love for the Father and for his brethren.

20:26. *Eight days later, his disciples were again in the house, and Thomas was with them. The doors were shut, but Jesus came and stood among them, and said: Peace be with you.*

The Lord has allowed himself and Thomas a little time before appearing to the gathered disciples on the second occasion. Thomas is given a respite, which he uses in order to persist in his attitude. And although the moment draws near, he does not ask himself what he would do if an opportunity to examine were not offered to him, or if the examination showed that the required markings were not present and, as a result of his demand, he became all the more strongly a doubter. Or if, upon closer inspection, the markings were found to have a different character from that expected. Or even if his doubting attitude had deprived him of the ability to recognize the markings in their factual objectivity. An estrangement could, of course, have taken place within himself in relation to these markings. For he has, through his doubt and the importance that it has assumed in him, moved away from belief. It could be that he has employed his senses so much outside of belief that they are no longer capable of recognizing that which belongs to belief. It could be that Thomas, through his demand for presupposing nothing, has assimilated so many presupposed concepts that he is no longer able to perceive the plain reality of belief.

The other disciples, then, who have already been consecrated, are gathered together, *and Thomas was with them.* And the Lord appears once again in the same mysterious way as before: when *the doors were shut.* The disciples, who are given over to belief and have joyfully accepted from the Lord the enlargement of their belief that was presented to them, have no eye for what is striking in the way that the Lord's appearance begins. They are already so caught up in the movement of their mission that they do not—and rightly so—dwell for long on the miracle of this appearing. At the moment when the Lord appears, in order to give them something new, they are not in contemplation. If they were, then they would perhaps have been open to this mystery. But since they are in action, it escapes them. And yet: if their love were even greater, they would nevertheless have had time to notice it. John, who was in love, noticed it (he recorded it, after all), although he, too, does not dwell upon it. In John, a kind of discreetness of love predominates. "Even that you can do," he seems to say to the Lord, "but I am not surprised because I know that you can do anything." He mentions the fact as a means of illustrating once again the Ever-Greater of the Lord and saying to his readers: He will do more for you than you believe; for he has always done more than we have expected. Through his deeds, he has left us a closed image of himself, but this closed thing has always been nothing other than a self-intensifying, open and transparent thing. At that time, it was a small symbol: he came through closed doors. But he will come through closed doors eternally. Not only will the Lord be greater tomorrow than today, but yesterday he was already greater, more binding, more fulfilling than we could ever have allowed ourselves to dream. We resolve to do better tomorrow than today; we forget, however, that even behind us everything outdistances us. This backward look is permitted to pure love, not to self-love. Already then, the Lord's relationship with every individual sinner was characterized by the ever-greater of his grace. And alongside and above the love between men there is a grace of the Lord, which stands their love in good stead because he was always more than they thought. A part of this mystery is contained in his appearing when the doors are closed. Our ignorance, our own closed doors of mind and soul are, if he wants to come, no obstacle to him. For the doors were shut, after all, not against him but against the Jews; and even when he is the one to be excluded, he can always and everywhere get through.

He stood among them. That his mode of appearing was an unusual one could be expected, that even his appearance itself should have an unfamiliar aspect. But it is as a man that he comes to them even though it was as God that he went through the doors. He stands among them as a man. He makes no sort of fuss about the fact that he can also appear in a different way than they. His form is the same as theirs. He stands among them; they stand around him as his representatives, and know themselves to be such. He has brought the whole of the Father's love into the world in order to redeem it, and he has entrusted this power of redemption to them. Indeed, so much does he stand among them that there is also the other sort of representation: that he appears as the representative of his apostles. There can be duties that can be performed just as well by one person as by another; and they have been taking over the task from one another in a reciprocal way for so long that, in the end, no one knows anymore whose task it actually was. If, for example, a guest who has lived in a house for many years always performs some given function in the household, then the head of the house has the feeling of representing the guest should he once perform that function himself. Thus the Lord has handed over to the disciples, as his representatives, the function of absolution. But he returns once again in order, with respect to Thomas, to take on this function himself. As long as he is still in the world and continues to have the opportunity of examining what his followers do, everything is quite transparent: the disciples know that the Lord is now exercising a function he has conferred upon them and that they will lose nothing as a result; just as the Lord knows that he is taking nothing away from his disciples when he grants absolution himself. In this situation of possible dual representativeness, the spheres of responsibility can no longer be distinguished: the Lord stands among those who are his, the priest among priests. He is the head of the Church, but here he stations himself in the ranks and does not disturb his own order.

And he said: Peace be with you. He arrives among them with the same form of greeting that he used before. From the very start, he places the whole course of events to follow in this light. He at once confers upon it the whole character of belief. He brings peace, and in fact, from out of their midst. Thereby, however, he also takes over the whole initiative for what is now to come. He possesses authority, and he shows himself immediately as love. He will now lead, lead wholly in love, and, without wasting a word, will provide an example of how to bring back again someone who is halfhearted, who has grown cold, who has been gradually driven away from belief and into the sin of doubting. One draws him out of his restlessness and into peace. But the Lord also brings peace to the others; for they are not to witness what happens as those who are uninvolved and curious, but as those who are blessed and loving. Since it takes place publicly, what follows is not confession in the proper sense. It is *correction* within the Church. The others, who have experienced Thomas' estrangement, are permitted to be present at his return. The whole thing is a Christian event. So much does it unfold in love that things never reach the point of rumor. Everyone knows how things stand with Thomas; everyone also knows where he himself stands. The task is taken directly in hand as soon as the wish for peace is uttered. Inasmuch as the Lord wishes them peace from out of their midst, he shows that he wishes them a human peace, the self-contained peace of Christian existence, the same peace that he received from his *Mother*.

When the Mother gave her word of affirmation, she uttered it wholly in human peace. She wanted only that which God wanted, and this sense of security within the will of God was so great a peace that it never again left her, not even in the greatest suffering. She will suffer in that peace which God's peace has assumed. It is a wholly simple human peace, because it rests in God; but in God it is transformed from a human to a divine peace. This human peace of the Mother is passed on to the Son. He possesses not only divine peace from the Father, but also human peace from the Mother. This is the peace that he wishes his disciples; they are to make their arrangements in it, they are to receive it from a priest among priests, they will be led back to the Father in it, for even the Mother's peace, after all, stems from God and rests in God. This divine peace is at the same time a *prayer*. The Lord will, in what follows, create order in the ranks of the disciples, he will give Thomas and the others instruction about the life of belief in the Church, he will clarify and consolidate various things; but he will bring all this about in prayer, since in wishing them peace he commends their souls to God. No one can correct error and create order in the Church unless he does so in the spirit of the Lord, which is a spirit of prayer to the Father. This prayer remains constantly necessary. That the Lord appears does not mean that all problems vanish without a trace. But whenever one prays, the Lord will always appear through closed doors, will confer peace, and in this peace all the questions that stir the disciples in the Church will then admit of being put in order. There is so much of the Lord's love present in the Church that it suffices even for all public and domestic problems, quarrels and doubts. Even there where we only pretend to be gathered in his name, he wishes to be among us. He tolerates in the Church no distinction between office and love, no "as if", no mere justice and objectivity, no compromising of love. Wherever something is being negotiated in the Church, the Lord wishes to be present, and he will always be strong enough actually to bring peace. He will always be able to effect the link between human and divine peace. He does this not merely, as we naturally expect, out of his divine-human center, but also with reference to his Mother, who realized this same divine-human unity of peace while a simple human being, who was there before he was and gave him what was hers. Out of this divine-human center that is possible for men, he draws the whole of peace together into one by neither conferring it on believers over the heads of his priests nor just distributing it to his priests, but rather, dispensing peace to all who make up the Church while he stands *among them* as her divine-human head.

The disciples might perhaps have had the opportunity, before the Lord came, of remitting or retaining Thomas' sins. But they still live so immediately in grace that they correspond to the Lord's will by waiting patiently. They do not attempt to anticipate grace. They let themselves be led by their impulses, they know that they can remit and retain sins only under commission from the Lord. And as long as the Lord is in the world, his commission cannot be fulfilled in any way other than through his making it known himself. Just as they, then, have to wait for a perceptibly issued commission, so the later holders of office will have to contact the Lord in spirit in order to know whether they ought to hear a particular confession or not. This means nothing other than that they may undertake dispensation of the sacraments only in the spirit of prayer, only in possession of the peace of the Lord. That is a part of their office. A priest who finds himself in grievous sin does not have the right to hear confession (although his absolution is valid) since he may exercise his office only in the peace of God. He must first seek, in remorse, the peace of God, the love of the Lord. Because that is indispensably necessary, not only does the father confessor help bear the sin of the one making confession, but also the one making confession helps bear the sin of the father confessor. Just as the former must make confession in peace, so the latter must grant absolution in peace. Within the oneness of the Catholic Church there exists this interchange, this reciprocal bearing. As personal as Catholic confession is insofar as it is acknowledgment, so impersonally catholic it becomes insofar as it is made in God and thus in community with all sinners in the Church. If someone infringes the traffic laws in a city, then he receives a corresponding fine; this is not, however, aimed at his person, but is imposed for the protection of the general public, and thus the fine, too, is paid for the general public by the general public, so that the social order might be preserved.

Only after the Lord has shown how strongly peace must be preserved in the bosom of the Church, the peace that he mediates simultaneously as God and as man, does he go on to concern himself with Thomas in particular. And yet, from the very start, in a special way, Thomas was already the object of this whole appearance of the Lord. It was he whom he had in view when he uttered his general wish for peace. In this situation is contained the possibility of ecclesiastical *intention*. The whole Church will profit from the Lord's appearance. For nothing in the Church can be separated off as private. But everything common and general can, in turn, be directed, devoted or applied to some individual case. That the Lord is thinking particularly of Thomas does not become evident to the others from what he says. This does not prevent Thomas from thenceforth occupying a special place in the Lord's thoughts. Thus, too, the Church and every Christian will have their special intentions in their prayers, particularly in Holy Mass. If a whole communion prays for the same thing within or outside of the Church, within or outside of Mass, then it still remains possible for each individual to offer both the common prayer and an individual prayer for his specific purpose. The priest at the altar has this right, and no less does the most unassuming little old woman in the last pew. Only a Catholic is familiar with these intentions, only he knows of this freedom: being able to bestow in prayer. That even the honoring of God, which is offered to him by the Church in divine service, can be *utilized* by God, in love, for quite specific ends. This freedom lies with God; but by giving us intention, he shares it with his Church. That God has his intentions is self-evident. That he also communicates this mystery of his love to the Church is pure grace. Moreover, he gives it to us in such a way that we can use it if we wish, but may also place it at his disposal. Thus one can have Mass read in one's own intention, but can also place it at the disposal of some particular intention of the Lord. Both possibilities embody the Catholic: being able to bestow in general, and actually to exchange gifts mutually between God and man. It is a work of love, of lavished rather than calculable love. This love extends from the grace of formulated intention all the way to pure mutual placing oneself at the disposal of the other; so that a Christian can, in the end, say to God: "Even when I come to you with my specific wishes, do with them what you will."

20:27. *Then he said to Thomas: Put your finger here, and see my hands; and put out your hand, and place it in my side; do not be faithless, but believing.*

Now the Lord turns to Thomas and invites him not only to look at his wounds but also, as he himself wished, to touch them. Thus the Lord accommodates himself to what Thomas desired. He places at his disposal precisely those possibilities of examination upon which Thomas made his belief dependent: proof through his eyes, through his finger and through his hand. Thomas recognized the Lord at once when he appeared; he has not for a moment doubted his identity. Now, however, he is to be allowed to do what he wished. And yet, by fulfilling his wish, the Lord offers Thomas infinitely more than what he had expected or was at all contained in his demand. To be sure, the Lord accommodates himself to the disciple's demand and thus apparently limits his offer. But precisely in this accommodation lies the much greater dimension to that which he offers. Basically, what he offers is to subordinate himself to Thomas, to place himself utterly at his disposal. He gives over to him his hands and his side and, with that, his whole person. And inasmuch as God the Son thus places himself at the disposal of the man Thomas, he demonstrates that being completely human is included in his sonship: his being human is tied to no sort of order of rank, but is free even to serve as an object, to subject itself to being inspected and touched. The Son lowers himself in his humanity so far as to become a proof that Thomas himself has laid down as necessary for his belief. He sinks to the level of illustrative material that man demands in order to arrive at divine belief. He makes himself into the proof of the proof, into what proves within the proof. And he diminishes himself, in a purely human respect, in such a way as to be practically nothing more these wound marks, something that answers to the eye, the finger, the hand of Thomas. With this, he shows the apostle the pettiness of what he has demanded. Thomas has reduced the Lord to something that can be encompassed within two small movements of his finger and hand. He has narrowed the whole possibility of belief down to something that answers to the tip of his finger and the feel of his hand. In order to confirm his belief, he allows no more of the Lord to exist than something that did not even belong to him prior to the Cross: the scars of the Passion. For Thomas, these signs of an external happening are all in which the Lord can abide. And inasmuch as the latter is prepared to be nothing more for Thomas than the wound marks, he reveals to the disciple, in an overpowering way, how low his belief would have sunk if these signs were really all that comprised his belief. Through the Lord's degradation, through his humility in accepting such degradation, he jolts the disciple just where he can be most profoundly affected: in his living belief from the time before the Cross. All at once, it becomes obvious to Thomas how great the disparity has grown. This becomes evident to him initially from the Lord. For the diminution of the Lord, in his humility, reveals just how great infirmity of belief has become in Thomas.

The Lord's humility is entirely human. He behaves as if he had forgotten that he is God and, especially, that the Father is in him. He behaves as if he really abided only in these three wounds. That his whole divinity is overlooked does not worry him. He is not now concerned with revealing the greatness of the Father in him. The wounds are the thing that men have done to him. They are the traces of human sin. And the Son condescends to allow the traces of this to stand as proof of his divine sonship. From this tiniest of spots, he wishes to allow the greatest, the infinite, to shine forth. If Thomas had demanded to see something purely human, the Lord would not have been able to show him that without simultaneously revealing to him his divinity and the Father. The wounds, by contrast, he can show to him because they are the signs of sin. All the more so since Thomas shares the blame for these wounds, and shares it all the more since, having been converted, his fervor turned cold once again.

The rest of the disciples do not really have any desire to see the wounds again: they want to be redeemed. For Thomas, the wounds are important but, in his doubt, he desires to see them as marks of the Lord. The Lord, by contrast, shows them to him as marks of sin. Thomas, who is inclining again toward sin, is thereby preparing the next cross of the Lord. Insofar as he does not believe, and thus seeks in the Lord only an external, human verification for his doubt—which, in the wounds, he also receives—the whole Passion could begin all over again. The Lord would be among men again, as someone who could be crucified anew, and it would be impossible to foresee why he would not, because of the new sins, actually have to be crucified. If Thomas, through sin and in sin, were to furnish proof of the Lord's identity, the only logical conclusion would be to crucify him again immediately. But the Lord, through his Cross, has redeemed everyone, and thus also Thomas; hence, the Lord's move toward Thomas cannot end anywhere other than in Thomas' believing. For the self-manifestation of the Lord *is* grace. It is, so to speak, a risk that the Lord takes here by demeaning himself in such a way; for he puts himself once again at the mercy of unbelief. But he does so while having God, grace and love both in him and behind him; in giving Thomas the wounds as proofs, he simultaneously gives him the redemption on the Cross.

The Son's commission consisted in taking sin upon himself. This is visible in the wounds. When the Lord shows the wounds, he shows himself as Redeemer and, at the same time, as the one who has fulfilled the Father's commission. What he shows to men in order to bring them redeemingly to belief also becomes visible to the Father, who recognizes in it the fulfilment of the mission. Inasmuch as he shows himself simultaneously to God and men, he proves himself once again a mediator: he is deemed by both the Father and men to have done right. He brings the views of both into harmony. Man sees the Lord as having been reduced most radically to these wounds; but the Lord leads man, who has brought him there, out from this most contracted point to the broadest view of the Father, to the view of the fulfilled commission. The Lord transforms the petty and absurd request of man into the supremely great because, in his revelation, he explodes unbelief (which is always small) into the greatness of belief.

Do not be faithless, but believing. Here, being faithless does not mean disputing the divinity of the Son, nor does it mean reverting to the faith of the Old Covenant; it means doubting the identity of the Lord. Regarding the Lord as dead while he is standing there among the disciples. Considering the Cross to be the end of the Son's mission, and therefore setting a temporal end to the livingness of Christianity in the world. Implicit in this temporal end would be the finitude of the Lord. The Lord's life, with respect to its duration, would be comparable to the life of any man. Given, however, that the Lord dies on the Cross for sinners in order to grant them a share in eternal life, so he proceeds anew into eternal life and draws men, too, along with him into eternal life. He does this, in his grace, in such a way that men are given a proof of it. And since it is an inescapable consequence of what men are that their belief constantly runs up against the finite, the Lord wants to provide them with evidence, through his visible return at Easter, that his own life, as well as their future eternal life, cannot hold to limits and deadlines that they set or calculate and that would, above all, be something irreconcilable with eternal life: human time-spans, humanly imposed finiteness. The life of the Resurrected on earth is his participation in eternal life become perceptible to us, and thus also an image and concrete illustration of our own eternal life, a proof of the redemption that was accomplished by his love. The Lord will bring Thomas to belief not through a miracle, but through the proof that was demanded by Thomas himself. He does not, however, leave this proof subject to whatever the apostle chooses and thinks best; he takes it over, he makes use of it for his own purposes. Thomas attempted to draw the Lord into his own sphere of doubting and proof. But by entering that sphere, the Lord has already brought Thomas into his greater sphere. Thomas will not be able to verify his specified conditions outside of what the Lord says. He will not be able to conduct his proving of belief outside of belief. Otherwise, an incongruity would continue to exist between the doubter's method of proof and the proven eternal love of the Lord. To be sure, the Lord permits Thomas his totally petty method of proof, but only in order, by so doing, to give him total belief out of the fullness of his love. He does this, however, by *requiring* him to believe. Simultaneously with the showing of the wounds is issued the demand to believe. It is quite different than it was before the Cross, when he from time to time called the disciples' attention to the Father's love and expanded the conceptions that they already possessed—of human love, of human possibilities of belief—into the greater sphere of his relationship with the Father. This kind of expansion is now past. What now obtains is no longer a gentle inviting. It is a most serious reminder of that to which Thomas has already dedicated his life. It is a demand for obedience of belief— one in which love is surely visible, although more visible to the others than to Thomas, who is just curtly told to believe at once.

Inasmuch as the Lord shows his sternness, he paves the way, in relation to his apostles and the coming Church, for unrelenting, exorbitant demand. Thomas, who is not some random sinner or unbeliever but one who has already believed and loved, can be compared with the baptized who should return again to the Church and the sacraments. Once, they possessed an incipient belief; but then they began wanting to determine for themselves the limits and attributes of belief. They stepped to one side, became halfhearted and cold; and now the Lord calls them back in stern terms. In relation to Thomas, he represents the position that a priest occupies in relation to a friend when he suddenly has to begin, in God's name, to make demands on him. It seems like a violation of the friendship yet is no such thing; for it leads back to that path which the strayer claims to be on but in truth is not. The Lord tolerates no halfway belief in those who have once believed and lived in grace. He would never treat seekers with a sternness so demanding. But for those from whom he exacts such demands, he simultaneously assumes responsibility. Earlier on, it seemed as if the Lord were diminishing himself, as if he were making concessions to unbelief. But at the moment when everything has been fully readied, the relentlessness of his love clearly emerges, which simply forces one to one's knees.

Inasmuch as the Lord shows Thomas the wounds, he grants him participation in the Cross. It is not as if Thomas were to have to suffer; rather, the Lord draws forth for him, out of the riches of his Cross, the grace of belief. And when it is almost mercilessly said: *Do not be faithless, but believing,* then this is because he draws upon what is innermost within him, his abandonment on the Cross, in order to give Thomas redemptive belief. It is not participation in the way that the women received it earlier: as inclusion in the abandonment itself. Rather, the reverse: as participation in the fruitfulness of the endured suffering. The Lord draws upon the fullness of the suffering that belongs to him alone in order to bring Thomas unfailingly to belief. When the Lord brought men to belief earlier on, it was always by referring, and reverting, back to the Father. Now he can avail himself freely of that which belongs to him (although he has the Father in him and has given everything back to the Father), namely, the proceeds of the accomplished mission. He possesses something like an authority of suffering because, with his taking over the mission, he has relieved the Father of concern about those in need of redemption and does not give them back to the Father again until after the redeeming act. He has authority on the basis of the suffering itself, by virtue of which he has the power both to accept the commission and to give its fruit back to the Father. Here, within a relationship of absolute trust, the Son enjoys independence with respect to the Father.

Be believing! In this statement, so terse and sober, to which nothing more is added, the always-more of belief is perfectly contained. Thus everything goes back to love, a love pertaining to eternal life that is pure opening. From the tiny locus of the proof, which starts with the wounds, the movement widens upward, as if in the shape of a funnel, till it opens into the infinite. The Lord summons Thomas to a movement opposite in nature from that into which Thomas wanted to draw him.

20:28. *Thomas answered him: My Lord and my God!*

In these words, Thomas expresses the whole of his belief. He recognizes the Lord and acknowledges him as his God. He no longer sees any distinction between the Lord before the Cross and after the Cross. He understands that Christ, as he now stands among them, is that Lord to whom he had earlier promised his allegiance. Both are one. At the same time, he knows that the Lord has arisen after having died, and in this Resurrection he glimpses confirmation of something that he already knew before: that the Lord and God are one. A perfect light has sprung up within him, a light that he cannot describe, but that all at once reveals to him the Mystery of the Son and that of the Father. He sees the unity of the Lord with the Father before the Cross, the unity of the Lord with the Father after the Cross, and the unity of the Father in himself as well as the unity of the Son in himself. He sees even himself, too, in this unity. He knows that the Lord belongs to him just as much as he belongs to the Lord. In his overflowing belief, he suddenly gains true insight into the essence of Christian life. Inasmuch as the Father becomes clear to him in the Lord, Christ becomes clear to him in the Lord and in the Father. He views an all-conquering unity. It is as if he were participating in the Resurrection, now, belatedly, after long hesitation, but nevertheless now so fully, so totally, that this Resurrection impels him into belief, and in fact, into the very center of belief and thus of eternal life. He undergoes in himself the utter counter-valuation of all values, the reversal of everything that he has previously experienced. Previously, he had been full of problems, attempts, reflections, initiatives and conditions; and now he experiences what it means to be suddenly thrust, by the Son who contains the Father, into belief. The man that he was before, with all his hesitating, no longer exists; only that one exists whom the Lord has made of him. One to whom nothing else occurs but the exclamation: *My Lord and my God!* One who has come to know unconditional grace. Out of the seeker that he had been has emerged a man redeemed, redeemed not only from sin and stress, but redeemed far more into the fullness of love. Previously, everything proceeded by degrees. Now he experiences it as if in a flash of lightning: The Lord in me must be everything! There is no transitional phase. All that existed before is replaced by an exclusive love of the Lord, to which he cannot adapt but which, instead, adapts him by shaking and stirring him through and through, filling out everything within him. The blind man will remember that he previously did not see; the lame man, that he previously could not use his limbs. From Thomas, by contrast, everything is taken away at once; within a second, he has to come to terms with the new man in whom there is no longer any place for the old and who belongs wholly to the Lord. Thomas goes through something that makes a mockery of all laws of development; he no longer has a past, but now only a future in the Lord. He now has only the Lord. It is more than a fairytale, more than a utopia. It is pure creation.

Thomas at once lays hold of belief, in the same instant that he is redeemed by it. The two embrace each other immediately, without anyone's being able to say that one preceded the other. This belief is so strong that it does not stop at the Lord, who has just redeemed the disciple, but moves on at once to God; and in God, Thomas perceives the Son just as directly as the Father. Never before has a disciple known such a totality as this. In the case of the others, it was always a setting out, a being led higher and farther, an extended process. Here, everything is only a lightning-flash: redemption from sin and initiation into complete belief. All the earlier stages that Thomas went through along with the others no longer exist. He is cast abruptly into the fire, into a fire that is simultaneously everything: the total annihilation of the previous man, the burning love of the Lord, the fruit of the Cross.

20:29. Jesus said to him: Have you believed because you have seen me? Blessed are those who have not seen and yet believe.

The Lord speaks these words not exactly as a reproach; but he cannot allow the fact to go unmentioned that Thomas, in order to arrive at complete belief, has made use of his senses. Even more: that he did not want to risk the leap into complete belief without making his own inquiry, that he desired to exercise control over the leap, that his prior devotedness was one hedged in by conditions, and that, had he kept to his path, he would have had to impose constantly new demands and conditions that depended upon himself. He would have installed himself in a belief that would, in the end, have had its deepest origin and its ultimate rationale in him himself. This belief would have drifted farther and farther away from that of the Lord. With every condition that Thomas had set, he would have stripped something away from the mysteries of the Lord. In the end, he would no longer have accepted anything that transcends and shatters human understanding. It is a characteristic of belief, however, that it often enough does not keep in step with understanding, which is bound by our senses. Both of these, belief and understanding, have a place beside one another and interpenetrate one another; but the final measure of understanding lies with the Lord, not with us. And we should always say at the start what Thomas says in the end: *My Lord and my God!* And only within this unconditional belief attempt to understand that which we are able understand.

Anyone who seeks to understand some person and his statements can start out from his own sensory experiences and perceptions, and use these as a bridge upon which to make his way across to the other. The Lord, however, desires not empathy, but belief. He implants this in us as something initially quite strange to us; understanding comes afterward, and in fact mainly in order that, through our understanding, we can lead our neighbor to where the Lord can once again endow him with primary belief. This we cannot mediate. We can perhaps pass on to another an enthusiasm for something true, beautiful or good; can infect him with our own enthusiasm. In belief, there is no such contagiousness. Through the Lord's grace, we can no doubt lead men toward belief; but on the way, we must grow increasingly more objective and detached, so that what corresponds to "enthusiasm" becomes increasingly a matter between God and the soul itself.

Thomas, then, had he not been called back by the Lord, would have turned further and further away. Grace was required in order to burst open his soul. Grace alone can effect such a bursting, and it does so every time that someone arrives at belief. Prior to that, religion can appear very beautiful, attractive and credible. The transition to belief, however, is a completely new birth, and in that, then, too, a fully new order of knowledge, even if it can justify belief no better afterward than before.

Blessed are those who have not seen and yet believe. They are blessed because openness toward the Holy Spirit is theirs. Those who do not see are, above all, those who *see through:* through the Lord's hands and beyond. Through and beyond to the extent that they no longer need to see the hands themselves. They have no need to produce proof of the Lord's identity: that the Resurrected is the same as the one prior to the suffering; they see through the hands and through the whole Lord to the mission beyond, or more precisely, to the one commissioned: to the unity of Father and Son. This is the work of the Holy Spirit. The Holy Spirit has his ways of bringing them to this point. At some time or other, it becomes clear to a person that everything which he recognizes as good in himself and in others does not stem from finite men. Someone has perhaps given alms, visited a sick person from whom he received no thanks or reward; he has forgone something dear for the sake of another. He knows that all this was not bad, that here something good has been done. But so far removed is he from being able to attribute it to himself that he will, instead, be grateful for it—for example, to the sick person whom he has watched over. A stirring of gratitude arises within him, a stirring of love which is not his own love; and in this stirring his readiness increases, his magnanimity to place himself at the disposal of the good. Within this movement, he becomes quite unimportant to himself. He is opened toward something that he does not know and cannot know, but to which he wants to give himself. This opening, even in someone who does not yet believe, is an effect of the Holy Spirit, who comes into play here with his various gifts and qualities: practical help, consolation, insight, piety. . . . The man who has been touched in such a way no longer sees himself. He is under outside direction. For his part, he sees only the demand and the result, without taking himself into account. He knows: this man here needs to receive alms (not: I must give this man alms); this distraught person must be afforded help; for this prisoner something must be done. In such self-forgetfulness apart from all reflection, the soul encounters the Holy Spirit, and the Holy Spirit leads the soul to the Lord, whereas, before the suffering, the disciples were led to by the Lord to the Holy Spirit. We have understood the Lord, on the basis of his Incarnation, as a man. The Holy Spirit, by contrast, imparts his

longing for belief to us even before we are burst open by belief, by
love, by the vision of the Lord. In this uneasiness of longing, we
recognize that the good transcends individual men. The sick person
whom we have watched over has perhaps died without recognizing
us, and still we are grateful to him for this experience of love: to him
who no longer exists. Such gratitude must therefore be redirected
onward, must be engaged elsewhere; we cannot keep it in ourselves
and for ourselves, lay it up in our souls as a kind of emergency stock
of goodness, be grateful to ourselves for the fact that we are grateful.
There is a residue here that remains unconsumed, and our seeing it is
an effect of the Holy Spirit, who, by opening the soul toward God,
prepares the way for belief. Without the Holy Spirit, all the good
that men do would inevitably lead them to self-deification. But the
Holy Spirit intervenes and makes of this a restlessness that points
toward God.

What takes place here is not without its dangers. The Holy Spirit
tries to gain a hold on the most insignificant element of good in man
so as to burst him open toward God, on the smallest rift in the soul so
as to bring it to the measure of *nonunderstanding* that founds belief.
But in thus furthering the good in man, the Spirit also forces him
into decision. He has to choose between belief and unbelief, Christianity
and godlessness. It is only either through God or through himself
that he can be good. Let us assume that someone has overcome
himself, conquered his flesh, in order to accomplish something spiritual,
to know something other than the law of the flesh. This turning
toward the spirit will be assimilated by the Holy Spirit. Whoever is
guileless will surrender himself to the *Holy* Spirit and effectively give
preference to God over himself. But whoever reflects selfishly will
attempt to interpret the Holy Spirit as his own "higher" spirit.

Whoever arrives at belief through the Lord himself is converted
quite personally: his personal concern is dealt with and put in order.
It is a personal gift. Whoever arrives at belief through the Holy Spirit
conforms in a way to what is required, surrenders all claim to
himself, becomes impersonal in love. Whoever is converted through
the Lord arrives first at the Bridegroom. Whoever comes to belief
through the Spirit encounters first the Bride, the Church; and his
spirit of gratitude, of devotion, is gradually turned into the spirit of

subordination in the Church. Whoever is converted through the Lord belongs to the Lord, and is hence included among the believers of the Lord. Whoever converts through the Spirit belongs among the believers, and thus to the Lord. The paths are different; in their endpoints, they amount to the same. We cannot, then, say that whoever arrives at belief through the Spirit is more blessed than whoever comes to it through the Lord. For in the case of the Lord, too, there is that which is invisible; one can surrender oneself to him, too, without seeing; and thus belief in him, too, is mediated by the Holy Spirit. At bottom, there is but *one* path to belief, whether it starts out from the Son or from the Holy Spirit; for in the Son and his wounds the Spirit exists, who is the one Spirit of the Lord; and in the beggar, the sick man, the prisoner, through whom the Spirit opens us, the Son exists likewise, because he is the Son of Man. Belief is a work of the Trinity, within which the three Persons are active together.

A fullness of possibilities obtains because the Lord never wishes to coerce, but always allows the freedom to take any good path. He throws open God's riches and leaves the choice to us. Even in heaven, each will be granted his own special preference. Thus we are free to let ourselves be led more through the Spirit to the Son or more through the Son to the Spirit. Thus, within the Church, there is sustenance through the Eucharist, through worship, through God's word, through contemplation and through brotherly love. All the paths lead to one another, each path is good insofar as it remains within the unity; for in the unity they all lead to the same endpoint. And the situation is similar for the paths to belief.

Blessed, then, is he who accepts what is offered to him. That means to believe: to allow the act of belief to be accomplished in him through the Lord in the Spirit. To pronounce the short Yes of acceptance, which is an echo of the Lord's Yes and is expanded by the Lord into his Yes. That means to believe without seeing: to forgo life in this world in order to be open to the beyond. To believe seeingly means: to adapt the beyond to life in this world. To believe unseeingly: to adapt life in this world to the beyond, where to believe will be to see. To believe unseeingly means: to forgo one's own eyes in order to see with the eyes of God, of the Lord, of the

Holy Spirit, of belief, love and hope. That was the belief of the Mother. She was so devoted to belief, so much the mere handmaid, that she had already forgone herself before she uttered her word of affirmation, because she possessed in herself room for the whole of belief. She was already pure, set out like an open bowl, placed at the service of what is to come. Thus she received, at one and the same time, the Lord and the Holy Spirit. No sooner had the Holy Spirit overshadowed her than the Son was also already in her. In her unconditional Yes apart from seeing, she was immediately a vessel for the whole of belief. She immediately gave up the whole of her life in this world for that of the beyond, and yet she is wholly human and not spirit: the perfect creature in the service of belief. She arrived at the Son through the Holy Spirit, but also at the Holy Spirit through the Son; for Father and Son together send the Spirit into the Mother. And for the sake of the sacrifice on the Cross, she is pure and has the readiness to receive the Spirit and the Son. In the inseparability of Spirit and Son—and most perfectly in the Mother—the nature of the mode of belief that does not see, and why it is blessed, becomes manifest.

SCRIPTURE AND TRADITION

20:30. *Now Jesus did many other signs in the presence of the disciples, which are not written in this book;...*

John has seen other miracles which he does not recount in detail but mentions only as a totality. He would shrink back from resolving the Lord's greatness into individual components and defining it. The Lord has performed all his miracles out of love; he has done them for the Father and in the Father, so as to lighten the work of redemption, so as to make men realize that something more than human is taking place here. John dispenses with detailed enumeration because he would like to let all these miracles blend into the light of the one miracle of the life of the Lord. For John, the absolute miracle is that the Son has come into the world as a man, has shared in our life, has done everything to show us that the Father deemed it not unbefitting to allow his Son to live as a man among men. The whole existence of the Lord is a work of unmediated love. The miracles of the Lord prove only this: that the Lord performs them in pure love, knows nothing other than love. If the evangelist wanted to attempt comprehensiveness, to recount one miracle after the other in order, so to speak, to cut facets onto the gem of that love, he would thereby only divert our gaze from what is essential. On the contrary, however, he wishes to direct light into the burning core of the love, into the core of cores of that love, into the love between Father and Son. He does not wish to stimulate our understanding, but to allow the words that the Lord addressed to Thomas to shine forth in this love. He is so overwhelmed by the love that he can by no means go on to relate more. It takes his breath away. *Now Jesus did many other signs* means nothing other than that he was love, pure love. It is as if the apostle stood in the midst of the love of the Father for the Son, of the Son for the Father. In his report, he has attempted to step back and recount things from a distance. He knew how inadequate everything remained; but he still had to try to impart color to the miracle, and form and life. Now he gives up. He can go no further. It is as if, in the innermost flame, he were able to utter only this sentence, which is meant to summarize everything unsaid. He has attempted to render objectively something supremely subjective. Now he renders subjectively something supremely objective. So subjectively that he cannot even speak anymore. He is like someone who, in the midst of telling a story, suddenly breaks into tears because everything comes much too alive to be describable in words. The helplessness of this sentence shows how naked the apostle stands before us.

Which are not written in this book. The book is an attempt by the apostle to provide a reflected image of what he has experienced. He has endeavored to diminish and also to magnify that which has, from all directions, drawn him into the speechless vortex of love. To diminish it inasmuch as, in each instance, he rendered only a few of the Lord's words, thereby allowing all the concrete circumstances to go almost wholly unnoted. He has barely described, almost only sketched, some particular situation or other in the life of the Lord in order that this might give rise to a situation for the reader. He has presented men of every state—including every state of sin, every state of love, of belief, of susceptibility to appeal—in encounter with the Lord. He has addressed himself to all whom he has acknowledged in the Lord's Prayer as his neighbors, and in every case, even when the portrayal was quite plain and unpretentious in its initial tenor, he tried to take, together with the reader and listener, the leap into the Lord's love. He always went along himself. He was the exemplification of what the Lord does in relation to God: he supplemented things through his love. God covers us with his love, he sees us in the Son's love that rounds us out. John loves the reader as his neighbor, appeals to him in the prayer of love, and arouses in him the desire to believe within love. He attempts to transform the unbelievers that we are into believers by showing us the Lord as *the* love while at the same time accompanying us with his own love as we move toward the Lord. Together with his objective message, he simultaneously gives each one something of himself to take along with him. Something that protects us, something that, as it were, softens the impact of the encounter. He does not interpose himself between the Lord's love and us, he only accompanies us on the way toward that love; by instilling a longing for the Lord in us, he also instills in us something of himself. In this lies the adaptiveness of John, his diminishment. It is an expression of his love that, in each instance, he begins quite simply, at some point where everyone can follow him, but then goes on to execute, in love, the whole leap between his starting point and the sudden disclosure.

At the same time, however, he magnifies, because he wants to take our love into account. He becomes a consummate bearer of the Lord's word. He leaves no room for mediocrity. He does not allow the response to be any other than his: a response of love. At first, he places himself in our position and, from that standpoint, shows us the beauty of the Lord; but as soon as we have responded in some way, begun to smile and to feel comfortable, he desires but one thing: that the Lord should draw us wholly into the fire. In his exposition, he shows that we do nothing, that the Lord does everything, that we are inundated with grace. But then he interjects: "*hence* we, too, must . . . !" He lives so much in God's love that he shows us what it means to live in the Lord's love. As little as the Lord can bear halfheartedness, so little can John. John the man is no attenuation of the Lord's love. He absorbs it as completely as possible, until what he radiates is no longer his own love, but really the love of the Lord.

The miracles were performed by the Lord *in the presence of the disciples.* He has, then, allowed them to participate in his miracles. There is a way of participating in the Lord solely through one's eyes, solely through one's being present. That is a mystery of the Church and the hierarchy. The situation is certainly not such that grace, too, increases in line with increasing levels of the hierarchy. But there is a grace that inheres in office. It belongs to office because it is intended to be mediated by office. Now, if the disciples had witnessed only a very few miracles, then they would have remained arrested by them as if by particular wonders. But since they have seen their fullness, they know that the sum of miracles constitutes the miracle of the Lord, and vice versa. As founders of the future hierarchy, they are to have these riches at their disposal. The Lord does not wish his Church to begin in neediness. He gives this wealth of grace, which lies concealed in the seeing of the miracles, to her as a dowry. Thus the foundation of *tradition* is also laid, as the living interpretation of Christ and explication of what is firmly established. Just as a teacher who instructs small children must possess a proper education in order to be able to give even the simplest answers, so the Church, from the very start, must have much more at her disposal than what she has to teach.

The individual miracles function here like the application of a basic principle, like its concretization: the miracle of miracles remains God and the Incarnation. But we would not understand it if it were not explicated for us, brought home to us. Through the individual miracles, we begin to understand. To be sure, as particularities, they divert our attention, but only in order to lead it back to the miracle in general. The miracles do not merely mount up to more and more; they raise themselves, as it were, to a higher and higher power, until nothing is left but the miracle: that God offers up his Son in love. This wealth of miracles is to be received by the apostles.

From out of this superabundance, however, also flows everything that is living interpretation of the Lord's activity in the Church: the sacramentals, the blessings that she dispenses, the repetition of gestures made by the Lord that the apostles have witnessed and remembered: how he walked through the fields, the nature of his bearing when receiving people, how he blessed children, consecrated the elements—a profusion of imponderables that are both ineffable and yet constitutive of the most living life. Also the profusion of everything that he did in freedom and left up to free choice without wanting to establish it as dogma. Inasmuch as he did it, he gave the Church permission to manage it further, to cultivate and regulate it. He committed to her the Kingdom of piety. It stems from the Lord, but it is structured by the disciples. They interpret things, they adapt things, always with a view to the Lord, whom they saw alive. In this is contained the Catholic. The Church is no religion of pure spirit, of dogmatic speculation. She is the Church of the Incarnated God. In every direction, she forges links to the perceptible and the everyday. The whole of our earthly life is to be touched by God through the Church, not the slightest thing may escape this touch; everything in our existence is to be brought before the Lord. A Catholic loves it when one blesses, when one consecrates earthly things, prays also for earthly things, lights candles in churches, donates money, makes pilgrimages and places holy water on burial places. . . . In a naïve purity, the Church is a unity of flesh and spirit. All the miracles of the Lord are performed before our eyes. We are affected on all sides. Everything takes place within a human atmosphere. Christianity is no mere teaching such as could have its place in a book; for in everything, man is to be drawn into the sphere of the miracle. In this sphere is lived the everyday life of the parish. It is not irreverent if, in many localities, mothers suckle their infants in churches; for Mary, too, suckled her Son while in prayer. Everywhere, the Church struggles against pure spirit. Everything in her overflows the literary, overflows that which *is written in this book.*

20:31. *. . . but these are written that you may believe that Jesus is the Christ, the Son of God, and that believing you may have life in his name.*

What is written is now directly contrasted with the life of the Lord. There exist, in clear differentiation, the two ways: the way of Scripture and the way of the Lord's life; both have the power of leading to eternal life. The Lord has lived as man and as God in the unity of his mission, and he has handed this mission of bearing witness unbrokenly on to the disciples. These have been charged by the Lord with the mission of writing. It was by no means left open to them either to write or not to write. Their activity is included in the Son's mission; their human contribution is at first a negligible one, which comes alive in a new way only within the divine mission.

Initially, the idea seems feasible that the Lord could have been able to perform his deeds and miracles simply *in the presence* of men, without their being written down. His mission could then have been passed on through the spoken word. But much would have become lost on the way. Over time, only a few sketchy outlines, some basic abstract principles, would still have survived; for men always tend to simplify. Therefore, he entrusted the whole of his perceptible mission to the evangelists, with the commission to write things down exactly as they had comprehended them. And just as the Son, in his mission, can never stray from the Father because he is without sin, so he has conferred on the evangelists the privilege of never being able, within their mission, to fall away from the center of that mission. He entrusted them with his mission in order that they communicate it. The personal coloring of the Gospels, however, is required by the

Lord precisely so as to exhibit, through the distinctiveness of each, the unfolding of his own plenitude. John, who reveals the Lord most directly, has the most pronounced individuality. But the differences between one Gospel and another are there only in order to indicate the fullness of possible ways of interpreting the Word of God.

The Lord desires that the evangelists should render objectively that which is objective in what they have experienced. They therefore transmit much that they do not themselves comprehend, whose depths they do not fathom, and they well know that they are transmitting more than they know. They transmit it, however— in a way befitting men—as intermixed with their own experience, or, so to speak, as a kind of "instructions for use". But one thing is strictly forbidden them (something that many preachers do with the word of God): they are not allowed to bring in ideas of their own, to indulge in paraphrase. They must hold totally to the Lord. And the Lord himself guarantees the inviolability of their mission. It was not possible that an apostle received a commission to write and that he might not have written or might have written something that did not lie within his commission.

The disciples had the good fortune to live with the Lord. But because the Lord handed over to them his entire mission, no one who was born later is entitled to complain. Things are not more difficult for us than for them. Anyone who will not believe on the basis of the Gospels would also not have believed if he were standing before the Lord.

But the Lord does not confine the evangelists to reporting only on his great mission. He also has them record a number of historical details that can still be authenticated today. He allows himself to be situated in space and time, among the people of his time, the places, the customs, the politics of his time. By creating this tension between the beyond and this world, he stimulates, so to speak, the interest of researchers, harnesses the attentiveness of the unbelieving world as well. The unbelieving scholar who studies the Gospels will find something or other in them that he cannot deny. A situation will become intelligible to him, an outline of truth will present itself, an impression, like a negative of the life of the Lord; his footprints in the history of mankind. The Lord desires that this verifiability of his earthly life should be available. No matter how much unbelief may carp about the Gospels and attempt to correct them, what is essential in them will prove unexpungeable.

The evangelists present only a selection. But in this selection must inhere, by virtue of the Lord's mission, the possibility that *every person* can feel himself included. If he does not, perhaps, recognize himself in the Samaritan, then he will recognize himself in the blind man, or in the centurion, or in the disciples during the storm at sea. . . . The force of the Gospels penetrates into every human life. It is unbroken because it is in no way exhaustible. It stands outside the laws of historical cause and effect. It grants men the need to recognize themselves in it.

In Scripture, the Lord constantly tells of his love for the Father. The disciples could not render this love if they had not themselves clearly experienced it. Their testimony must be a testimony of love. Above all a testimony to the love that the Lord had for them, and yet also a testimony of their own love for the Lord. This love becomes most visible in John, but it is not missing anywhere in the Gospels. Now, throughout Scripture, the vitality with which the Lord loved his disciples and which was an expression of his living love of the Father is vividly retained because the situation that is described remains always the same: the Son of God offers his love to men. The "immortal tales" of literature have a meaning for us only if we find ourselves in a mood or situation that makes us responsive to them. The Lord desires, however, that we should always be in the frame of mind that will enable his stories to speak to us: in the frame of mind of a sinner before the Redeemer, who is telling him of the Father's love. This tale is no merely one-time phenomenon like other tales, by which one is fully affected just once and then, at best, in one pleasing repetition. The Gospel always retains its full force and relevance. One can never say that one is no longer the blind man who sits begging at the temple, or the female disciple who listens to the words of the Lord. The compellingness of the encounter would always have to persist here, and it *can* do so as well, because in the Gospel everything comes from the Lord.

It is impossible for a person not to be affected by the Gospel. Since the entire mission of the Lord is contained in it, a commission to every man is also contained in it; involuntarily, every man is called to account through Scripture. Reading Scripture forces one, sooner or later, to come to a decision. One must identify oneself. It takes hold even of those who open the book for some quite worldly reason and begin to read it. They are touched by the fire of the Lord. They no longer belong to the unsuspecting. They have been "enlightened". A girl can excuse herself and say that she had no idea of the consequences of her yielding; but that is of no use to her: the consequences are nevertheless there. One cannot remain without response to the Gospel no matter how removed in time one is from the Lord when one reads it.

Just as the situation at that time was always constituted by two parties—the Lord and some other, who becomes the occasion for him to discourse on the love between Father and Son—so it is, too, in the Gospels. In them, the Lord and the respective evangelist always work together. The evangelists are priests. Those among the disciples of the Lord who are only priests and not evangelists must draw, for their apostolate, upon the same source as the evangelists. Even if they do not possess the mission of writing, their mission of assimilating is nevertheless the same: they draw upon the same substance and transmit the same. Thus, from the very first, both missions stand counterposed: the mission to record things in writing for those who come later, and the mission, without writing, to transmit the content of what is written. The source of both is the same, and thus both must necessarily harmonize. If Thomas tells his listeners what he knows and has experienced of the Lord, then his account must be identical with what can be read in the Gospel. He is quite at liberty to give things a different emphasis now and again, to recount in detail something that was summarized, to treat summarily something that was set out in detail; the substance, however, which stems from the Lord, must appear in his account in such a way as to correspond precisely to what can be found in the Gospel. But what applies to those apostles who have not written also applies to every priest who comes later. The first thing required of him is that his preaching should correspond precisely to that of the Gospel. He is not permitted to release himself from the totality in the way that heretics do. He may add nothing that he has freely contrived, reconstruct nothing in line with his own subjectivity. Any priest who did not derive the standard for his preaching from the Gospel would, for that reason alone, be a bad priest. The Gospel is the substance of the life of the Lord, and this alone should and must be communicated. He should transmit only the living presence of the Lord. Anything that a priest does, says or writes must reflect in some way the essence of the Lord. He cannot allow himself anything that would stand completely apart from the Lord's life. Ultimately, all of Christian life, too, is nothing other than a commission to bear witness to the Lord, even in the world, in the worldliest calling. Just as the evangelists had to give their testimony through their writings, so every Christian must, albeit in another sort of writing, bear witness to the essence of the Lord. His life is subject to the same law as is the Gospel; only the alphabet in which the life of the Lord is written here is the alphabet of life. Every Christian life is like a prolongation of the mission that the Lord gave to the evangelists, namely, to set his life down in writing. The particular way in which man accords with this mission—whether he turns his attention more toward men in order to lead them to the Lord, or whether he goes first to the Lord in order to proceed on to men together with him—is something secondary, as long as in every life the movement toward the Lord ensues.

The commission to promote this movement is issued to all: to priests, to laymen, to everyone whom the Lord calls and to whom he allocates his mission. And in the end, mission and Eucharist are the same movement: the Father separates himself within the mission from the Son, he sends us the Son as food that comes down from heaven, and the Son distributes himself as bread throughout the world. But just as boundlessly as his flesh, he also distributes his mission, which he has received from the Father and which is the content of the Gospel. The same vitality is characteristic of both. The disciples lived so much in grace that full correspondence between the Gospel and their mission was a matter of course for them. The more widely the mission is distributed, however, so much the more must Christians take care to ensure that, at any given time, they still stand within it. What serves them as a criterion for this test is the perfect mission—as perfect as men are at all capable of performing—the Gospel. If a Christian in parish office would like to do the Lord's will and also has some knowledge of the Lord, he could easily become unsure about whether he still stands within the mission. But he possesses a touchstone: he should look to whether he is the one who encounters the Lord in the Gospel, namely, the sinner, the blind man, the sick man . . ., and whether, in these stories, he actually encounters the *Lord*. This test on the part of the individual does not hinder the Church herself, insofar as she has office, from interpreting the evangelical mission of the individual. He is not permitted to move inordinately into the subjective. Every mission is Catholic and remains Catholic. Many a sect attempts to live according to the Gospel, but because it lacks office, it ultimately works out for itself a gospel according to what it thinks best. And only from the center of sacramental life outward is one able to inquire and decide. If a Christian's sacramental life is in order, then his mission will also be in order. There might be a danger that one could become falsely enraptured with something mysterious in the Gospel. That would, however, be prevented through correct reception of the sacraments.

That you may believe that Jesus is the Christ, the Son of God, and that believing you may have life in his name. For anyone who reads the Gospel, there can be no doubt that the Lord is really the Christ and that through his arrival on earth a promise has been fulfilled in the sense of a real conclusion. The movement of the Son away from the Father and back to the Father is eternal, but the sojourn of the Lord as a man on earth is a closed episode. There is thus no question of our once again expecting the birth of the Son or of his sufferings once again becoming necessary. He is the promised one, in a finitely self-contained mission, which nevertheless, in eternity, does not lie behind us. A single link in the chain has become visible; the whole chain lies within the invisible-eternal.

What we were given to see remains alive in the Gospel, so alive that it provides us with the basic substance for everything that we are still to be given to see, and that it contains all the demands that the Lord can place upon us. All these demands, numerous and unlimited though they seem to be, nevertheless always issue in the commandment to love. This, however, is a commandment that never admits of being regarded as self-contained; it is constantly open in both directions: toward man and toward God. It affords us an insight, at one and the same time, both into the image of our neighbor and into the image of the Lord. But this insight never becomes a static image; rather, if it is true and mediates truth, it remains movement, and this movement it draws from trinitarian life. The Son is *the Christ* because he is One of the Trinity, and must embody the entire Trinity for us and bring it closer to us. Thus it is that cessation nowhere occurs; any cessation would be estrangement, not relaxation, not rest. Belief, as the state of having one's own life taken up into the Trinity, is at bottom never a fact that one can regard as established or concluded; rather, it is always and forever mediated by the Gospel, which derives its life here from the life of the Lord. To believe means to be willing to share in the trinitarian process. One can know nothing in belief without committing oneself to this.

The mission is distributed eucharistically, that is, within the conferral of the Lord himself, which means, in turn, the conferral of trinitarian life. If *Jesus* is the Christ, as is laid down in Scripture, then anyone who sees and believes this must participate in trinitarian life. It is no longer merely the movement of the Lord as a man through which one is turned in the direction of God. Initially, no doubt, the common basis of the human encounter with the Lord remains. But this section of the path, which appears so understandable, also begins to trail off here: into the Trinity, which we no longer understand. Much of the earthly visibility of the Lord was a concession of the Trinity to us. Christ became visible because he is the Son; it is not, however, because we know what a son and a father are that he is the Son, but rather, he is the Son in his deepest origins. And the love that binds him to God is the love of God the Son for God the Father. In this, it possesses, from time immemorial, a character that is related to what we call love, we creatures and sinners. And since it lay in the trinitarian decision that men were to be brought home, were to be given a share in eternal life, in the movement of the Trinity, then—if men were at all to understand what sort of offer was being made to them—something comprehensible to them had to take place. By some sort of word, movement or demand, they had to be reminded of something for which they would discover, somewhere in their innermost selves, a counterpart, a response. That lay in love. Love is a reality in us. None of us can say that he does not know what love is, that he cannot recall having ever encountered love, having ever thought about love. And this thing that we know is what the Lord lives out before us. In him there is both: the life of the Trinity that is incomprehensible to us, and this loving sojourn among us, neighborly, poor and needy, brought up by a mother, cared for by a foster-father, surrounded by disciples whom he loves and who love him. We understand all that; it does not leave us apathetic, for it is, after all, one of us who accomplishes, through means familiar to us, what we understand, sanction and admire. Thus the Lord links up with men in order to draw them over into trinitarian life.

He is the Son of God. Inasmuch as we know *that Jesus is the Christ,* we also immediately recognize in him the *Son of God.* And inasmuch as we know that he is in the world as our brother and yet is the Son of God, we know beyond doubt that we must be children of God. Thus we know that recognition of what he is implicitly contains the absolute demand for us to be that which we are in his eyes: his brethren, the Father's children. It is not a choice that we are free to make; we cannot assume the one thing and then act as if the other had nothing to do with us. Acknowledgment of the first means being unconditionally and totally subject to the second. It is a demand that we cannot review and define, which does not find its fulfilment in terms measurable by us; it is a demand that simultaneously means unconditional fulfilment. If the Lord is the Son of God, then we are also children of God.

Anyone who wanted to deny this would want to prevent the Lord from being his brother. He would want to prevent Redemption and the Cross. He would want to hinder the Truth from coming into the world. If all that is prevented, then it is also not true; then the Lord has lied. Then I am right and do not need to believe. But there is one place that the rebellious ego cannot reach: the relation of the Father to the Son in heaven. The decision was taken there without men's having been consulted, and in what was decided between Father and Son, in this reciprocal love, the redemption of the world was from all time implicit—so implicit that I, with my personal, divergent truth do not advance toward, do not arrive at, do not penetrate into the shrine of divine truth. Hence, from primordial times, the power not to be children of God, the power to prevent the

Lord's being related to them as brother and to the Father as Son, has been denied those who are predestined to redemption. No matter how much they try to present themselves as laying claim such power, they do not possess it. That they do not possess it is the greatest gift that Father and Son, in the Son's mission, have given them. Inasmuch as they have denied them this power (which would only be powerlessness), they have saved them and given them in its place divine power, which is a power of truth.

And that believing you may have life in his name. One can have life only believingly and only in his name. What we would regard as life if we did not believe and were not in his name would be, at best, a succession of vital functions whose common element would lie in the fact that they would all have death in them. In belief, however, and in his name, we live. Death is not only alien to belief and his name, but contrary to them. Both belief and the name of the Lord are open-ended progressions in God. Both leave death far behind them in order to strive more and more vigorously toward God, to turn more and more fully toward his life. Belief is contained in the name of the Son. Belief is the living principle, the core of love and hope, the seed that sprouts and grows toward God. One could almost say: it is the flower and God, the root. As soon as one understands that the origin lies not behind us but before us, that we strive toward the origin from which we stem, one has also grasped that life in belief is the opposite of earthly life: earthly life proceeds toward an end, life in God toward the beginning. That is the meaning of Scripture: to turn us toward the beginning. Earthly life is life that grows old. Eternal life is eternal rejuvenation because, in it, one becomes increasingly a child of God, until ultimately the whole weight of our existence lies no longer in our beginning, but in the eternal beginning of God. Earthly life advances up to a certain point, toward a climax, in order to go into decline again, to live from memories. In God, there is no zenith of love, but only an eternally more.

THE BARK OF PETER

21:1. *After this Jesus revealed himself again to the disciples by the Sea of Tiberias; and he revealed himself in this way.*

John starts off once again. He shows by this that he is a real human being: a human being involved in striving, a human being who never has enough. Although he had previously concluded his accounts of miracles in the belief that he had said all that was necessary, and had finally tied everything together in a summary knot, he begins once again with an account of a manifestation of the Lord. He wants to round things out. He fears that he has perhaps still kept too much of what he knows to himself. His love would like to give everything.

That the Lord reveals himself *to the disciples* contains a mystery of all subsequent manifestations of the Lord in the Church. He shows himself to those who love. He chooses for his appearance the place where his believers, his disciples, are present. In these manifestations after his Resurrection, the natural and the supernatural occur side by side, but in such a way that the supernatural predominates, just as, in the visibility of the Lord prior to the Cross, the natural predominated.

He revealed himself in this way. Whoever loves someone is interested in the smallest details of that person's life. He can never get enough of experiencing everything. Where someone else sees only one case among a thousand, love recognizes something unique. It regards it in the light of love, of individuality. Thus it is when we regard the life of the Lord in belief: everything becomes significant to us, the smallest actions — for instance, between Mother and Child — become important to us. And this is so not on the basis of natural sympathy with the Lord, but on the basis of belief, which is supernatural illumination of his supernatural mystery.

All the stories about his life before the Cross were simultaneously natural and supernatural; and if we had lived at that time and possessed loving belief, we would have seen them in a light that would have shown us their inner infinitude. But we would still have had to gain access to the supernatural through the natural. Now, the

Lord has concluded his earthly mission; we can therefore no longer observe him within his unfolding earthly mission. We see him now only in belief, quite as the real Lord, not merely as a vision; we see him no longer as facing heavenward from earth but earthward from heaven, and thus solely in belief.

He appears to the believer. That means there, where there is already movement toward God, and this movement he increases. Where believers are gathered together in his love—that is his place. He appears as coming from the Cross. Hence, with his solitude behind him. Were he to appear to those who do not have love, then he would appear to solitude, move into solitude and, with that, once again toward the Cross. But this lies behind him. Thus he appears only where there is love, in order to nourish it further and to take it with him to the Father.

The appearance is real, not visionary. But since it is still precisely to believers that he appears, he thus lays the foundation for later visionary appearances, and, in fact, for visions in which a commission is conferred. Now, he always appears for the purpose of accomplishing something, of furthering, of bestowing. This will repeat itself throughout the course of the ecclesiastical period. He always appears within a two-sided relationship. So, too, the conversations that are conducted in these appearances are of a totally different kind from the Lord's conversations prior to the Cross. They are no longer one-sided talks by the Lord that often seem almost like monologues, but true conversations in which the participants share through the grace of the Resurrection and the Holy Spirit. In each particular case, then, they amount to a prayer together with its fulfilment. So it was for Magdalen; so it will be again for Peter. The disciples seek and find the Lord within belief; they are thus, at any given time, already in conversation with the Lord. That is the thing which will live on in the Church. It is confirmed, on the one hand, in the behavior of priests and believers and, on the other, in the behavior of believers in relation to unbelievers. The instruction given before baptism is quite different from the guidance after baptism. The former remains a one-sided preparation, the latter is always a two-sided process. In relation to unbelievers, the Church always maintains her reserve. She cannot speak with them about her innermost mysteries. No real conversation comes about. There are forms of the Lord's manifestation that a Christian does not share with an outsider: for example, the Eucharist. To administer Communion to him would mean degrading the Lord, because one would expect from him a form of surrender that can only be two-sided. And one would only bar the way to the Lord for the unbeliever; for he must first learn to know the supernatural Lord in love. Everything that binds him to the bodily, historical manifestation of the Lord must first be transformed into the supernatural. Whoever allows a man to approach the Lord with his own earthly standards, instead of with those of belief and love, blocks the way to the Lord for him.

In this way the Lord appears: as concrete presence, as vision in belief, as purpose and commission, as prayer. All these appearances in belief have as their basis the positing of life, regardless in which form. In this, believers must only render him the service of standing receptively before him, of accepting him, which means simply: of believing. He became a man in order to communicate himself to men. This communication always remains, even when he returns to the Father, a communication on earth. What he did and said at that time on earth—that remains. Ever since he has been present in the form of the Eucharist, however, he stands not merely as a man before other men, but as someone who wishes to be accepted by them. He has placed himself like a nonentity in their hands so that they might permit him to be God again in themselves. He advises them to keep the belief and love which he came to bring so alive that he can return to earth again at any time, that he can change earth into heaven. To allow belief to wane so little that it should not be exhausted until the whole world has become Christian. The Lord left twelve apostles behind, imbuing them with belief and giving them the commission to convert the entire world. He wants no figures, no statistics. But he wants them to allow the love that he brought them to go on being fruitful until it returns to God. Individual successes can perhaps be measured externally, but love, which is infinite, can never be. One cannot say, after one has converted six people, that one has half of the Lord's love. His whole love lives in believers, and with that, his whole commission is also conferred on them. In this bestowal of commission lies proof that he loves us *totally*. He would have loved us less if he had accomplished everything himself, for then we would not have had the opportunity of proving our love to him. In the Lord's commission, however, we live inwardly in love, and therefore he appears solely to believers within this love and this commission. Love wants to grow and effect actions. The highest thing for the Lord is to bring something to the Father, and this highest thing he shares with us. He does this in a supernatural way, namely, by depriving us of the ability to oversee and measure deeds and successes, and that is the way in which he reveals himself.

21:2. *Simon Peter, Thomas called the Twin, Nathanael of Cana in Galilee, the sons of Zebedee and two others of his disciples were together.*

A number of the Lord's disciples are together. The first named is Peter, immediately presented in a kind of contrasting relation to Thomas. Peter, who denied before the Cross, is opposed to Thomas, who doubted afterward. They stand there as two regenerates, those who have arrived at full love only by circuitous routes. Peter is named first because the Church will play a special role in this scene. He is given precedence as the representative of office. Of the rest, some are also identified by name while others are submerged in anonymity because, although their office and love were known to the participants, they become anonymous for the Church as a whole. For the participants, they have just as clear and precisely formulated a commission as the others. For the Church, they embody, so to speak, alongside the officially prominent Peter, those who, in their name-lessness, were alive at that time. Those identified by name are, so to speak, the ones upon whom the others lean for support. Those who have sinned by no means appear in a bad light. They are redeemed. They exist so much in the Lord's love that they are not at all in arrears. Thomas, for example, has made confession before his friends; he stands before them as wholly open, and this openness implies not the slightest inhibitedness between him and the others. The actual truth never comes between men so as to estrange them from one another. It does not occur to the others to look down upon Thomas, for they, too, have been enriched through Thomas' absolution. They all live from the same divine grace, from the same treasure-store of the Church. Together, they form the one Church of the Lord, which has many members: those that stand in bright light and those that stand less in the light, the clever and the simpleminded, sinners and saints.

21:3. Simon Peter said to them: I am going fishing. They said to him: We will go with you. They went out and got into the boat; but that night they caught nothing.

The stimulus comes from Simon Peter, the head. He wants to go fishing. He thinks of fish; John, who is describing the scene, already sees this as implying men. Everything that Peter does he does in the name of his office; everything that the Church seeks and effects has some relation to the work of the Lord. In the work of the apostle, there is no ultimate separation between external and internal activity. Even when he works in his own name, he can do nothing other than work in the name of the Lord.

Peter does not invite the others to go with him. They know, however, that they are not only welcome to go along, but even have a duty to do so. As long as a mission has not been demarcated more specifically, it must be carried out within the framework of the Church as a whole. Whatever the Church does in general must also be done by the individual. If the Church celebrates Easter, then the Christian celebrates it, too; at the hour when the Church celebrates Mass, the Christian is also found in attendance. Everything that belongs to the total picture of ecclesiastical life makes its claim on the individual, even if that claim is not directed at him in a personal way. It could be that Peter wanted to arrange things differently, but since he does not do so, the others go along with him. Here, fishing stands for every sort of ecclesiastical activity: for action, prayer and contemplation, for the business of casting out and pulling in under commission from God.

The others go along without asking where they are going. They stand within an obedience that is given no special emphasis because it is a matter of course. And although they stand in obedience to Peter, this obedience is nevertheless handled in such a way that they feel themselves primarily obedient to the Lord. They know that the ties uniting them to Peter are the same that bind them to the Lord. They know that all of them form a unity in the Lord, and that, within this unity, there must be order. This order poses no "problem" for them at all, not only because their numbers are still few, but mainly because the Lord dwells among them. Because the Lord is totally alive in them and they therefore have the opportunity to inquire, at any time, whether they are acting within his commission. This inquiry has nothing rigorous about it, nor does it imply anything embarrassing; a glance at the Lord is enough to let them know whether they are in accord with their commission. To be sure, they still remain sinners, but they are much more those who have been commissioned. They live in love. They do not ask themselves how much the Lord is giving them and how much they are giving him. They know only that they have received a clear request to live in his love, while their own love will always be only a striving toward his. But this love is so fresh and living that it is fully at one with obedience. They are like children who were never disobedient because it never entered their heads to be so. That is true freedom. In this obedience, they have freed themselves of everything that could block their path to the Lord. It is a naïve obedience that consists entirely of love. One cannot increase the love of those who obey by imposing a cleverly devised system of obedience. Rather, one must live in fully naïve love in order to be able to obey completely. Love obeys wholly of itself. At the beginning of many religious orders in which obedience has become a cleverly devised system, love was originally present, and obedience was then a fully naïve consequence. Still, it is difficult, after centuries, to reestablish the initial freshness and naïveté. So it is, too, in the Church as a whole. And yet, today just as then, we have the opportunity to have the Lord among us, in the full naïveté of our obedience, if only we want to.

They went out and got into the boat. They go out into something new. That new thing is unknown to them, but they approach it in unity, in the will of the Lord, in obedience and love. They entrust themselves to the Lord's will; they will do what is demanded of them without knowing how great or how small what is to come will be. They step out of a situation that is clear and into a new one, but not without first having inquired. Because they are in obedience, they do what the Lord expects of them; they do it simply, through the movements and means of everyday life.

That is the timeless situation of saying Yes to the Lord. The Mother was able to say Yes once and for all because she was in order before God. After it was spoken, God took over total responsibility for her life. If she had not been so perfect in love, her word of affirmation would have remained only external, and internally a No would have been present somewhere. As she who is wholly pure, however, she can speak the wholly pure word of affirmation. The disciples, who are setting out to fulfill their mission, have to be in love; they have to be settled, ordered. Otherwise, one cannot *get into* any mission of the Lord. For one would then surely do something that is not required of one. This applies to all who come later and have a mission. They must stand at the center of their commission and must, in addition, be in order: the eye of their purposiveness must be focused purely upon the Lord. Anyone who possesses a specialized mission may perhaps recognize it quite well initially; he could, however, still fall away from it if he began to perform it mechanically; the work would remain, externally, a "work of God", but the man would no longer be thinking of the Lord. He would be doing a work of his own and no longer that which the Lord had originally envisaged. Before the disciples get in, they see that all is in order and that the coming work lies in the Lord. But this knowledge must accompany the whole of their activity. The Lord's catching fish must not gradually turn into their catching fish. This applies as well to all who have a quite ordinary mission in the parish. Things are easier for them; they are not specifically required to get into the boat and sail away. They can simply live within the sphere of the Church. But they, too, are constantly threatened by the danger of Pharisaical confusion, the danger of settling comfortably down into becoming a mechanical Christ. There is something in the constitution of the Church that contributes to this danger. The only non-Pharisee has always been the Lord.

The Lord himself allocated only a number of specialized missions. His other disciples had to symbolize the communion. At the time of the apostles, however, specialized missions were always predominant. Today, their comparative number has become much smaller. Not because the Lord commissions less, but because we pay less attention to mission—we, the communion of believers, and we, the ones who are called. The average Christian considers himself lucky if he is left in peace and spared any special missions. Many knew once that a call had been made. But they found it more comfortable not to hear it. Thus, many are in disobedience. Perhaps, in their youth, they had heard the call, but then they drowned everything out until, in the end, they smile about those who are called. And perhaps they do all that they can to render other calls from the Lord inaudible. They cannot bear it when the disciples who go fishing with Peter want to establish full orderedness, to stand as wholly transparent before the Lord and place themselves wholly at the service of what God determines. If they once make an attempt to learn his will, they immediately wrap their soul in a multitude of veils so that his glance might not fall upon it. And yet, how easy this would be: instead of posing endless questions about God's will, instead of searching one's conscience in a complicated way, simply to open and offer oneself: *I am going fishing. We will go with you.* Simply to do that whose essence corresponds to the essence of the Lord's mission. We at one with the Church, and the Church at one with the Lord.

The disciples know that what is involved is a fishing expedition. But they do less planning than Peter, who bears all the responsibility. Like him, they know the worries of a fisherman; yet they leave it to him to direct and supervise things. They get *into the boat* with him. They have gotten into fishing boats often before, but today they get in differently. They are the Church, gathered together for the first time for a new voyage. It is as if the *history of the Church* as an active entity were beginning with this voyage. And thus the relation of the individual to God also enters a new phase.

Previously, they were schooled by the Lord; through his talks, they were instructed in his Cross, in the undergoing of suffering. Then they experienced his Resurrection; and, through all of this, they matured into priests. Now, the period of schooling is over; theory is transferred into practice. So they stand, as it were, once again at the beginning. They are the Church, which offers herself to God anew and to which God offers himself anew. Now, too, they do not proceed immediately to action; in a changed way, something of the earlier course of events repeats itself. They enter into a kind of contemplation, no longer that of Christ, but rather, of God. Just as, after the first weeks of marriage that were spent together by the partners in secluded intimacy, the husband returns to his job, reestablishes his connections and brings his friends and interests into play again, while the wife has to adapt to this new, widened circle and rediscover her husband in all that she at first finds unfamiliar, and just as, in this new phase, the element of the intimate must also be secured in a new way, so the Church must now readapt herself to the Lord, to the broadened horizon that has come about through his return to the Father. As long as they lived exclusively as a couple, all misunderstandings could be clarified and put right at once. That, too, now becomes different: one no longer has the opportunity for constant discussion of things; one may perhaps need to sense from the context, from the situation, from the others who are present, whether one has made a mistake, and attempt to avoid it. And if the wife was previously able to acknowledge these mistakes to her husband at once, she cannot do that now, in the presence of strangers. There are certain constraints upon openness. Thus, too, a superior in the Church cannot simply bring charges against himself openly; he must find other ways of redressing the injustice. In the boat of Peter, it is no longer just the immediate relationship to the Lord that prevails. And the Church must take possession of herself anew; the Christian must now accustom himself to finding the path to God via the Church, the sacraments, the congregation. From out of the objectivity of the Church, God must once more be won anew.

The apostles necessarily approach their task with certain preconceptions: this and that are to be achieved. These preconceptions are not God's plan itself; God takes control of them so as to turn them to his purposes. Their intention is to go fishing. What in fact initially occurs is something else, namely, that they find themselves together at night on the sea in the boat. That they form for the first time this religious communion in relation to a new God who has dominion over them as a communion. It is no longer "my personal faith", "my God", that I have found, that has found me. It is now our common life in faith. Everyone had his own, personal way of arriving at God. Now, in the boat, what was personal for each must merge into a communion. In this state of togetherness, they move toward the Father with a view to winning him anew. The beginning lies with the Father, for it is, after all, the same path as before, which must now be traversed in a new way. Not because the communion would have made the individual personally insecure, but rather, because a new cycle of events has begun to unfold. They are about to win for themselves a greater God, to surrender themselves to a greater Lord. God appears so much the greater the more there are that believe in him, because more then accords with him. This, however, always implies a depersonalizing of belief, for the sake of the only Son's position before the Father. Belief becomes standardized. If each individual at a table were to order his own favorite food, then all the orders together would not amount to a menu for everyone. If we want to partake of a common meal, we need to reach an agreement, balance things out, exclude some things. So the Church, too, in her position before God, needs to become something unified that can be made manifest. Even that within us which is most personal must now be colored by the communion.

In this process of selection with a view to the communion, the Holy Spirit enters upon a new function. The Son brings God to man and man to God. The Spirit, however, brings *measure* into this process. Not a measure that makes smaller, but measure as rhythm, as uniformity, proportion and balance. A balance that we do not know, do not comprehend. We know only through the Spirit that God is order. Thus in private devotion, too, he evidences measure: between action and contemplation, between enjoyment and penitence. This measure always possesses the highest degree of freedom and elasticity. But it is a measure of the communion. My God must become your God and, at the same time, the God of the last sinner who does not know God. In himself, God has long been this, but now he becomes this for us, through our togetherness in the boat. Previously, we saw the Ever-greater of the Father and the Son. Now, we see the Ever-greater of the Spirit, and indeed, precisely in the fact that he becomes smaller and smaller in this infinitely ongoing process of adaptation, although only in order to hand each of us back, enriched and expanded, to the Spirit in God and the Spirit in the Lord. The adaptation of the Spirit is one so thorough that he is like a schoolteacher, persisting with the lesson until it almost appears as if the pupils had understood more than he, exercising patience for as long, going into the ever-smaller for as long as is necessary for the impatience of pupils who have understood to be aroused to go into the ever-greater. Here, the pupils usually overlook the fact that even the analytical progression into the ever-smaller already serves, of itself, to extend their knowledge into the ever-greater. The new leads further ahead, but in such a way that it seemingly leads further back; and, in this very leading back, it offers the decisive step into the decisive leading ahead. A teacher can challenge those pupils who have understood their $3 \times 3 = 9$ to count next all the nine units together and to attain the same result in another way. What is basically one can appear in a variety of forms. And since they all make up a class, they must, without abandoning their own conceptual approach, also incorporate the conceptual approaches of the others into their own. Then they will also be in a position to explain the principle to the largest possible number of others later on. What remains uniquely important is that the principle be objectively correct. The particular way in which one demonstrates or remembers it is basically of no concern. The teacher attempts to make each pupil grasp the principle in the way best suited to that pupil, but also, at the same time, in such a way that all the pupils together will be able to understand it, discuss it and pass it on to others.

The Lord has not yet appeared. He is now the path to the Father through the Spirit. But the general commandment to love is present, so to speak, cryptically, as something enjoined by the Lord and implanted in the disciples. No one thinks of calling into question the conception that the other has of God. He respects it as highly as his own. The commandment to love is what expands the truth from a personal into a collective one. It is present only latently. This latency is also what allows the individual to comprehend God latently. While one converses about a particular quality of God in order to comprehend it in some way, one will not forget that the other qualities are also present. Every religious truth that one explores retains a latent interconnection with all other religious truths. Hence, the boat is like a forerunner to a council: its occupants make an effort to understand what God is, what his truth is, by understanding one another in way that reconciles divergences, thus excluding everything personal that would be in heretical opposition to the communion.

In the adaptation by the Spirit lies a core element of the apostolate. Being opposed to any exclusiveness between self and other is intrinsic to the Spirit, because he always exists within the trinitarian process. Everything that he does, attempts or realizes goes back into the unity of that process. If I come to know you in the Spirit, then I know that you are as little closed up within the Spirit as I am. At first, I know only this: we both have a common goal, namely, the return to the Father. I know that about you because the Lord gave you to me as my neighbor. And that could be enough, if the apostolic requirement were not also involved. If we wanted simply to repose in our mutual love, then we would still not really have encountered each other in the *Spirit*. If, however, I possess a mission, then I have need of you. Should you be a believer, then you are important to me from within my mission, just as I can become important to you from within yours. Both of us are valuable to the Lord, as instruments. That you have arrived at belief—perhaps through me—does not mean that my task regarding you has been completed. Precisely now you become meaningful to me, for it is now that your love of the Lord begins to be fruitful. Therefore, I, too, must know you and be aware of how your love is constituted. Those who carry out the Lord's mission along with others must, then, come together on a common plane of love, in a kind of exchange and neutralization of the loves that are personal to each. They must do so for the sake of the mission. Only through this exchange of knowledge *within* love does it become possible to grasp those things that stand outside of belief and love. The Church's concept of God must be broad enough to supplement, develop and incorporate all approaches to God, all notions of God, that exist outside. Hence the joint conversation in the boat.

The Spirit, who gives us measure, also gives the measure of time, of the duration of the conversation in the boat; the measure of the formative process in the community. He gives himself to us within measure. There is no reception of knowledge and no exchange of knowledge that goes on endlessly. Here, too, a norm exists, and it is possessed by the Spirit. Thus he mediates not only the measure of knowledge, but also the *measure of ignorance*. In the latter, he shows us the Always-More of God and the always-more of love and of the

Spirit in the Church. If a man wanted to store up knowledge in himself without the Spirit, there would be no reason for him ever to conclude his amassing of things to be known, and he would never move on to the sphere of action. He would find a counter-argument for every argument; he would become bogged down in research, in controversy, in dialectic, in the systematization of everything knowable. The Spirit determines the stopping point. He is the Spirit not only of knowledge, but also of *wisdom;* and in wisdom the decision is contained. The Christian must decide; that is what the Spirit requires in the boat of the Church. John would certainly have been able to say much more about love, and Peter much more about office. But they did not say it. It becomes submerged in the measure of the Spirit, which, for the Church, is necessarily a *middle measure.* Top-level achievements are not excluded, but are only possible if they have their foundation in the achievements of the communion, and these remain "middling" ones.

This is the first excursion by the Church: it takes place without the visible Lord. It is the first move toward self-reliance. The first test. The first responsibility assumed by the communion. The venturing of the first step. The beginning, too, of theology.

But that night they caught nothing. As experts in fishing, the disciples had expected success from their nighttime excursion. In so doing, they had no idea how much everything was directed toward their apostolate. Night is darkness, night is stillness, night is lack of distraction, night is often a peculiar configuring of all that concerns us most deeply and most personally. Night is the ebbing of ordinary preoccupations, and in this night, the Christian works. It is now not at all the "night of the senses". It is the night of lacking all view of the work as a whole. It is that which happens when nothing happens. It is the time when we catch sight of the absolute, the solitude, in which everything stands out in relief and seems larger than life. It is the opposite of a momentary enthusiasm, namely, a growing sobriety in the face of eternity. This night is especially important in the boat, where the fishermen all become more or less invisible because they have become parts in a unity. The oppositions, the sharp edges of their individual natures, are blotted out. By day, all things appear single and disconnected. At night, what is essential glimmers forth from the day's confusions and takes on the countenance that God himself defines. Life's continuity appears in the night. So, too, the new unity of the Church is established at night. Night binds together much more than day. It binds personal missions together into one ecclesiastical mission. Lovers who want to spend the day together are constantly disturbed; at night, they belong wholly to one another. Everything at night is more exposed, less protected. During the day, we endure everything alien; at night, the only thing alien one can endure is God. Night is withdrawal into the open, the all-pervasive, into the one solitude that is more densely populated than the streets. It is the time of surrender, of abandonment, of simplicity, of relaxedness, when love no longer consists in a thousand individual proofs and acts. It is the time when God's love appears and everything becomes transparent to it. During the day, man works; at night, God acts. During the day, one must inquire; at night, things become clear in God. During the day, one can reassure oneself; but the knowledge of presence is stronger at night, when one sees nothing. Thus prayer at night is something different from prayer during the day. As loving, we are closer to the Lord at night than by day.

They caught nothing. Nothing visible. It is as if they had spent this night in the boat to no purpose, as if nothing at all had happened. And yet it will later emerge how much did happen in it, because much was prearranged in the Lord, provided for by the Lord. But because it is night, everything is enclosed in the Lord. And nevertheless, they should have caught something. From the human viewpoint, the time was favorable for a catch. But they have achieved nothing more, have nothing more to show, than their having waited and hoped together to see and evaluate together the result of their efforts. It was part of the Lord's plan that they caught absolutely nothing, obtained nothing to see and evaluate, so that they might later be able to see the effect of his being present among them.

Many a person thinks that his intention is to work solely in the Lord, and this is subsequently shown not to have been true. But if his intention is really pure, if he has labored away out of love for the Lord, and not out of love of his own work, then the *nothing* that he has caught can still be much. For the apostles, that muchness is, on the one hand, what is to come, but also, on the other hand, the fact that they have persevered through the night together and that this perseverance has brought them to the Lord. It has forged them more strongly into a community; in their present unity with one another, as well as in their coming unity with the Lord (which he will effect), they have gained experiences, Christian ones, and therefore living, fruitful ones. In this lies the point that is common to all those experiences in which things did not turn out as expected. The blessing of misadventures, the blessing of the supposed sterility of the apostolate, the blessing of pure capitulation (so utter as to occur without any comprehension) —all this comes together in this night. To have ventured forth in the Lord, even if in the invisible Lord, was the precondition for the blessing. This blessing is not intended as a consolation for the unfruitfulness of the world. For even unfruitfulness itself is fruitful in the Lord. Everything took place in him and is thus a preparation for the miracle to come.

21:4. *Just as day was breaking, Jesus stood on the beach; yet the disciples did not know that it was Jesus.*

The disciples have spent the night in the name of the Lord; it was the first time that they were, without the Lord, gathered together in him the whole night through. The fulfilment of this night consists, without their knowing it, in the fact that, the following morning, Jesus is standing on the beach. More than the Lord's being there they could not expect. It surpasses all expectation. Even though they were in the boat in order to draw closer to God in a new way, and knew quite well that Jesus was the way to God, they still did not expect to find him there in person. The last times that he appeared among them, his appearance had been a wholly supernatural one; he arrived suddenly, through closed doors. (Nevertheless, the supernatural aspect to his appearance had not surprised them; they had, perhaps, scarcely noticed it.) In a certain way, they had contributed to this supernatural event, since they were gathered in his name when he arrived. Now, of course, the element of their being gathered together is present even more strongly: they had been together, after all, the whole night through in order to serve him in a new way. Thus the conditions for the supernatural appearance of the Lord here stem more fully than before from *their* side. But they are unaware of this.

Strangely enough, they play a larger part in the Lord's arrival than they did the previous times, but their expectation has nevertheless grown smaller. Whoever puts a question to the Lord for himself alone, such as pertains, perhaps, to his mission, may expect an answer from the Lord that falls within his own particular field of spiritual vision. But when there are seven together who possess a common task, then each one of them does not expect a personal answer from God about how the work is to be done. In their common task, in their common questioning, the answer is contained in a transpersonal way. Both in the question and in the assessment of the Lord's answer, there is something like a *ratio communis*. The sense that each one personally possesses for the Lord's answer becomes here a communal sense and a communal faculty of reason. Thus, for example, an individual can have the right to allow himself to be killed if the Lord's commission puts him in danger of this; but he no longer has that right if the task is an affair of the community. In this, admittedly, lies a great danger for the Church: the communities become accustomed to dividing up the answers of the Lord, to always turning the communal answer into a means of security for the individual. The answer still comes from the Lord, and just as immediately; but it should be administered by the community for the community, because the community, too, is immediately in God. What is daring, what is truly alive in love should not suffer because the answer is given to the community instead of to the individual. It must not be that only the individual Christian is afire while the community remains lukewarm. Otherwise, there is a danger that those in the boat will not recognize the Lord.

And yet they have set out to find God, and in this way they find the Lord again, who awaits them in God's innermost core. Being led to God always occurs through the Lord. There are a thousand ways of leading a community further on its way, but only one means of really leading it into God's inner being: the Lord. For the present, the apostles do not at all need to know it; the Lord knows it, and for that reason he is there. Everything is as it has to be, whether the Church knows it or not. The Lord, who is love, the most binding thing that there is, is unrelenting when what is at stake is the way: he stands there over and over again. He stands there all the more, and all the more unrelentingly, the more that they require him, even though they do not expect him. There is no other way to God than the Son. So certain is this that, in every case, the Lord is always already standing there, thus sparing us any seeking of the way in our seeking for God.

He stands at the place of arrival; he is thus the end of the way to God. He is this because, in his Person, he encompasses, and is, the entire way of the sinner toward God. He is this insofar as he is the conclusion of all futile seeking, and the beginning of finding. The further stretches of futile seeking he has paid for himself; he spares us them. That becomes very clear in confession: a man can have gone astray for fifty years before he encounters the Lord; as soon as he has him, all that happened earlier is immediately over and done with; there is no possibility of comparison between the way to the Lord and the way that is the Lord.

That the Lord is there, unexpectedly, is his gift to the disciples. They have come together in order to serve him better, and implicit in that was something like a prayer, a request for the gift of the Lord. If a lover asks for something, suddenly and unexpectedly, the other may perhaps have nothing with him just then; quite frequently, he will not have with him precisely the thing requested. In its place, he can perhaps only give something wholly inadequate, perhaps he will even ask for something from the one making the request simply in order to give it to him as a gift and to show him his love. Thus the Lord, too, in his response, seldom gives precisely what was requested; often, he gives something unexpected, and if a community petitions him, then he will give it that which it already has: his love. He will make the same thing a gift once again. The community would not seek God if it did not already have the Lord, and it would not have the Lord if it did not seek God. If an individual asks the Lord, "Give me something", then he does so seekingly, without anything specific in mind. The prayers of the community are different from this; they must have a framework, a form, a direction, they are parts of a specified act of worship. Just what sort of fulfilment these specified prayers and entreaties by the community will receive is much less knowable in advance. The larger the community is, the more definite the formulation of its prayer must be, but also the more indefinite the nature of the fulfilment remains. The fulfilment itself is certain, though usually different than we think. The situation is the same regarding both those revelations that are private and those that are intended for the community. But regardless of what fulfilment the Lord may bring, he stands on the beach and points the way.

That the disciples do not know the Lord is also due to the fact that, as a newly formed community on its way to the Lord, they still have no fully developed communal sense-organ for the Lord. That they are on their way, they know; but that the Lord, having already arrived, is waiting for them, that he stands on the beach while they themselves are still out on the water, that he will be the goal for their whole community again and again, always standing anew on the beach—this they do not yet know. They still think that they can survey the Lord's life as a historically unique phenomenon. This narrowness of outlook is now to be taken from them. What the Lord will now communicate to them, from the place where he stands, is a new possibility of entry into eternal life. There is only *one* eternal life, but an immense number of ways of arriving at it. On their way, while they are gathering new knowledge in order to grow, one thing mainly is demanded of them: that, in growing, they keep opening themselves anew. Were they to remain the same, occupying the same place, were they to regard the Lord always from the same point of view, then they would ultimately come to think that they knew and comprehended him, and surprises would no longer be possible. But the Lord does what is greater: he awaits them on the beach—in the "beyond" of all their possibilities—with new possibilities that they have not at all taken into account. The fact that they fail to recognize him shows only that they are still not open enough to recognize him in every situation. Earlier, when they set out, everything was quite simple: they pushed off, and knew the way as such. Although they have now moved farther on, everything has become more difficult. The Lord is no longer on the way with them; he stands on the beach, which, as opposed to their way, always remains the beach. Earlier, they had a key; now, they no longer have one.

21:5. Jesus said to them: Children, have you any fish to eat? They answered him: No.

The Lord addresses them as children, as children of God, as his children, who have been entrusted to him. Implicit in this form of address is a signaling of his identity. But they are so preoccupied with their new position, with their newly discovered point of view, that they see everything from this perspective and assume that everything strange fits into it. Hence, the Lord's form of address does not, for the time being, serve to open their eyes.

Have you any fish to eat? The Lord initiates contact through the simplest of questions in order to open a path for them to his understanding. As if he did not know that they are his disciples, that they are involved in an apostolic journey. As if, like just any neighbor, he merely wanted to strike up a conversation with his neighbor. In so doing, he gives them a lesson about how they themselves should initiate contact: as simply as possible, in order only afterward to enter into the greater. They should descend to the necessary level, should attempt to be all things to all men, in order to pass on later to more far-reaching topics. People who do not yet know how to handle love, who are not yet really acquainted with it, cannot suddenly be set upon with the profoundest mysteries. One must begin quite carefully, and gradually move up from the level of the inessential, the normal, the universally human. One must not ask too much all at once.

The Lord is the one who begins again. He sees that they are in belief and yet still do not know him. So he lowers himself and places himself at their level. To the disciples, that is a humiliation. As long as love and humility are living, they are in constant interplay. That the Lord humbles himself is a sign of his love. No love would grow if it did not have its counterweight in *humility*. But humility is never an end in itself. It has its meaning only in love. So, too, the Lord makes use of it here only in order to render the disciples open to love, to instruct them in that self-surrender which, at bottom, is already identical with love. Just as Christ, by presenting himself to be recognized, is the Lord and the male, so the Church, which recognizes him, is the female, which must know humility in self-surrender and availability. Love wants only love, it does not want reciprocated love. Whether or not the beloved wants my love today does not affect my love. Whoever believes must grant the Lord the freedom to come when, and as, he wishes. Perhaps he wants something different, something new. This granting of freedom is humility. There are, perhaps, some forms of humility that man can learn to control by his own efforts, "exercises" in humility through which he can arrive at a kind of mastery. But the measure of humility lies ultimately not with man, but in the Lord. And we know this: he is love; therefore he humbles, when he does so, out of love. One experiences the humiliation as such, but only because one is not yet sufficiently open to love. Anyone who possessed complete love would also have complete humility, and could no longer be humbled. Still, this point at which love and humility coincide is not a static pole; it is always in motion. Humility is inclined from the start to look favorably upon the opinion of a friend or neighbor. It extends credit. In her word of affirmation, Mary placed everything in the hands of the Lord; that was her humility. The humble man is also not taken aback if someone humiliates him, indicates his short-comings, enlarges him. He will accept it in love. But humility has no eye for, and no measure of, itself. No one can say, out of humility, that some task is too great for him. He would then be reviewing his own capabilities, without conceding room for the Lord to be able to do, in his soul, that which he himself cannot do. Hence, humility is, at the same time, the will to obedience. Humility never apportions or calculates; that is not to say, however, that it is unknowing. All its knowingness just lies in the Lord. When the disciples answer the Lord by saying "No", they thereby concede room for everything to him. He can do what they cannot. Hence, in them, humility is not an end in itself (when something is in the process of vanishing, so, too, our look must not be directed at the process of vanishing as such): it just opens up room for obedience and love.

If the Lord humbles the disciples, then that is merely a necessary transitional event. Also, the negative, the state of not knowing the Lord, is not humility. The distance between us and the Lord, between temporal life and eternal life, between the sea and the beach, is not the measure of humility. Anyone who sought humility in that would never make the transition from confession to Communion. In Christian seeking, the finding is always implicit as well. Out of the humiliation, there always emerges a greater nearness to knowledge of the Lord.

The Lord, who reveals himself to the disciples from within eternal life, lets them know that he is nevertheless someone who dwells among them and has needs. He does this so that, afterward, when they recognize him, they will understand all the better the duality of his life in this world and in the beyond; and also because he has need of their answer, their *No*. He requires this No as the summation of what preceded his appearance. They set out to go fishing; they caught nothing. One cannot, however, catch anything, engage in any fruitful apostolate, if one does not possess dynamic belief. They believe, but their belief is static. They have all been consecrated as priests, but they are still enveloped, as it were, in the atmosphere of the seminary. They know life only by hearsay; their theology has yet to be tested. They must first take in a setback. Their nets remain empty because things much greater must come about than what they, in their (well-meaning) self-directedness, had been aiming at.

Their No is an unqualified one. They have attained absolutely nothing, and are also not even just at the point of catching something. Their No implies no hope of an imminent harvest. No sort of mitigation is possible. To say it straight out: *Nothing!* This, once again, is a humiliation. The first humiliation was in the sphere of knowledge. The second lies in that of life. The first lay in theory; the second lies in practice. The first lay in their inward, personal mission; the second lies in one that is directed outward. In both, they have failed. First, their contemplation failed, then their action. They thought that whoever believes knows the Lord, and that whoever knows the sea can haul up what is in it. The Lord permits this failure, just as he permitted it in the case of Martha. The apostles, like Martha, mean well. But meaning well does not suffice. The Lord has greater intentions and must, before he enlarges, expose what is narrow and wrong-headed.

Their No also implies their disappointment. Although they were together the whole night long, they experienced nothing essential, saw nothing of substance and have nothing that they can show. They do not know that, to the Lord's ears, their No sounds like a Yes. They possess the insight, even if it is still inexpressible, that they cannot do anything without him. To be sure, they ventured forth together with the intention of committing their boat to the Christian destiny. But they lack the experience of prayer, of meditation, of encounter. In their No is contained that which they have humanly comprehended; in the Yes that the Lord hears is contained that which his grace will make of their failure. The night of their unsuccessfulness will be reshaped in such a way that, precisely from their failure, the fullness of grace will stream forth. They stand there as seekers, and in this seeking, they leave their own finding up to the Lord. He will find for them. It is not as if the Lord hears in their naked No, a naked Yes. Rather, he fashions from that No, a Yes; he makes of their lack of success the full success of his grace. What is essential does not lie mainly in their having the right attitude, and also not in the (for them coincidental) presence of the stranger; it lies in the *hearing* of their answer by the Lord. Man can be ready and still not know; the Lord confers the meaning, the value, the fulfilment. At the decisive moment, things are such that man's word and deed (his No) and the Lord's response to that both take on their meaning only through him. At the moment when man desires to surrender himself fully in this new form, the Lord adds what is missing. Seen from the viewpoint of man, it is true self-surrender. The No is no mere negation, but a real offer, something opened up by the Holy Spirit that is ready for more, something serious, a real assumption of risk, a transference of rights, a withdrawal from the field. I determine, in fact, that the Lord should determine. And it is not without me that the Lord fulfills this will, above and beyond my will. In the No, the whole abyss yawns wide—between what man is not and what God is—but that abyss is at once filled in with the whole fullness of the Lord's grace. If one answers objectively and soberly, one answers in the way that one *must* answer when the Lord questions. One does not complain about having caught nothing. If one receives a mission and obligates oneself, immediately and concisely, then one simply leaves the field free for the Lord, without explanation, without apology. Otherwise, one would only be a hindrance to that which the Lord wants to place into one's soul. No matter how much man may have accomplished—at the moment when he stands before the Lord's question, "What do you have?" he must say, "Nothing."

21:6. *He said to them: Cast the net on the right side of the boat, and you will find some. So they cast it, and now they were not able to haul it in, for the quantity of fish.*

The Lord's answer contains a clear directive. He would not have been able to give it if they had not been fully prepared for acceptance of what he said. After he has established contact and permitted them to describe their situation to him in detail, after he has understood, in his own terms, the answer that they gave him, he answers them quite humanly, but in such a manner that all his divinity shines forth from his words. Until now, the conversation had proceeded like a discussion between man and man. Yet in it, the entire path that they had covered on the way to him was already marked out, so much so that they could do precisely nothing other than find him and his answer.

From the very start, two lines of development were unfolding alongside each other. In one, there are human fishermen, who describe their situation to a man standing on the beach—who is somehow familiar with their occupation and the local conditions— and expect some advice from him, and in fact, because he had spoken to them first. As when someone on the street does not know the way and asks a passerby, whom he assumes to be familiar with the locality. In the other line of development, they are the apostles, who steer the ship of the Church on toward the new life, fulfill their mission as well as they are able, arrive at what appears to them to be a negative result and, in doing so, encounter eternal life, the complete divinity of the Lord—unexpectedly, even though that was precisely what they were seeking. Their situation remains that of every Christian who has encountered the Lord, who has to lead his own life and also seemingly does lead it, yet hands it wholly over to him; he is affected by the grace that he had always wanted to strive for, though without being able to imagine that it might actually be possible for him. The disciples believe, and they serve, and they want it to be so; they are apostles. That was the way things were arranged even before the Cross. Already then, they had given a word of affirmation with incalculable consequences, although they still possessed a certain insight into the Lord's human life. And perhaps they thought that they had even been granted a certain feeling, an instinct, for the Ever-Greater of the Lord. They pictured to themselves that everything was unfolding within a (perhaps ascending) progression. So, perhaps, too, within a constantly increasing act of renunciation that remained, precisely in its degree of increase, incalculable. Now they suddenly learn that the incalculability is a reality. A reality that the Lord shows them from on the beach. They had imagined this incalculability to themselves. Now they experience it; now they are thrown into it. They thought that things would perhaps turn out otherwise; now, the Other itself shows itself, and in fact, precisely *as what is other.* With that, their whole being becomes swallowed up in the being of the Lord, not only their expectation, their openness to exalted possibilities and perspectives of some sort, but utterly their whole persons. In this whirlpool, however, when God has become everything, there is clear directedness. At the moment when their knowledge is overpowered, when it is their fate to be swept away, comes something concrete, something small: *Cast the net on the right side of the boat.* It is like the tiny penance after the infinite absolution, like the banquet after the newly ordained priest's first official celebration of Mass . . . : the insignificant sacrifice after the total self-surrender. They are prepared, as a community, to place their feeble powers at the disposal of the Lord, and the Lord is prepared to allow them, as his complete brothers, to take on his divine commission. Man is permitted to let himself be taken into rapturous transport if he is prepared, at the same moment, to take on sober directedness. One just as much as the other comes from the Lord. The Lord never checks full self-surrender with his directives, he never disciplines it; surrender to the utmost degree is allowed, but it flows on into mission.

And you will find some. He not only gives them a command; at the same time, he gives them a promise. Command and promise are inseparably one. He does not tell them what they will find. But they will find that which is contained in his directive: the fulfilment of what he intends. By doing his will, they will receive the fruit of his will. This promise is made to all who encounter the Lord in this way. The command is quite precise: *on the right side of the boat.* The Lord prescribes quite concretely the form that their self-surrender is to take here. He does so at the moment when they still do not know he is the Lord. They know only that the stranger has something to say, inasmuch as he began speaking to them. In this, they show something like an implicit cognizance that consists largely in trustfulness, in a willingness to refrain from acting on their own even if they have the feeling that, as experts, they would perhaps understand the matter better. One surrenders oneself and one's opinion even when one does not know the other. This fluid willingness is poured by the Lord into a wholly solid mold whose form *he* determines. They entrust themselves to this form even before they receive proof that their trust is justified. They do not inquire before they believe. They are in love and, with that, are on the right path. They possess the naïve movement of the good toward the good. Only when the Lord finds such trust can he realize his intentions: this is the bridge that leads into his own Ever-Greater. Not only into the greater that I expect, but much more still, into that which he *is*. Just what form this takes he does not say; that remains open from mine to his. My own always-more is the seeing of how, from every point that I know, every point where I stand, infinite perspectives keep opening up (so that, in the end, one could write a thousand books about every sentence). But this is still by no means the Always-More of the Lord, which begins totally beyond my progressions. Not only my "I become" but also my "I do not become" must disappear into his "he becomes".

The disciples follow the Lord's directive; they perform, in gratitude, an action that he told them to carry out, and to that extent, his will and their action coincide: he commanded it, they carry it out. At the moment of its accomplishment, however, what they are capable of doing ceases, and all that is left is what the Lord does. Here, that which happens every time someone attempts to obey the Lord becomes clearly apparent. He does what the Lord demanded of him, what is contained in his brief words; as soon, however, as he is about to do what comes next, there is only one person left who can do it: the Lord himself.

They cast the net. But they are no longer able to haul it in. One can lead a man to belief, by way of instruction. But as soon as he actually begins to follow, asks, reads, learns, the teacher loses control: the learner stands before God, and here only the Lord can be of further help. It is he who will convert my converts. Latent in the work that he commanded is its own bursting open.

The disciples *were not able to haul it in, for the quantity of fish.* Thus, the previous total emptiness stands in clear contrast to the present superabundance. God's fulfilment never corresponds to the measure of man's expectation, no matter what form the latter takes. For everything that we expect from the Lord is always subject to *his* law of fulfilment. The fulfilment between Father and Son is, from eternity, something constantly richer: they have always surpassed their mutual expectation. At the basis of their relationship of love is lavishness, the incomprehensible, indeed, a not at all wanting to comprehend. When a man wishes to comprehend another's love, then he is already more concerned with himself than with the other; there is, however, no concern with self in God. If two are really in love, then each has no time for himself; the fact that neither looks back upon himself gives them the opportunity to lavish themselves fully on one another. And thus there is also no exclusivity in their love. Their lavishness is not cut to the measure of the personality of each; it is a simple overflowing from both sides. So it is, in complete measure, between Father and Son, with the result that, when the Son brings the Father's grace into the world, he thereby also performs an act of their mutual lavishness. The *amount of the fish* testifies to this lavishness: in it, the Lord has given the disciples a share in his own lavishness. They are inundated by it. Not only does the Lord *give* more than they expected; they also *receive* more than they expected. Hence, there arises a unity of lavishness in which God and man are involved together.

With this, the disciples become possessors of a dangerous teaching: that the Lord always gives more than we expect; more and, at the same time, in a different way. His love is not exhaustible, just as little as is his capacity to give. But he gives in ways that he deems good, unpredictably. In this giving differently than expected, then, lies a removal of the possibility of prediction and thus an averting of the danger for men. The Lord reserves the right to give as he wishes. He confers sufferings and he confers joys; to him who asks, he gives gifts that he intends to be given, in turn, to others. Nothing can be definitely established except the one fact of our inclusion in the lavishness of the Lord.

In casting the net, they use their own strength, but not without the strength that he gives them. There is, then, something that they both have at their disposal and place at his disposal, and there is something that is more: what the Lord disposes. His effects on them, in them and, even more: his effects through them. When they cast the net, they are actually casting their whole personalities into obedience; they obey the Lord immediately and totally, they do not simply feel their way toward what he commanded, they do not try to make something out of it. Rather, they allow the Lord to do that. Not, however, as passive onlookers; instead, they allow the Lord to work within that which they have prepared for him. They allow the obedience that they have placed at the Lord's disposal to become living through him. They allow the Lord's commission to shape itself into fulfilment through him. This is the true, the lavish humility; as soon as the Lord and his commission are there, one no longer thinks about one's own humility, one has become oneself a commission of the Lord, and thus a new livingness in the Lord. The self-diminishment is only a preparatory stage of adaptation to the Lord. When man has placed himself at the Lord's disposal, adapted himself to him to that extent, then the Lord adapts himself to him and does so without limits.

Also inherent in obedience is fulfilled and fulfilling hope. A sinner, an irresolute believer, can perhaps nurture quite justified hopes which he expects will someday find fulfilment. Regardless of what these may be, they exist, in the one who hopes, as a future possibility that hovers before his expectation. He has some quite specific hope that aims at some quite specific fulfilment and discharges itself in that. In obedient belief, however, all separating walls between expectation and fulfilment collapse. The hope has such vitality that it is constantly fulfilling itself, and because it always hopes for fulfilment in the beyond, it possesses no bounds. The situation is similar to that regarding adaptation: both are always in process insofar as both are in God. In such hope there is no "enough", because it is unending and always fulfills itself, even if we do not always know how it is fulfilled.

The obedience of the disciples is structured by the Lord. He, too, is always an obedience in process. He is the narrow track along which they walk, and at bottom, it is the Lord who carries out this obedience in them. He becomes the bearer of their obedience in an ultimate kind of reduction: man contracts into a point that is subsumed by the Lord. This "personal" obedience, as an instrument of the Lord, exists behind all perceptible acts of obedience. It is an abdication at the source of action. The gap, the abyss between the casting of the net and its filling lies *wholly* in the Lord. Here, the obeying man has become imperceptible. In his adapting, his expecting, his hoping, there always still lay an attempting, an engaging, an acting. Here, everything has been absorbed into the action of the Lord. One no longer avoids anything, one is no longer concerned with anything negative, one is taken up into the positive act of the Lord.

The cast net is man's placing himself at disposal, which is then filled by the Lord's grace. Between the casting out and the hauling in, between the sowing and the reaping, lies the gap that is left up to the Lord alone. The disciples do not know what will happen, whether they will catch anything, which fish will appear. It is a suspension, a night, a pause between question and answer. In it, their having placed themselves at disposal hangs suspended. The human part has been done, but the Lord has not yet come forward in his response; it is as if the invisible response must first concentrate itself into a visible sign. How long the net will remain in readiness is not said. Man has to wait. Were he to press more strongly for God's response, then his attitude would be less devoted. It is like the case of a lover's proposal: once the question has been put, any further urging can only serve to distract. There are acts that one cannot intensify, cannot redouble. The Lord said: *Cast the net on the right side of the boat.* This they have done. More than to obey they cannot do. Now, both remain silent until the fulfilment. For his part, too, the Lord adopts that extinguishment of self which they made use of earlier. Only this grace is still at work. It is a situation that can be found in all the sacraments. The acknowledgment of sins has been made, the role of man has been fully acted out; until absolution is effected, the pause endures. Or the host has been received, and the response of the Lord follows a moment later. Or the priest to be consecrated has flung himself down wholly with the net, and awaits that anointing by the Lord which will be the fulfilment of his life. The pause, the caesura, is like the drawing of breath by the Son in God. Before he effects anything visibly, he works within the concealment of the Trinity. For us, it is like a vacuum. For him, it is our invisible assimilation into the Trinity. The two forms of readiness come together: that to receive and that to give, both rounded out, each adequate to the other, adapted to one another through the grace of the Lord. This is what gives rise to the pause, in which both are in the process of uniting. And in each instance, it is a new, creative act of the Lord.

And now the miracle. *They were not able to haul* the net *in, for the quantity of fish.* As long as it was a matter of readiness, obedience and hope, everything seemed clear: one could see where the Lord stood, where the disciples stood; between the acts and powers of both there existed a kind of relationship. Now, when the actual deed eventuates, in which the powers of man become measurable against those of the Lord, it is manifest that man is at once no longer able to do what is required. He had been sure of his powers (although he had still not caught anything and thus had not had any opportunity to test them), but these powers fall short at once: *they were not able to haul in* the net. Not because their strength had waned so quickly or deserted them so suddenly, but simply because no kind of relationship exists between their strength and the strength of the Lord. As long as they did not have to test their strength against the strength of the Lord, they were certain of it. Now, when the Lord has effected his deed without any perceptible effort, they are no longer able to do what is required. Their strength was not to be called into doubt as long as it still remained untested. Working the whole night through without catching anything was an achievement that demanded all their strength. Then, at that time when they caught nothing, they were completely convinced of their strength. It is like the situation prior to temptation. As long as someone has not been tempted to steal, he can believe himself incapable of stealing: his strength is victorious. But if temptation comes, then his strength will succumb or the strength of the Lord will win out in him. Or as long as a man does not know the Lord, he can assert much about himself, perhaps even correctly. But once he comes to know the Lord, he can assert nothing more about himself because, in the end, the Lord is his assertion. If he does not know him, then he can place something of his strength at his disposal. But if he knows him, then he knows that the Lord has command over him in every respect, and all measuring of strength immediately ceases. As long as the self applies its measuring stick to the other, all kinds of rivalry are possible, one can hold a contest of strength, and I will always find an excuse if I happen to fail. I am, perhaps, superior to the winner in some other area, and this balances things out again. Everywhere in the world, there is a measurable relationship of strength that has its limit in the maxim that "one can do no more than lose or win". But between the Lord and man, there is no contest of strength, no comparability. Here, man loses in the sense that his highest powers are no longer anything at all, and God wins in the sense that his effortless victory surpasses all conceiving.

The pause now takes on another aspect. It becomes the space in which the event occurs and the confrontation between man in his failure and the infinitely surpassing Lord takes place. Thus there lies hidden in the pause a kind of alignment, the support, so to speak, that man has need of, the staging without which he could never again compose himself, the site plan that he can later bring out again. An order is established, a situation that first makes what the Lord does understandable. The abruptness of the encounter is overcome by introducing an adaptive shift, a quick becoming accustomed to things, which in fact only serves to heighten the element of surprise. The disappointingly brusque, the plainly incomprehensible, is removed, so as to allow the true Always-More of the Lord to be glimpsed. The Lord does not want to "trick anyone into" what he does. Belief is always a kind of understanding between God and man. This exists, too, between the Lord and the Father: on the Cross, when nothing is left but the remoteness of the Father, the Son still recalls that it all came from the hands of the Father. What was lost is still present to consciousness, and this is what first constitutes the loss as such. Thus the Lord deprives the disciples of their supposed strength (as measured against his, they have none), but does so by giving them his strength, which drove the fish into the net. As they become conscious that their strength has failed, they discover, in retrospect, that this fiasco is founded on their earlier fiasco, when they had caught nothing. It was not until, in their obedience, the Lord had lent them his strength that they caught something. Strength and weakness, achievement and failure, are always related to each other in such a way that man fails at those times when he both wishes and acts for the best. He catches nothing even though he has the will. He cannot haul in even though he has cast out. But the endeavor was a good one only because the Lord turned it to the good at the time and transformed the emptiness of their net into an overfullness. Turned it to such an extent that all their robustness as fishermen is dashed on the strength of the Lord. He gives them the two, both strength and powerlessness, in a chain of paradoxes. When they think that they can do something, they are able to do nothing; when they think that they will fail, precisely then they prove able. If they do their own will, then they do not do his; but if they do his, then they do something else in turn, namely, the will of the Father. Were this not so, then it would be impossible to see why the Lord should not leave them to their own will, out of love or in order to show them what good Christians they are. But he himself does not do his own will, but only the will of the Father, which is also his divine will. Hence, they must learn to distinguish between their human and his divine will. He opposes a Yes to their No, and a No to their Yes. They are to realize that he knows only the will of the Father.

The amount of fish is so great that it no longer bears any relation to the strength of the fishermen. It is already the harvest of the Lord that they have to haul in. The harvest of the Lord is always something different from what was expected. Part of what one had expected is perhaps included, but the whole is strange, incomprehensible; it is the Lord's. They had set out to go fishing; they had entrusted everything—themselves, their belief, the Church—to the little boat. They had staked everything on the one card. Thus the catching of fish becomes an image of their apostolate. In the fulfilled mission, however, everything immediately goes back to the Father. Here, too, just as before, there is the moment when things hang in suspension: the symbol of fruitfulness is present, but one does not yet comprehend it, has not yet caught sight of the prey. In this vastness, what first becomes visible is solely the origin of the mission: the Father. The Father sent the Son in love: redemption lies in the mission, the disciples' apostolate in the Lord's mission, and their individual deed in their apostolate. So they gaze now, through this individual deed, upon the fulfilment of the whole mission in God, which is emblematically signified by the fish. The Son performs the miracle for the glorification of the Father, and the miracle contains a surprise even for the Son, because at the moment when he glorifies the Father, he is always also glorified by the Father. The Son knows exactly what he is doing when he performs a miracle, yet he still leaves the overseeing of it to the Father. His whole life is a miracle. He is the miracle of the mission that is initially the Father's; he is so fully given over to the Father's commission that he organizes the miracle within it, but as the Father's miracle rather than his own. Thus it remains a miracle for the Son as well, even though he himself effects it. Not that the number of fish would be astonishing to him—rather, he sees in the mass of fish the benevolence and magnificence of the Father. It is not the amount of fish that goes beyond him, but the love that he receives from the Father. He always expects everything, and yet everything that he receives is always different and more, because in his expectation he never runs ahead of the Father. The glorification of the Father that the Son intends is in every case exceeded by the glorification that the Father confers, just as the glorification that comes to the Father through the Son is in every case more magnificent than could have been foreseen. Already during the pause of invisibility, while the net is under the water, the Son knows that the Father will grant more love in the miracle than the Son requested. The Son does not, after all, dispense the miracle on his own, but effects it in the power of the Father; thus he lays claim to the Father's love in order to perform the miracle in the Father's name; before anything becomes visible, he already goes back to the Father. There is a power of the performed miracle that is inherent in the miracle but cannot be calculated. There is no analysis of a miracle in terms of cause and effect. The power of the Father effects it in the Son and through the Son. But the origin and end of the miracle is the Ever-Greater Father.

The disciples understand that the fish contain not only the miracle of the large number, but also a miracle of promise. They know now that even between their own expectation and that which the Lord sends them there lies the whole, forever unsurveyable fullness of the Lord's love. Whether these men are regarded as fishermen or as apostles, they are simply an expression of what the Lord is able to do in love, but does in such a way that he uses them to help. Despite their failure of strength, they are allowed to assist in hauling the fish out of the water. They feel themselves renewed as instruments of the Lord. But that feeling remains insignificant as opposed to the knowledge, radiating over everything, that the miracles of the Lord are always miracles of love, miracles of his love for the Father.

All this is still unclear to them. They have, after all, still not recognized the Lord. It is the last stage of their preparation: they are ready for the new form of love. But this can be communicated to them only through love itself, and in fact, through the love in their midst: John.

21:7. *That disciple whom Jesus loved said to Peter: It is the Lord! When Simon Peter heard that it was the Lord, he put on his clothes—for he was stripped for work—and sprang into the sea.*

It is significant that the love that is necessary for knowledge comes once again from the Lord. John describes himself as the one who receives the love from the Lord and thereby becomes capable of returning that love. Love becomes the catalyst for belief and knowledge, an opener of the soul. Externally, a whole succession of events has unfolded; but only the innermost love is able to interpret them, only it participates in the light and can transmit light. From this can be inferred the nature of knowledge in the Lord, its inner order and structure. Here is a man who is occupied with a multitude of problems, all existing alongside one another; but not until love is added does knowledge penetrate them, illumine their interconnections from within, and turn them into questions for the Lord. If they exist in this light, then they also already abide in the answer of the Lord. Question and answer come together in the soul, so swiftly that, at the moment when the question arises, the answer, too, is already there. Not only prayer is constituted in this way, but also every instance of Christian knowledge. No one who believes can stop at this or that partial object; he is compelled to integrate it into the whole, to bring it into the light of the Lord. He can, of course, occupy himself with some subproblem, but even the most specialized research remains for him ultimately a component of knowledge of the Lord. Everything with which he concerns himself he wishes to relate ultimately to the Lord, to know in love for the Lord. Thus Catholic research always presses, in love of the Lord, toward the totality of things. And it does so not on its own initiative, but because the Lord himself comes forward and offers—indeed, sends—his answer. Whether the sub-problem is solved quickly or slowly or not at all is a matter of indifference; if it is posed in the Lord, then it will lead to some sort of knowledge, perhaps lying in a quite different area, but ultimately being what the Lord wanted to communicate and also not remaining, for the Lord as well, unconnected with the original intention. Even if a Christian were to progress much less further in his research than a non-Christian, his activity would still have a quite different illumina-tion; it stands in the light of the Lord, and receives from there its outlines and contours. *"Ama et fac quod vis"* applies here, too: one can pursue any occupation, conduct any sort of research; if it occurs in love, then it is good and the Lord can receive it.

The loving one, who recognizes the Lord, tells this to Peter, the official. They stand in the same relationship as often before: love has recognized something, but what it possesses it must immediately pass on. And thus we can see that it possesses a commission that has no end. There are resting points in its mission, whenever it has fulfilled some commission. But this resting is quite temporary, for the next instance of knowledge is already on the way, and with it the next commission. The loving one does everything that he does in love; he cannot cast it off, he cannot grow weary of it. The forms of love can change; the meaning of life, however, remains the love that persists with constant intensity. This essential condition of love, because it is in the Lord, is not surveyable as a totality; only particular acts that bring it to surface become visible, such as, for example, this report to Peter. In the Gospel, external actions by John very rarely become evident: a few words, a few instances of being present; but since everything is summarized in the fact that the Lord loves him, these meager externals are paralleled by a consummate inner fullness. Out of this fullness, John will function again and again to activate the official Church and set it into motion without himself being moved. For love is already movement by its very nature.

John accomplishes his commission with perfect sureness about what he has to do, and in fact, without having received a perceptible commission from the Lord. Love acts in an obedience that has its source and sustenance directly in the Lord, apart from all mediation. It is the Lord as God from whom John draws his mission. Were it the Lord as man, then the others would have noticed it. Hence, only John himself hears and knows it. What he has received, however, he passes on, without diminishment, in the uninterrupted power of love.

Peter, who will represent the Lord, receives his commission either from Christ as man, who represents Christ as God, or from John, who equally represents God for him. For John lives so much in the beyond that he can mediate it to office. Through his office, Peter is so strongly rooted in this world that he needs John in order to grasp the beyond. Perhaps, for John, the Lord is so much in the love of the Father that his appearing is hardly necessary for him anymore. He recognizes him by the traces of love that he scatters and leaves behind. He sees straight through the manifest love and beyond to God. That which is direct for John remains indirect for Peter: he acquires contact by means of John.

Inasmuch as the Church offers believers the Eucharist, the door to love is opened for them. Thus the Church does not save up the love that she receives in order to keep it in reserve for an indefinite period and for unknown purposes; rather, she passes it on, and in fact, in the form in which it will immediately take on new life, as love, in believers. The Church receives the love both from the Lord and from believers, and passes it on in abundance and undiminished, just as she has received it in abundance. She receives it, however, in a certain form and passes it on in another form, and in this the first is not immediately recognizable. She must, so to speak, subject personal love to centralization in the sacraments. She must offer it in a form that possesses the capacity for transformation. The love that an individual presents to the Church may perhaps contain something very fervent, very personal; but as soon as the Church takes possession of it, that same love is given an almost official, anonymous character, and it is in this official form that the Church gives back the love received so as to allow it to develop itself personally in believers yet again. She gives it, so to speak, in a neutral form, as something having the potential for being formed into the most varied of things. The passing of love through the official sphere of the Church is necessary; otherwise, the love of Christians for the Lord would stray off into the private. Indeed, it would remain sterile; it would not be the love of the Bride who awaits the Bridegroom. Ultimately, it would have to degenerate into self-love, only to run itself out in an unending idling process. The passing of love through the Church does not serve to break the personal relationship with the Lord; on the contrary, it first really establishes that. No one can say that he is bound to the Lord so personally that he does not need the sacraments. All Christians are dependent on seeking personal contact with the Lord there where he himself designates it, namely, in the sacraments of the Church—which does not prevent the Lord from also conferring grace in other ways as he deems fit. A living Christian who would vest all his encounters with the Lord in reception of the sacraments would be no poorer than one who had still other means of access to the Lord. No matter how the Lord's measure of grace may be constituted, if someone lives according to his directives, then the measure of grace intended for him by the Lord will also be fulfilled. That fulfilment is not measurable, and is sure to be richer than its recipient has any right to expect. And whether it is fulfilled perceptibly, with experienced grace, or imperceptibly, in complete aridness, it is fulfilment as long as the person lives in love and faithfulness. Here, the *unity* of the love of the Lord and the love of the Church becomes apparent. When a hundred Christians receive Communion together, each of them approaches the Lord with a personal love, and the Lord, in divine freedom but in some way that is appropriate to the personal devotedness of each, will bestow himself on each personally. And yet the Church interposes herself here by effecting an absorption of all the personal loves into one, as it were, anonymous love, which she presents to the Lord as the unity of the Church's love in order to receive back from him the unity of his love, which she then personalizes anew, but differently, in the sacraments and their recipients. The individual sinner's love is absorbed initially into the love of the Church as Bride, but in such a way that, when the Lord receives it, he still recognizes in it the relevant personal note. And contained in his response to the Bride is also his individual response to that sinner. It is directed at him not insofar as he is a sinner, but insofar as the Lord loves him in the Bride, as the presumed friend that the Lord sees, and accepts, him as being. The sinner receives the love of the Lord as the one who he is, as the sinner; the love that he receives is meant, however, for the friend that he must still become but that the Lord sees in him and takes into consideration. In all of this, the role of office is both to intensify and to temper. Because a wealth of living love is always available to the Church, she presents individual love to the Lord in a condition of heightened livingness. She evens things out and adds what is missing. It is impossible that today a hundred men should receive Communion in the Church with supreme love while tomorrow a hundred should do so in utter halfheartedness; that today the Church should have a proper bridal gift to give to the Lord while tomorrow she should be standing before him with empty hands. She lives from her wealth, and to live, for the Church, means placing her wealth at the disposal of the Lord; and because her wealth is one of love, she never becomes impoverished, even if today she has more to reinforce by drawing on her wealth than she had yesterday; she remains, in a certain way, forever rich. Her mystery is not only one of this world, but equally, too, one of the beyond; her source lies in the Lord and in the Trinity. Even if she were one day to consist of nothing more than a few believers, she would not therefore be any poorer, at bottom, than she was at the time of her greatest external development—her essence in the Lord is the same, the mystery between her and the Lord is inviolable—even if we would have to regret the apostasy of many.

Hence, office lends to every believer's personal love the intensity that is still lacking, and, after this supplementation, the Church offers the Lord what is most her own: the fullness of ecclesiastical love. This makes her capable of also assuming another supplementary role which is usually overlooked: conveying the Lord's love to the individual in the form that is suited to him. A sinner cannot endure direct contact with the naked flame of the Lord. Were he to receive the Lord in Communion just as fully as he offers himself to him, he would be burnt; he would have to die or lose all his senses. The office of the Church is there in order to temper. This function can become dangerous; the Lord can be received by sinners in a way that is all too tempered, all too abstract, so that he is not allowed to have any influence on life. But office must exert this effect in order to remind the recipients of their own office. When receiving grace, the Church transfers something of her impersonal office to all laymen in order to bring them, by so doing, into renewed unity with herself as well. Ecclesiastical office is not an end in itself; it has the task of ordering love, it is a yeast that must rise in the love of believers. A priesthood without laymen would do away with itself, but so would a laity without office; everything would fall apart without the unifying function of ecclesiastical office. Office reminds love of the fact that Christian life as a whole is also official in nature, that the Christian Faith is an official mission in the world.

Within the Church, prayer has the least clearly stipulated place. From office, from the Mass, the liturgy, the life of the sacraments, there derives a certain minimal regulation of prayer to which all believers have to conform. Between this minimum and the highest degree of prayer regulation—such as one can find, for instance, in contemplative monasteries where the whole day's work consists of organized prayer—there are all levels and shadings. The amount and manner of this prayer can thus be subject to an ordering that depends, in any given case, upon both office and love. From office comes what can be formulated: one is able to communicate to others what and how much one prays. But alongside the quantitative stands the qualitative, the substantial ordering of prayer that depends primarily on love. Office establishes external forms that love fills and often overfills.

Love fulfills everything that can be imagined in love of the Lord. Office must consider the community and lend expressions of love a form acceptable to everyone. For example, it will permit certain declarations of piety only in private prayer and not in the Church. But also, every Christian can embody for another the Church's official function. One will behave differently in dealing with the Lord when one is alone than when one is not alone. For in the communion, discretion is always necessary.

John calls out: *It is the Lord!* Peter hears this call. Thus office and love come together, and the two form a synthesis in the Lord. The Lord carries them both in himself. He embodies them as God, and also, as a man, becomes for his Church both perfect office and perfect love. And by becoming a *unity* precisely at the moment of this meeting between John and Peter, he shows the Church his superior divinity. He shows it to her in such a way that, precisely at this moment of unity in the Church, he becomes a unity *for the Church.* Inasmuch as the two characters of office and love converse with each other here in such a manner (the one conveying something, the other receiving it) as to melt into a unity, something new arises: the living synthesis of office and love in the Lord. The Lord had always been that unity, but at this moment he begins to be that for the Church who receives him. He who is always that unity nevertheless does not want to be the one who he is for the Church without her belief. Hence, both being and becoming are involved here.

Precisely at the moment when office and love become one in the Church, the Lord becomes present to the Church, he is received by the Church that was founded by him and that has its existence through him. And precisely at that same moment, the mystery of *transubstantiation* comes to pass: in the coming together of office and belief. For what John says also signifies the absolute belief of love, that pure knowledge of the Lord which is mediated only through love. Without love, John would know nothing more than that a man was standing there on the beach who had just done the fishermen a service on the basis of certain things that he happened to know. Because John possesses love, he possesses essential belief and is able to know that it is the Lord, the one whom he loves. Through love, he makes the leap into belief. Hence, it is as if the Lord arises here out of belief, as if he, who is present *by his very nature,* becomes present *for the Church* through the loving belief of John and the official belief of Peter. So, too, the host becomes living in the Church through the unity of loving belief and official belief.

Before the transformation, the host is initially "something or other", similarly to the way that the unrecognized Lord on the beach is "someone or other". The praying priest blesses the host by sacrificing it. He thereby gives it the highest thing that a man can give. He consecrates it to God, he separates it off from its natural use; and along with this, he sacrifices and denies himself by forgoing its use, detaching himself from it, leaving it free so that it might become the body of the Lord. Sacrificing it is like a farewell. It is not, however, committed into nothingness, but rather, into the Father. And inasmuch as one gives it back to the Father, offers it in the way that the Father expects, the Father can give it back to man in the living form of his Son, which the Son assumes in the farewell-ed, blessed host, in this host that has acquired an indescribable share of the prayer of the priest and the believers. It had lain in an atmosphere of prayer upon the altar, it had absorbed into itself the sacrifice of the Church. This quite distinctly tinged host, almost saturated with belief and with the sacrifice of the Church, is filled by the Son, he adopts it as his body; the process of transubstantiation, which is a free act of the Lord, should not remain unrelated to belief and to the sacrifice of the Church. For this process to *occur,* the emergence of the process from God and its existence in the belief of men must form an inseparable unity. The priest who acknowledges that the host has become the body of Christ and contains his life actually confers, by virtue of his office and in the name of the Father, life upon the host. The Father gives the Church a share in his power to make the Son present. Thus belief and life become a unity here. It is a meeting point, even more, a synthesis, a flowing source of the Son and of belief. Time and eternity come together; temporally, the transformation is one moment among others and definable as such. But the second at which the transformation occurs contains in itself the value of an eternity: the whole of nontemporal and nonspatial eternal life is projected into the small-sized host. But so, too, the belief of the Church, which lives on impersonally throughout the centuries, which comes from all places and enters into all times, is personified in this priest and makes contact in him with the host. When John says, *It is the Lord,* he utters, as it were, the first *"Hoc est corpus meum".* Both sets of words say the same thing, spoken by the mouth of the Church, which is the unity of office and love. Both are the words of the Church's belief. Then, as now, the Lord bestowed belief, love and office; but he did so in order to become in the Church that which he already is in himself. If he is actually to be the Lord of the Church, he must receive belief back from the Church at both times—in fact, a belief that is simultaneously a belief of office and a belief of love, John and Peter; a belief of the Church—just as, at that time, the boat was the Church and just as, today, the transformation is possible only in the Church. He would not be there if love did not communicate to office that it is he; but he would also not be there without office, which administers his presence, recognized by love, in the Church. And in fact, the mystery of this presence arises at the exact moment of the *communication*, as a negation of isolation and a founding of communion in the Lord—of the communication precisely between love and office. For the Church, the Lord's becoming present lies necessarily in the coming together of the mutual necessity and dependency between love and office. This is a mystery of his free determination; because he *wills* love and office, he is thus to be found where office and love meet. Wherever these two come together, one can be sure that the Lord abides with them; and where the Lord abides, one can be sure that office and love come together. All this has shown what the Church ought to be: the synthesis of office and love in the Lord. And therefore the Lord also expects of his Church that the two should meet in him again and again.

When Simon Peter heard that it was the Lord, he put on his clothes, for he was stripped for work, and sprang into the sea. Peter becomes the central figure. Without pushing John aside, he assumes the leading role. He hurries to the Lord; afterward, he will haul the net out of the water. Everything now proceeds irresistibly in and through Peter. He, and not John, hurries to the Lord; he, and not John, brings the harvest in. No one thinks of trying to deny him this privilege, this primacy. For him, it has become a matter of course to have love in himself, to distinguish no longer, within his role, between office and love. The two merge into one another. This unity must only be such that the vitality will stay preserved in it. If the two were left standing side by side, it would possibly be easier to measure oneself against both. Each would be defined in contrast with the other, and one could discern one's position in relation to office and in relation to love. There would be two touchstones, two norms. However, because the Church must be a complete unity of office and love, there is only a single norm, and the Church remains, in a sense, untestable for the Church. If her essential core could be tested by the believers, she would not be the Catholic Church. This core must be enduring vitality in the Lord, a vitality that is so great that it can only consist in the unity of office and love, of anonymity and personality. The

Church must be anonymous, and yet she is not permitted to settle into this anonymity; at the same time, she must be supremely personal life. Men come to the Church with their personal love in order to make themselves personally available for service; yet as soon as they have been admitted to the Church, their love is integrated into office, and in this integration it can no longer be measured, no longer recognized. It almost appears unkind that John recognizes the Lord whereas Peter is allowed to be the first to go to him, and yet John wishes nothing more dearly than this, and that his office should merge with that of Peter. This involves no dissolution of the person: in total dedication to what is official, in full submergence in its anonymity, the whole requirement to be personal remains in effect. For in the Church, too, the Lord remains— quite personally—the Lord, who takes his Bride, the Church, and every individual sinner as a member of this Church, personally. Although we, as sinners, are the extreme opposite of the Lord as the head of the Church, we must nevertheless attempt to be as personal as the Lord himself, and to love as he does. Were the Church to consist of none but the righteous, she would have no need to emphasize her anonymous side, into which sinful man has to disappear because the Lord, too, enters into it when making his sacrifice. That the Church possesses this side is connected with the provisionality of her earthly form, with the abasement of the Lord and the necessity of purifying sinful Christians in this bath. Were mankind to consist of none but the saintly, were it not fallen, there would be direct contact with God; when two came together, they would be gathered from the first in the name of the Lord, and God would be among them. The whole apparatus of the official would not need to have been developed, nor also the whole structuring of our life into sacramentals, forms of prayer, regulations and rituals. As it is, however, there is a need for this sphere in which purification takes place, and indeed, precisely in the form of anonymity. There is a need for the great transpersonal that absorbs the sinner into itself. When a sinner asks God for something, he does not expect God to overthrow the world order for his sake. He dares to hope for fulfilment of his request only inasmuch as he commits it to the larger, sustaining, all-enveloping spiritual vision of the Church. He places his prayer in the lap of the Church and draws simultaneously upon her wealth, which is a general, anonymous one. Precisely as a sinner, he needs this shield of anonymity. At the same time, however, he knows that what is his personally does not therefore become invisible to the eyes of the Lord. He must give his whole personality over to the Church and adopt her form of life as something anonymous in order to receive it back again from her, but now as externally impressed with the stamp of the Church. She puts the Christian into a kind of uniform, and he will not expect that, just for him, this garb would have to be especially soft and comfortable. Suffice it if he knows that he receives the garb that God has intended him to have. The sum total of all the uniforms should certainly present a unified effect, while every individual wearing one is recognized quite personally. In a Christian hospital, the sick are given an opportunity to receive the sacraments before dying. But the Church is not only a place where one "has an opportunity" to encounter God's light. She herself has a light at her disposal to which all within her must expose themselves, whether they want to or not. Precisely because the Lord, without having asked men, died for all men without distinction (and therefore also for me), the possibility of choice is taken from me: no matter what, I must acknowledge my being affected in an objective form in which, by inclusion, the anonymity of the ecclesiastical form is recognized as well.

In this scene, Peter represents the whole Church. When he has recognized the Lord, he goes to him in the name of all. Insofar as the Lord is there for all, and Peter goes to the Lord on behalf of all, he is similar to the Lord. The more differentiated some mission in the Church is and the more difficult, accordingly, it becomes to allow oneself to be assimilated into already-existing forms, the more consciously the official side of the Church must be recognized and affirmed as well. For Peter must, in fact, go to the Lord, and through Peter, the love of all who want to stand by love.

That Peter clothes himself before he goes indicates the dignity of his office. Only as clothed can he appear before the Lord. Regarding souls, one can always say: the more nakedly they stand before God, the better. But when office appears physically before the Lord, the reverse applies: the more dignifiedly, the better. Peter must make himself ready before going to the Lord. This small delay is proper.

Because the Church is official, she needs ceremonies; she must impart an official gloss to what she does, a certain solemnity. To be sure, it may seem strange that Peter dresses himself precisely before springing into the water; even the Church could perhaps swim better if she had fewer clothes on. And yet this is essentially connected with office, with representation of the entire multitude before the Lord, with the delay that arises from the fact that everything must be given its fitting place within the general whole.

He sprang into the sea. He chooses, despite the delay, the quickest way. He goes to the Lord, attired in the dignity of office, carrying in himself the living love that John has given him, which has made his belief living and enabled him to spring into the water with hope, hopeful because he must now actually fulfill what the Lord expects of him. He acts alone, he detaches himself, as the bearer of office, from the congregation by springing in and going to the Lord.

21:8. *But the other disciples came in the boat, dragging the net full of fish, for they were not far from the land, but about a hundred yards off.*

The boat that ventured forth in order to reaccommodate itself to the Lord, turns homeward. The Church had put to sea in order to test what she could achieve; she was able to do nothing; but the Lord was able to do everything. It is because she made herself available and the Lord was able to fulfill—everything and above all measure—that the way things end looks so very different from the way they began.

Two distinct groups emerge: on the beach, the Lord with Peter, and on the sea, the boat containing the others and their catch. One cannot say that the Lord with Peter—that is, with his Church—has estranged himself from the boat and the catch by standing on the beach. In this separation into two, as apparent to the eye, there lies instead a sure sign of unity. The unity of the Church is so constituted that every kind of movement in her is not only possible and permitted, but required: she is a unity embracing constantly new variations and constellations. The boat that is apparently separated from the beach is still steering toward the Lord, in a movement that was anticipated by Peter only because he knew that the others would be following him. Even if the others were to feel themselves isolated—they nevertheless know that they are involved in carrying out their task and are thus united with the Lord in the mission, that they have to bring in the catch presented to them by the Lord, and that this gift from the Lord came to them in the midst of their commission. It would be nice to be together with one another always. But there are these separations, distinctions, directions, which cannot be at all judged outside the Church but belong to the living inner life of the Church. Seen from the outside, it looks like schism and discord; from the inside, one is gladdened by precisely such divisions because one understands that, through them, every individual is fulfilling his task.

The disciples in the boat drag laboriously after them that which the Lord has given them. They still cannot see what they have caught. It is enough for them to know that the mysterious content of the net stems from the Lord. Their net contains precisely that which the Lord wanted to allocate to them, and for this they are grateful. Thus should our gratitude always precede our seeing. We often press to see the fruits of our apostolate, to receive from the Lord confirmation of our work in the form of our success. But we should already be giving thanks when everything is still unseeable. The disciples sense by the weight of the net the bountifulness contained within it; we could recognize by the weight of our mission the bountifulness of the Lord. They row toward the Lord in order to present him with the yield, to give to him what he has given to them. They drag in something whose nature they do not know, with no other task in mind than that of bringing it all to the Lord. Peter, who is already with the Lord, will be the first to pull the net out and to examine and view it officially. From the vantage point of the beach, with the Lord, facing those who are hauling the net in, one has an awareness, a certain larger view of the activity. Without any supervision at all, things cannot succeed. From time to time, one must receive renewed certainty about the correctness of the way. It is not sufficient just to keep moving in the direction of the Lord. Occasionally, one must regain oneself in the Lord. Those in the boat are engaged in action; Peter, with the Lord, is engaged in contemplation. Action is always without supervision; that is mediated by contemplation. Striving takes place in ignorance; arrival (even if provisional) is in knowledge. But nothing would be more dangerous for the Church, and especially for office, than to stand constantly with the Lord on the beach.

Of the Lord, we know only that he occasionally stands on the beach and allows his Church to look out from there at the rowers in the ship. Usually, he assumes that the unity of his Church is not there where he stands, on the beach, but rather, in the community that is steering toward the Lord. The unity of the Church is not one of quiet possession and enjoyment, for her main task is to be there where the fishermen are at work, who possess nothing but the unknown gift from the Lord that they are to bring back to him. It would be wholly wrong if the leaders of the Church were to devote themselves mainly to observing how the others toiled away, to evaluating their achievements, to making compilation of statistics their favorite occupation, to looking down on the work of the others from the elevated standpoint of contemplation and not returning again to actual, dragging, wearisome action. That Peter stands on the beach does not mean that he is the true Church, that the others are only a subordinate band of servants. Peter's view out from the beach is the exception; the boat with the struggling, sweating and groaning workers is the norm. Only for the space of a second is Peter allowed to stop; immediately, he will *have* to return again to action. Many callings and missions come to naught because those who possess them no longer want anything but to rest. Here below, to have arrived at the Lord does not yet mean resting with the Lord. Otherwise, one would put aside one's mission and, in so doing, at once incur loss of the intimacy of the Lord. As soon as one has succeeded in finding, one is cast by the Lord back again into the surging waves of the seekers. He himself disappears from the beach, and it would be wrong to imagine that, because one saw him standing here yesterday, he would have to be (invisibly) present, precisely here, today as well.

The disciples are not far from land, and they drag in the net *because* they are not farther away. They bring the Lord what belongs to him for the very reason that they are so close to him. The Lord gave them a catch that was not far away from him: precisely those fish are directed to them that were already close to the net of the Church—those believers, too, who had grown cold but can be brought back through word or example. It is not forbidden to want to lead to God even a man who stands far away; one can pray for him. But really binding him to the Lord first becomes possible only when he is no longer far away from him. The closer the net is to land, the less that is lost on the way.

In a sense, it also seems as if the boat had divested itself of office. And in fact, it has done that, in order, namely, to bring the fish to office, to go with the fish in the direction of office. The fishermen divest themselves, in a sense, of their official character when they set out on their fishing expedition. From out there, they can point to the beach, to the Lord and the Church; they point toward these without constantly emphasizing the fact that they are themselves of the Church. They are able to do this because John is among them, who has, to be sure, handed his love over to Peter officially, yet has retained it personally. To personal love, nobody has any objections; in the context of the catch, it does not arouse the same mistrust as office. The only part of love that Peter has taken with him is that which fits the mold of the *Una Sancta*. The rest remains in the boat in order to love those men whom one must lead to God, and in order to lead them, precisely through this love, to the Church.

THE MEAL

21:9. *When they got out on land, they saw a charcoal fire there, with fish lying on it, and bread.*

The disciples first see the meal of fish and bread when they land on the beach. This meal seems like a contradiction to the question that the Lord had directed to them previously, namely, if they had any fish to eat. Thus he already possessed what was needed before he demanded it from them. He has what is needed, he demands it from them and he presents it to them. And his gift is of such dimensions that their strength was inadequate to the task of hauling it in. And yet his *hunger* is never constituted in such a way that he would need more than he already possesses; the question that he put to them was not an expression of his need, but, without their being able to perceive the fact, more an expression of theirs. He wanted to arouse a certain hunger in them, to allow it to arise as a result of his commission. Their hunger was to be a hunger for him to act, for increased knowledge of what he is able to bring about and ultimately, simply hunger within his commission, without any palpable object.

The Lord can arouse a longing in us that is simply longing, and not until he appeases it does he reveal its essence. To the false longing of this world, which is the complete opposite of the longing of the Lord, everything appears dull, unsatisfying, empty, worn-out. Turning toward the Lord is a turning away from the dullness of everyday life in the world toward a fervent longing for the Lord. As seen from the outside, both conditions can seem quite similar; both express a need that cannot be satisfied by this world. But one is weariness and satiety; the other is a bright, flaming longing that comes from the Lord. In man himself, there is always only something like a tentative beginning; only the Lord first brings fulfilment, but in such a way that, in each case, he also rouses an unknown hunger, quite essential needs that had previously remained concealed to man. They are his needs, yet far more still, the needs of the Lord. All the things that he brings—his joys, for example—bear the stamp of his nature, his quality of openness toward the Father. A purely human teacher may perhaps have very ideal aims, but they remain finite, limited to the human. A Christian teacher has, as his ultimate aim, an open one: to bring the children under the influence of the Lord, who has his own aims for them. But the Lord, too, has an open aim: the infinite openness of trinitarian life. A true teacher, who has some favorite student, would always like, at bottom, to make more out of him than he himself has achieved; he knows his own limitations, and would like his student to avoid and transcend these. If he is only a human teacher, then he will perhaps elevate his student to the position of his "God", and attempt to fulfill in him the whole of his ideal. Ultimately, however, he will have to impose some limit on his ideal, on this product of his life as summed up in another person. There are Christians who think of the Lord in a way not very different from the way that this teacher thinks of his student. It may be, of course, that they expect more of the Lord than they themselves are willing to give to him; still, they ultimately serve the Lord as if he were their own ideal, which means that they must impose the limits of their understanding and imagination on the fulfilment they expect. And these limits they determine themselves. They believe them to be very broad. Only true fulfilment would first show them how narrow, in fact, they were. But whether what is adored or worshipped is a student or the Lord, the fact remains: as long as the limits of the set ideal are merely one's own, it is disguised self-worship, a projection of one's own ego. If, however, a Christian worships the Lord in truth, then he knows that all shaping of things comes from the Lord himself, can never be finite because it stems from trinitarian life, takes place in the Holy Spirit and has its source in the Father. Everything remains open and an expression of the unpredictable, sovereign will of the Lord. If a teacher loves his student in a Christian way, or a father his son, then he knows that even the best he can do for him remains something merely secondary, and that it will become fruitful only if the Lord adds his contribution by scattering his seeds on the tilled soil. Anyone who might think that he had definitively comprehended his student or his son would be mistaken; the side of his pupil that is turned toward God would always still elude him. And if one cannot see all that there is to even a man, then far less can one do so regarding the Son, and far less again regarding the Father. It is like a progression of noncomprehension, but a progression into the grace of the open incomprehension. It is enough if God understands; the infinite comprehension of Father and Son in the Holy Spirit imparts to the whole of human incomprehension the character of peace—despite everything that remains incomprehensible, despite all the expectations that go unfulfilled—because nothing comes to an end; everything continues to progress unceasingly in God. Precisely this is the true longing that simultaneously means fulfilment: the unceasing continuation of life in God, which God also communicates to us. The eternal process of moving further ahead that characterizes Christianity presents the sole possibility left to the Christian for resting satisfied with things as they are.

What we see now is the preparation by the Lord of a quite simple, ordinary human meal. And the disciples come simultaneously to him and to this meal. They come with the miracles of the Lord, with this superabundance of food that the Lord has procured for them. If he sends apostles out to fish for souls, then that occurs under commission from him, but also, at the same time, under commission from the Father. He wills something, but, at the same time, his will is at one with the Father's will and is satiated in that will. And when those who were sent out return home with their catch, when the fishermen draw near with what they fished, they see that the Lord's need has already been satisfied. They see the opposite of what they had expected: he has long possessed everything that is being brought to him. To be sure, the Lord needs . . . ; but he nevertheless always has all that he needs. He always has the beginning, he already possesses the Church, and in a sense, too, in perfect fullness, inasmuch as she is enough for him. And yet that which he has is only a beginning, because he wants to have everything in it, would like to catch everything in it. For he came, after all, in order to save everyone. Thus there is a kind of disappointment at the fact that the Lord already has everything, that he who comes to him is actually superfluous. But if this disappointment is a Christian one, then it allows itself to be resolved into the longing of the Lord. And precisely if someone is disappointed, then he has still grasped nothing of the fullness that constantly increases; hence, it was high time that he came in order to allow himself to be integrated into the Spirit of the Lord.

In the meantime, the fish are already in the net, not yet utilized, but already caught and available. They are like catechumens who wait in captivity, no longer in freedom, until their time has come. And every person in the Church, at some place and some time, is in this condition: he has been captured, that is clear; but still unclear is just what use, in particular, the Lord will make of him. That is part of the essence of the longing: this twofold determination of how one is to serve. In the tension between the two lies the element that bursts open in belief: the arousal of thirst and its quenching are not congruent. Such congruence would not be fitting in a religion that issues in infinity.

Many apparently fully developed images are now present alongside one another: Peter standing on the beach, the fishermen in the process of arriving, the hauled-in catch, the paradoxical answer of the Lord to his own previously asked question. All these images are present without coming together to produce any final, comprehensible image. Only in one respect do they all agree: that there where they share a common effect, they all point toward openness. Where the answer is awaited most urgently, it must turn out that no answer meets the question that was posed. After all the problems have been pursued as far as possible, one reaches the conclusion that they all issue in something else that one can no longer reach conclusions about. And in fact, on the most varied sorts of plane. There is no unitary level to which they could all be raised or reduced. Each of them comes to an end at its own special level. The only one who knows but a single level, a level that we are not capable of grasping, is the Lord; and only this much is evident: that his grace will surely bring all these problems to a solution. But the solution lies only in him. In each case, how far it must go to meet them will differ, but just how far can never be measured.

21:10. *Jesus said to them: Bring some of the fish that you have just caught.*

The Lord issues a brief command. These are the first words that he has spoken since indicating to them where they were to cast their net. Everything that has happened seems to have been intended, thought through, planned by him to such an extent that not the smallest room for surprise is left in him. Now he continues to command. He takes control of the fish as if they were his (which, after all, they are), he takes control of the fishermen as if he knew of their readiness to serve him effectively. And he exercises control without expecting any kind of objection, without being prepared for any kind of resistance. But he exercises control not only as unrestricted Lord, but also under commission from the Father. His commission and the mission of the Father are contained in him, are his. He draws on their power, which he receives from the Father. Thus he is the image of authority, of the unbroken authority of the Father in the Son. The Son, who otherwise never acts in a domineering manner, makes use of this authority like a tool; it rests in his hands like something that belongs to him completely. Just as a well-bred person dining at a stranger's table partakes of everything that is set before him, so the Son helps himself to all the qualities of the Father that have been made available to him. He does not choose only what tastes best to him, for example, love and mercy, but is also happy to represent that in the Father which shows him to be the Lord. Just as a Christian ought to receive all the sacraments that are available to him, and should not be selective, so the Son makes use of everything that the Father places at his disposal.

Bring some of the fish. The disciples are not first to come, then only afterward to bring. They are to come as bringing. He wants to receive them as they now are: as those who have something to bring. He makes no allusion to the fact that the gift was already his before they had it. For that which they bring and that which the Lord has combine to form a Christian unity. If someone works under commission from the Lord, then everything that passes through his hands can belong only to the Lord. It belongs to him so much, and so self-evidently, that he can, for that very reason, entrust it to his workers as something that is his. There is an obvious interplay in possessing things, just as a wife buys the groceries with her husband's money and the husband eats the meal that his wife has prepared for him. Everything belongs to us because everything belongs to the Lord. And between both, a trustfulness prevails that does not wish to be constantly either demanding or rendering account. Between mine and yours, there is simply no distinction made. Everything is *one* large commission, and all the lesser things that occur become components within it. And in any case, the outcome rests continually in the Lord.

21:11. *So Simon Peter went aboard and hauled the net ashore, full of large fish, a hundred and fifty-three of them; and although there were so many, the net was not torn.*

Again, Peter takes the lead. He climbs back into the boat; he goes out to meet the others and hauls the net ashore. In bringing in the fish, the main role falls to him. But what is essential, in the first instance, is that he goes out to meet them. He, who embodies the Church, goes out to meet the others, the ones who are simultaneously returning home with what is awaited. Not the Lord. The Lord occupies an unalterable standpoint. He stays there where he is. Peter's going back and forth, however, his moving first toward the Lord and then back to the boat, his first leaving the boat, then again leaving the Lord, then again finding the boat after having found the Lord, all illustrates the movement of the Church, her process of development, of accommodation. It points to the element of the human that attaches to the Church; but to something human that unfolds before the eyes of the Lord, before the eyes of the immovable Lord. As if the Lord were remaining immovable primarily so that the Church can take her measure by him. So that Peter can observe him from both on the beach and in the boat. So that the difference might finally become clear between the Lord and his one Church. For Peter remains the one; he embodies the one Church whether he happens to be standing on the beach or in the boat. He has talked with the Lord on the beach, and now he is at work again in the boat, but under commission from the Lord.

What he does is real work: Peter hauls in the entire net. The Lord appears no longer to do anything but issue commands, no longer to take things in hand himself; for the time of his earthly, physical work is past. In the time in which he now exists, he merely perfects what he has previously done. He does it from his position on the beach. His taking things in hand occurs differently from the way it did then; it comes about now *through* the Church. The Church is the one that makes the efforts. There are some directives from the Lord that she can fulfill where she stands, and others that bring her into movement and can be fulfilled only through movement. Some things are clearly specified, others come to light only in the course of carrying out the commission. And the Lord says: *Bring some of the fish;* but he does not say how. Yet even regarding the how of the carrying out, the Church should remain just as precisely at the center of the commission. By doing that, she accepts the measure of the Lord: that she live in obedience, toward the Lord and outward from the Lord, in the full livingness of being Christian at the place where it is most intense, namely, in the Church.

Her activity has the appearance of a series of little waverings, and the Church can certainly not allow herself very wide swings in any direction. But she needs freedom of movement. Above all, she must never have arrived. Over and over, constantly anew, Peter must take things in hand. If he wanted to remain standing with the Lord, and do nothing more than worship him, he would be denying that the Church is living. She is living, however, through both her turning toward the Lord and the path she must follow from the Lord, and in this movement lies the unity of freedom and obedience. And Peter hauls the net ashore; he performs the observable action even though the commission was issued to all. But there are certain ultimate things that the Church reserves to herself, things upon which she must impress the seal.

And inasmuch as the Church fulfills the commission, the greatness of the Lord also shows itself to her more definitively. She grows through his commission, and thereby the Lord—though not in himself—grows for her. Inasmuch as the Church grows, it becomes evident to her that the Lord is no longer comprehensible by her. So great is he. And because the Lord, at every stage, is always greater than the Church, the latter, in order to grasp this, must constantly remain living. The last commission from the Lord will never be fulfilled; never will she be able to say of herself that she has no further commission left to fulfill. Even were it to pertain just to the understanding of dogma.

The net that Peter hauls ashore is filled with the miracle of the Lord—so full that human strength alone, without the office of the Church, would not be able to bring it onto the beach. Men alone would not have been able, when Peter was still in the boat, to haul it in. They are capable of that only after having received the commission to do it. Previously, they all had attempted to drag the net in; now Peter alone does what all had only attempted. The commission confers, once it is present, the strength to carry it out. And there is no longer any relationship here between the strength before the commission and the strength under the commission. Previously, the strength was comprehensible; now, the strength relationship has been displaced to such an extent that the strength is no longer measurable—it is enough that it is there, as a component element within the commission. It is a strength deriving from the threefold life of God, but an absolutely differentiated one, directed toward the particular mission conferred. If, at that moment, Peter did not have the commission, then he would perhaps have been unable to move even a quarter of the net's weight. A part of the strength also lies, however, in the object: this will *allow* itself to be moved. The man who can be converted will allow himself to be convinced. Thus the weight is affected from both sides and is brought into motion, precisely because the commission stems from the triune life. The commission always transcends the commission: both in respect of its origin, for it has its meaning in a much greater context, and in respect of its purpose; the commission, as a restricted one, is only a part of an encompassing, perhaps immeasurable, whole. In every Christian commission, the vitality of trinitarian life is contained. For every divine commission from the Son stems from the Father and acquires the strength for its execution from the Holy Spirit; although all three Persons accomplish the entire work together, there is still something like an apportionment of roles: the Father bestows the meaning, the Son the love and the Spirit the strength. Every mission that the Son confers bears the characteristics of the mission of the Son, who lives in the Father and acts in the strength of the Holy Spirit. And everyone who carries out his mission is thereby taken up into the mission; he stands at the end in quite a different place than he did at the beginning, because, in the meantime, he has taken part in the movement of the Son away from the Father and back to the Father in the Holy Spirit, even if without realizing this—just as the earth unconsciously revolves around the sun.

Whoever observes a man who accomplishes his mission no longer comprehends him entirely. He knows only that this man belongs to the company of the Lord; but just where he stands within his mission is not fully comprehensible. Apparent only is the fact that he has changed his position, has become caught up in a movement, now stands in a place, that is specifiable neither by even himself nor by the observer. The situation of a novice, for example, at the end of his novitiate, is no longer graspable by his relatives. They see that he has become different; but his real position is a secret of the Lord. The transplanted one himself can attempt to trace the path he has described in order to work out his current position; but even he will not be totally successful.

The number of the *hundred and fifty-three fish* bears no relation to the number of participant fishermen, just as little as it bears any relation to their expectation. Quantitatively, the number means, at the same time, an enormous sum and a countable number. It represents the numbers of men whom the apostles, under commission from the Lord, have to bring to the Lord through the Church. From this moment on, no one will any longer have a relationship to the Lord that does not find its main pathway within the Church and her relationship to him. This pathway will now always be one where the *Lord* calls and those *who are his* bring. All who are brought can be individually counted, but they form, in their total number, something that remains beyond correlation, because the nature of the devotedness of the individual to the Lord never becomes totally transparent to the Church. And yet this untransparent thing is nevertheless clarified and rounded out before it becomes visible to men, because the command was issued by the Lord, to individuals: Bring *me* the fish!

One can also understand the number of fish qualitatively; then it includes the kinds and styles and paths of love as they have been explained in this Gospel. Were one to add up these styles and paths, one would perhaps arrive at this number. All who are coming are contained in the net of the Church; the net reduces them all to the same state, they are caught within the net. But each individual still retains his character, his personal nature. And if each came into the net, and to the Lord, by virtue of the unitary command of the Lord, each had, up to the point of arriving at the net, nevertheless traversed a quite different path. The Lord's command can be expressed uniformly, and yet, in the case of each fish, he has provided for his individual path. And all the disciples have dragged in the one net. One cannot specify just how the doing of the work was divided up: whether this one had more success with casting the net, whether that one pulled more than the others when dragging the net in. Each one tried, in his own way, to obey the Lord's command, and within this common obedience, each acquired his own relation to the work, his own characteristic approach. Thus a hundred and fifty-three fish were simultaneously caught with the single net; but they were not brought to the Lord until Peter went out to get them. This oneness of being brought remains the same throughout all centuries. The oneness of the time of bringing lies in the command of the Lord and in being caught in the one net, in the oneness of Peter, who hauls the net ashore; just as it was *he* who, at the beginning, went fishing. But the oneness of the net is not enough for the Lord; he counts the fish individually, he pauses over each individual one. Within the impersonal, there is room for what is most personal, for the fish as well as for the fishermen; all particular and differentiated commissions have their place within the all-embracing unity.

And although there were so many, the net was not torn. The net of the unity of the *Una Sancta* does not tear, no matter how much, quantitatively and qualitatively, is to be found in it. It contains the most varied directions in itself, without thereby being split open. Perhaps some parts of the net have suffered damage; perhaps, because of the enormous mass, even some of the fish have suffered in some way—sacrificed a fin, lost a few scales. But they are all there and are all counted. Because the commission of the Lord is what is decisive— the love of the Lord for the whole net, for its entire contents, for Peter and the fishermen and for every individual fish—the fishing expedition as a whole is the answer to the Lord's question: *Children, have you any fish to eat?* Just what purpose the individuals are used for is a wholly indifferent matter; the only important thing is that they are all in the net and occupied with the net, that they are all available. The Lord's love applies just as directly to the individuals as to the totality; it is both particular and universal. In this, it distinguishes itself from love between men, which is at first merely personal, and only later, in a sense, expands. The Lord's love for the individual flows over to mankind in general; but his love for mankind in general always fulfills itself as love for the individual. Were a man to love a hundred and fifty-three persons, he would somehow divide them into groups, and the unity of the hundred and fifty-three would then exist solely in him, the one who loves. The Lord, by contrast, makes them all into an objective unity: the net. Thus Christians, too, who carry in themselves the love of the Lord, should not split up too much into groups, but should allow their love, in every instance, to expand all the way to the anonymity of the net, not placing too much importance, within the totality of the *Una Sancta,* on subsidiary organizations lest, for a profusion of particular groupings, they become no longer capable of seeing the unity of the Church. The Lord embraces all in the oneness of the net, in the oneness of the one Bride of Christ.

21:12a. *Jesus said to them: Come and eat.*

The Lord addresses them once again; but he had not stopped speaking to them, since his words had remained alive in them the whole time. They are Christians, and therefore hear his words in everything they do. But this hearing—as Christians have to hear the Word of the Lord—is always a hearing through to: not only a sensory one, with the ears, but one that extends beyond, into the wider context of the commission. If a hungry man begs for bread, then his words will continue to exert a living effect on the one who offers it, throughout every stage of the deed, until such time as the hungry man has eaten enough. The new words that the Lord speaks now are a consequence of some words that he spoke earlier, namely, his question about bread. And between the two lies the entire commission; and included in that commission are now also these hundred and fifty-three fish, along with the net in which they are caught. In all this, the reality of *prayer* becomes manifest.

Prayer is both the constant occupation of one who is under commission from the Lord and a drawing of the whole Church into this occupation. The fish are there by commission from the Lord, and the first commission from the Lord, to anyone who is a living member of the Church, is prayer. The prayer of those who belong to the Church always has this twofold character: that deriving from the commission of the Church, which, in the name of the Lord, issues a commission for prayer, and that deriving from the commission for individual prayer, which is carried out within the Church. The former is commissioned praying, and the latter prayed commissioning.

The Church immediately places those who are arriving into a framework: she gives them commissions to pray for something, and to grow into their framework through prayer. Yet the one who thus prays will not overlook the prayer that is expected of him, for it is a part of a larger commission. His prayer is almost an administrative prayer. Above all, the Church gives him the commission to participate in her business, which is that of prayer; and only after he has allowed himself to be fitted into this almost incomprehensible praying, through which he grows into the Church and the Lord, does his personal differentiation begin, does the individual become capable of bearing the word of the Lord. This bearing the word of the Lord is now simultaneously the carrying out of the commission for prayer and the capacity to do so; for in the Lord's commission for prayer, the question and answer are always simultaneously contained. Only in prayer do the questions of ecclesiastical life allow themselves to be resolved. And in the end, a Christian, no matter what he does—be it scientific research or organizing the state and the family—should carry out everything in prayer.

Every word that the Lord utters in this world is a prayer to the Father. It is also *essentially* prayer, and hence also prayer for the one who hears it, namely, commissioned prayer; it can therefore only be heard and carried out in prayer. Everyone who really hears what the Lord says hears it as having a meaning that accords with his own calling. It is infused into the various commissions and derives its livingness from those commissions. If a man asks for water, it can be for a thousand different purposes—to drink, to wash, to paint and so on. And it is according to the meaning of the commission he issues that the one commissioned will hear his words and carry them out. The fullness of the meaning of anything that the Lord says always lies in God, in the life of the Trinity; and it is back toward this meaning that each of the individual meanings contained in the different commissions must always ultimately point.

Everyone manages words as best he can, or at least ought to do so. We have grown accustomed to giving words a clearly defined meaning, to making our ears and our minds a filter, to ignoring or denying or forgetting words that we do not understand in this schematic sense. It seldom happens that we trouble ourselves seriously about any word: going behind the schematics in order to understand just what it means, here and now. But no word of the Lord's can ever be schematized, for none is ever understood in its fullness. Behind what is understood, there always stands the ever-greater truth. And if the Lord now draws the new arrival into the prayer of the Church, which is his own, he simultaneously shows him, by the magnitude of the framework, that he has to trouble himself about the meaning of his words. The commission that he issued to the fishermen, namely, to cast their net in a certain manner, is a commission that he issues to every individual: to try to approach things, and to carry them out, in a precisely specified manner. To appropriate as much of his words — that is, of his prayer to the Father — as one is able to apprehend in such a way that they might continue to be effective in the prayer of the hearer and, in that livingness, find their way back to the prayer of the Lord. Every word that the Lord utters, and that is addressed to the Father as well as to men, is, in the one who hears it, a call for unity — in the Father as well as in us — and is aimed at returning into the unity out of which it was uttered. It is not, however, aimed at going back empty, but together with us, the ones who hear it. This is the meaning of the words of the Lord: they are aimed at binding the Father and men into their unity, into the unity of the Son. Thus the Son becomes the absolute fisherman.

Every word of the Son contains the Father; it is disclosure and glorification of the Father. And inasmuch as the Son confers participation on us — which is just what prayer is — he confers participation in the revelation and glorification of his Father. Through this, he draws us into the unity of the *Una Sancta,* which must be realized within every individual life. He forms the life of the individual into an ongoing prayer, and also, through that, into an ongoing revelation and glorification of the Father within the unity of the Church.

As long as someone has not yet been taken up by the Lord into his commission—and this commission begins with being taken into the net, into the Church—he can arrange his life in the way that he himself deems good; he can, insofar as is possible for men, exercise control over his life. But once he is in the net of the Church, participating in the Lord's commission, his life is controlled by the Lord, who divides it up into its main component aspects, and only within that structure is he still left free to exercise control himself. This now means that he must adapt his life not only to the commission in general, but also to understanding the commission. But through having his life controlled in this way, he has gained sight. He has lost his blindness, with the result that these controls over him acquire a manifest meaning; he is active within his commission, in the Church, and this withinness means freedom. For he is given the freedom of prayer, of belief; and everything that he does in it is illumined, in a way, from within, through the conferring of commissions by the Lord. For in the Lord, the conferring of commissions and the granting of belief are one.

The individual fish that comes into the net will find other fish in it; he will have to move in a community of others that share his orientation and belief. The net was empty as long as men were alone, as long as they had not yet received the commission from the Lord to fill it. So, too, as long as one fishes only for oneself, the net of the commission is empty. But if one fishes under commission, the fishing expedition becomes an activity of the community, which leads to a communal catch that fills the net. And not only the fish—those men who have been led to the Church—but likewise, too, the graces, the prayers that are part of the commission, thereby become communal. In the Lord, and solely in him, everything is fruitful, everything related to everything else, everything living; while everything that is not touched by the grace of the commission remains dead and unfruitful.

Everything that is done within the commission is opened toward the Lord, and this opening gives birth continually to new openings. One cannot have the commission to lead some person to the Church and then, once that has taken place, be left standing there with no commission. One cannot have the commission to assume some ecclesiastical office and then, once having assumed it, find that the commission has ended. Rather, every commission necessarily continues on further, is intrinsically unlimited, so much so that it lays claim not only to the personal life of the one commissioned, but also to all of his relationships, acquaintanceships, spheres of influence and interests. To be sure, the origin of the commission lies in the personal: one must allow oneself to be possessed by it, alienate oneself from oneself in order to allow oneself to be received by the Lord. In this self-alienation lies the finding of one's personal "salvation of soul". It is salvation to the degree that the one pardoned forgets himself in favor of commitment to his commission. Whoever is entirely redeemed is at once put to use in a coredemptive capacity, because neither in redemption nor in the commission is there a setting of limits. If someone who had been redeemed wanted to regard that as an accomplished fact, then he would thereby have imposed a limit on the commission from the Lord. When a man is set totally free from the power of sin by the Lord while still in this world, then that is primarily in order to make it possible for him to participate in his redemptive work while still in this world. Everything that he effects in us is passed on, through us, to others; if he gives someone a living belief, he does so in order that it might become living in others as well; if he frees someone from servitude to sin, he does so in order that others might be freed through him. Here we have proof of the fact that, in Catholic life, everything is destined for continued life. Just as little as the Baptist was permitted to keep his disciples for himself can any Christian utilize for himself alone anything that was entrusted to him. This is inherent in the nature of love. Just as the relation between man and wife gives rise to the child, so there arises, from the love between the Lord and the Christian, something new, fruitful. Whether the life be active or contemplative, as a Christian one, it is always a life of ongoing generation. Every instance of action demands new action, and also brings it about. And every instance of contemplation is a seed that the Lord uses for new sowing. The more the Lord has control over a life, the more fruitful it is. It may be that the Lord by no means wishes to control every particular thing; in the case of marriage, for example, he leaves the arranging of this aspect of life largely up to the person; he takes over only one part, and only illumines and colors the other, suffusing it with his Spirit. From there, different levels of devotedness and controlledness become visible: for instance, those of a lay apostle, a secular priest and a monk. And the greater the part that the Lord controls, the more fruitful the life will be. Even within monastic life, there can still be special controls: one can enter an order with the intention of converting black Africans or of sacrificing for poor souls, and this control can be imposed by the Lord and the individual jointly. The control will be at its most perfect when the Lord alone controls everything, and any differentiation of the mission occurs only as a consequence of his having control over the full indifference of the one controlled. Still, this state of existence is not intended for everyone; each person finds what is right for him in responding to the prayer of the Lord, and this prayer is heard personally, and differently, by each.

The Lord shows us that every word he speaks is a prayer in order that we might learn to make a prayer of every word that we speak to him, no matter on which level of the commission and the mission. Whoever does not have love, and does not give the Lord the possibility of forming his words to the Lord into a prayer, is tempted to speak with the Lord in such a way that, in this conversation, no sense of prayer is any longer perceptible. The human words no longer integrate with his divine words, which go to the Father. An egoistic request to the Lord is no prayer if the Lord does not, in receiving it, transform the egoism into love. A prayer that becomes prayer only for reasons of external duty, only for the sake of performing it, is no prayer. Prayer first arises when the wish is present, in the background, that the Lord might hear even these feeble words in such a way that they can be transformed, in him, into true prayer. Then the Lord can fill in the emptiness with his own fullness. And yet there is, in the Church, the obligation to pray, and with that, obligatory prayer: there is penitential prayer after confession, and the liturgy of the hours prayer of the priest. Obedience and love, closing and opening, come together here, and the two must measure themselves by one another. The net, after all, is closed as well; but on land, it is opened before the Lord's eyes and its contents counted. Form and spirit must converge within the unity; even though the form may seem constricting, the spirit can expand it and burst it open, but without destroying it, without detaching the one who prays from the form.

The Lord's discourse is always aimed in the two directions: toward the Father and toward men. Each of his words is spoken in glorification of the Father, and thereby becomes, for us, an admonition to glorify the Father likewise, in him and with him. All his commissions always ultimately come down to this glorification of the Father. Therefore he now expects us, who have received his commission, to carry on his speaking as well, to take up as our own the discourse that we have heard from him. Thus every word that we direct to any man should, at the same time, be a prayer to God. During his life on earth, the Son had always looked both toward men and toward God. Even if he cannot bestow the vision of the Father in the same way—for no one but the Son has ever seen God—he can still give us the substance of his mediating position: that none of our words should die away unheard. Whether our words are directed to a believer or a nonbeliever, they are Christian words, which means that they are presented by the Son to the Father, and are therefore prayer. When the Son speaks, he knows the Father and us. When we speak, the Son mediates to the Father what we say, thereby allowing it to become fruitful in relation to men. Through him and in him, we, too, can speak to the Father with every one of our words. That is a great relief to us, for, of ourselves, we have no conception of the Father; but the Father, with whom we speak when we address ourselves to men, is the Father who sent the Son, and who thus hears the words in the way that the Son pronounces them. If we speak within the Son's commission, then our words have, for the Father, the sound of the Son's love, and he no longer needs to weigh them, but can receive them as words of the Son. Not as if the trivial words that are exchanged among Christians were to acquire the weight of eternal words—and yet the core of their talk is God, and this is so thanks to the presence of God's Word in the midst of all that talk. Even in the human partner, after all, the Lord is present, and that partner can, through his knowledge as well as his ignorance, always serve as a reminder that the conversation must be conducted in God.

When the Son invests any man with his commission, that occurs for the glorification of the Father. His aspiration is that man, too, should aspire to God. The longing and the desire that the Son arouses in him can never cease to be longing and desire because they possess no other object and goal but God.

For that is what Christians strive after. They do not strive primarily after their sanctity, their blessedness or any other sort of personal state, some "level of prayer" or of perfection. God alone is the goal. Anyone who wanted to strive after something other than God would, in the end, be striving after himself. But whoever strives after God strives least of all after himself. He also does not desire a synthesis between himself and God. The Son never took his own sanctity as the goal of his striving; his sanctity was to accomplish in everything the will of the Father. To strive after one's own sanctity would mean, once again, to set and measure limits. But it is only when all possibility of measuring is lost to us that each thing we say becomes truly a prayer, because it becomes submerged in the striving of the Word of God that is the Son. There is no measure for prayer, for the measure of prayer is the Son, the boundless Word of the glorification of the Father.

Come and eat. After the Lord has demonstrated the immeasurability of the commission to the disciples, and after they, despite this immeasurability, have arrived at the end of one stage in the commission, he invites them to come to him and to eat with him. The simplicity of this invitation seemingly bears no relation to the sublimity of the commission. They are to come, since they are already near; to eat, since the food is already prepared. The invitation might appear like one pertaining to a small, shared feast. But it remains to be noted that he himself had asked for food, and that the disciples are now to eat the food they have brought. Once again, the situation undergoes a reversal. The Lord declared a need to eat, and now it is they who are to satisfy their hunger. Whenever the Lord has some need or other, then this is only in order to arouse it in us or to make it serviceable to us. In so doing, he makes use of that which we can understand in order to open perspectives for us onto something that we cannot understand. And again and again he breaks things off, as having gone far enough, by again and again giving his demands and explanations some concluding formulation. He is, as it were, satisfied if we get no further than arriving once again at the notion that everything is, after all, greater than we thought. He does not like things to be concluded by us. He himself concludes things. He does this, in a sense, in order to give us some relief, but while also taking advantage of our wishes for rest and conclusion by making something out of them that corresponds to his purposes. At these moments, he brings us his human nearness. He is, after all, not only God, but a man like us. He is the man who must show us God, but also the God who must show us man. And everything that goes to make up our humanity is granted us and left as it is, if only we nevertheless strive for knowledge and glorification of the Father.

21:12b. *Now none of the disciples dared ask him: Who are you? They knew it was the Lord.*

This is very unexpected, and yet, for John, very characteristic. John is so much the lover that he always wishes for confirmation in love, but, on the other hand, sees in lack of confirmation the exalted greatness of the love. He has recognized the Lord in love, has passed this knowledge on in his communication to Peter; but the other disciples have not been informed. They know that it is the Lord, but dare not ask him. They dare not request confirmation of their love. To question would mean being deprived even more of their rights by love, being overpowered. Daring to question would mean forgoing their right to the questions and answers to come, to the whole conversation. Loving or engaged couples perhaps keep silent about certain things in order that a door might still be left open. And the disciples refrain from asking in order that they might not be drawn into something all too great. They know that, were they to ask, the answer would take hold of them like something colossal. They hang in a state of suspension, and the question would start things swaying, would perhaps force them into making incalculable decisions. If the woman asks the question before the engagement, then the man's answer becomes inescapable. The Lord's answer, too, would be inescapable; it would be the firmest of bonds. They well know that this state of suspension cannot be a permanent one. But they want to do nothing on their own initiative to end it. They dare not. They dare neither to hurl themselves in nor to be hurled in. They are like those believers who cannot accept the ultimate consequences of belief without first examining them, because they realize that this would be a surrendering of all security. But this condition cannot last long. For soon the Lord will begin to speak.

That is a Christian situation. One has recognized something, but one lacks the courage to accept the consequences of that recognition. Every Christian is, in a sense, like this. We attempt to postpone things by not asking the Lord, but waiting instead until he himself speaks. We love our state of equilibrium so much that we see any determination by the Lord as a disruption of our situation. Through what he said previously, the Lord had brought something to a conclusion. Now it is the disciples who cannot conclude things. For they sense, no doubt, what lies before them. So it is with respect to being called: one has once, no doubt, heard the voice of the Lord; but one would like it to express itself a little more clearly. And until then, one remains quiet, out of fear of being taken seriously. How many callings are thus ignored! John does not know this fear because he has love, because he immediately passed on what he recognized. Now he sees the fear in the others, but it is not his task to tell them that. He waits for the Lord to do so, which does not prevent him from observing that they are lacking in daring. A girl who knows no sort of selfishness has no fear of confirmation of her engagement. And John ridicules that fragile state of equilibrium because love has its own equilibrium. Only that which is not yet fully love requires assuring, even if the assuring consists in the fact that there is no surety to be had. We continually offer everything to the Lord, yet nevertheless make secret, fearful qualifications: But only not that! Love gives everything without any fear of being robbed.

They knew it was the Lord. They are in a state of latent recognition. But they want to keep to themselves their own knowledge of his identity, to mark out the dimensions of their recognition themselves. They hope that, if they refrain from asking who he is, they can make of him something that they understand, something that they would like him to be. Then they would not need to learn that he is *the* Christ, whom they do not understand.

21:13. *Jesus came and took the bread and gave it to them, and so with the fish.*

The first thing to happen is that Jesus hands them something that was already present, something of his own, which they have not brought with them: bread. It is not the first time that he gives them bread; since his having explained, and presented, to them the eucharistic character of the bread that is distributed in his name, they can, however, no longer eat any bread without thinking of him, without knowing that, when he gives them bread, he simultaneously presents them with what is his own and initiates them into his living mysteries. The first thing that the Lord gives them is what he himself possesses; for in everything that he presents to men, what is his always remains essential, even if what is ours belongs, in a secondary way, to what is his. By handing them the bread, he gives them his presence. Were he to give them only his presence, without the bread, they would not comprehend the grace involved; for this, they require a sign that is simultaneously something real. Thus he presents himself to them doubly in concrete form: in himself and in the bread; and in this doubleness lies the nucleus for presenting himself infinitely in concrete form. Also, in this way, he gives them that confirmation which they had not dared to request from him; and this, too, bears his character, namely, that of overflowing grace.

The Lord himself distributes himself as the Eucharist: he gives himself to men as the one who gives himself. This doubleness will no longer be necessary in heaven; there, we will no longer need any earthly confirmation of the presence of the Lord. And yet: inasmuch as he himself administers Communion, it is as if he were simultaneously giving heaven and earth. He opens up both perspectives: the view toward the Father through his presence as a man among those who are his own, and that of his abiding with the Father on earth through his offering of his bread to them. But inasmuch as he gives them this twofold gift, he gives them a third, namely, that which is his absolutely: the inseparable, everlasting glorification of the Father. Between the Lord who gives the host and the Lord who is in the host lies the giving as such, the movement of the Father toward the world in the Son, the breath of trinitarian life, as if that which, in his hands, is force and movement, that which, in his hands, holds the host together, were the effective life of the Father in him. As if it were the making visible of the Father in him. When the host is living and radiant in his hands, and he himself is living and radiant, then what unites him with the host, what turns both into a single ray, is not some qualitative likeness through which the two would blend (as if after the fact) into a common radiance, but the one life of the Father in him. It is so much the life of the Father that it has neither beginning nor end in him and, in the handing on of his own bread to these fishermen, possesses a movement that not only has the character of the personal movement from the Father to the Son in the Holy Spirit and back again to the Father, but, at the same time, also signifies a visible conferral of participation in the essentially eternal life of God. It is as if, in what is projected between the Son in himself and the Son in the host, there were the complete, infinite projection of eternal life, as if one had caught the whole of eternal life in one momentary image, as if the whole of eternal life had concentrated itself into that moment.

Also, the handing out of the bread serves, in turn, to make visible the commission of love. Anyone who sees two lovers embracing can infer much about their love from the way in which they move. From the gestures of the Lord as he distributes the bread, still infinitely more can be gleaned about the essence of love. The eternal Son, in the form of one of the Father's creatures, bestows himself in the form of the host, that is, in the communicability, lent to him by the Father, of an eternal life in the world. Everything lies in those gestures. On the basis of this little scene, one could reconstruct the entire Gospel of John. How else could the Lord honor the fisherman, after they had completed their commission, if not by presenting himself to them? By giving them what he has, the bread, and bestowing himself, in his own act of offering up, as he does so? By bestowing himself as presenting and presenting himself as the bestowed?

But because he surrenders himself in this way, his act of offering up becomes a possession of the Church. *Holy Mass,* too, takes on this twofold aspect. The priest who celebrates it is, on the one hand, the sinner who acknowledges his guilt, but then, immediately afterward, the official of the Lord who absolves. He is the spokesman of the congregation when he sacrifices, but the brother of the Lord when he administers Communion. This twofold orientation he receives from the Son, for in the Mass, after all, he is his representative. He ventures the sacrificing of the Son to the eternal Father. He does not sacrifice himself. For the reason, to be sure, that the Church must live and draw sustenance from this pure sacrifice, which is the only worthy sacrifice before the Father. But that is not all. During the sacrifice, the Lord is next to the priest, in him, around him. And at the moment when the host becomes the Lord himself, he takes, as it were, both priest and congregation, those whom he embodies before the Father, with him into the host. For a fraction of a second, Christ, priest and congregation seem to have become but one thing: that which is offered up to the Father. It is impossible that the Lord should embody himself in the host, enter into its form and being, yet not take mankind with him. He enters into the host only as simultaneously taking with him his commission: as taking with him both the priest and the *office* that is embodied in the priest, as well as the congregation and the *Bride* that is embodied in the congregation. Even if the priest were to say Mass alone, without the congregation, the Lord would take the congregation, as the Church, with him into the host. And even if the priest were to perform consecration as an unbeliever, the Lord would nevertheless take with him as much of the priest as is official and belongs to the Church, and even something of his person as well. The Lord never sacrifices himself alone. Not without us did he enter into his bloody sacrifice on the Cross: we were there with him, as the guilty, the reluctant, the dragged-along, the also-crucified. This mutual participation in the Cross is carried over into the unbloody sacrifice. Just as he is himself one and the same both on the Cross and in the Mass—the one who went forth from the Father in order to lead creation back to the Father—so he can never again, having once entered into creation and become a member of this order of creatures, return to the Father alone: he takes us with him.

In his sacrifice, the Son who comes into the world does not want to be only God, only the one sacrificed as God by God. He wants to suffer as man, and his sacrifice should take place within the abasement of being human; thus he also wants to be sacrificed by men. In this abasement lies a reversal of his path. For us, he is the path to God. But for him himself, there is no other path back to God than that of being sacrificed by men. He not only becomes the path for us; he will make use of us as the path upon which he returns to the Father. In this abasement, he has fallen from himself and into our hands, into a state of utmost self-surrender, in which he is now nothing more than something that is controlled by us. He allows himself to become an object of men to such a degree that he wants to lead men back to the Father through the host, in which only belief recognizes him, but which unbelief totally overlooks. He now becomes the continually Incarnated, no longer once only, by the Holy Spirit in the Mother, but in a mysterious and concealed form that is repeated daily in numberless places. His enemies do not recognize this coming; they see nothing but a piece of bread. Only his friends know about him in belief. And if his initial Incarnation was already visibly a relinquishing of his divine magnificence in the bosom of the Trinity, then his abasement in this new form of coming goes much further: it is like a reduction to nothingness. But only in this way has he fulfilled everything; and inasmuch as he allows himself to be consumed as a piece of bread, both by those who believe and by those whose belief is halfhearted or dead, he allows himself to be accepted within the whole range of gradations that extend from nothingness to God. To the sinner who does not believe, he is nothing; to the Father, he is God.

He owes his life in the host to loving trust, but to the loving trust of the Father, who alone recognizes the full divinity in him. The Father's loving trust in the Son exists in unity with the Son's loving trust in the Father and with their mutual love. And if it is as life that the Son receives the Father's loving trust in him, then he sacrifices back to the Father that which the Father has given over to him from eternity. The life that he owes to the Father from eternity he owes to him in the host as well. But in the host, he also has his human life, so as to be able to give lavishly of himself in gratitude to the Father and to offer it up to the Father. Into this he draws the whole of his redemptive sacrifice by men on the Cross and, in the reenactment of Holy Mass, the whole of humanity as Church, priest and congregation. He reveals his magnificence as Bridegroom in such a way as continually to bring it forth in the Church, his Bride. The Father is continually involved in generating the Son; the Son is continually involved in bringing forth the Church; but the Church, too, is continually involved in giving birth to the Son in the world. It is an eternally self-intensifying cycle of life. It is as if the Son, in acknowledgment of his love for the Father, were to keep inventing constantly new forms of love; and the culmination occurs again and again in transubstantiation.

If a man and a woman love each other, then they, too, will think up constantly new forms to express their devotedness. But it is impossible that they could ever present each other with new life continually and substantially. Between God and man, however, such an exchange of most genuine life comes about inasmuch as the gift that they give each other is life itself, in the form of the Son. In the new, sacramental form of life that the Son receives from the priest in the grace of the Father, that is, from a creature who is a sinner and has committed the offence of sin against the Father, he obliges that same man, by allowing him to bestow life upon him in the Mass and to sacrifice his life, to give back to the Father that which is dearest of all to the Father but which he has sacrificed for the benefit of man: his Son. Thus he takes man up into the focal point of love, into the center of the essence of the love that no man will ever understand. For no priest comprehends what he does when he celebrates Mass.

Among men, one cannot take love between friends so far as to lend one's own wife to one's friend so that, if a child comes, one would not know, in that love, whose it was. But when the Lord permits himself to be born and sacrificed anew by the priest in every Mass, by an immense number of priests into a still much more immense number of millions of hosts, all these acts that bring about the Son's presence point toward the one eternal Son who returns to the one eternal Father; and the Son who receives this life from an immense number — an immense number of priests and, together with them, a still more immense number of the faithful in the communion — returns us, and all those for whom this life is intended, personally, as his brethren, to the Father.

From this perspective, the celibacy of priests becomes understandable: they must renounce personal procreation in order to be able to participate in the bringing forth of the Son. He who marries exercises active control over his procreative powers. But in the Mass, the priest must subject himself wholly to external control, must be the entirely subordinate one: risking the attempt to be, in relation to the Son, that which the Son, in the host, is in relation to the Father. The priest is the subject of control by the Church, just as the Son, in the host, is the subject of control by both the Father and the Church. In the host, the Lord distributes himself as that which he is: as God and as nothing. He is simultaneously the supremely active, which bestows, and the supremely passive, which is nothing but the sacrificed and bestowed. He is simultaneously the supremely personal and the supremely anonymous. In this, the priest should attempt to become like him.

And so with the fish. The Lord gives the fishermen not only his food, but also their own. They, however, have brought only fish, and not bread. He had already presented them with this food when he told them to cast the net, the food that belonged to them when they hauled it ashore, yet becomes wholly their own only after he gives it back to them. Thus the gift of the fish stems from the Lord, is offered to the Lord by the fishermen, and is given by the Lord to the fishermen. Here lies, in contrast to the priesthood, the founding of the essence of Christian marriage. Partners in Christian marriage must first give themselves over to the Lord so that the Lord might give them back to one another. Even someone who is seeking a marriage partner casts his net by command from the Lord. He does so in the direction that the Lord indicates to him: he will look for a fellow believer and someone who loves. But what he has caught on this fishing expedition he must first bring to the Lord in order to have it presented anew to him by the Lord.

Both of the two, virginal priesthood and marriage, bread and fish, have one thing in common: the aim of bringing men to love, of grounding what is common to both love of God and love of men in love of the Lord. Although virginal priesthood is on a higher level than marriage, everyone can nevertheless realize something fully valid under fully valid commission from the Lord. It is not we ourselves who choose our station in life; it is the Lord who distributes the bread and the fish.

21:14. *This was now the third time that Jesus was revealed to the disciples after he was raised from the dead.*

He reveals himself to those who have come to maturity since his Cross; he treats them as those who have received the three sacraments: confession has been instituted, Communion has been distributed and confirmation is likewise already present conjointly with the ordination of priests, even if its fullness will first be revealed at Pentecost. The disciples have matured: they have made confession and are now those who seek him in love. John, who recognizes him standing on the beach, represents here the archetype of the person who has made his confession and has grown so pure in love of the Lord that he seeks to recognize the Lord everywhere, and he makes himself available for every sort of commission, even when not specifically summoned. And although John immediately handed the commission on to Peter—thus, at that moment, accepting and carrying out a specifically defined commission—he nevertheless reverted at once to the anonymity of love and its attitude of open readiness. All of them serve as an archetype of the second sacrament, the Eucharist: for the Lord accepts from them and distributes to them in equal measure that which he has received. And that they have received the strength of confirmation conjointly with ordination as priests he makes evident by meeting them at the moment when they are steering their boat toward the hardest stage of their task. In coming to them three times, the Lord demonstrates that he has accepted them as a group, that they belong to him as a group, that they form a unity with him and that he himself, within his own commission, gives this unity its particular stamp for the glorification of the Father.

This third encounter exhibits the character of all future encounters of the Lord with Christians. It is only within their belief that believers will any longer recognize him, and only love will make evident to them that his appearance is real. Even if a man were to see the Lord with his eyes, that could still only come about within belief and love; and if he were to communicate it to others, that, again, could happen only within a commission that was grounded in belief and love. The same love that allows John to recognize the Lord also leads to his communicating what he sees to Peter. And the precondition for this love is belief. But this belief and love are one. Anyone to whom knowledge of an appearance of the Lord is communicated must see the love in order to be able to accept the appearance as true. The disciples who saw the Lord nevertheless saw nothing at first but John's love, and only through this love did they learn about the presence of the Lord and thereby arrive at the vision of him. The first two appearances of the risen Christ were also, of course, appearances in love. Since his sacrifice of total love on the Cross, he can no longer appear in any other way. And because they are appearances of love, they are always really an appearing and never a vanishing. No appearance of the Resurrected has any conclusion; none has any limit to its efficacy and fruitfulness. All these appearances, which have belief and love as their preconditions, contain as their consequence, their germinal core, perpetuation without end in belief and love. Were someone to want to forgo one of these appearances, to erase it from the essence and memory of the Church, then he would be robbing her of part of the wealth of belief and love that its bestowal on the Church was intended to enrich. Perhaps it is not easy to elucidate the innermost meaning of each of these appearances in such a way that it becomes understandable in its distinctiveness. But no matter how monotonous they may perhaps seem because of their number and their simplicity as external happenings, each of them is, according to the intention of the Father and the Son and the Holy Spirit, nevertheless unique and crucial. So unique and so crucial that, if we are unable to understand and describe it, then this merely attests to the poverty of our spirit.

And further: since the appearance of the Lord to the fishermen lay hidden within the love of John and came to light through that love, the appearing of the Lord is from now on bound up just as much with men as with the Lord himself. Not only in the sense that love on the part of man is from now on a condition for the appearing of the Lord, but also in the sense that, just as the Lord deemed it fitting to be represented on earth by Peter, he can also send representative appearances. Not only he alone can appear, but also those whom he loves—his Mother, his saints, his redeemed ones—can appear in the same efficacy of his love. Hence, he allows those whom he has redeemed to participate as much in the giving as in the receiving of the appearances. In that way, he imparts new forms to men's love for him out of the fullness of his own love. He breaks through finite laws for the sake of love. He dissociates himself and those whom he loves from these worldly laws. He invents a new law that has its place solely within his love, that cannot be defined and interpreted in any way other than through his love. Under this law, which he possesses in the Trinity, everything is, in a sense, from now on possible, insofar as it is merely purposed by him. One can almost say that, as long as he lived on earth, he had accepted our laws and accommodated himself to them, all but allowed himself to be regulated by our laws, but only in order to allow us, in his new life after death, to participate in the fullness of his own law of love. This act of breaking through has its entire meaning only in him, and should make us understand that neither the Son nor the Father can ever be circumscribed by us; and that, if they ever subordinate some part, some speck, of themselves to one of our laws, then that happens only for the purpose of both opening and subordinating precisely that law to their own expansiveness, which is the expansiveness of love. And just as this third appearance did not exhaust itself in the mere appearing, but served, through the miracle of the fishing expedition, the glorification of the Father through the Son in the Church, so, too, all subsequent appearances in the Church always serve the summing up, the interpretation, of his earthly life, whose sole meaning consisted in glorification of the Father by means of returning the love of men to the Father—a returning even if the whole of the love that the Son brings back to the Father was kindled by the Son himself. Thus every appearance in the Church is ultimately reaccepted and handed on by the Son in the sense of the Son's mission.

The Lord no longer appears in the visible way that he did before his suffering, for example, as he appeared to the Samaritan woman who did not yet believe. Now, he owes it to his Bride, the Church, to appear only in the context of love and belief. By conferring office on Peter, he thereby also gave him certain guarantees. He already ignites the love before he appears, so that love has effectively become an indispensable condition for his appearing. This does not, to be sure, guarantee that anyone who loves will also see the Lord, but the reverse holds true: only those who love have seen him. The Lord allows this precaution to prevail for the purpose of reassuring office.

After he was raised from the dead. From all the dead taken as one: as if the Lord had shared something with them from which he had set himself free again through his Resurrection. And yet: not only did he separate himself from them, but he took something of them back with him into this world. If the dead are now mentioned in connection with the Lord, it is because they have some quality in common with him, and in fact, a quality that they acquired from him by virtue of his having shared their condition of being dead and having set himself free again from that. For the Lord cannot encounter any man, including any dead man, without imparting something to him. And this something always bears the seed of life. What he imparts always has an inextinguishable character, for it bears something of the essence of his own Person and thus remains, even when it has been imparted, with him. That which he bestows, and from which he seemingly separates himself in order to lavish it, remains more living than ever within him. It is almost as if that which he gives away were to take on its own life in him, in the fullest sense, only through his giving it away. And if now, in the case of his third appearance, his rising from the dead is mentioned once again, that is because these dead, from whom he separated himself in order to come back, as well as the men to whom he now appears for the third time, have all been presented with something that lies hidden in his Resurrection and in his appearing. There is a quality of love in the Lord whose core lies both in his appearing and in his Resurrection, one which forms a living bond between the dead and the Church to whom he appears. This bond is so strong that it is no longer possible to separate the dead in the Lord from the Church in the Lord. From now on, the Bride is no longer thinkable without the dead. Those who are in death, who have been redeemed by the Lord through his participation in their fate of death, remain forever tied to the fate of the Church. Inasmuch as the Lord journeys from the world to the dead, he brings the Church to them; and inasmuch as he returns from the dead to the Church, he brings the dead to the Church. He claims the dead for the Church. The dead are not discharged into some vague, self-enclosed heaven, but into heaven for Christ and the Church. They participate just as much in the Son's passage through the world and back to God as do all believing men on earth. Whenever the Lord now comes down from heaven in order to appear to the Church, he comes from a heaven in which his redeemed ones now dwell. The communion that he has with us in this world, through the Eucharist, he has with those already redeemed, directly and without sacraments, in heaven. Thus, in his appearances, he also brings heaven down into the world. In him is the unity of the three realms: of heaven, of earth and of the netherworld.

The appearance of the Lord is real. It has nothing in common with the appearances of spirits and ghosts. And because it takes place in love, it provokes no false curiosity. And love will never attempt to force such an appearance of the Lord. It does not think of wishing to penetrate the mysteries of heaven. It receives the Lord just as straightforwardly as he presents himself. It will love him just as much regardless of whether, at any time, he appears visibly or not. For the Lord also appears without one's seeing him. Every Christian prayer includes an appearance of the Lord, every Christian word that a man utters in prayer is heard and answered by him. In prayer, heaven stands open, and whether belief is to perceive visibly or nonvisibly, to meet with the Lord on this or that level of visibility, it leaves entirely up to the Lord who appears.

THE PRIMACY

21:15. When they had finished eating, Jesus said to Simon Peter: Simon, son of John, do you love me more than these? He said to him: Yes, Lord; you know that I love you. He said to him: Feed my sheep.

They have eaten together in a communion that can never again be abolished. The entire Church was present: the Lord and those who are his. Previously, the tasks were distinct: the Lord was there, having appeared in love and been recognized in love; and he had, out of his divine love, given the disciples the commission to go fishing, also issuing, within that commission, a separate commission to Peter. Then, in the course of the meal, a kind of merging into one had come about in which none was any longer different from any of the others. But this condition was a temporary one, spent in expectancy. And now the Lord brings it to an end by starting a conversation with Peter. This conversation has the character of all future conversations between the Lord and his official representatives: it is not prompted by the Church, but rather, initiated by the Lord. In every conversation involving him, the Lord has the first word: it is he, the one who answers a prayer, who appears, who lets himself be heard, who issues a commission to someone who loves and thus allows him to act in his place. The Church is drawn into the conversations that the Lord conducts in her midst. And in order that such a conversation might really acquire an ecclesiastical character, and not lose it again later, the Lord must be the one who originates it. The Church cannot just suddenly come up with some question for the Lord. It is always she who is questioned and must give answers to the questions of the Lord. If something becomes a topic for public discussion in the Church, then that is because the Lord has manifested himself somewhere. He is the one who has raised the problem. One can, no doubt, raise a question in the Church, but only insofar as one simultaneously declares, and proves, that this question is posed in the sense of the Lord. On the other hand, no one can come forward with the claim that he has to engage in private conversation with the Lord about ecclesiastical questions if he does not already possess a commission for this, and the commission will then always be an ecclesiastical commission. The Church as a whole is subject to the leadership of the Lord; personal individuality is to be preserved in the Church, but never outside of the ecclesiastical commission that she administers. The livingness of the Church and also the livingness of her problems stem primarily from the Lord, and only quite marginally from the individual, who is perhaps quite troubled by the averageness of the Church. No individual is allowed to use his personal questions and problems to attract the attention of the Church or influence possible directions for her renewal. Even the most burning questions of the day—the social question, for instance—cannot provide the proper starting point for the formulation of questions in the Church, but solely the question of the Lord. If the Lord raises the social question, then she is obliged to concern herself with it, but only then. For the Church, all personal, political and cultural problems always remain incorporated in, and subordinate to, the questioning of the Lord.

If the Lord, from his position on the beach, from the place where he arrived, now starts a conversation with the Church, who has behind her the experience of the expedition and the miracle, and if he turns this conversation to the subject of love, then this conversation contains something very significant, something definitive. The Lord did not come into the world nor onto this beach in order to solve peripheral questions, but rather, to unfold the most burning, most serious question that exists in heaven or on earth. The emphasis of his conversation must not be shifted; we must leave it there where the Lord places it. The conversation takes place with Peter, who emerges from the ranks of the others, who is given preference. But the importance of Peter's office was generated out of John's love. It is not only because the Lord calls Peter to the fore, but also because John's love moves into the background that the figure of the primacy now becomes so crucially prominent. Peter stands between two burning poles: the divine pole of the Lord's burning love and the human pole of John's burning love for the Lord. Peter is the representative of the inarticulate mass of believers; but inasmuch as he becomes their articulation, he must come to terms with the Lord and with John. He is the representative of the whole Church, and thus he also has to receive John's love into himself in order to open the way for it to the Lord.

The situation of the Lord is clear from eternity. But both the situation of the Church and the situation of John within the Church are new. For now the Lord converses, not with the one who loves, but with the representative of the Church, and thus only indirectly with John. Even when the Lord needs love—and he needs it now more than ever—he turns to the official representative of the Church and expects the Johannine response from him. He wants to hear it from Peter, who not long before had betrayed him, who outwardly possesses nothing but the character of office and has just previously performed his office by hauling in the net. The new thing is that John, who is present, does not speak. He knows that he is included in the answer of Peter. Inasmuch as it was through John that he arrived at recognition of the Lord, Peter received a gift from John that continues to live in him. Primarily this: that both the finite, human love of John, which had previously issued in the infinite love of the Lord, and the finite power of Peter, which was exercised within the infinite power of the Lord—that these personal qualities and gifts of the disciples do not first come together in the otherworldly infinitude of the Lord, but rather, already attain infinitude and unification within the Bride, the Church. Previously, John had loved the Lord in the way of a man, but the Lord was God and burst that love open. Peter had obeyed him in the way of a man, but the Lord was God and thus this obedience acquired a divine character in him. And now the new thing can occur: through the common activity of love and office in leading toward the Lord, the widening of both in the Lord is shifted so as to occur already in the this-worldly context of the Church.

A transformation of both love and obedience is brought about inasmuch as both must pass through the Church. The Church, as the binding entity between the believer and the Lord, exerts, on the one hand, a retarding effect, but on the other, so to speak, a hastening one. She resembles a class of pupils: all of them have to learn the same material, so the most intelligent are held back while the least intelligent are overtaxed. The curriculum is not quite suited, personally, to any of them. And the teacher's approach to the class perhaps contains something that does not wholly satisfy any individual and gives each of them some cause for complaint. Only once the class has ended can the teacher allow that "something" to drop—for instance, once everyone has mastered the set material—and then he stands as a person vis-à-vis the person of the pupil. The anonymous averageness of the class disappears as soon as the purpose of the class has been achieved. And yet not entirely, for it also contains an end in itself. It creates solidarity within the class. Through it, the best pupil is obliged to help the slowest. He cannot simply rush on ahead as his talents allow; not only must he show consideration for the average pupils, but he must place himself at the service of this averageness. The equalizing, neutral focus of the class becomes a decisive means of education in selflessness and love. Through this process, the good pupil does not become ungifted, nor does the bad one become more gifted; but both receive something that is shared, something communal. And that which the teacher, as teacher of the class, imposes on them remains evident later on in their personalities.

The Church is in some ways like that class. The Lord himself must take on something of the nature and aspect of that teacher; for he did not come in order to redeem only individuals, only the gifted, but to redeem all. And he came, first and foremost, in order to bring the individual's love, as part of a communion of love, back to the Father. He must give this love the opportunity of unfolding itself within his redemptive work and his commission, which is nothing other than a commission of unity and unification. That is why Peter, the representative of unity, has assimilated the love of John. In his conversation with Peter, the Lord wants to call attention to the new form of cooperation, of coassistance, while at the same time providing education about it. The spirit of the class is a means of educating each individual for later life. And the spirit of the Church is a means of educating the faithful for eternal life. But something of the spirit of the class is taken along into life: the loving readiness to help. And something of the ecclesiastical spirit of mutual accommodation will enter into eternal life.

In creating the Church, the Lord makes concessions, readjusts, balances things out. This third thing between him and the individual, this class, this neutral and anonymous aspect of the Church, is the distinctively Catholic. It cannot be understood from the outside, but only experienced from the inside, in the experience of the Lord. It goes so far that every personal guidance given to a seeker outside the Church always refers, at the same time, to the seemingly impersonal sphere of the Church, and every personal attempt to imitate the Lord occurs only within this balancing framework. Let us assume that a sick man demands to be operated on by a famous surgeon: he is admitted to the hospital, and becomes a "case" who has to conform to what seems to be a pitilessly impersonal system. The famous doctor is surrounded by nameless assistants and nurses, instruments and daily routines, and the patient has to submit to all this. For the doctor, he is perhaps more a person; for the other staff, he is a case. For the doctor, every case is a particular one, whereas the staff tend to see in the patient something general and constantly recurrent. The patient will regard the whole impersonal system around him as almost a necessary evil; but it is only the system that permits the doctor to concern himself usefully with the patient. It is in this way that the Lord makes use of the visible Church and her system in order to encounter the individual.

The Lord has the commission to redeem all men. He does not have a commission to educate all those in the class in such a way that they become exemplary pupils. The class is as it is, and will, as such, be largely mediocre. The Son is not supposed to alter creatures in order to lead them to God. He is supposed to lead them to the Father just as they are. For this, he does not need to impose uniformity by raising them all to the highest level. He has not received any authority from the Father to turn them all into exceptional men, into saints in the special sense. He came not in order to dissolve the work of the Father, but in order to complete it. He does not touch men with a magic wand. He leaves them with their human path, with their seeking, groping and erring. He does not encroach upon their freedom. He does not simply place them at the goal, but makes himself the path for each. He also does not interfere with their personal gifts; he shows them what is possible in the framework of the understanding that each of them possesses and can realize with his grace. But inasmuch as he bequeaths to all of them the commandment to love, he obligates them to come to him no longer as individuals, but as a communion; he expects each one to share, in accordance with his personal gifts, in helping them all to traverse their common path to God. The love that he adds to this contains every possibility of coassistance and cooperation, everything that is capable of leading toward the Father. Through this love alone, the sense of communal responsibility, the "feeling of the Church", is created that brings about a balance between all.

Thus arises—as in the relationship between the gifted and the ungifted in the class—a relationship of mutual subordination of the members. On the basis of his gift, and because the teacher himself does not do otherwise, the gifted one has a duty to direct his support more to those less gifted. And this not because he is holier, more advanced or more capable, but it is based on the teacher's equal readiness to help all. The less another is able to absorb grace himself, the more he must be ready to communicate. For the grace of the Lord has this sort of readiness. Anyone who wants to turn his giftedness to his own advantage comes close to being expelled from the class of the Lord. In the mystery of this balancing out lies the starting point for understanding the "treasure of the Church". It is part of the mystery of that communal spirit of the Church into which all personal shortcomings and advantages are assimilated and balanced out in love. In the class, the gifted one must assist the teacher. When he has understood the material, he is not allowed to leave until the others have caught up—not even if all the others know that he has already understood, that perhaps at home he is already studying quite other things than those that are being studied at school. Even those other things must be put to use by him in some way for the benefit of the whole class. For he is only a pupil, and it is up to the teacher to determine what is to be done with his surplus of knowledge. In relation to the teacher, he is still, despite his special giftedness, just one of the class. Thus the Lord claims for his Church every richness of grace that a Christian possesses.

The first question that the Lord has to put to the official Church is the question of love. For the moment, this question extends only to the Lord: *Do you love me?* It is strange that the Lord, who has risen from the dead, who has his suffering behind him and nothing now but the path of magnificence before him, wants to assure himself above all of the love of his Church. And in fact, of the personal love of the official representative of the Church, in relation to him personally. Outwardly, it looks as if one human being were asking another about the extent of his personal love. *Simon, son of John,* although he is the official representative of the Church and, as such, carries John's love within him, is questioned about his own love for the Lord, even though the Lord has installed him in his office and even though the Lord himself is in possession of the Father's love, of a proven love such as he has not experienced in this degree of fullness throughout the course of his earthly commission. Nevertheless, the first thing that worries him now is Peter's personal love, the intimate, almost private relationship of this disciple to him.

The Lord demands personal love from this impersonal Peter. He wants friendship and confirmation of this friendship by Peter. He did not ask about this love on the Cross, but now he asks about it, when he enjoys the love of the Father. He asks not about neighborly love, not about the communal love of the Church, but about the personal love of the official Peter. He requires this precisely because Peter is to become the administrator, indeed, the administrator of the love of the Church and, with that, of love of one's neighbor. Love must not become in the Church something unsubstantial, free-floating, impersonal; it ought to be something tested and proven, between man and man, and also between Christ the man and Peter the man. Every instance of love must include the surrender of the person; for every instance of love embodies the whole of love, however insignificant its individual occurrence may be. And through Peter, love is to remain living in the entire Church. The whole of love is to be summarized and concretized in the love between man and man, which has as its root, however, the infinite love between God and God. Every love between man and man must be a representation of the infinite concrete love between Father and Son, its reflection, a living focal point. At the moment when the Lord reaches the culminating stage of the revelation of his divine love, he looks into the Church and speaks with office about love. By doing that, he demonstrates that there is only one love. That the love between Father and Son is the sole force behind the love that he places at the disposal, in its unaltered form, of the Church and the individual and, at the same time, necessarily expects to be returned. And in fact, the love between Peter and the Lord is to be unbrokenly regainable, in the way that it lives in the Trinity. Absolute love is placed at the disposal of men; it is near and concrete and graspable by all, and dwells in our midst. It is nothing transcendent, highflown, but rather what is nearest.

Do you love me? He asks about himself, not about love of the Father. He assumes the right to determine matters regarding the Father's love in the way he would if it were his own. He takes over this love of the Father in order to show that it is his own. And that any form of love in the world is conceivable and acceptable as long as it issues in the love of the Trinity, in infinite love. He knows that love of him, the Son, includes all things in itself, the Trinity as well as the world. Otherwise, he would not be allowed to restrict love by relating it to himself in this way. When he speaks of himself, he speaks of everything.

And the love of Peter must be made clear. It is the foundation for all that is to follow. It must be an explicitly stated love; nothing can be left vague between him and the Lord. Without full mutuality of love, what is being constructed cannot be taken further. It is the objective and indispensable foundation. In a marriage, love can be the starting point but then undergo many changes that follow on from that beginning; the initial love can later give way to a great mutual respect, to this or that moral sentiment or to a state of habituation, and on that basis the marriage can perhaps be developed further. In the life of the Church with the Lord, there is no such ongoing development; her life in the Lord is possible only if life and love meet within the Lord himself, form a perfect unity in him. The gift of the Church and the gift of the Lord must never be able to be distinguished. The gravitational center, the midpoint, of love always lies hidden in the Lord, because the Son rests at the center of the Father. In this hidden place of the Lord, where love continually flows forth as from a wellspring, the love of men for the Lord is also harbored. The love between him and the Church is not like a chain in which one link succeeds another. Rather, all the love is concentrated into the midpoint of the Lord, and everyone who loves receives the love from that source. It is like the ground color upon which all the rest of the picture is painted—even more, into which everything else merges and is balanced out. Just as a fish can live only in water, so the love of an individual man can live only in the love of the Lord. Just as a father can divide his property up among his underage children, yet take something from it for himself if he needs it without anyone's anxiously calculating how much of this and how much of that, but viewing it simply as a broad total sum, so the totality of the love of the Church is always at the Lord's disposal.

Every love that is offered to the Lord is useful to him; indeed, it acquires by that very fact its quality of usefulness to him. That which we call love, but which does not bear his stamp, cannot be accepted by him. In man, there exists initially something that can be called his "natural will", something which he is capable of offering of his own accord and which then, through grace, coincides with the love that the Lord kindles in him. But only the unity of both, of the modicum that is mine and the infinitely-more that is bestowed upon me, can be received by the Lord as love. When the Lord is in a position to question Peter about his love for him, he already introduces absoluteness into the question and expects it as well in the answer. He can expect only absolute love in response to his question, and he can expect it only because he gives it. He gives it to Peter; but John, too, has given his love to Peter. Previously, the love between the Master and the disciple of love was immediate; they stood face to face, and they loved each other. Now it is as if the immediate path from the Lord to John had vanished into the path between Peter and the Lord. And in fact, Peter has absorbed into himself, and thus made to disappear, not only the personal love of the Lord for John, but equally the personal love of John for the Lord. He represents the sphere of anonymity and neutrality into which the two personal poles of love are consigned and lost. Inasmuch as the Lord created this situation—and he creates it through his question—he depersonalizes himself and becomes the Bridegroom calling his Bride to account. The love itself acquires an official stamp. He asks not for attestations of friendship, but about the objective status of the love. It is the head of the Church that questions the body. And it is the Lord, as the one who accomplished the mission to men, who questions Peter, the fruit of that mission. Between the mission as act and the mission as fruit lies something objective that participates in each; and this—no matter what the ultimate consequence for the bearers of the love, indeed, of a love that is no longer personally claimed or bound to persons—must henceforth present itself as love in general. For this love, which is now perceived in a direct encounter between head and members—this love is the thing that offsets the humiliation inflicted upon God by creation and forms the meaning of the whole of redemption. In every human love between men, there is always much that is personal and changeable: warmth, enthusiasm, a certain degree of self-surrender, of expecting, of anticipating. Only later, when the love has long matured, does it clarify itself into the great love that is, at bottom, comparable only to the great pain that can fill a soul entirely. In human love, too, there is a stage at which it becomes in a way objective, and the lovers no longer engage in taking one another's measure. This comes to perfection in the love of the Lord: on the one hand, it embraces the Father in the Holy Spirit; this love is objective and, with that, the objective measure of all love. On the other hand, in relation to Peter, it makes the absolute demand that goes above and beyond all his human declarations and enthusiasms. Everything humanly personal is in some way finite and has to expand itself into the transpersonalness of this love. The great depersonalization of love is a mystery between the Lord and Peter—one that comes close to the tragic and upon which the shadows of the Lord's impersonal journey through the netherworld fall. It is so much a mystery that it remains mysterious for both. It is as if both were to veil themselves from each other. For the Lord and for John, this mystery of impersonality is perhaps difficult. To Peter, it causes no suffering. He is the one simply predestined for his function here. Although it is to him that the mystery remains most impenetrable, he finds it least difficult to bear, because for him it virtually lacks any power to draw him in. He is himself the vessel of the mystery, yet it troubles him least of all because his office is that of office.

Inasmuch as the Lord produces this mysterious, previously unknown quality of love out of the transparent love between himself and John, he still does not produce it out of nothing. The basis for this possibility, too, was already inherent in his love for the Father, and was reserved for his use. For the love between the Father and Son is not only something infinitely personal and specific; it is also, equally, something absolutely general and normative. God is, of course, love, and thus God's love is the general norm for all love. Hence, every personal love that stems from God's love must, at some time, commit itself back into the generality of this uniform love. A father possesses a magnificent library, and he gives his son permission to lend as many volumes to his friends as he likes, but under the condition that all the books must ultimately be brought back again. Thus each person who receives a book will be enriched in a different, personal way; but each will know that what he has read could also have been read by others and that everything stems from a single source to which it must also be brought back again. Peter is the representative of this oneness in the manifold of personal ways of participating in divine love.

To someone who observes the official Church, it is as if John's personal love had disappeared by being absorbed into office. But John has, of course, not been deprived of his love by the fact that he has presented that love to Peter. On the contrary: his love only increases through this presentation. But he also comes to experience that the love itself has taken on an instrumental aspect. It is not something that he keeps for himself and that he has at his own disposal; so much does it belong to the Lord that the Lord utilizes it as he wishes without even asking John. And if the Lord takes charge in this way, then it means that Peter has need of Johannine love. Hence, it still lives on as John's love for the Lord. But the earthly phase of this friendship has reached its end, and the Lord hands its fruit over to Peter like a legacy. It contains something of the most beautiful that the Lord has experienced during his earthly sojourn, and he does not want to keep its fruit for himself, but presents it to the Church. By doing that, he demonstrates to John the magnitude of his thankfulness for the fact that he was permitted to have him as his friend. There is nothing wistful in this act, for naturally the Lord takes this friendship with him into heaven. That he makes use of it for the benefit of the Church can only bring joy to John: his love will become fruitful for all others. The Lord shows him that he regards their mutual love as able to bear so much weight that it can be walled up in the foundations of the Church.

The existence of Johannine love in Peter, in office, is not always comfortable for him. He cannot rest satisfied with just managing and organizing things. Love is explosive; it tends to thwart him everywhere. His plans are repeatedly shattered and frustrated by it. It is the thing that he has to administer first and foremost, and it does not permit of being administered simply through legalistic paragraphs. As office, he must force himself to gain a certain comprehensive view; but precisely love is that which never admits of being viewed comprehensively. Being by nature incalculable, it continually sweeps right through all his calculations, like a hobgoblin scattering his well-ordered documents. The Lord has set Peter an almost unsolvable task: to unite in himself both office and love. As office, he must define and determine things, yet realize at the same time that love can never be defined and determined. When the aspect of office in him is tempted to force love too much into a supernatural system, then the personal character of the love between the Lord and John awakens in him and becomes living in a way that could not have been foreseen. There always remains something more for office to regulate, and what is left cannot be regulated because it must remain living. Good sense dictates that everything should be regulated. But to regulate everything would mean the death of love and, with that, also the death of the Church, for the living core of love between the Lord and John remains the core of the Church as well.

The impersonality of love in the Church has its counterpart in the impersonality of sin in the world, which includes in itself, and transcends, all the personal sins of individuals. The sum total of sins is more than the sum total of all the personal lapses of individual men; and this moreness has a mysterious character of generality and anonymity. And yet, in considering sin, the personal element can never be excluded, nor can the responsibility of the individual be lessened on the basis of this transpersonal dimension. For every sin is an exemplification of the nature of sin as a whole. From this viewpoint, too, the Church can be understood. Within the stream of love, a place for each one who loves is reserved in such a way that the whole of love always derives its stamp from every individual. The Church counts on individuals, and is willing to leave to each one the special place that has been reserved for him from time immemorial. In this place, he may be what he is; there, he may develop himself within the total stream of love, develop himself in such a way that, through grace, he can realize his best possibilities within the Church. And the more fully anyone occupies the place reserved for him within love, the more distant and obscured his corresponding place in the realm of sin would be. For every individual, there is a place created in the sphere of the Church that is perfect in itself, and occupying it wholly would mean perfection. This place, this possibility, has been created through the reciprocal submerging of the Lord's love and of John's love in the figure of Peter. If the love of John, who now embodies those who love and believe *en masse,* is perfect, it is so because it is completely accepted by the Lord; and in this acceptance, as in the renunciation by the Lord when he allows this love to become submerged in Peter, he creates for each individual the possibility of wholly fulfilling that which the Church expects of him. But if, through this renunciation of love, a personal mode of activity, a personal place, a personal love is offered to the individual, then the individual can effect, possess and be all that only if he himself is prepared to undertake Christian-Johannine renunciation in favor of the Church. In the Church, then, he receives the greatest measure of the personal, of that which is reserved for him by God, only insofar as he hands it itself, to the point of its becoming anonymous, over to the communion of the Church. Because the Church is essentially built upon this renunciation, no one can enter her with the demand to be able to retain and develop himself within her, to regard her as a means to the end of attaining his personal goals. Instead, he must realize that, for the time being, he will have a kind of temporary character in the Church, and that, in her as an institution, he has to understand obedience as the form of love because the institution is adapted precisely to his temporary condition, his earthly finitude.

On the one hand, then, the individual has his personal commission, which he must consign to the sphere of the general in order to receive it back from the Church in a new and different form. Here, the anonymity of the Church would be the temporary thing. On the other hand, this anonymity is dependent upon the whole temporal span of its earthly existence, and thus remains what has finality on earth, since each must allow his temporal life to be submerged in the Church in order to participate in the infinitude of eternal life. As long as the soldier serves in the army, he must remain in uniform regardless of whether it pleases him or not. And only in the context of being uniformed does he become aware of how varied, beneath their uniform dress, the characters of his comrades are. The distinctions become more inward, more intimate, and one gets to know others better than in civilian life, where it is the custom to distinguish people only outwardly, on the basis of the clothes they wear.

The individual thus comes to the Church with a fullness of personal attributes, wishes and outlooks, and this individuality has to be submerged in the communion of the Church so that it can then be given back to him, as a newly crystalized personality, by the Church. The Church has the duty, and therefore also the power, to remold the individuality of each person in such a way that it subsequently reemerges as a personality that bears the Church stamp of the Lord and his mission. No one lives in the Church for the purpose of self-development. It is the Lord who unfolds himself in him and makes use of his personality as an instrument for realizing his plans. In this process, the responsibilities are distributed quite unequally. The Christian, who allows himself to be submerged, undergoes very little risk: he has the guarantee of the Lord that his self-surrender will not be in vain. For the Church, the responsibility is substantially greater: she may not dissolve what is personal any further than is necessary in order to be able to impart the mission of the Lord. She may not take the depersonalization too far. She may not plead that the individual would nevertheless still retain his direct relation to the Lord and would be saved by virtue of that. She must also form in him, and save, the intermediate life of the Christian, by virtue of which he must be a member of the Church and commission-bearer. And she must do this out of the core that is embodied in Peter, and may not allow the ecclesiastical in the life of Christians to degenerate into superficiality.

It may be that there is some person in the Church who does not have love, who has perhaps stolen his way into her for the sake of external advantages. The Church will have to attempt, without thereby doing violence to his conscience, to keep him with her, because the love that inheres in the order of Peter is greater than the personal love of the individual. It is not a lapse for someone to leave the Church who subjectively believes that he has good reasons for doing so. But it can be a lapse for someone to continue to live in the Church for bad reasons; even more so, for someone who thinks that he cannot accept certain articles of faith, who is irritated by much in the Church. But if he possesses, or seeks, love, then he is forced to try, through his love, to assimilate that which he can no longer, or not yet, rightly comprehend. The Church may not, of its own accord, bring force and brusque treatment to bear on anyone, but the individual should allow himself to be taken firmly in hand by the Church until such time as his subjective love acquires the proportions of objective ecclesiastical love. What is essential is: finding the Lord lovingly within the love of the Church. Every way of relating to him should allow itself to be regulated in this form, as desired and founded by him.

The ordinariness of the Church must not give fright to anyone who loves. It is based on the fact that the Lord and John freely deprived themselves of what is highest in order to allow it to become submerged in the middlingness of Peter. They are trees who sacrifice their most beautiful branches so that some kind of general fire can be kept burning. Thus it is ultimately the mark of true love, both of the Church and of the individual, that it freely surrenders itself in order to burn in this middling, undifferentiated fire, knowing that, within it, there are some who flare up in red-hot flames, while others only pretend to, or slowly smolder, but would have grown cold long ago were they not still situated among the burning.

Do you love me more than these? The Lord expects that Peter should love him more than the others do, more than John, who is nevertheless love personified. And he should also have personal knowledge of this *more*. This expectation constitutes an immediate overtaxing of Peter, an overtaxing that begins here and will reach no end until the end of time. Peter is now supposed to know already that his incomplete love has been supplemented by the divine love of the Lord and the love of John that strives toward the Lord, and that his own love, despite its earlier tepidness and its denial, has now really become a burning love. He is now supposed to have already at his disposal the Lord's and John's surrendered love. He is supposed to make all three forms of love fuse into a single unity within himself. And this not in a way roughly characterized by impersonality, not as something that concerns him merely from afar, that somehow takes place objectively of its own accord, but expressly, in such a way that he immediately stamps it with the qualities of fervent, demanding ecclesiastical love. In this more that the Lord now demands lies something like a mirroring of his own quality of being Always-More. Every time that believers ran up against his mysteries, he explained to them that more lay behind those than they grasped. He knew that they could never comprehend him, and he taught them to make allowances for this moreness each time they thought they clearly understood. And now the Lord demands of Peter that the love of all the others, the perhaps little emphasized love of the bystanders and the select love of John, should be so clear and transparent to him as to enable him to make a comparison between those loves and his own love. He thereby demands two things: more love and a judgment about the others' love. Thus the Church has received the power to judge through the fact that she has been given, and must give back, more love. Inasmuch as the Lord has submerged both his own love and John's in the Church, he has implanted in the Church, precisely through the gift of Johannine love, the possibility of vision, of scrutiny and judgment. The intermediate organization that the Church represents as Bride of Christ, through her having been equipped with supernatural gifts, has also been endowed with the possibility of seeing through things. And in fact, not with a varying, relative power of penetration, but with an absolute, *infallible* one. For the Lord expects of Peter no casual, approximate answer, but an infallible one.

The Lord sees through the Church; he sees her entirely as she is. That is part of his love. And when he submerges his love in the Church, he also gives her something of his power of penetration. He presents her with the possibility of looking into the particular and the individual. This possibility is not distinct from the Lord himself; rather, it is bound up with him like the runner of a shrub that, while sending out visible or underground roots from which new plants are generated, does not lose its connection with the mother plant. What the Lord sets into the Church comes together there with what John has planted in her; the divine of the Lord meets with the human of John in so intimate a way that it metamorphoses into a new structure in Peter. Peter, as a personality, was undoubtedly mediocre. But he assumes, through that which grace gives him, an enduring character. Considered as a man, he will remain mediocre, but as the Rock of the Church he becomes a saint of the Lord. As a man with a human endowment, he is given permission to remain mediocre. But he will nevertheless have to measure himself constantly against this position of love in which he now finds himself. This laborious task stands before him. His mode of service springs from an initiative of complete love; but for purposes of performing it, he remains the Peter that he always was, even if equipped with a new grace. He is expected to swim in the stream of love, even if he does not know how to swim: he is thrown into it under prohibition of sinking, indeed, under command to swim the stream with controlling skill. But there is also absolutely no possibility that he will drown, since the Lord's grace engirdles him like an invisible lifebelt.

The Church is the neutral sphere between the Lord and John, into which they have committed themselves. Peter must interpose himself at the plane of intersection between these two loves; there, he participates in the unassured sureness of love and in the infallibility of its judgment. But he participates in the impersonal form that the love of the Lord and of John has acquired through their sacrifice. Regardless of how average the Church might be, how full of external shortcomings, there is still the possibility for each one within her to position himself at this point of sureness, and Peter himself has a *duty* to do that, since he has a duty to love more than the others. He can distance himself personally from this point and thus err as a private individual. But insofar as he is *placed* at the precise point of intersection, he cannot err, because there love is infallible. In this connection, the consecratedness of office resembles a fireproof cloak that allows the one who has received consecration to stand at the very centerpoint of love without being burnt. Only thus can any man stand there, and by standing there he fulfills what is demanded of him. No Christian is *prevented* from positioning himself there. And if Christians were really to position themselves there, then Christianity would lose its mediocre character. But it is a frightful place: the place of the fire of love, of belief and of hope, and furthermore also a point of death, of the boundary between this world and the beyond, of the fulfilment of all hope, because it contains in itself the whole of faith. It is God's answer to life, the fulfilled existence in the point of intersection between love of God and love of man. Just as, at the moment of death, all of one's life experience becomes visible as a whole and is surveyed as such, and indeed, as stripped bare and displaying its essential core and complete meaning, so this point of intersection is death, as a surveying, at the instant of being opened into new, eternal life, of all that has previously been. Every pronouncement that is made within infallibility bears the character of conclusiveness regarding earthly things and of being opened into eternal life. Everything now defined is ineradicable, but is to become the seed and bud of new, future activity. However, it can be open to the new only if it flashes forth in the light of love. This flash is an absolute engendering. There where the love of God in its wholeness and the whole of human love are submerged and Peter representatively stands—there is engendered the infallibility of the Church. In this, John must be devoid of all mystery: he must be able to be penetrated completely. The Lord, however, from his side, brings with him the mystery of trinitarian fruitfulness and submerges it in the new thing that arises in the Church. Thus the moment at which infallibility arises becomes an impenetrable and mysterious one. It participates in the mystery of the grain of wheat that dies in order to live. Here, too, death and fruitfulness are very closely related.

The fruitfulness of the Church is recognized only by someone who stands on the inside and simultaneously knows that everything ecclesiastical that does not allow itself to be moved toward the point of love is halfhearted and doomed to death. Whatever allows itself to be moved toward that point will be summoned to life and fruitfulness. Fruitfulness in the Church is the endeavor to set as many things as possible, as often as possible, in motion toward the centerpoint of love. Everything that strives in that direction is fruitful, and even more fruitful is everything that facilitates such striving. But if there were no infallibility, then the fruitfulness of the personal encounter with God, of the personal point of intersection, would always be just a quite limited one. No final blossoming would eventuate, no direct process of ongoing generation. Within infallibility, however, every fruit is immediately destined to exert a continuing influence on the abovementioned movement. The ripened fruit bursts open at once like a seedpod and fructifies the movement anew. Just as the official words of the priest become fruitful in the communion in the sense that, through them, more fruits of love immediately arise, so infallibility engenders continually new fruit within the Church as a whole. Everything that lives for itself and its own perfection is sterile. Only that which is immediately presented, in turn, to someone else is fruitful. The fruitfulness of infallibility is similar to the fruitfulness of the Eucharist. Just as the Lord bestows himself in the Eucharist, so his representative has to bestow himself in the infallibility of office. This infallibility never has, or at least never should have, the character of mere purposefulness, but always, in addition, that of love. When the Pope passes a judgment, when the priest utters a fruitful word, then it is only so as to allow love to become more living in the Church. The love that is harbored in office is the driving force behind everything that happens in the Church. Office may well be a clumsy apparatus, which the sinfulness of its representatives tends to impair even further, but its infallibility, which springs up out of love, transcends everything human and cannot be prevailed over.

More than these also means: more than these who have previously known only personal love. They are to be outdone in their personal love by Peter. Official love is not to efface personal love, but rather, to perfect it by rising to a higher level. From the love of the others, which is to remain in existence, Peter is to take an example for going beyond it. Both modes of love are to remain in existence alongside each other. Only this, after all, can be the meaning of the act in which the Lord submerges his love in Peter and permits John to let his personal love likewise become submerged in Peter: so that Peter's love might thereby become even greater and more fruitful. Since the Lord's love is the perfect as such, he cannot separate himself from that love. He can present it to Peter only in order that it might flourish all the more in him. Not in the sense that Peter would now become more capable of love than the Lord himself. But Peter will, to the eyes of believers in coming ages, represent that love more visibly than the Lord. Time and again, the human and visible sides of the Church and her love will serve to attract men and lead them to the divine love of the Lord in her. Thus the Lord expects of Peter that perfect personal love will be found within his official love; that he will be able to administer this love and allow it to flourish in him in such a way that its entire fullness and breadth will be recognizable, and that, finally, even in those areas where the mass of the half-hearted move, traces of this love will still be found. Precisely because the Lord admits the immense number of sinners, half-believers and objectors who do not wish, or are not able, to understand this love, and adds them to the immense number in the loving Church, he expects that his love and John's love will be cultivated all the more painstakingly by Peter, so that even those will be touched by it who continue in a state of insufficient receptivity. When the crowd of those who more or less only join in without comprehending what is essential weighs so heavily, then it is all the more urgent that, from the side of the Lord and John, love actually be bestowed upon Peter and come to expression in him. Were the halfhearted capable of outweighing love, then the Church would have to cease being the Church. But she will not cease, because the love that the Lord has at his disposal is always greater than all the halfheartedness of men. If he has the ability to convert unbelievers to belief, then all the more does he have the ability to preponderate over lukewarm believers. And finally, were the Church to consist of nothing but those who love in equal degree, then, given the way that the world is made, fruitfulness would wane quite rapidly. The slope in things would no longer be present. A constant irrigation process, so to speak, is necessary, as much conduciveness to flow as possible, in order that the halfhearted might be affected, too. Peter must draw even the barely suggested movement of the mass, which hardly deserves the name love, into the love that he has received from the Lord and John, and also attempt to form it into that third thing which the Lord has already produced in creating the Church. He must create, within the Church, a projection toward the Church. He must make out of these halfhearted ones something that can fit itself into, reflect itself into, what the Lord has created. He must integrate the greatest and the narrowest sorts of love into the one ecclesiastical love.

Every Pope and every administrator in the Church has the task of reconciling the loves of the Lord, of John and of the mass, the task of bringing these into unity. That is not easy. He may not diminish the love of the Lord, he is supposed to make proper use of the love of the saints and the fervent and he should not treat the love of the half-hearted brusquely, but rather, attempt to set it afire with divine and sacred love. And perhaps the most troublesome thing is not how to deal satisfactorily with the halfhearted, but how to see that the love of the saints does not suffer any more than necessary. All this is so difficult that nobody ought to become annoyed with the slowness of the Church's processes and that everyone should try to understand the immense magnitude of her commission and to defend and support her in her mission—especially given the fact that she is the product of the loving suffering of the Lord. No one can say that this official body is a matter of indifference to him, that he has to concern himself with it only peripherally; for to belong to this body of the Church means to live from the redeeming love of the Lord, who has, through his suffering, spared us our suffering. Everything previously said, which as yet took no account of this suffering, only outlined the character of an institution that did not ultimately affect me. But when it becomes evident that the Lord suffered for me personally and, on the basis of this suffering, founded the Church for me personally, that he would not have had to create this third and intermediary thing if the sins of every individual, including mine, had not compelled him to do so, then it first becomes evident that the Church is the locus of the ongoing sacrifice of the Lord and, as such, can never be a matter of indifference to me. She is the result of the Cross, and in her the Lord is daily sacrificed anew. He is sacrificed in love. Sacrifice and love are so much one in the Church that, if the love alone cannot draw me towards love, then the sacrifice—for which I am responsible—must surely do so.

In the obligation to love more that is placed on Peter there also lies, then, a requirement to do this in the name of those who love less. And he receives this more from the commission that arises directly out of the mission of the Son.

He said to him: Yes, Lord; you know that I love you. Peter responds to the demand put by the Lord and acknowledges it totally. He acknowledges that he loves and loves more than the others. He acknowledges it at first quite objectively, by recognizing the content of his mission and, at the same time, by crediting the Lord with knowledge of the moreness of his love. Both pieces of knowledge stand as mutually complimentary: that he loves more and that the Lord knows about this. They form an indivisible unity. This unity, which Peter now has knowledge of, is proof of the fact that he understands exactly what the Lord has done. It is a masculine kind of knowledge, all of a piece. He forgoes all grumbling, all misplaced humility (as during the washing of the disciples' feet), all distinguishing and classifying. He leaves the unity that the Lord has created as it is, even though that renders the disproportion between office and person in Peter all the more gaping. This split is present in every priest. He may pardon sins in the name of the Lord, may dispense him, interpret his sayings, administer all the blessings of the Lord in the eucharistic sense; but if he sees himself alongside this office—no, within this office—as the sinner he is, then he must be seized most profoundly with terror. He knows exactly how often he has denied the Lord, how unsuited, therefore, he is to representing him. But he also knows that he has not selected himself for this office; rather, the Lord permits it, bestows it, is willing to dwell in him in such a way that the evil is inundated by his grace, that the man does not need to measure himself against him but may risk an attempt to be an answer to his question. Were he to measure himself, together with all his sins and inadequacies, then the priest—and anyone else along with him—would only arrive at the conclusion that he is the least fit person of all for this office. And he would have to answer the Lord with a No. But Peter knows in the end that the Lord has produced that love in him about which he asks. The Lord himself utters the Yes when he asks. He is the living love that lives in Peter, and inasmuch as the latter answers that he loves the Lord more than the others, he merely acknowledges that the Lord's love is greater than his own.

The Lord does not allow Peter to dwell upon this answer. He does not allow it to dissolve away into itself. He gives him no time in the human sense, but continues on immediately in an official vein and issues the instruction: *Feed my sheep.* From Peter's having greater love it follows directly that he must feed the sheep; this means that love is the force placed at his disposal for the carrying out of his coming commission. The greater love of Peter has no other task than to feed the sheep of the Lord. To watch over them and look after them in such a way that nothing untoward can befall them and that, above all, they will remain sheep of the Lord.

Previously, the Church appeared as something intermediate. Now she acquires the entire concrete aspect of the communion, of the members. That third thing, namely, the institution and the organization, has now all but faded; nothing more seems to be still living than this one thing: the welfare of each individual in the communion of the Church. Each one is to receive his proper share of love, each one is to receive the love of the Lord directly from Peter and each one is to allow Peter to participate in his own particular love for the Lord. Now, it is as if the Lord and John had depersonalized themselves in order to make it possible for each individual to preserve his personality. And as if Peter had the commission to ensure that such preservation remains possible. Here, everything that will be, in the future Church, a form of caring for the affairs of men is given its place: welfare, charity, the social question, everything that the incomprehensible love of the Lord translates into visible earthly love and help. In all this, however, the highest principle remains in force, namely, that every sheep must really be fed in a way that points toward the Lord.

But Peter also has to mediate prayer, he feeds his sheep on prayer. He leads them to prayer within the sphere of his Church. He imparts a public side to even this most private of things. In the Church, knowing about the prayer of someone else is no indiscretion. It is unimportant whether I like or dislike the person whom I meet with in prayer: we are praying, and thus we belong together in the communion of ecclesiastical prayer. In the unity of the praying Church, everything personal recedes into the background, human nearness and farness give way to a common nearness in God. All take part in the same conversation conducted by Peter with the Lord. This ecclesiastical prayer is part of the commission to feed the sheep, and inasmuch as Peter feeds the sheep in a flock, all defects of love and all criticisms are reduced to silence in him. In the same act of prayer, all recognize one another in their attribute as sheep of the Lord. Out of communal prayer, through which the Church feeds the individuals, the pastor awakens a common love in them and thereby forms the communion in the Lord. Non-Catholics strive only for a personal relationship with the Lord; they are happy to forgo the "holy place" of common prayer. With that, they forgo the invisible but very real world of prayer that is the air, the atmosphere, of the Church. Someone is almost always praying in Catholic churches, and the solitary person who goes there to pray will at once be caught up in a communion of prayer. There are also summary forms of prayer by the pastors, such as the intentions of the Holy Father or of the bishops. Or one has prayers said in monasteries or dioceses for common and personal concerns. Thus, even the mediation of priestly and monastic callings is never just a matter of personal grace, but requires affirmation by a communion of prayer and also the submission of an individual to the choice made by the Church. The position of a monk in a monastery is doubly mediated by the community: not only did he say Yes to God, but the Church said Yes to him by recognizing his calling and the monastery by granting him, the applicant, admission. Thus, in the Church, the personal is communally molded from all sides. Private prayer is pushed more and more into the background, the personal quest for sustenance is taken over more and more by the Church which feeds. Prayer does not thereby become weaker or less direct, but the thoughts and interests of the Church, which are those of the Lord, gain ascendancy in it.

This feeding becomes most visible as liturgy. The one being fed is more and more strongly integrated into this prayer, too, while, on the other hand, it accommodates itself to the feeding. It intercepts with its objectivity what is subjective in those who are praying. At some time or other, they grasp that they are enclosed within this objective prayer. The Church created the liturgy inasmuch as she wanted to embody in it the love that she holds for each one of her sheep regardless of what its particular condition might happen to be. In the endless succession of her prayers and ceremonies, she has taken into consideration every stage, every situation in the lives of Christians. She offers something for all the major sorts of event, but no less, too, for the minor and petty matters of everyday life.

This totality, humanized into care and prayer, intermixing the objective and the subjective, Peter gives back to the Lord, thereby fulfilling his commission to feed. He feeds not only by receiving from the Lord and giving to men, but equally by receiving from men and giving to the Lord. He himself, however, inasmuch as he has accepted his commission, has simultaneously accepted the condition of never again being alone. The community is not one that he can either belong to or not belong to, but one that would no longer be thinkable without him. He is carried by it, taken along with it, never again released from it, for he has to present it continually to the Lord. The movement of the love of the Lord and of John is directed into the Church, and Peter must bring back the result, not only to the Lord and to John as persons, but to everyone. He must take the rays and form them into the sun that shines on everyone. If the Lord embraces the Church, then the Church, by way of response, may embrace not only the Lord, but at the same time all those who are in her.

21:16. *A second time he said to him: Simon, son of John, do you love me? He said to him: Yes, Lord; you know that I love you. He said to him: Tend my lambs.*

Once again, the Lord puts the question about love, but more briefly, more concisely. He omits the element of comparison with the others. He omits everything that could in any way be understood as involving estimation or measurement. He throws love as fully back on itself as if it were naked. Thus the second question becomes significantly more serious, more binding than the first. It is the explicit demand for a detached, absolute love. The question has become so absolute that it almost no longer has need of the man Peter as respondent, but almost more as someone to whom it is directed, who apprehends it. The question has become more essential and therefore, in comparison with the answer, much more absolute. Also, it becomes clear that it begins to imply a reference to the threefold denial of Peter, who must, through giving a threefold Yes, more than atone for his threefold No. Peter, however, cannot atone for anything; only the Lord in Peter can do that. That is why the question sounds more and more relentless, more and more absolute. Here, one must see in the question itself its inherent seriousness. Precisely because it is outwardly a repetition, it is inwardly an endless intensification. It sounds almost as if the Lord had given the whole of his personal love away to the Church with his first question, and as if he were now questioning from within the trinitarian love that is at his disposal, as if his human love had been left behind in the first question and he were appearing now as transported into the second Divine Person; as if he had withdrawn himself from his human attributes so as to be no longer anything but the Son under commission from the Father and the Holy Spirit; as if he no longer possessed anything but the *office* that lay at the basis of his commission, and now embodied, in relation to Peter and his ecclesiastical office, the full character of trinitarian office.

In the first question, love had effected everything. Now, it seems to stand wholly in the background so as to give full scope to divine office, situated between the relentlessness of the justice of the Father and the relentlessness of the sin of men. In the first question, love enveloped everything in soft contours. Now, as Peter's denial begins to come to the fore, the question no longer avoids the conflicts. In two directions, that of the sublimity of the Trinity and that of the horribleness of sin, the horizons are rent apart. Had the man not been prepared by the first question, he would not at all be able to bear the second question. Previously, he saw the magnificence of the love and everything that he would gain through it. Now, he sees the burning demand and everything that he will have to lose. The human is rolled back in order to allow the divine to become manifest. Peter must forgo the Lord's human love—which has been given away—in order to learn to understand his divine love. The earlier situation was right just as it was: the man had learned, through the Lord's sojourn on earth, to love him and, through him, to love the Father. But now comes the moment when the Son returns to the invisible Father and Peter has to learn to love the invisible God in him. The Lord is still visible, but he already wholly embodies the trinitarian side of his Person. Previously, Peter no doubt knew that the Ever-Greater lay hidden behind the Lord, that there was the opening toward the Father. As things stand now regarding his love, Peter must, to a certain extent, overlook the Lord whom he knows so as to learn to love the Lord in the Trinity, whom he does not know. He will have to give his second answer to a Lord about whom he almost no longer knows anything, who has withdrawn himself into the Ever-Greater, who has, as it were, hidden his countenance in God. Previously, Peter knew about the incomprehensible background aspects of the

Lord, but thought that the Lord would show them to him in some-thing like a comprehensible way. Now, the Lord himself recedes into the sphere of incomprehensibility. Previously, the Lord had revealed that the meaning of his coming lay in the glorification of the Father, and this, in turn, in his love of the Father's commission. Now, it is as if, as a result of his return, he were no longer able to describe the love that moved him to accept that commission because he stands at the center of its source, at its indescribable origin. He can no longer personally represent the glorification of the Father because he no longer stands out as distinguishable from it. Previously, he guided those who were his, step by step, through the land of love; now, they are swept up into the reality of an unrecognizable Lord. What is now demanded is no longer the Yes of love, but the Yes of belief, which is required to show itself to be stronger than any experienced love. The Lord takes advantage, so to speak, of the moment when John has given away his love to make his demand for naked belief: for belief in love.

The demanded Yes is a whole one. Peter can no more say Yes to a partial love than to a partial teaching. There is a unity of the whole of belief and of the whole of love, and in fact, one in which the unity of belief occupies the foreground as the unrelenting demand. Who-ever comes into contact with belief at any point does not get free of it until he ends by giving his full affirmation to full belief. As long as the Lord was training his disciples and leading them slowly, step by step, closer to belief and love, it was he who set the measure of what was to be believed. He and his representatives cannot demand every-thing all at once from someone who is just coming near. When, however, office has been established and has attained its full significance, he cannot expect that he who holds it would still need instruction about essential points. The individual, including the priest, will certainly always have to wrestle with the meaning of the profoundest words of the Gospel, but he must always do so from the standpoint of the truths of faith, and no longer on the basis of mere reason. Those assistants of the Lord who have charge of his truth, inasmuch as they officially disseminate it and hand it on to others, can, in certain circumstances, communicate only parts of it, but they must possess the whole of it, and that they can do only within their undivided, absolute word of affirmation.

This is the point of the absolute demand in the Lord's second question. Inasmuch as he transports himself to heaven, he deprives Peter of the possibilities of human empathy and adaptation. He takes back with him a whole part of Peter's essence, which he harbors in himself. The Lord now *exerts an attractive force,* just as the sun draws moisture up toward itself. Thus, in the context of the second question, Peter is already, without willing to be so, the provider, whereas, in the context of the first question, he was wholly the recipient, namely, of the Lord's love and of John's. Now he is like a rubber band whose one end is held by the Lord and is pulled with him when he withdraws. Peter has said Yes for one, first time; now he must experience the consequences. He must leave his customary place in order to go where he no longer stands at a distance, because much of himself has disappeared into the Lord. He wanted to be taken seriously, but now the seriousness becomes uncanny. He, who always thought of administration and accountability, of clarification and translation, has lost all possibility of overseeing things. He has to give an answer to someone who is in the act of withdrawing. He has to direct what he says at something uncertain, incalculable. Within this mystery of belief he stands as Pope: wholly taken up into that which is inconceivable, cotransported into the endlessnesses of trinitarian truth. Only in that way can he in truth mediate divine truth. Much of what he must pass on to others he does not himself wholly comprehend. He often resembles someone who has to deliver a message in a sealed envelope without knowing any more about it than that it is very important. But now, in asking his question, the Lord expects Peter to stand by this message, to sanction its contents, to be certain that its effects will be the right ones, even though he has but a feeble inkling of what, at bottom, he is doing in mediating it. Love must take on the form of blind obedience. One might almost be tempted to try to stop the Lord because he seems to be demanding things of Peter that no man is capable of achieving. And yet he knows exactly that he himself will achieve in Peter what is required. But Peter is put to the task, and has to answer both as a person and as a representative of office. He has to make a decision in favor of participating, without comprehending what that involves, in the whole life of the Lord, of committing himself along with him to everything that will be required of him.

One after the other, in the way that the Holy Spirit deems fit, the Lord will make available to Peter participation in all the mysteries of his mission and life. Some aspects of these mysteries will be clear to him at once; there will be others that will remain forever opaque to him. It will be participation in the joys of the Lord and in his sufferings, in his being as human and in the mysteries of the threefold Divinity. Since the place from which the Lord demands this participation is a place at the center of the mystery of the Trinity, he can allocate these things only in the name of the Holy Spirit; what is primary in this allocation will no longer be the Lord's love for his Church and his disciple Peter, but will be grounded in the plans of the divine Spirit. Participation in what is transparent will not be difficult for the Church because, in relation to that, she will be able to rely implicitly on the support of those who love these mysteries. Peter may never, namely, act alone; his activity always occurs together with others. But when what is required is participation in wholly opaque, and perhaps even awkward, mysteries, then the threefold God will first request the participation of those in the Church who love, going through them before taking the matter to a Peter who well knows that he, too, will ultimately have to say Yes to it. There are things that come to him secondarily even though he has said Yes to them primarily. And he has to remind himself, when they reach him, that he has consented to them. It is as if the encounter between the Lord and John were to be repeated once again somewhere in Peter himself, in some place that is wholly incomprehensible to him. And yet it must be he who gives his affirmation to it, knowing that it is presupposed and that this meeting point within him must be right. Peter harbors in himself a mystery linked very closely to Lord who withdraws himself back into the Trinity.

He said to him: Yes, Lord; you know that I love you. Your trustfulness, Lord, knows that my belief is in it. Your divine cognizance knows that my human cognizance allows itself to be enveloped and determined by it. Even more: your overtaxing is so great that it can overtax me only from within itself, in its own self-sureness. Peter is aware that, if the Lord demands a Yes to his love from him, then the Lord will assume responsibility for that Yes. It is as if Peter were now suddenly to understand the Lord who is distanced within belief. And with this realization, he also knows that the Lord can do it only with his word of affirmation; because the office that he holds is so much the Lord's that all of its content and its trinitarian mission are part of a mission that lies in the Lord. Peter the man has now understood that his entire mystery is played out at the supernatural level, that all his power derives its sustenance continually from the Lord in the Trinity, and that the duration of the Lord's mission in the world depends on the duration of the mission of Peter. That the Lord has submerged his m ssion in the mission of Peter. That the mystery of the love of the Lord and that of John, both of which have been assimilated into his office, did not at all have the finite character that he, Peter, could understand, but became part of the everlasting mission that the Son took over from the Father, which seemed as if it would come to an end with the Ascension, but in fact lives on in the mission of Peter in a way not totally different from the way that the Son's mission will persist within the bosom of the Trinity.

Thus the love that the Lord now demands from Peter is a so love of the mission. Just as he took over the mission out of love of the Father, so he now gives love to Peter in order that he might derive sustenance from it for his earthly mission. This love is more than merely human love; it is unrelenting divine love that is linked to the love of the Father, which inherently contains justice. It almost has the objectivity of a doctor's love, which undertakes everything that is necessary even if it is painful.

When the Lord came into the world in order to accomplish the Father's mission, he said Yes to this mission in that trustfulness that will also be the most precious aspect of Christian belief. Within it, he knows that he will be able to accomplish the mission. And if he knows that, despite the Cross, he is on a course toward certain success, then that is because he possesses the same loving trustfulness that he brings to men. It is into this "belief" that the Lord now draws Peter.

He said to him: Tend my lambs. Peter must take over responsibility for the sheep. A responsibility in love that nevertheless, at the same time, goes above and beyond love. A lover can somehow explain, if not the limit, then at least the objectivity of his love, in the sense that his love, even if it were to widen in scope, would always be encountering new persons and objects. He loves, for example, his friends and the friends of his friends, or he loves the neighbor whom he meets. Responsibility, by contrast, can dispense with this sort of objectivity. There can be a Christian responsibility for things that one does not at all know. The Lord—who now, from within his state of divine transport, confers responsibility for tending his sheep upon Peter for a second time—surveys a field of responsibility that lies far beyond Peter's horizon. Peter is drawn into this broader field and becomes responsible at a place where he is not at all present as a person, but present only through his relationship to the Lord. There is something neuter in him that he cedes to the Lord, yet that the Lord administers not alone, but only in coresponsibility with him. It is implied in this second sentence that Peter should also make himself available for, and devote himself to, tending the sheep even there where, for purposes of human visibility, it is not he but the Lord alone who tends these sheep.

Previously, Peter was agreeable to doing anything that the Lord could justifiably demand of him. Now, he has to do as the Lord tells him without being able to express an opinion about the matter. He allows the Lord to act out of and with that which the Lord has taken from him. The Lord makes use of Peter's spiritual gifts in order to reap a mysterious, incomprehensible harvest. Peter has placed himself— his freedom, his memory, his understanding and will—at the Lord's disposal, and in fact, in the spirit of a pastor; and the Lord makes use of him in order to tend his flock. The Church's anonymous store of prayer is further expanded, but in such a way that the element of the personal that was absorbed into anonymity appears, from beyond the anonymity, once again as personal.

As seen from the outside, this sort of use can almost seem like an abuse: in circumstances where Peter offers his finite powers, the Lord appropriates them in an infinite sense and uses them in a way that perhaps runs quite contrary to Peter. He will experience how, in his name, the Lord will accomplish things that have nothing to do with what had been his own intention. There is a tending in the name of the Lord whose ultimate consequences are taken wholly out of the hands of the pastor, present a wholly different aspect from what he had imagined, may even perhaps appear wrong to him, would have to oppress him with a constant feeling of guilt, had he not heard the command of the Lord: *Tend my lambs.* Perhaps, from an earthly viewpoint, everything goes amiss. Perhaps all the care lavished on some soul has only made it more obdurate. Perhaps the pastor ultimately comes to believe that he should have done everything differently. But if the Lord gave the command, then he will not leave Peter on his own. He is there tending, too. He has chosen the pasturage, appointed the pastor and he knows his sheep. Everything is, from the very beginning, in his safe hands. The pastor must know this, even if the Lord is now transported, if the link with him is less clearly discernible and he is left more dependent upon his own limited understanding and will for finding what is right. In his attempts, he must acquire a growing sense that the Lord is overseeing everything, while to him, the pastor, it all remains strange.

Here, it also becomes clear that the Church must have an external form with steadfast laws. On the one hand, because she must be accommodated to human averageness; on the other hand, however, because she must not forget that the Lord is greater and more incomprehensible. The Church cannot simply adapt herself to the Lord dynamically. There is a point at which man's "good will", or what he deems "well-intentioned", becomes ridiculous. If someone should want to entrust a princess to a dairymaid so that the latter might instruct her in good manners, then the dairymaid might try as hard as she could, yet the inappropriateness of the arrangement would only become all the more clearly evident. Similarly, the Church will always remain inadequate. On the one hand, there is nothing perfectible in her; all her undertakings fall short in view of the ideal that was to have been attained. Thus existence within the Church seems to be sheer uncomfortableness. On the other hand, the Christian knows, in belief, that the Lord rounds everything out in his grace, and this could be a reason for him to experience existence within the Church as something comfortable. But at bottom, it is wrong to divide one's evaluations in that way. The Church, in her humanity, makes things somehow comfortable for those who only straggle along, who never catch up, whereas those who give their best perceive the inadequacies in what they achieve. On the other hand, anyone who measures his achievements must feel himself uncomfortable in the Church, whereas he who leaves everything up to the Lord finds himself relieved of all discomfort. The Lord wants us, in a childlike manner, to bring everything that is ours to him so that he himself can mold it into whatever he likes. He wants us to be humble enough to work together with him even though we know that all our best is as nothing to him. *Tend my lambs.* The most reprehensible thing would be to let everything drop in despondency so as to leave it up to the grace of God. An authentic dialogue ought to occur, not a monologue by the Lord. The Father has created the partners for the conversation and hands them over to his Son, who takes them seriously, who not only wants to speak with them as a man but also, through his divine Sonship, educates them for participation in the unending conversation between the Father and Son in the Holy Spirit. We are expected to join this conversation. If we refuse, out of false humility, to take our part, then we are refusing to do the will of God. Our attempt to participate consists in our bringing—actively and passively—that which is ours to the Lord, who forms it into whatever he likes. Out of our not refusing he forms our having a say. The Father, too, did not refuse the Son when the Son asked him for permission to effect redemption. And the Father left it to him to make his own decision. He could have said No; he could have found that the Son was demanding too much. But—to speak in human terms—he relinquished certain rights stemming from his Fatherhood and his love for his Son in order to allow the Son his act of supreme self-surrender. Further, God has created us to be images of himself, and the Son would like to reawaken this image in us. Out of the Father's nonrefusal, he presents us with the possibility of not refusing, so that the same thing might be accomplished in the Son through *our* nonrefusal that has already been accomplished in him through the Father's nonrefusal. People often react with affected politeness when they receive a gift and say, "It is too much!" They thereby show that they place their ability to measure above the love received. It may well be that, objectively considered, the gift exceeds the means of the one presenting it. But if he really wants to present it out of love, then measurement by limit-setting reason has lost its justification here. Thus, when the Son makes his offer to him, the Father does not say,

"It is too much!" He relinquishes, so to speak, his right to judge and oversee things, and leaves full scope of judgment to the Son. It is into this attitude of mind that Peter is drawn when the Son permits him to tend his sheep.

It may be that a loving person who has given a great gift will feel himself deprived and disadvantaged afterward. Perhaps he has given away his only writing pen and must now write with a pencil. But if the love behind the giving was genuine, then even this constraint and hindrance will become for him, through his thoughts of the beloved, an impetus to growth in love. At the moment of the giving, his sacrifice was not hard. But it is a growing sacrifice, which had merely its beginning in the gift. He will perhaps start missing what was given more and more. And he will be able to regard this increasing sense of absence as a sign of his increasing love, since authentic love is in growth. Indeed, the growing sacrifice will offer the lover an opportunity to be growing in love because precisely that which he misses will remind him more and more of the beloved. Whether the pen that the latter took away with him is actually of any use to him he does not ask; it is enough that it is at his disposal. As little as it would have been fitting for the beloved to refuse the gift on grounds related to its usefulness, just as little does the lover feel himself driven, from a need for verification, to inquire into what the beloved does with it.

Thus the Son, too, during the time of his sojourn on earth, will, as it were, be missed by the Father; and the more he is missed, the more the Father will appreciate the magnitude of his love for the Son and of the Son's for him. For the Father also needs the Son and cannot be without him. Perhaps the Father would have had other suggestions, other ideas pertaining to redemption that would not have made the abandonment of the Cross necessary. But he does not express them; he leaves redemption up to the Son. In love, what is best is always what the other wishes. But the Son, too, goes along wholly with the will of the Father inasmuch as he makes ready to embark upon his redemptive course. They love each other so strongly that their wills always coincide, not in the sense of meeting somewhere in the middle and uniting, but within an eternal, absolute unity in which each one forgoes what is his and each is in agreement with the other from eternity, not within a rigid, dead identity but within that eternal life of love from which everything that bears the name of grace flows.

A gift can often be quite impractical; but if it is presented in love, it must also be accepted in love, and one sees in it only the love that has presented it. Perhaps the loving person who has offered the gift had imagined that the loved one would enjoy possessing it as much as he himself would, which means that he has projected himself into the loved one and thus created a unity over and above the gift. This identity, established by way of the gift, is love. In it, the Persons in God remain distinct and yet form one essential unity.

Here, too, the mystery of the Eucharist emerges in its issuance from the Trinity. The Father allows the Son to give himself to the world, and in fact, for everyone and for each individual, in order to awaken, from within the world, the love of all individuals for God. In doing this, the Father relinquishes his Son and himself gives his Son eucharistically: behind the sacrifice of the Son stands the consubstantial loving surrender of the Father as the source of the Eucharist. The Son takes men up into this mystery, and they surrender themselves to him believingly and lovingly by relinquishing what is their own and permitting the Son to give them over to the Father. This permission is a permission for sacrifice, with one's own cognition and will being surrendered into the unity of trinitarian life.

It is the Son's decision to allow himself to be sent forth by the Father in order to redeem the world as a man. And the Father permits the Son this so fully that he expands the limits of a human life boundlessly so as to give the Son the opportunity to have his sacrifice continued all the way to the end, to the very limits of the world. With that, the Father makes possible the Eucharist. The Son requests the duration of a human life, and the Father presents him with the duration of the world. He lends, so to speak, transtemporal, divine forms of being to his worldly existence in the Eucharist. Also, he now generates his Son continually within this eucharistic form. The Eucharist is not merely the Son's concern; otherwise, the Son would be involved in it alone with men. It is also the Father's concern, and therefore the Son mediates the Father in the Eucharist and is, in the

21:16

process of his eucharistic generation, always linked to the Father. In the Son's eucharistic form of being, too, the Father continually imparts something of his own essence to him. And he constantly receives back what he has bestowed, since the Son continually sacrifices and presents his eucharistic life to the Father. Between the Son's decision to take over the mission and the Father's decision to participate in the Son's eucharistic life there exists a kind of perpetual cyclical process.

Thus there is something like a reception of the Father in the sacrifice of the Mass. We sacrifice the Son to the Father just as the Father offers and sacrifices him to us. We place back into the Trinity that which lives in the Trinity.

Peter is introduced into this mystery and, together with him, the Church. It is the Catholic mystery. As long as man seeks God alone, the whole of his activity remains something private. But when God allows his grace to descend on a man, it splashes off him like a drop of rain and onto all those standing nearby: the grace itself has a eucharistic character. That is why Peter must tend the lambs. His love for the Lord is transformed into eucharistic love. His relinquishing love. He has to administer the Eucharist eucharistically. He has to administer the Eucharist eucharistically. He has to administer incomprehensible grace without comprehension. He must dispense grace as one who is himself dispensed. He must be both the individual who is affected and all those who are affected, and beyond that, must also administer— as administrator of the superabundance that is characteristic of grace and the Eucharist—the drops that land on no one. He must not allow any aspect of office or grace to become lost. If, for instance, the Mother of the Lord appears to a certain few, he must ensure that this grace also affects a large number of those living then and born afterward. He must distribute things and balance things out, keeping everything flowing within a process that resembles, from afar, the trinitarian process.

He has to forgo any ability to see things as a whole, but the Son, too, had forgone that on the Cross. Peter can never unroll any long-range plans. There is no strategy of the Church. He can only tend his unsurveyable flock on its way toward an unforeseeable destination.

382

21:17. He said to him the third time: Simon, son of John, do you love me? Peter was grieved because he said to him the third time: Do you love me? And he said to him: Lord, you know everything; you know that I love you. Jesus said to him: Feed my sheep.

The Lord puts the question a third time; in view of his threefold denial, Peter is to confirm three times that he loves the Lord. To give assurance three times, within a single conversation, that he stands by him. As in all conversations with the Lord, however, the Lord brings the answer along with the question, and man is placed in between the two, within an immense expandedness. But what is now important is less the expansion of Peter and his answer than the absolute breadth of the question and answer of the Lord, which are much broader than Peter will ever be able to grasp. They are, after all, words that the Lord simultaneously directs at the Father, words that must therefore always remain measureless in scope and that the Father alone can understand in the sense in which they were intended. The Son supplements the shortcomings of the sinner when he presents him, as his brother, to the Father; and this rounding out is completely unintelligible to us. But the Father likewise rounds out the human words of the Son and hears them as divine, and this rounding out also remains incomprehensible to us. In any consideration of the Son's words, there always remains a mysterious surplus that no amount of contemplation can exhaust, a mystery between Father and Son.

The Lord questions three times because—and this becomes fully evident the third time—he is questioning in the name of the Trinity. He questions within the justice of the Father, the knowledge of the Spirit and his own love. And he expects that the reply will be maximally adapted to the context of the question, that Peter's reply will be not only a reply of love to his own love, but simultaneously a reply to the Holy Spirit and the Father, knowing well that, given the distinctness of the Personal aspects, the triune reply must result. He also knows that Peter is never in a position to see the whole of the question or the answer, but that he, the Lord, will place the question and answer at the service of the Ever-Greater. That Peter is prepared to accept any instruction from him, not only through him as God incarnate but also through him as God in unity with the Father and

Spirit. This readiness of Peter is a living one, which will remain living as long as Peter is prepared to accept the Lord's question. And the Lord's question is not a question that might have temporal limits somewhere; rather, it is an eternally asked question that is eternally, even if silently, answered.

Inasmuch as the Lord endows the question and answer with this burst-open significance of the trinitarian spirit, he confers upon Peter the enduring possibility of inquiry. Peter, who always has to hear and answer the question in the name of the Church, will continually have the possibility of inquiring: not only into whether he has heard and answered correctly, but also into whether the Spirit that the Lord mediates to him through his question remains constantly living, constantly capable of adapting to the hidden Spirit of the Lord. He is hidden because the Lord will not always ask the question aloud, and Peter will not always give the answer aloud. The conversation must continue even in silence. And here speech and silence are transformed into action and contemplation. The question of love and the answer of love manifest their livingness in the eternal relation between action and contemplation. There are both possibilities: the question can be taken as action and the answer as contemplation, but also the question as contemplation and the answer as action. For a contemplative person, the question of the Lord is action; for an active person, it is contemplation. It is not the case that, in this conversation, action and contemplation are constantly opposed as distinct. Both for the Lord and for Peter, the two can exist in a kind of mutuality, in mutual integration. But inasmuch as action and contemplation present themselves in the Lord's third question, it becomes manifest that both action and contemplation are always fructified by the mission of the Trinity, that they receive the life that is most properly their own not just from the personality of the Lord but equally from the trinitarian mission: from the Lord's mission within the unity of the three Persons. There occurs now, as the Lord is at the point of returning into the Trinity, a manifestation of what he had taken with him, and incorporated into his mission, from the Trinity. He became a man, a man with his own special nature, with the divine character of the Son, yet this character was never separable from the divine character of the Father and the Spirit. He never relinquished, in the course of his mission in the world, those qualities which—circulating, as it were, in God—pertain to the three Persons. Not only did he come as one sent by the Father, but he also took with him, as incorporated in his mission, qualities of the Father and the Spirit; and this made it possible for the Father and Spirit to participate in the mission.

It is in this trinitarian sense that action and contemplation are spoken of here. Contemplation is the kind of prayer that is not complete in itself, that does not repose in itself in the way that, for instance, it is enough for a prayer of supplication to have reached the Lord; rather, it is an open prayer that draws its substance out of the Trinity itself. When the one who prays takes nothing earthly with him into his prayer other than himself, so as to surrender himself wholly, and expects nothing other than what God will give him, then such prayer leads him into contemplation. This readiness is like a bridge. Peter steps onto the bridge when he shows himself willing to answer any question from the Lord. For he is ready not only to work for the Lord but also to allow the Lord to work in him. It is like the readiness of a bride for everything to which the bridegroom will lead her. And since the Lord, within his trinitarian mission, can no longer be satisfied solely with what he could demand as one who loves, but must also demand what he has to bring back to the Father and the Spirit as proof of the faithfulness of his Church, he questions for a third time. He lets himself be given the ring by his Bride.

In the case of the first question, there were two partners facing each other in a conversation. In the case of the second question, the Lord hears the answer more definitely, because *he* gives it its full sense. In the case of the third question, because he is in the Trinity, he hears it as a witness. He receives it as a vow. When he asks for the third time, he accepts this vow from the Church in the presence of the divine, threefold Majesty. Just as one takes monastic vows in the context of Holy Mass: in the solemnity of a liturgical act in which the Lord assumes the role of witness. Indeed, the Lord stands opposite himself as witness inasmuch as he differentiates himself into both the Second Person in God and the incarnated Lord.

But Peter has denied him three times, and the Lord does not just pass over this in a spirit of redeeming love. Despite the overtaxation that he expects Peter to cope with, he still shows him that his love recognizes justice. He does this because he is also questioning in the name of the Father and the Spirit, and everything past and future must be included in the question and answer.

Simon, son of John. Each time, Peter is addressed by his full name. The Lord addresses him as someone whose whole existence he must, each time, confront him with again, one whom he must make remember exactly who he is, and one whom he must also show that he, the Lord, knows exactly who he is. The whole person is implicit in this name—not so much the human person as the human bearer of office. From this, Peter recognizes that he is not merely giving his answer for himself, but rather, in the name of his whole Church, and giving it in such a way that it is binding, binding for all those who are entrusted to him. As soon as he realizes this, he understands that, from a purely human standpoint, the answer amounts to an unparalleled overtaxation, not only because he must answer for all, but also because he expects of the Lord that the Lord will accept the answer as valid for all those who will later believe in him. Hence, it is an overtaxation on both sides.

Do you love me? Implicit in this question is an infinite hope, and in fact, a hope of Peter and a hope of the Lord. The Lord expects from Peter not a love that corresponds to his stature, but a love that knows about the unclosable nature of trinitarian life. He should also love the Father and the Spirit, and indeed, love them in hope, in a hope that represents the element of growth in love, the element of the unsurveyable that allows belief and love to arise like ripe fruit, that belief and love can draw nourishment from as from a root, and that would be an answer even before any question is asked. In a hope that has its center no longer in Peter, but in the Lord.

This third question is asked not in relation to time, but in relation to eternity. Peter hopes for full redemption, for eternal life, for the vision of the Father, for initiation into the mysteries of the Trinity; he hopes for the whole side of the Lord that he does not now see, that he has heard about only through things that the Lord has said. His hope is based on the visible side of the Lord and aimed at his invisible side. He hopes that the finite conversation with the Lord in this world might open, in the beyond, into an infinite prayer to God. He hopes in the way that children do when they are being told a fairytale and expect to be transported into fairytale land itself by the storyteller. He leaves all control over his expectation to the Lord; he loses himself in what the Lord promises. One is so utterly surrendered in contemplation—whether one is now seeing or not seeing—that one cannot even adopt an attitude toward seeing or not seeing. In this spirit of contemplation, Peter must now say Yes to the Lord.

In the Son's life on earth, the period of contemplation—the thirty hidden years—is manifestly distinct from the three years of public activity. The years of contemplation represented not only the Son's contemplation but also the Father's contemplation as directed toward the Son, the trinitarian contemplation; just as the Lord's public activity also represented the Father's activity through him in the Holy Spirit. Now, as the Son returns again to the Father, contemplation and action, as separated entities, return again into God's unity of contemplative action and active contemplation. But the Lord bequeaths to his Church a participation in his trinitarian contemplation and his trinitarian action, and Peter has this in himself when he answers. This trustfulness and this hope can be had by every Christian: that, in giving his word of affirmation, he also participates in the Lord's contemplation—even if he sees nothing and feels nothing—and that his affirmation will be passed on by the Lord, not only in his role as a mediator who gives it to the Father and the Spirit to be divinely expanded, but also as the eternal representative of the Father. For his mission can be understood as the element of action within trinitarian contemplation, so that, on the basis of his own essence, the possibility remains open for him, in terms of his mission, to give what he has received back into the Trinity.

Peter was grieved because he said to him the third time: Do you love me? Peter recognizes quite clearly the connection between his denial and the thrice-asked question. He senses in it something like an accusation, something like a continued dwelling by the Lord upon a matter that could perhaps already have been regarded as over and done with. He thinks that he has matured so much as a result of the Cross that he might have been able to compensate for his three denials by means of a single answer; that he has become, through the Lord's Resurrection, someone whose word of affirmation has full validity. Even if he cannot express in words the transformation that has taken place in him, he feels it, he can almost grasp it with his hands. Precisely because he was one of those who brought the Lord to the Cross, the Easter message is fully valid for him. Thus he is forced by the change in him to look first of all at himself, in order to see just what, in fact, constitutes the transformation that has occurred. Since the Resurrection, he lives within a new grace that he can no longer fall away from. And now, to this new man Peter, and to the highest ecclesiastical office that he now represents, this question is nevertheless put. He feels that the Lord does not, at the moment, doubt his personal faithfulness, because he himself has conferred faithfulness upon him. But in the name of his Bride, the Church, the Lord must create new foundations, foundations that must endure throughout the millennia and cannot be laid strongly enough. Peter is reinstalled in his ecclesiastical office, but now as the administrator of a transformed Bride of the Lord that has gone through the experience of the Cross. In the name of this installation, he must learn no longer to take personally that personal feeling of unease which he might interpret personally as a distrust of his faithfulness on the part of the Lord, but rather, to objectify it until it becomes submerged in a knowledge of his new responsibility within that clearly outlined mission which transcends any redemptive grace granted to him personally and guarantees him the objective grace that has been promised for the objective Church. Previously, Peter had been required to adapt himself to the Lord personally. Now, from within office, he must be adapted to office all over again. All his personal feelings must be absolutely subordinated to office until every question directed to him is perceived and understood as an ecclesiastical question.

It is from within this new official consciousness that Peter answers: *Lord, you know everything; you know that I love you.* "You know everything" connotes, in Peter's mind, not so much the fate and thoughts of individual Christians or of the many enemies of the Church as the Lord's knowledge of his evolving Church. The Lord's knowledge of the foundations that he is now laying, of the developments that lie in store, of the interplay between office and love in the newly instituted community. Once Peter recognizes this knowledge of the Lord, he is more prepared to subordinate himself to him, to devote himself to the Lord officially in such a way that he truly assumes his share of the responsibility, no longer as a personal friend and disciple but, finally, as the Rock upon which the Lord can build. Now, something absolutely immovable has arisen in the relationship between the Lord and Peter, something so solid, firm and seamless that no insight into the distribution of powers between the two can any longer be sought; a unity that was, to be sure, created solely by the Lord, but one in which Peter's contribution can no longer be seen as something separate. He, too, must now give back to the Lord in superabundance that which the Lord has given to him in superabundance. So much are they an amalgamation that, between them, there is only *one* knowledge, one clarity. That is divinely dispensed infallibility. No one can any longer withdraw from this relationship. Peter the sinner, the man, remains the person that he was, but he has acquired an official face that fades off into the earthward-turned countenance of the Lord. The Lord always has two faces: one turned toward the Father and the other toward the world. What passes from the Lord to the Father and what he receives from the Father remain entirely unrestricted. What has been changed is that, from now on, the Lord's graces all arrive on earth by way of the Church. Everything that he pronounces in his name, and in the name of the Father and the Holy Spirit, enters strictly into the Church. The long path that Peter had to traverse before he arrived at recognition of his official role would have to be traversed, in one's own way, by anyone approaching the Church from outside her: one has to recognize that the Lord has freely bound himself to Peter.

The Church, which now arises out of this firm bonding, is the testimony to the unity between the Lord and Peter: a living, continually developing testimony, which remains subject to all its evolvements, passes through the most varied sorts of phases, endures in tranquillity and restlessness, but can always be traced back to this point of the thrice-elucidated and strengthened relationship between Peter and the Lord. It is there that the apex lies; everything else must be determined with reference to this apex. At the apex, Peter receives the blessing of the Lord, which he will have to diffuse throughout the whole Church, *urbi et orbi*. Here is the knot, the act of drawing together, into which even the other apostles present at the time are tied. If Peter is given the commission to administer the totality, then it is impossible that the others should be ranked parallel with him and be able to do as they choose independently of his commission. If apparently parallel authorities were to do something wrong, then Peter would still be held responsible in their place.

You know that I love you. Peter now answers in the name of the Church. The Church loves the Lord; Peter attests to that. It is probably the first answer that is given in the name of the Church and that must nevertheless be definitely understood as the testimony of an individual. The loving Peter and the loving Church require together nothing more than a single declaration. Peter's voice serves for them both. As a Christian, Peter has provided proofs of his love; despite his denial, he has remained faithful and loving ever since the Cross. Now, however, when he has absorbed the office of John's love into himself, he is entitled to make a declaration that includes, beyond his own person, all present and future followers.

A man can be committed to loving another and can promise him faithfulness. And every time he makes a pledge to be faithful, he believes that he will keep it. Though others may prove unfaithful, they would be the sort who do not know love in the way that he knows it. But when he himself later becomes unfaithful, he will quickly come up with numerous excuses both for himself and for unfaithfulness in general, which supposedly accords with the ways of the world. But whoever draws the strength and fidelity of his own love from the Lord's love for him cannot become unfaithful, because he draws on a store that is inexhaustible. If his love really springs from the Lord's love, then it will have no end. And just as Peter is certain that, from now on, he will never again separate himself from the Lord, so he is certain, in the name of the Church, that she will always abide in the life of love. Since having received the eyes of office from the Lord, he sees the sources of love much more clearly than before. He can almost observe with his bodily eyes the development of the Church as the fruit of the Lord's bond with him, and if he has absolutely no need to comprehend also why precisely he was chosen to be the administrator of the Church, he nevertheless sees no less clearly that she is a work of the Lord.

It is not hard to imagine the personal element in the Lord's love for every individual lover and sinner, nor to think of the sorts of courses that these different pathways of love will take. But it is difficult to form a picture of the impersonal element of the Church within this love. When the bond between two lovers gives rise to a child, that is not only the start of a third being alongside the first two, but, beyond that, the arising of something wholly new that is simultaneously both abstract and concrete: a family. This is something substantially different from the personal love between two human beings. A wholly new order emerges, with new, firm laws to which the laws of the parents' personal love is subordinated. Family life and love of the family come into being. It is something no longer wholly graspable by the individual, insofar as the family now acquires a destiny of its own. Thus there is, in the Church, something like an objectification of all—of the Lord as well as of Peter and all the others who are in her. And this objective element passes on to the following generations: here lies the origin of *tradition.* Hence, various forms, rites and laws must now already be created that are not necessary at the moment, but that will be indispensable for the continuance of the new objectivity of the Church—just as the Lord instituted the Eucharist at a moment when it still seemed not at all necessary, since he himself was still there. Much was instituted by the Lord that acquires its significance only in the course of time. And much was also arranged by the Church, in his name, that becomes important only for the future. This is not to say that it is necessary for all rites to have been instituted by the Lord himself at the very beginning, but only that whatever has once become tradition in the Church expresses something that was intended from the very beginning.

Thus Peter really promises love in the name of a Church whose mature form he still does not know. He promises it for all eternity. And he assumes the responsibility for this love. He commits the love that the Church both owes the Lord and shows him through Peter to a duration that will be equivalent to the duration that the Lord has foreordained for the Church. He adapts the love of the Church to the will of the Lord, so everlastingly that he promises it everlastingly in the name of one who will be everlastingly present in the Church. That anyone should promise himself personally to the Lord for eternity is, in itself, something incomprehensible. But that anyone should, on behalf of all men for millennia to come, on behalf of all sinners, seekers and strivers, find a word that sums up everything that has permanence and validity before the Lord—that is something dizzying. It is the belief of a Church that sees the Lord as capable of anything and gives herself as security for that belief. *You know,* says Peter. And if you know it, if you possess such knowledge, then your knowledge about me and the Church cannot err nor falter: out of this rock of your knowledge will flow our certainty of loving you eternally.

21:18. *Truly, truly, I say to you, when you were young, you girded yourself and walked where you would; but when you are old, you will stretch out your hands, and another will gird you and lead you where you do not wish to go.*

After the Lord has assured himself of Peter's faithfulness through his thrice-asked question, and after Peter has understood how seriously he has obligated himself, the Lord goes on to trace the implications for the later life of the apostle. He begins with his youth, which, like all youth, was still indeterminate, still lacking in commitment, yet equipped with the freedom to make decisions. The Lord uses two examples to illustrate this: first, girding oneself as an expression of shaping one's own personal life; and this self-girding has remained, up to the present, a matter of course for Peter. Second, walking where one would as an expression of shaping one's activity and occupation; and this second example already begins, given Peter's new situation vis-à-vis the Lord, to be called into question. Through the Lord's reference to youth as something generally symbolic of the stage of still not having decided, it suddenly becomes clear to Peter that decisions of the gravest sort have now been made, decisions in which he participated through his thrice-given affirmative answer, but that were brought about by the Lord because *he* posed the thrice-asked question. The emphasis that was implicit in the repetitions now assumes for Peter the finality characteristic of a vow. From now on, he is no longer free, he can no longer survey things as a whole, and above all, he senses the guidance of the Lord with a new seriousness. The Lord has brought him to this position; the Lord also reveals to him that he knows the course his life is to take and that he has him in his hands. Henceforth, Peter is someone whose destiny is predetermined by the Lord himself. About the present, the Lord says nothing. He only points back to the past and ahead to the future. Previously, it was Peter's own will that determined how he acted, and this will arose out of his own strength and capacity for decision. This strength and capacity are not taken away from him today. But his will itself has been transformed. It has become a part of the will of the Lord. In the spiritual sense, he has given everything that was his to the Lord. Therefore, he must undergo a new subordination in the material sense. He must be newly integrated into the new forms of his mission.

At the start of his discipleship, he had given his first word of affirmation. Now, after his denial, he must expiate his guilt by giving a new word of affirmation three times over. By virtue of its very threefoldness, this leads him much more deeply into his responsibility: just as every denial had imparted a more serious character to the preceding one, so now every affirmation acquires more weight from the succeeding one. And this intensification has an immediate effect upon the scope of the mission, so that Peter is thereby initiated more and more into his ultimate mission. Previously, he had always thought that his Yes and his No, his vow of faithfulness and his betrayal, had a primarily personal meaning. Now, in the light of his new affirmation, he sees that, at each point, his entire mission was also involved. This mission is only now, through the mercifulness of the Lord, disclosed to him in its full scope, to the extent that his word of affirmation becomes stronger and deeper. Similarly, the owner of a business may perhaps have long since chosen to make his son the inheritor of his entire firm, but, before telling him this, has been charging him with minor tasks and responsibilities. And it is not until the father puts him quite seriously to the test that he comprehends what sort of commission is actually proposed for him and grows into the role in its full scope. The more one becomes engaged in it, the more the commission grows.

And it is, in fact, a commission that can, and should, grow. Martyrdom is not something that one must gradually adapt to through practice, but the apostolate is: one has to grow in the knowledge that one must exist unreservedly for the sake of the mission. This knowledge does not have the character of self-assurance or self-confidence, but that of a constant petition, of a plea. The more one really grows, the more the element of active training gives way to fervent pleading that the Lord might accomplish the mission, in me, against me. Here it should be noted that the mission of love, like that of John, is much more delicate than the Petrine one of office. Love can never assure itself, whereas office can constantly assure itself. It stands under a law that assures it. One can be sure of having done that which is required of office, whereas it is infinitely more difficult to have done everything that love requires.

In Peter as he now stands there, shaken, moved, the Lord sees not only office, but also, included in that, the office of John's love. And if he now speaks with him in such detail about what is to come, then that is in order to show him that he also recognizes the love in him. He will die a death of love. Peter, the awkward one, who does not at all feel adequate to the demands of his office, who despite his word of affirmation bears the heavy burden of his denial, will henceforth be permitted to live in a great hope: to die for the Lord. The Lord's words are descriptive of both his youth and his old age, which means that he holds both. Peter has been given an assurance that he will be the Lord's right up to the end.

When you are old, another will gird you. He will no longer be able to do it himself. Perhaps because he will no longer possess the strength and dexterity to do it. Perhaps, also, because someone will prevent him from doing it; because he will become so dependent that he will no longer be able to perform even the most everyday tasks, the most routine movements, at his own discretion. This second possibility is hinted at in the words *stretch out your hands.* From that time on through endless time, this remains, for Christians, the movement that the Lord had to make on the Cross, the movement not of action, but of passion. *And lead you where you do not wish to go.* The will of Peter himself will not welcome death, will fear the crucifixion. But the will that lies with the Lord, which he must from now on recognize as his own, will cause him to allow himself to be led where he does not wish to go. Just as the Lord himself, in his suffering and through his own will as deposited with the Father, allowed the will of the Father to be done. In what he foretells, the Lord establishes Peter as similar to himself. It is a tremendous parallel, which lies much more in the inner will than in the external cross. Peter sees that his mission, too, encompasses his entire will, just as that of the Lord encompassed his will, and in such a way, in both cases, that the will was not lost, but was taken up into the will of the Father and Son.

Peter will be led, not of his own free will and yet willingly, where he does not wish to go. He cannot, and may not, choose his martyrdom with his own free will, but if the Lord has chosen it, he may choose it along with him. Thus what is demanded here is consummate indifference. As long as the mission lasts, the one commissioned is to remain willingly within it and not seek death even though he perhaps sees it in his reach and would find it simpler to die; rather, he is to die willingly at the moment when death is actually extended to him. He is to evade his enemies as long as possible even if he thirsts for martyrdom and to remain still willing, at the moment of martyrdom, to go on living if God should demand it. No one may wish to take up his heavenly mission as long as he still can, and may, carry out his earthly one; and in the course of that, he should nevertheless joyfully anticipate his heavenly one. If he is conquered, then he will rejoice at going to God; until such time, he will joyfully fight, using every resource, to prevent being conquered.

Peter is led. He will not go himself. He will be forced into passivity. But even now, he no longer goes where he wishes; even now, he is being led. When his being led by the enemies of God eventually occurs, it will be like a continuation of that which always was, and Peter will see in them and their opposition to God a still more intense obligation to endure this being led. He will not think that he has become separated from the guidance of God, but will recognize in the guidance of the enemies that of God.

This being led happens to Peter, to the Church, and to every individual; and it is always a being led *where you do not wish to go*. For every Christian instance of being led is preindicated in these words of the Lord; in Peter, the Lord has illustrated and uncovered and recondensed what guidance means, from youth until death, in a Christian life: being more and more strongly directed out of self-determination and into being led. What the Lord illustrates through Peter is not personally intended, but is a model of the guidance that will live on in the Church and whose main characteristics, thanks to the way that Peter entrusted himself to guidance, she will always be able to infer for herself.

The close connection between guidance and mission is clear. The one commissioned has constant need of guidance, and the guidance must in some way correspond to the mission. Between the two, a kind of unity should arise, a unity conducive to the freedom of both. A mission of love has need of the guidance of office; but because a eucharistic quality already attaches to love as such—it knows that it is there for the others—this guidance will not be difficult. If, however, it is a mission of office, then it is subject to the danger of becoming petrified within laws and barriers, and so it requires the guidance of love. And when Peter now undergoes investiture with the office and love of the Lord, it becomes clear through this once again how much the two—office and love—form an absolute, radiant unity in the Lord. In his final encounter with Peter, the Lord must make this unity light up once more in all its compelling clarity for the whole of posterity, because afterward, when he will no longer be in the world, Peter and the Church will be the image of this archetypal unity. He must do this in order that the impression will not later arise that office and love have become divided in the Church, that there are some individuals who have received the "gift of office" and others the "gift of love", with it then being left to men to try to form a unity out of the two that would prove, in the long term, impossible, or perhaps even to seek a new unity, a new equilibrium between the two, outside of the existing Church. The Lord is the archetypal unity, and he confers on Peter both the opportunity and the obligation to reflect this archetype in his Church to the best of his ability. In the Church as a whole, not only in particular missions in which a special gift for office or love is evident. And the Church must always be conscious of these two things: on the one hand, that office and love, in the visible manner appropriate to her as Church, were present, wholly and archetypally, *in the Lord* (that, for instance, the official side was not imparted to her later or made necessary by circumstantial factors); and on the other hand, that this unity was transferred by the Lord, from the very beginning, to *Peter,* and that the Lord desired, and himself effected, this unity in Peter, making known, by the unattenuated manner in which he transferred it to him, his will that what Peter received should also be passed on to the later Church in an unattenuated form. These two things are thus, at bottom, but one: Peter embodies nothing new vis-à-vis the Lord; rather, he embodies in the Church, for all time, the twofold office of the Lord himself.

21:19. *(This he said to show by what death he was to glorify God.)* And *after this he said to him: Follow me.*

That the death is part of the mission is a matter of course for John. The death of à Christian differs from all others by being included in his service. And every Christian service derives its substance from the Lord's service, which consisted in glorification of the Father. Everything that he did, said or suffered took place for the glorification of the Father. His life as a man was framed by his birth and his death, which, like everything else, were testimonies to the Father. And if Peter will meet his death on a cross and his death will acquire the manifest qualities of glorification of the Father, then those qualities will be lent to it by the Lord's death on the Cross. But the Lord does not desire merely a kind of external copy, a poor imitation of his destinies in the Church. Just as he himself lived the whole of his inner life in glorification of the Father, as the Man who is wholly in God, so he wishes to give his believers, too, the possibility of taking up service of the mission in an inner, personal and freely-willed way. Each believer is allowed to glorify the Father in his own personal way. His glorification is the response of the most unique thing that he possesses, the response of his whole being in faith. And precisely because it is so personal, and in a certain sense left wholly to the discretion of the Christian, it is as if it were a collected component of the will of the Son. And here it becomes manifest that the Son, in his own glorification of the Father, already knows—as though it were the substance of his own mission—about the mission of the Church and of each individual, including its uniqueness and personal achievability. Long before Peter knows that he will be prepared to die on a cross, the Lord knows it and leaves it, despite his knowledge and certainty, up to Peter. Peter will accept, of his own free will, that which is intended for him by God. And it is only because Peter is a model, a precursor, that his whole pathway is revealed to him in advance, in order that he might be given an inner certainty that his example is necessary. The Lord even discloses more than that to him. He shows him the inner connections within his mission. Because he has said Yes three times, the Lord relies on him, is quite sure about him and shows him his own certainty, so that, when the time comes and it would perhaps be easy, falling back upon his earlier betrayal, to become disloyal again, Peter might himself have the certainty that he cannot become disloyal. He might know that the Lord is counting on him; he might know it so well that he can infer from this knowledge the additional knowledge that he will assuredly remain loyal. Inasmuch, then, as the Lord makes Peter's death integral to the latter's mission, he thereby leaves active determination of this death to him. Peter is permitted to determine the happening of this death; he is permitted to suffer this death for the glorification of God and to know about this determination in advance; already now, when this death still lies in the distant future, he is allowed to be certain that he will offer this death to God.

It is only now that the Lord says to him: *Follow me.* Even though Peter has already been following him for a long time. But this is a new kind of following, just as it is a new kind of mission, a conversion within the conversion that has already occurred. A new belief within the belief that has not become obsolete. And the new mission needs the old as a kind of birthplace. Not, however, out of free determination by Peter, but out of that by the Lord, who confers, guides and shapes the mission, who absorbs it into his own at the point where he has accepted his own from the Father. It is like a flowing fountain of missions: a constantly new gushing forth from the central source. And because the Son desires that every mission should serve the glorification of the Father, he does not have the missions link up with his in a peripheral way, but rather, lets them arise centrally, out of his own center. There is a succession in office, but none in mission; in the latter, there is nothing derivative.

With that, the Son renounces something: a renunciation of having his own disciples in the sense of his own fatherhood. He could have had disciples whose mission was born out of his own mission; and those disciples could then have engendered further disciples, who would have been offspring of their mission. But the Lord does not want that. He wants to let every mission issue from his having been sent by the Father. He does not want every disciple to have, like a planet, his own system of moons around him which, in order to arrive at the central sun, would first have to ascend along with the mediating planet. Inasmuch as he does not desire this, the Lord is the exemplary saint. He mediates the mission, to be sure, but does so into the very center of the Father. And by that, he teaches everyone who is sent to lead those who are entrusted to him directly to the Father. That alone is true Christian mediation. In working out a mathematical problem, one must occasionally introduce an external quantity in order, through it, to arrive more directly at the solution. Similarly, the Lord introduces himself in order to lead to the solution of the Father, and that is what every saint will do within the Catholic Church. Were the Lord not to do that, then he would separate his human mission from his divine one; he would be active alone, instead of in unity with the Father. To be sure, it might still appear outwardly as if he were making his mission of becoming a man serve the purpose of leading to the Father; but its inner trinitarian meaning would be excluded and, above all, the Holy Spirit would be impoverished and deprived of his function—he, the one who is the Lord of mission. The individual would then possess merit in himself if he devoted his life to his mission; but it would no longer be Christian merit, because this always lies in God, just as the mission stems from God. The merit is, after all, fully dependent upon the being in God of the one who is sent. Therefore, all responsibility is wrested away from the man in matters pertaining to holiness and merit. Even if he thinks he knows that he can see none of the two in himself, claim none of them for himself.

Peter has received everything: the whole of love, the whole of office, even the whole knowledge of his own faithfulness to the end. But he is not thereby released into pursuit of his new mission, but rather, newly bound into new discipleship. If one wanted to regard his threefold Yes to the Lord as his three vows, then these would now be transformed into a final, absolute binding to the Lord. The new freedom that is given to him through the vows is no longer freedom of personal development and self-realization, but freedom of ultimate binding to the one whom he wishes to glorify. The *Follow me* amounts, above all, to fulfilment: the recognition by the Son that Peter now bears his stamp. Far more is involved here than the paradox that freedom and binding are the same thing. From this position, one can see the logical consistency of this unity shine forth with an unequaled inner forcefulness.

PETER AND JOHN

21:20. *Peter turned and saw following them the disciple whom Jesus loved, who had lain close to his breast at the supper and had said: Lord, who is it that is going to betray you?*

Peter has hardly finished speaking with the Lord when, by turning around, he apparently turns away from him. But now, for Peter, there is no more turning away in the inner, essential sense. He is so bound to following the Lord that he can now do whatever he wishes; he will always be following. He is secured. Not in the sense that, if he were to undertake something against the Lord it would nevertheless be for the Lord, but in the sense that the Lord guides his actions. He can no longer want anything that would not be of the Lord. No one may, then, attempt to cast a bad light on Peter's turning away here. Peter believes; he believes in such a way that each one of his movements is an expression of his belief. Belief therefore recognizes, even in Peter's apparent turning away, something logically consistent with its belief. He knows that his belief can no longer be found existing outside of unity with his action. In order to subject the office of love and the office of office, which are now both represented in him equally strongly, to any real criticism, one would have to place oneself outside of belief and within unbelief. From now on, Peter is someone who is bound personally all the way to death; he is Saint Peter, and at the same time, as such, he is officially the Rock of Christ's Church.

In turning, he *saw following them the disciple whom Jesus loved.* This is the first thing that he perceives in turning to look back. He sees the disciple from whom he received and assumed the office of love. And although that disciple has, to a certain extent, become submerged in him, he sees him carrying on independently his life of one who loves. Peter sees himself, with his newly assumed office that includes the office of love, almost brought into confrontation with the office of love that has remained in John, so that the situation discloses a kind of preponderance of love. A situation that has to persist just as does the situation of the newly received mission. An eternal, a Christian situation, the eternally furthered opening of the mission into the mission. A letting go of freedom by entering into the freedom of being bound. And to a certain extent, too, the birth of action out of contemplation. In turning around, Peter makes a transition from vision of the Lord to action of his own—something which had its origin in contemplative discussion with the Lord and whose first result is that Peter encounters the Lord's love in another person.

When Peter catches sight of John, the first thing he realizes is that this is *the disciple whom Jesus loved.* John, who records this, knows that Peter is very conscious of his office and that he has to be so; that he now sees in John less the one who has mediated the office of love into his office of office and more the disciple who possesses the Lord's love. He sees in John the one who he would like to be, the friend, the privileged one, of the Lord. Not for personal reasons, but to a certain extent for the sake of office. That he would like to be this is now a sign of his having understood. For it is, after all, difficult for office—which also loves and is so gripped by love that all its efforts are directed toward passing this love on without loss—to remain within the bounds of office, to create the kind of unity between love and office in which the official is given its due. Peter, to whom the Church is now entrusted, is weighed down by an awareness of his responsibility and the knowledge that he has become the administrator of the unchange-able, firmly integrated structure of the Church. In him, who has personally thrice made denial and thrice again made promise, there is so much vacillation that it is now doubly difficult for him to embody this fixed, unchangeable character of the Church. A fixedness which, to be sure, must always be enlivened and kept flexible by love. And thus, when he catches sight of John, he is reminded of the fact that there are other kinds of commission that spring entirely from love and are involved with the law in a quite secondary sense only; missions that are given sustenance, again and again, by the Lord himself, and furthermore, in a way that can be seen, felt and experienced.

And then he recognizes in John the one *who had lain close to Jesus' breast at the supper and had said: Lord, who is it that is going to betray you?* the one who had called the Lord's attention to the betrayal, the one who had used the love he both received from and returned to the Lord in order to remind the Lord of the betrayal. And Peter knows that it was not a question asked out of curiosity, but a question asked out of love; one that perpetuates itself, Christianly, enduringly. It is not office that calls the Lord's attention to the lurking danger. It is love. And it is not love at the moment of drawing back, of distancing, but love at the moment of giving itself; a love that would prefer to speak only of love, to become nothing but love wholly and fully, yet that nevertheless, in this situation of supreme intimacy, asks about the betrayer—indeed, has to ask, on the basis of a privilege and a duty. Of a privilege, insofar as this love of John lightens the Lord's human outlook on his coming suffering. For through the question, the Lord also comes to know that he is loved. Of a duty, since John, by virtue of his position of love to which Peter had appealed, is forced to remind the Lord of the betrayal. The office of love knows nothing strange, alienating. It enters into everything that is difficult and mysterious, whether it be a matter of external destiny or something inward and personal. And it also has, as office, a desire to take cognizance of what is difficult and, with that, to recall the difficult to mind. Love cannot behave otherwise: wherever there is danger approaching, it must see it and call attention to it. Love's clairvoyance desires to be used for that; it does not understand itself as a luxurious clarity that is sufficient unto itself. And the fact that John's love is clairvoyant has also not escaped the notice of office; that is why questions of office are constantly being put to the Lord through John. Would it not have been more appropriate for office to have called the Lord's attention to the betrayal? But because love constantly gives and receives answers, we know: no, it was a matter for love. And yet this answer still does not silence the question of office. Here, too, an eternal, continuing situation has been created. Not a situation, naturally, of personal jealousy, but one of objective, continually effective fruitfulness. Precisely in office's continuing to question further (would it not have been its turn to ask?) lies fruitfulness, for by so doing, office learns not only that love, too, has its duties and requirements, but that office itself has an obligation toward love.

21:21. When Peter saw him, he said to Jesus: Lord, what about this man?

Peter has learned of his own destiny. He is far from comprehending it. But he has grasped the one essential thing: what awaits him does not belong to him; it belongs to him who comprehends it. And it is sufficient for that one to have the comprehension. Once again, he feels himself in the hands of the Lord. Himself and his office and everything that he does not know. That was the wonderful outcome of their conversation. He had been downcast about his denial and the fact that it was necessary for the Lord to ask him three times. But now, everything that was unclear and worrying to him has disappeared into the great certainty that everything is the Lord's. And implicit in this knowledge is the fact that everything that is John's or every Christian's is equally the Lord's. The Lord also knows, and has with him, the destinies of everyone else. At this point, it is the part of office to ask the Lord what will happen to John.

It was the part of John to ask the Lord who was going to betray him, to understand love as office. Now, it is the part of Peter to ask what will happen to love. In the concomitance of the Lord with love, in divinely dispensed love, John had to understand what he was to do: to place his love at the service of the coming suffering. That was the responsibility of love. The responsibility of office is no less great. Peter cannot just stand there as the privileged one who has experienced the unprecedented grace of knowing his Christian destiny. He cannot know that and yet not ask about the destiny of the others. For he is responsible for John. He is responsible because he holds office and because he has taken over love from him. And finally, he is responsible to the Lord for showing him that he has understood everything. He must give something like a proof of his official competence. He must also accumulate experience, make preparations for later on. Precisely because John is an important disciple, Peter needs to know about his destiny. He now receives him into his office anew, no longer as the giver of love but as the subordinate. He takes his justification for this from the words of the Lord. The Lord should be put at ease: he will be able to go to John through Peter; Peter has accepted John as one of his children. John will not cease to be a child of the now founded Church, regardless of whether he receives further communications from the Lord or not. Peter shows the Lord, so to speak, his own attestation. The Lord does not need to certify things and to issue a commission: Take care of John. Peter says of his own accord: I will take care of him.

John himself does not ask what will become of him. His personal destiny does not interest him. He is the self-surrendered one. Taking care of things falls to office. John goes through the world in utter poverty; the Church must take care of him. The Church must enwrap him in her cloak. But she is not allowed to break off the love between him and the Lord. She may not do so, and she cannot do so. She will only help where she both can and may do so as office. And in this, one recognizes that Peter has love. He asks not only for purposes of office, but also out of love, out of a love that cannot do other than show itself to the Lord.

When Peter now sees John as the one who had lain close to the Lord's breast, it is not out of a desire to imitate him in this, not out of wanting to experience the same sort of affection from the Lord. He remains objective, but wholly replete with love, with a love that does not permit him the intimacy permitted John. For such intimacy is not something that one can claim for oneself; it is freely conferred by the Lord. Peter loves the Lord through the whole structure of office. And he loves him in his successors. He can claim nothing for himself that would not also be claimable by all those successors. Precisely now, when he is all aglow with love, when this image that he has long carried in him rises again before his eyes, he must remain conscious of his office before the Lord. But through this love and this vision, any rigidity or aridness of office is made impossible. The vision and the image give him an animating soul.

Peter's betrayal occurred after the Last Supper had taken place. Already then, during the period of the Cross and through to the present day, he has carried this image in himself: the image of the Lord and of this friendship, of this love; and has superimposed upon it the image of the sudden, unexpected question. He kept it with him like a few lines on paper, a sketch for which he still lacked the final completing elements. Now, when he has been wholly opened to love, thereby recognizing that he no longer needs to give that which the Lord has already completely appropriated for himself (*You will be led where you do not wish to go; follow me*) — only now does everything within him take on full form and prompt him to ask his new question. It is as if John's countenance acquires a new expression when Peter regards him in this way. Earlier, Peter was with the Lord in so human a manner, in the joy of being allowed to be a part of things, that he still did not really notice the enormous responsibility contained in love of the Lord; and thus John, too, was just another member of the Lord's circle. Now, in his new responsibility, everything has grown together into a unity: the Lord, the Church, the Cross, the teaching, the manifestations. . . . And when he now looks into John's face, he sees in it the unity of love, which senses in joy the impending suffering and in suffering the all-overflowing love. The smallest details of the Last Supper take on, in the eyes of Peter, a new significance; everything becomes transparent toward the Lord, is organized toward the Father, toward eternal life. And it is as if, at this moment, the many supports that he had been lent so that he might better understand (and he has to understand, after all, a tremendous number of things) have fallen away, thereby suddenly throwing open his line of sight to God. He experiences this at a moment when he is with the Lord, and with that, he establishes another basic situation. No one can comprehend and be broadened in his understanding other than when the Lord is with him. Every question that one directs to the Lord is answered, as it arises, by him in such a way as to open up the questioner. In unity with the Lord, that is accomplished which must be accomplished with him from a Christian standpoint.

21:22. Jesus said to him: If it is my will that he remain until I come, what is that to you? Follow me!

A second time, the Lord requests that Peter follow him. But this time, it is after Peter has directed a question to him which the Lord rejects with a kind of reprimand. It becomes clear that it will always be difficult for office-bearers to get definite indications from the Lord about the position of those who love, even though this is part of their office. But Peter has not received his office from the Lord as something settled and complete. He has received a principle, a beginning; and he should allow time for it to develop. Much will be unfolded through the interaction between the Lord and Peter. Peter, even though head of the Church, remains a man; and all his conceptions remain developing ones, capable of supplementation. He has asked his question out of a sense of responsibility. And yet the Lord, who desires to see him grow, reprimands him as if he had allowed himself too much. He rejects the question, even though it was not out of place, even though it was more than justified; he wants to show that there will always be conflicts between office and love, that he, the Lord, can do things that the Church can never completely investigate. He has instituted the Church and office, and believers are bound by what has been instituted by him. But he, the Lord, does not allow himself to be bound by something that he himself has created. He remains the Lord of the Church. He will never be coextensive with ecclesiastical office. This disparity between the Lord and Peter had not yet been felt by Peter; hence, it must now be made emphatically clear. Almost as if through a reversal of the situation that existed between the Lord and John at the Last Supper. Now, it is the Lord who warns office, at a moment when office is doing what is appropriate to it. But still, at a moment when office does not yet possess the maturity that the Lord will largely communicate to it through his words. Office must understand that the Lord is not among those things over which it simply has control. The Lord will always remain the Ever-Greater, the one not bound by the Church, who follows the laws of the Church as a matter of course because he generated them all out of his relationship with the Father, but who instituted them in such a way as to allow himself, as God, to accomplish what falls to God in the glorification of the Father.

If it is my will that he remain, says the Lord. This is no assertion that John will remain, for the Lord does not say: I will it. His words amount to the opening up of a possibility: it could be within my will, it is possible that he might remain. With these words, he deprives Peter of any power to comprehend John's destiny in its entirety. And in so doing, he still announces something extraordinary to him. He gives him one of those answers that can never be exhaustively understood, not even now, after John's earthly destiny has long since been fulfilled and his mission in the Church has also become clearer. We know much about the traces that John has left behind, about the effects of his writings and his apostolate, about his remaining in the Church as a saint. And yet we do not know in what sort of love he exists with respect to the Lord nor what sort of love he receives from the Lord in eternal life. Again and again, there are new rays of hope and perspectives when we concern ourselves with him as believers; but there is much more that we do not at all know. Inasmuch as the Lord throws open the possibility of his remaining, and expresses it in such a way that the reality can be envisaged, he directs the gaze of believers, and thus also the gaze of John, to what will happen to the beloved John between his earthly life and the Second Coming of the Lord. He can remain. Not as one who continues living on earth, but certainly as one who continues to be effective, not only through the completed contribution that he bequeathed to the Church, but primarily through his remaining, at the same time, in the Lord and among us. And that means: through his holiness as active for the world. A holiness that is completely enclosed in the will of the Lord. At this point, it is clear to what extent holiness is a gift of grace from the Lord that he willingly mediates — *if it is my will*, he says, and thereby directs Peter's attention to his will. Directs it so strongly that Peter must almost hear it more as a rejection of any interference than as a foreshadowing. It is as if he were thereby creating a focus of unrest, even though this remains, at the same time, contained within the consummate placidity of his will: in the remaining of the holiness until the end. There is an inviolability, an untouchability, an immutability in this remaining of the holiness within the Lord's will.

And yet the question asked by office, prior to what the Lord said, is still there. A question that seems overhasty when seen from the viewpoint of the answer, yet is quite justified when seen from that of the office of the questioner. A certain gap becomes visible between the duties of the Church and the expression of the will of the Lord. This gap does not, however, become a split, but is given full justification through the fact that the Lord, by means of his answer, evidences his will and himself creates the distance between John's destiny and Peter's question. John, who knows exactly how he is regarded by Peter, and who knows all the more intensely the kind of love of the Lord he dwells in, does not comment on these words, but records them just as he perceived them. He does not give any hint about the extent to which he becomes aware of what awaits him.

Previously, when Peter's future path was disclosed — and disclosed in such a way as to enable him to sense that he would be guided to the very end—that was a necessity for office. It was not done for Peter personally. John does not need such a foreshadowing because, to a certain degree, he continues to be guided by the personal love of the Lord; since, on the one hand, he becomes submerged along with his office in the office of Peter, and yet, on the other hand, remains completely free in obedience to the Lord. If we compare the two paths, then Peter's path appears as if truncated: we see only his earthly pathway, which was preindicated up to the point of his death. For John, by contrast, the Lord has lengthened the pathway, extending it up to the point of his Second Coming. Peter's path is a path of unrest even in the will of the Lord. John's path, a path of rest in the will of the Lord. This does not prevent their paths, both on earth and up to the Second Coming, from being largely one common path. It was not necessary that Peter's path after death be disclosed to him; it was, however, important that Peter should know about the later path of John. In his hinting at the nature of this path, the Lord acknowledges a certain right of office to know something about the matter. John would not at all have needed this answer. It is office that needs assuring, needs to know that both paths are right: the short one that ends in the death that brings all one's preceding earthly days to a proper conclusion, and the immeasurable one of the enduring love that is concealed solely in the will of the Lord.

Along with the answer, Peter is given a kind of reprimand, not unlike what occurred in the case of Martha at the tomb. Her objection, too, was not out of place. And yet she had to be reproved. As the active one, she needed this humiliation. So, too, office in the Church should never get the feeling that it is able to deal with the Lord on the basis of one equal with another. The Lord must humiliate it again and again. Peter holds the highest office in the Church, and yet the Lord treats him like a novice. Here, too, he is still educating him in the submissiveness that even the highest office needs—and how much more the others. These concluding verses of the Gospel are the proper subject of meditation for the Popes. Peter has just been conclusively installed in his dignified position; he will follow the Lord, and he will die for him. He is enthusiastic; he is full of rapture. But in the midst of this bliss, he is hit once again by a sobering word from the Lord; he must never lose for a moment his readiness to be humiliated by the Lord. And there is something unrelenting in the way that John discloses this. But it is the part of love, of the office of love, to hold this mirror up to office. Here, John anticipates the role of a Catherine of Siena, who holds the truth up to the Popes. And Peter experiences here something of the laws of monastic life: of uncomprehended humiliation, of a new and different kind of obedience.

Follow me! With that, the Lord puts the seal on his whole relationship to Peter. He is to follow with a new reassurance, since the Lord commands him to follow, but not to forget that inherent in it is the uneasiness of never fully being able to understand, the disparity between fulfilment of office and the greater demand of the Lord, between guaranteed dedication to office and the greater dedication, above and beyond this, that the Lord still demands personally. Peter can also never comfort himself with the thought that he is fulfilling the requirements of his office as well as he can, and is uneasy only at the personal level, about things bearing on his personal relationship with the Lord. The uneasiness goes deeper. It affects Peter as a whole, including his official side. Although the validity of office is secured by the Lord against any unworthiness, no matter how great, on the part of the office-bearer, the latter, in view of the disparity between his office and his person, will still never reach any final reassurance and complacency.

With his first *Follow me*, the Lord had adumbrated the personal destiny of Peter; he thereby asked him for increased personal dedication. There, no split between the person and the office became visible. With the second *Follow me*, Peter is required to follow together with his office. From then on, he will always have to do both at once: to administer something limited, but with an unlimited commitment to the mission. Whenever a new Pope is selected this becomes clear: someone is designated for a function that, in principle, each of the others also could perform; but an attempt is made to combine the individual's personal mission with the function in such a way as to bring about that unity which the Lord both demands and founds here.

For Peter, it is in a way painful that the Lord must repeat his demand to follow him, while no such demand is made of John at all.

For John, things are not painful. He, after all, can simply remain. He exists in love, and therefore everything is in order. Peter, because of his office, will always have a path ahead to be covered, gropingly perhaps, stumblingly and seekingly. This implies nothing at all about the human perfection of the two apostles. It is a different mission, a different way of possessing love. John possesses it in such a way that the Lord rests content with this love. He does not mold him further through words. He knows that the love in John is powerful enough to mold him wordlessly, that he is prepared to accept the Lord's love without resistance and, should there be anything needing improvement, to effect that on the basis of love. When anyone really lives for the love of the Lord, his whole ego vanishes; he wishes for nothing more than the Lord in everything. He possesses the tenderness of love: one glance from the Lord is enough to let him know what he should do. He reads off from love what is required. By contrast, Peter acquired love to a certain extent in a secondary way, on the basis of office. In his case, that which he has to achieve must be clearly shown and outlined to him. And at the same time, in order to keep on striving, he must always clearly sense how far he still must go. With someone like John, who loves, these two things are not necessary; they could even prevent him from giving his full love. Peter remains to the end a servant, who must constantly undergo retraining, even in the highest thing that there is, namely, love.

Also, love will ask of its own accord. It need not be pushed into doing so. Office, on the other hand, must be schooled in questioning. If only for reasons of succession, Peter has much more need of marked experiences that he can hand down. In John's office, by contrast, there is no norm that could be passed on to others. Love is always in its origin. With it, there can be no succession.

21:23. *The saying spread abroad among the brethren that this disciple was not to die; yet Jesus did not say to him that he was not to die, but: If it is my will that he remain until I come, what is that to you?*

A rumor arises about John. Who started it, who passed it on, is not mentioned. But the rumor starts from the same general perspective from which it will always start throughout the whole life of the Church: from the notion of a personal formation of mission by the

Lord that is so personal that associates and bystanders do not comprehend it. And the ones who start the rumor are the brethren, the believers. The rumor could possibly be connected with the beginning of a split among them. For the rumor is a finite, human interpretation of an infinite statement by the Lord. Precisely this statement by the Lord, however, needs no interpretation beyond his own. Therefore, John does not really bother himself about the whole matter. He is so firmly established in love of the Lord that he only looks to love in everything. Those who started the rumor, by contrast, distance themselves from love. The forming and spreading of opinions that do not correspond precisely to the truth, and indeed, in the sense of a conclusive interpretation, is an offense against the Lord's love, which always remains open toward greater truth. Not, of course, in such a way that everything begins to totter and nothing is any longer known for certain, but in such a way that the knowledge becomes increasingly deposited with the Lord, increasingly a participation in his knowledge. It is not my knowledge that extends all the way to God and, so to speak, sees through him; rather, the tree of God has put down a root that extends all the way to me.

When the brethren say that John will not die, they have understood something of the word of God and translated it in such a way as to give it a place within their belief. But there, it is only this-worldly things that have any place. The disciple's remaining in the beyond until the Lord comes again means nothing to them. They have to materialize everything in order to understand it, including the destiny of the disciple of love. All the words of the Lord stem from his dialogue with the Father; they therefore have a meaning that far transcends what is angled toward men. The brethren are not capable of perceiving them in their eternal resonance. They hear them in a curtailed form brought about by the diminishment in obedience.

The brethren also grasp something of the office of Peter. It is, in a sense, clear to them that a Church has been founded here; that Peter administers it; that they have to subordinate themselves to him and thereby themselves acquire new functions that are connected with Peter's office; and that a certain conformity is required of them. And they are quite happy to have received, at last, their ordered place.

Actually, they have grown tired of being left to themselves and repeatedly running up against the incomprehensible. And if they now sense that the Lord will soon be disappearing entirely, then they are greatly comforted by the thought that someone is there who will watch over the newly-commenced traditions until his Second Coming. They really look forward to life in the Church, in which all things will revert once again to peace and order. The Lord is going back to heaven; he will, in a way similar to the situation under the Old Covenant, be separated again from the world; and John will remain on earth—so they think—as a reminder of him. The other connection between heaven and earth, as was hinted at in what the Lord said about John, they fail to see. And they would like, by means of the rumors they start, to contribute to building the Church: to make it, as soon as possible, just as rigid as it had been under the Old Covenant. They dream of a Church in which one can live undisturbed. They tell no lie with their rumor. What they say in it is what they understand. But with a definite will to understand nothing but the finite in the words of the Lord.

John continues his report objectively: *Yet Jesus did not say to him that he was not to die.* He raises the matter of the rumor in order to negate it. But he does not commit himself to any interpretation. He merely asserts what the Lord did not say, with a view to making clearer what he did say. So much does he do this in his office of love that he pays no attention to himself at all. It is of no importance to him just how the Lord's prophecy will ultimately turn out for him. He desires only one thing: the truth. And in order to bring it to light, he places it beside the untruth. That suffices. He gives no information about his death; he has himself received none and requested none. He knows this: if the Lord has foretold the death of Peter but not that of himself, then knowing about the former is important, but knowing about the latter is unimportant.

John's not dying, in the sense in which the brethren understand it, would be an exemption from earthly death. Despite death's having been overcome by the Lord on the Cross, and despite their knowledge that he overcame it not only for himself but also for them, they continue to look upon death in much the same way as before. They think of it with fear. And when John places the words of the Lord beside the interpretation of the brethren, it becomes suddenly clear to him how great the gap is, how little room the brethren have left for love in their souls, given that they can think so narrowly of the Lord. Although they claim to love, they want to have a say in everything, to oversee the whole, to have the last word. They understand belief as a kind of argued discussion with the Lord; they consult with the Lord, but only insofar as they can make use of what he says. They accept what he says and also pass it on to others, not, however, by making themselves subordinate to it, but after adapting it to themselves and rendering it amenable. And the death which they thus deny will come to John is a reality that defines and restricts the whole of their being. Their belief has validity for this mortal life; what will be the case in the beyond, how their belief will be transformed in the beyond—about that they choose not to worry.

Their belief and John's belief stand opposed in the present passage. John's belief is a belief that endures beyond any death because it consists of love. It is no provisional, mortal belief that would have to be replaced afterward by a complete, otherworldly belief. Here, John has already opened himself completely to otherworldly belief and allowed it to live in him as otherworldly, so that he will remain, along with his belief, in the Lord until the Second Coming. The opposing of the two forms of belief thus indicates a direction, a path. The path of living belief lies in a kind of understanding of the Word of the Lord in which death is annihilated. Death is of no importance for love. It is no limit to love. It is an occasion for love to grow, to make increased room for what it has received, to let itself be wholly possessed by it. John leaves to the words, which he simply repeats, their quite otherworldly sense; he takes from them as much as he can understand, and remains, in the whole of his soul, open to that which lies beyond him. He, too, feels the limitations of his earthly existence— more strongly, in fact, than the others; but he also knows that, as soon as they become manifest and are felt, they are, as it were, eradicated by the greater love of the Lord. They are there only in order to reveal to the weakness of human love the infinite strength of divine love, and in such a way that the revelation of this also serves to mediate it. The small love of the one who loves and the great love of the Lord no longer stand opposed as here to there, but believing love now already undergoes acceptance by, absorption into and eternal endurance within the Lord.

John remains within love. And yet there are moments when he gently brushes against his own limitations. But the Lord never allows this restrictedness to become really painful. Awareness of such limitations can never become consolidated in John. Whenever he feels them as a thin veil that has been thrown over him, the veil is no sooner felt than it is withdrawn; so that he knows only: there was a hindrance here, but it is no longer present. He never sees the hindrance as lying before him, but always as only behind him, as something that the Lord has already overcome for him. This forms part of the way that he is wonderstruck, astonished and overwhelmed by love. It is characteristic of the state of astonishment that things lose their sharp contours and refer transparently to a deeper mystery. And if the astonishment is about the love of God, then who would want to restore the lost contours? For why should the astonishment come to an end? Inasmuch as the Lord himself removes the constraints, he relieves John of any desire to reconstruct them. In return, he gives him only the pleasure that lies in knowing: there was something here that has now been overcome, something that the Lord's love has dealt with conclusively. With powerful extractive force, something has drawn all that is limited out of the disciple's love and into itself, where it vanished utterly. And this same process is the thing that John experiences as the center of confession. He senses, no doubt, his own sin; yet it never takes on wholly sharp contours for him. The Lord does not worry about it. He absorbs it all into himself. John dwells in his love as in a perpetual absolution that is always present and so constituted that it does not permit—especially not now—any backward glance at past sin. At the moment of absolution, one undoubtedly still knows more or less what one has confessed. But it lies behind one, as something overcome. And in the case of the love of John, any shortcoming of that love lies continually behind him, overcome through the greater love of the Lord. He who is in complete love no longer looks back at his sin, and he also knows that he will never commit it again. He receives absolution, as it were, continually; whereas one who loves incompletely receives it as if through an act effective for one time only. For him who loves completely, it is an enormous obligation, rising above all others, to know that he dwells in love. He understands the demand completely to integrate his whole life into that love. For him, sin actually lies in the constantly renewed failure to achieve comprehensive integration. One who loves incompletely will tend much more to look for his sin in individual actions. As long as love looks to the Lord, it has an abhorrence of sin and cannot comprehend how one could ever sin again. It is no longer attracted by sin. Incomplete love, by contrast, does not look so exclusively to the Lord that it could not also be attracted by sin.

John's remaining in the Lord is not, however, a solitary one; as ordained by the Lord on the Cross, it is a remaining together with the Mother of the Lord in a new communion. He will share a life on earth together with her that is wholly concealed in the Son, that has become a function of the life of the Son. And at the same time, his own remaining in the Son—this otherworldly, spiritual one—will occur together with participation by the Mother. Both share their remaining in common, which has its effects in both and radiates onto all those entrusted to them. John's priestly office is commended to the Mother; she includes it in her prayer and takes over those of its difficulties that a woman can better bear and overcome. And this womanliness is not only tied to the human, but also preexemplified in the whole immaculateness of the Mother and in her service to the Son: she effects in John what she has already effected in the Son; she gives him what was the Son's in her. She is the first one to whom priestly office is given over to be practiced as prayer. She represents the womanly function within the priesthood. John's priestly office is not based exclusively on his relation of friendship with the Lord. It is a proper office. And the Mother is included in that office. The Lord, after all, has himself entrusted her to John. Her fruitfulness had to be involved in the eucharistic expansion of the Son; because she gave birth to him, she had to play a part in the birth of the Church. The Lord gives her this part in John. Through John, she acquires a share in the mission of all Christians. Just as John's mission of love never remains purely personal but is given an official and eucharistic character, so, too, the universal meaning of the Marian mission will be fulfilled in its entrustment to John. And because the Mother is human, the

Lord avails himself of a human being in order to allow her fruitfulness to enter the Church. The Lord is now going back into the inaccessible Divinity. And thus, had she not been given John, the Mother would be left as if lacking a son. But she is, in her whole nature, so much a mother that she cannot for a moment be lacking a son. Through John, she remains tied to the human reality of the Church while retaining her own reality as a mother, but all by virtue of the Lord's love. Rather than being transported into the divine, she remains. She remains together with the remaining of John. Through this tie, however, she retains her openness toward the Ever-Greater of the Son. Once, she had opened herself fully in order to receive the Ever-Greater Son into herself. Now, she assists the Son's Ever-Greater to realize itself within men. Hence, by virtue of remaining with John until the Lord's Second Coming, she is simultaneously integrated more fully into humanity and included more fully in the Son's mission.

During his life with the Lord, John received so much direct love from him that he always knew the nature of love. He never had to ask himself what one does if one is to love the Lord. It was made easy for him. He unquestioningly accepted the love he received, and unquestioningly returns it with his whole soul. And now the Mother has been handed over to him. The Son, desiring to show the Mother his love by giving her to the Church, has entrusted the disciple with an office of love for the Mother. And John loves the Mother. He knows that the Son loved her and, at the same time, he knows that the Son's love was something quite different from the sort of love that he can show the Mother. On all sides, he runs up against the always-more of the Son's love of the Mother. And he must earnestly learn—in order to fulfill completely the office that the Son gave him and to represent the Son vis-à-vis the Mother—to love the Mother, as a human being, in the way that the Son had loved her. He must learn to love in the Lord's way without constantly receiving assurance from the Lord that he is doing so correctly. In relation to the Mother, he must practice something that he has to pass on to all those entrusted to him. It is like a school of love in which the Mother is the subject matter to be learned—by no means a random one, for she has, after all, experienced the full love of the Son; and she is now supposed to recognize, in the love shown to her by John, the love of the Son who has, out of love, entrusted her to John. In no respect must there occur any accommodation, compromise, resignation or shirking of the task. Everything must be carried out in the perfected form of love. And at the same time, the Mother is the first who has to recognize the Son in any of her neighbors. In the life of these two together, the commandment that the Lord gave to men is fulfilled: they love one another because he wanted it so and because they each recognize the Son in the other—although it is naturally harder for the Mother to recognize the Son in John than for John to recognize him in the Mother. But their mutual love remains in the Lord and becomes in him what he had intended: inasmuch as they both, through the remaining of their love in the Lord, rediscover the Lord and his love in the other, it becomes clear to them that the love presented them by the Lord, which they are to recognize as his, is really the love of the Son, which returns through him to the Father. The Eucharist and love of one's neighbor are represented exemplarily, in their unity and interpenetration, by the two human beings who were closest to the Lord—as close to the source as anyone could ever be.

And this love becomes itself a source and draws all of us into it. It is authentic, Catholic mediation which, as such, illumines the Catholic teaching on saints. In one way, negatively: the Lord did not establish the communion between Mary and John in order that they might be happy together. Of course, the Lord's loving care for his beloved ones is also evident in his having establishing it. But that is not the ultimate reason for this ordained love. Above all, he entrusted them with this gift so that they might distribute it to others. They receive it in profusion in order that they might hand it on in profusion. And this communion is no wall behind which the Lord would seclude those who are his. Rather, he is so infused into these two that, in them, in their relationship which he himself established, we run directly up against his love and recognize from it the existence of a consummate possibility of realizing neighborly love and eucharistic love, of realization of the command to see the Lord in one's neighbor. The Lord not only rounds us out through his love before we are presented to the Father; he also shows us, in Mary and

John, that the love bestowed by him can be, and is, a fullness. Without this example, hope of the promised rounding out of our fragmentary love would perhaps remain for us something unlikely. With it, however, proof has been given that it is possible, that the Lord's grace can enable it. And precisely this is the role of the saints. They are proof of the possibility of Christianity. They can, therefore, be leaders along an otherwise impossible seeming path to complete love. And inasmuch as God has established every kind and form of saintliness, he has opened up infinitely many pathways, some of which, at least, are sure to be traversable by me. In authentic imitation of the saints, the always-more of Christian love follows as if of itself. For a saint never signifies a boundary, a stopping point. Even in imitation, after all, we never succeed in reaching his saintliness, since that itself is not something concluded. The introduction of the saints is an assistance granted by the Lord, a concretization of his command, a pointer of the way about which nobody can be deceived. And it will not be the case that one consults this direction-giver only at the start of the path, and then continues on afterward with the Lord alone. The saint accompanies one by becoming, of himself, constantly more transparent toward the Lord; he does not need to be pushed aside. Of himself, he allows the Lord to become constantly more central. For the essence of all saintliness consists in remaining in the Lord until he comes again. And through his saints, the Lord takes everyone up into the communion of love, which he founded and which is, in the world, the sign of his having been here and of his coming again, but even more the hidden sign of his remaining among us. In this remaining of the Lord and remaining in the Lord, all have their own mission, as corresponds to the mission of Mary and John; one part of this mission is visible and determined by the Church, while the other is hidden and lies in the Lord's invitation to remain with him.

The remaining is a remaining in the Lord, but also with Peter in the Church. And the two-sided unity of this remaining is called *prayer*. Every one who participates in it in any way—as a seeker, believer or saint—prays. Every prayer has a form that exhibits its ecclesiastical origin, a form that the Church knows and that lives from her office; and yet, because of the prayer's remaining in the

Lord, it is, in relation to its content, both incomprehensible to and uncontrollable by anyone but the Lord. It arises at some visible place, yet unfolds itself at once into the sphere of the invisible. Everyone who prays has knowledge of a certain structure of his prayer, of the words, thoughts, intentions that he brings to it. But as soon as it has been realized, it is taken from him and, through remaining in the Lord, is so transformed by the Lord that it becomes fruitful in the realm of the eternal and invisible. Here, the Lord effects something like a Eucharist of prayer. Even a prayer that was spoken only to him is accepted by him as his words; and his words are there in order to glorify the Father, although not in solitude with the Father but in the handing over to him of everything that belongs to him: including our prayers. And with them, also our selves. In this act, the Lord takes over our prayer in order to expand it according to his meaning, in order to place it wholly at the Father's disposal and to receive it back from him in the sense of his mission as Son. And he, the Son, certainly knows what he has prayed. We perhaps know what words, what wish, we expressed. The actual substance of the prayer escapes us. For if it was really prayer, after all, then its substance consisted in losing its own substance in order to be wholly accepted in the Lord. The Lord desires that our prayer should remain in him.

Previously, every believer was expected to recognize the Lord in his neighbor. Now, the Lord must recognize himself in every neighbor. Above all, in his prayer. Not in the sinful nature of men can he recognize himself, but in their prayer. What he does here is something like the opposite of the Incarnation. He became man so that we could recognize him. Now, he wants to recognize himself from us, in men. He makes out of him who prays something like an extraction, like the opposite of transubstantiation. He divests him, so to speak, of his crass humanity and fleshliness, in order to expose him in the essence of his prayer. The possibility of doing this was purchased by him through his Incarnation. It cannot, however, be understood in the sense that I would remain, on earth, the man that I always was, and would transmit something superhuman out of myself that the Lord receives. Inasmuch as the Lord receives me, receivingly transforms me, recognizes himself in me, he gives me back to myself as transformed. Through his grace, I have become another person. This mystery is very closely related to that of Holy Mass. For the transformed host is not sufficient unto itself, but aims, in a kind of reversal of the transformation, at living in us, at converting us to itself.

The heard prayer, then, in which the Lord recognizes himself, he returns to us by presenting us with something of his essence, which was imparted to our prayer through his hearing it. In the most extraordinary cases, this movement toward the Lord and then back to him who prays becomes conscious to us; it happens at the borderline of comprehending his love, of being overtaxed by his love. And yet everyone who prays, everyone who meditates, even if he is no mystic, knows again and again those moments in which he becomes lost to himself, runs up against someone greater than he is, experiences contact with him, without being able to say how that greater is constituted.

But because this happens through the recognition of the Lord in us, it is also presented to us when we look at a believer. One contacts and encounters in him something of the immensity of God, but without its being able to be fixed in concepts and words. It is not this special individual grace that the other has received, not this quality, this virtue, which absorbs us; but something else, something incomprehensible. It can become visible when we unintentionally intrude upon someone who is praying—less in church (where, from the outset, a certain adaptation to the communion, a kind of insulation from one another, is required) than in solitude. This prayer-giver is caught up in something like a transformation that is effected by the Lord and cannot go unnoticed.

The Lord, who returns the prayer, at the same time retains it. The two are not mutually exclusive. That which the Lord accepts is so increased by him that he can both return it and retain it without dividing it in two. That is why the efficacy and stewardship of prayer remains entirely with the Lord. Not as though the Church were given to see nothing of its fruits. She can, in a true sense, see them, but she can never oversee them, because the returning of prayer and the fruits of prayer to the world is conditioned by their simultaneous remaining in the Lord. The whole being of the believer—his intentions, his prayers, everything that constitutes his belief—is affected by this remaining in the Lord. All this was always the property of the Lord and will remain so. However, it is no motionless remaining but a participatory remaining, a remaining in the things that the Lord does; and because he is constantly at work, is on the move within trinitarian life, continues to dispense his Incarnation and his Eucharist, redeems the world without pause—for that reason, this containedness is one of exposedness: he gives us what is his by using what is ours as his. By offering us our remaining in him, he presents us with his remaining in us; but that can mean only his going out into the world and returning again to the Father, his flowing forth in all directions, into which he sweeps us along as well. His being eternally Ever-Greater, into which he draws us with no possibility of standing still.

And this *until I come.* Then there will be a caesura. For then the world will be conclusively redeemed. Then his remaining in us and our remaining in him will undergo a transformation. Everything that is now a striving-toward of longing will, from that time on, be a remaining in complete fulfilment.

JOHN THE WITNESS

21:24. *This is the disciple who is bearing witness to these things, and who has written these things; and we know that his testimony is true.*

The same one who is bearing witness to these things is the one whose remaining Jesus has heralded. John has thus experienced it all, and his experience grows into his testimony. He expresses the words of testimony that belong to the Lord, grow out of his remaining in the Lord, are drawn into the strength of the Lord and contain the love of the Lord in the way that the Lord himself means and represents it: as developing and communicating itself. Indeed, John's very experience is formed by his testimony, by the Word of God. And in reporting about precisely this remaining in the Lord, he sees that he still has before him a growing experience of this remaining, that he will receive constantly more of this remaining and that it is a remaining that develops. Less than ever does he comprehend his destiny. He does not know what will become of him. He does know, however, that the Lord watches over and makes use of this becoming. And he continues in his position as a disciple and in the total devotedness that wants to let itself become more and more like the Lord, while at the same time realizing the impossibility of attaining complete likeness to him, yet not being troubled by that since his remaining in the Lord is guaranteed. He himself is unimportant to himself. He has become lost to himself. But his remaining in the Lord is important to him. It has, after all, become for him the reality of his life, the demand of the Lord made visible in him. The Lord needs this remaining; he shapes it, represents it and, to a certain extent, defends it against Peter. John sees, moreover, that the place at which he must stand cannot be outlined in human terms, that no conclusive resolution can be expected to the new question evoked in Peter by the Lord's answer. And John stands, in relation to Peter, as the cause of the latter's being disquieted by the Lord, as one who discovers that his remaining in the Lord must become a question for Peter, but who nevertheless longs for this remaining regardless of how the Lord will grant it to him. And it is as this one that he gives his account. He exposes the starting point for a possible conflict. But he does so as *bearing witness to these things,* and he writes them down, identifying himself as the one who creates the possible distress without ceasing to bear witness to that. In this unity of bearing witness and causing distress lies the germ of his further utilization by the Lord, even for such tasks as will perhaps strike the Church as dreadful: above all, for the Apocalypse. With the Apocalypse, the Church will receive a gift from the Lord that she will never exhaust and that perhaps will not be merely agreeable to her.

Because of the distress he has caused, through which he also became the focus of the rumor, John is in a delicate situation. But in deciding once again in favor of pure witness-bearing, he undertakes a new renunciation of self. Through this, he becomes ready for the office of the Apocalypse, which will not be understandable in the same way as was the office of love, the office of remaining together with the Mother, but will be, instead, an unfathomable, all-exploding office. Previously, in the company of the Lord and in the communion of the Church, the growth of the disciple had, in a sense, taken place organically; and it was necessary that this should occur first. So much so that John was all but absorbed into the office of Peter. But this organic, ecclesiastically foreseeable state of affairs can once again be totally burst open by the Lord so as to result in fully incomprehensible things. And this new readiness of John is an openness no longer in the ecclesiastical sense, but so absolutely that the Lord can undertake even the most inscrutable sorts of thing with it. The apostle himself will not thereby be placed outside the Church. He will never be able to make separate appeal to "his" transecclesiastical law. Even the new eccentricity that John will be catapulted into remains in John, from the viewpoint of God, a mode of service to the Church.

For most Christians, being prepared for anything remains somehow a theoretical matter. One wants to affirm what is unknown as well, but in such a way that one also attempts to portray in one's mind the most extreme cases possible. And one does not really want to believe that it all could be meant quite seriously. John knows no such constraint. He has wholly forgotten himself in his word of affirmation.

And who has written these things. He has lent to his testimony the enduring manifestness of the written word, expounded it in such a way that it remains examinable at any time. He has not allowed it to become fragmented and crumble away. It can be brought before one in its entirety at any time. In this way, he has also fended off the rumors. And he has included himself in his testimony because, at many places, he crops up personally as part of what is being attested to. He has learned not only to know himself, including as an instrument of his testimony, but also to depict himself.

And we know that his testimony is true. John and the believers know this together. John does not shift the responsibility for this knowledge of the truth onto others; he does not distance himself from it. He does not force this truth upon them from the outside, without their participation in it. And on the other hand, he gives this testimony not as a solitary individual, but in communion with the other believers: they all know with equal strength, equal depth, that it is true. They participate in this truth not only through what they, too, have experienced, but also through their testimony that it is true, and not just through the mediation of what has been written down. Their testimony gives the truth its force. Their testimony places the truth in the proper light. They speak of the truth not only as of a possibility or a reality; they represent it in such a way that they simultaneously engage themselves for it, speak from within it, simply attest to it and can, through this, first represent it in its truth. And they do so by giving information not only about the truth but, at the same time, also about themselves. And since it is a testimony of love, it is therefore a testimony of being in the truth.

Even if John puts himself last and wishes only to be the servant and instrument of the truth, he is still unable to disengage himself from that truth. He must bear testimony to the truth into which he has been drawn, which has thereby become his truth, a truth to which he belongs. In Christianity, there is no merely theoretical truth. Of course, the truth exists, even when men deny it. But when man affirms it, he cannot do other than to exist together with it. Here, belief, love and obedience appear as a unity. If love is present, then the readiness is there to accept as one's own the truth of the one whom is loved. Precisely this is belief—which, in forgoing autonomous determination of the truth, is nothing other than obedience. And this is John's position in relation to the Lord: he bears witness to the Lord's truth because he loves the Lord; therefore he believes and obeys him, and at the same time passes this truth on, as one with which he identifies, in his testimony.

And if love has belief and knows the truth, then it cannot rest so long as it has not succeeded in bringing others to share that truth with it and to believe, too. It is part of its office to bring others to that very place where love itself stands. It does not, of course, present the position it occupies as the goal. The apostle remains the path; the Lord alone is the goal. But John's love knows no rest until everyone has reached this goal, that is, until completely the same truth exists for everyone. And now he says: *We know that his testimony is true.* He says this even though he alone has done the writing and the others cannot join with him to monitor the correctness of what he writes. But he extends credit to them; he admits them, as coknowers of this truth, into a circle that he defines. At the same time, he thereby makes them owners of this same truth. He knows that they endeavor to love and that, in belief, the endeavor to love is the same thing as love because both have the same directedness toward the Lord. And it is part of love that it does not exclude but, on the contrary, includes, does not leave things behind it but takes them with it. And further: when he claims that they know the truth, he confers some of his love on them in order that their capacity for grasping the truth might be increased. Through this capability, they become more prepared to believe even that which goes beyond them, if it only be accepted on the basis of love and attested to through the witness of love. Thus it is no longer difficult for the believer to believe even what is incomprehensible. And he is still not uncritical, since he has tested love, the sole medium in which this exchange of transcendent truth is possible. Naturally, there must be a basis of insight so that the readiness to accept more can be present. But it is then love that mediates this more. John possesses something like a power of attorney: he is authorized to sign on behalf of the believers. He can make the statement that the believers know about this or that truth even when he knows that they perhaps still do not know about it, because his exceeding love assumes responsibility for bringing them to recognition of that truth—especially since, as believers, they are already on the path of love, that is, the path of recognition of all of God's truth. The Church inculcates in believers a certain understanding of what it does. In this connection, the office of the Church is essentially satisfied if believers are willing to believe even that which they do not understand. Love, by contrast, does not rest satisfied with this; it wants everyone to understand the mysteries of love. And no doubt it also assumes for a moment, representatively, that the brother already understands; but only in order to be able to initiate him better into them. And the believer feels himself so attracted by this behavior of love that, even in cases where understanding is perhaps still lacking, he arrives at authentic belief precisely through it: at unshakable belief through love. He has come to learn that God is greater and can accept into his truth even those who do not understand. He finds the testimony to this in the one who loves, and he will himself attest to this truth. He has also understood that criticism outside of love can only be false and has to take place within love, because full truth also exists only within love.

Every believer knows that the beliefs of another believer are true, because, in love, every believer has the possibility of recognizing the direction of the other's belief. And that this direction is one toward God guarantees the authentic presence of truth. Even if the truth of others has a different coloring and stamp, everyone must have this certainty: that not only he is in the truth, but others as well. This certainty is not least of all a guarantee of remaining in the truth. When previously unacquainted believers meet, they have a rapport in the truth from the first moment on, with no need to test and define where each of them stands.

John speaks as one believer among many. But he also speaks as one who possesses an office and, with that, a responsibility. By including the others through his *we know*, he enters into a guarantee for them. Initially, this guarantee seems to cover only the assertion that his, John's, testimony is true. This testimony is, however, only a part of the truth that is contained in the knowledge of all believers. Thus he does not shrink from allowing his own testimony to become part of the testimony of the others, from allowing it to be attested to for himself by those who are in the truth. In his instrumental function, he can vanish so much beneath the testimony of the others, but also, on the other hand, come so much to the fore in their testimony, that he makes himself an indispensable part of their testimony. It would be no real service for him to want to disdain his testimony and leave it aside so as to allow only that of the others to be recognized. On the contrary, he must put himself wholly to use in the service of his task, so much so that this self-utilization could appear shameless. He refers to his own testimony and to his truth, and he makes a fuss about the belief of the others for the purpose of bolstering this truth. In so doing, he shows that he must exhaust every possibility that his office has to offer, right up to the last; and that this last is no concluded last, but an open and growing one. He made use of his earlier mission—as it was when the Lord still dwelt on earth—in order to bear witness from within his present, greater mission as evangelist; and he places his greater mission in the framework of the still greater mission of the Church (which is part of his mission) so that the Church might bear witness to his Gospel. He is so instrumental that he not only behaves like an object in God's hands but also works with himself as an instrument in God's service, with an instrument that is, at this moment and as if coincidentally, he himself.

21:25. *But there are also many other things which Jesus did; were every one of them to be written, I suppose that the world itself could not contain the books that would be written.*

After John has spoken of the truth of his testimony and has, so to speak, concluded that truth by declaring it to be contained in the testimony, he breaks through that conclusion one last time in order to come back to the Lord, to the Lord who—even in the most beautiful, most extensive and most complete testimony—can never be exhaustively represented. Actually, it is not John who breaks out of his own testimony, but rather the Lord—through the simple presence of his Ever-Greater and in order that no sense of repose in having arrived, no feeling that the truth now experienced is enough, no attitude of complacency about what has been achieved, might allow the testimony and its content to become rigidified. The Lord himself can burst open the testimony and expand it; in the grace of the Lord, John can do so, too. And precisely his mission is one that never comes to rest. He would be denying himself if he wanted to bring his Gospel to an end with a concluding testimony and thereby proclaim, in a certain sense, that everything had been said, that everything was contained in the words recorded by him. He has become so much a part of his mission, exists so much within the Lord's commission to allow everything to keep on expanding, that it is a matter of course for him to allow everything said so far to be burst open by the Lord—though also with his own cooperation—in the direction of the infinite. It is a merit of John that he does this, but a merit in grace. In this act of breaking through the closed Gospel by John himself, the point also becomes visible at which grace and merit are no longer separable. John breaks himself open, but in oneness with the grace that breaks him open, thereby demonstrating the bond between his mission, that of the Lord and all the other missions. Through his Gospel, John has fulfilled a mission, and the Lord was contained in that Gospel. But he is not closed up within it; he is more, he stands above it; and because John, with his mission, is in the Lord, he remains available for any further task. And it is self-evident that this further task will eventuate, that it will mean moving further ahead together. There is by no means any need for a new summons to set John to work on a new undertaking for the Lord.

John is conscious that, in the whole of his Gospel, he has not represented the Lord and his teaching in the way that he shows himself to a stranger, an outsider, but rather, in the way that he has experienced him himself; and that, within the mission accorded him by the Lord, he has also repeatedly represented himself as a cosubject. He is one of those in whom the work, the efficacy, of the Lord has become visible. Therefore, he must also allow the effects of that work to become visible through his allowing what he has brought to conclusion to be burst open. *But there are also many other things which Jesus did.* He does this precisely at the moment when he uncovers the never-to-be-concluded unfolding of his truth and of witness-bearing by those who are his. And at the same time, John wants to direct attention to how profuse the works of the Son have become, how they have left traces behind everywhere, beginnings, seeds, all of which contain the potentiality for elaboration and development. The

Lord does nothing, and bestows nothing, that could not be brought, through him, all the way to the Father.

The Lord has done things that made everyone uneasy: the believer has been broadened; the nonbeliever has been stirred up, confronted with questions and set on a path. All these seeds contain the potential for blossoming into complete belief, complete love. Even he who has only heard from a distance that someone has come from God and has described the pathway to God carries such a seed in his heart. And all those countless ones who have heard the Word of the Lord but of whom it is not known whether they arrived at belief and at their mission, and even those who do not at all know that they have been called—they, too, belong to the *many other things which Jesus did*. But John does not aim at a diffusion into endlessness when he throws things open; on the contrary, he wants to show how the unsurveyable manifold of missions that arise from the Lord's mission is actually tied to the Father. All the widely dispersed works that have been accomplished find their nodal point in the Incarnation of the Son, which is *the* work. And yet this work is dependent on another work, namely, that he created for himself the Mother, that he no longer used dust in order to create but the Mother, in order to allow himself to develop out of her. It is from here that all the works of Jesus issue. And what he has done, he has done from time immemorial; from the very beginning, he has never ceased to show the path that leads to the Father. He already showed it before his Incarnation, when he was still the content of the promise. From the moment when the Incarnation was decided upon, he already stood out as the one who discloses the paths to the Father. And afterward, it was his activity that he allowed to be accomplished through the Annunciation to the Mother, until he himself arrived and took that activity more into his own hands. But he determined the activity and development of the Mother as well. He was the one who, during her lifetime, was active in her in such a way that everyone who turns his gaze to her thereby looks upon him and even upon the Father; he was the one who, during the period when he was still withdrawn behind her, shaped her essence into the form that it will forever retain. He fashioned her so as to ensure that, no matter where she exists and is sought and is venerated, he will be standing in the background. The mission that he fulfills for the Father he entrusted to her so that she might fulfill it for him. She became not only his Mother, but the eternal Mother of all believers, since she always refers maternally to the Son and represents the Son maternally wherever his presence has not yet been recognized. One can come almost unsuspectingly to the Mother and end up allowing oneself to be led by her to the Son. For devotion to her as Virgin or Mother, or as understanding woman, trusting girl or comforter in misfortune, is never exhausted solely in itself. As little as anyone comes to the Son without being led by him to the Father, so little does anyone come to the Mother without her referring him to the Son. In the whole of her representativeness, in the alleviation that she confers by being the always approachable one, she acts solely for the Son. It is the eternal Christian mystery of mediation: of allowing oneself to be interposed and allowing oneself to be removed again, of being a path, of instrumentality. The whole essence of belief, the essence of the Father, of the Son, of the Spirit, can never be grasped. It can only be sensed, after one has already been placed on the path of truth. And one station on this path is called Mary. She can be attractive and understandable to those who are still far from wanting to have anything to do with the Son. She can be the first explanation. It would be idle to object here that Catholicism likes to conceal its ultimate intentions and to entice people through attractive things placed in the foreground. Christians always aim at glorification of the Trinity. But because no one wants to understand this aim, they do the same as the Son, who made the Mother the beginning of his path and, as it were, placed her to the fore so that she might prepare the paths of the Incarnation for him. The Mother is a creation of the Son. Even the image of the Father, who eternally generates the Son, is, in the world, such a creation insofar as his eternal love of the Son is revealed in the world by the Son. And the Mother is reflected in the Son as the eternally enduring Mother.

In reflecting the Father, the Son makes himself wholly man; in reflecting the Mother, he makes himself wholly God. As if he were to attribute the characteristics that he inherits from each of his parents to the opposite one, saying: I resemble you, Father, because the Mother gave birth to me; and I resemble you, Mother, because I stem from the Father. He resembles the Mother because he stems from

God and because God created men, in grace, according to his own image, an image that he nowhere finds in more perfect form than in his Mother. He wanted, after all, to reestablish this image of the Father in men, and for that he had need of the willingness of men. And the first one he found who had always been willing was his Mother. So he resembles her. And inasmuch as he found the willingness of the Mother already existent at the time of his Incarnation, he possessed something like a precedent; he was able to prove to the Father that his creation was not hopelessly lost, and that he, precisely because he was born of the Mother, already resembled the Father. For the Mother is continually reborn, in grace, out of God; her motherhood is a grace that is never concluded; and this grace that is conferred on the human Mother has a source quite closely related to the gift conferred on the divine Son when he is eternally generated by the Father. And inasmuch as he owes to the Mother that which is God's—drawing, as a man, his similarity to God from the Mother—he shows her that God lives in her, and shows men that God really abides among them. And to the Father, he shows that men can be good. And thus the joy that the Father and the Mother take in him is similar to the joy of earthly parents: the Mother is happy because the Child is like the Father, and the Father, because he is like the Mother. But because his parents do not discuss things with one another like human parents, the Son takes the place of this discussion and shows his parents these similarities in him. He does this when he is still a Child; he does it continually in his teaching and in his life, constantly leading men to the Father and the Father to men. And yet he is ultimately HE, the Incomparable, the God-Man, precisely because God and man have brought him into the world. He has allowed this unbridgeable opposition to become a unity in him. And he does so not as a concluded work, but in a love that develops constantly anew. It is the eternal truth of love that he has done that.

This is his work, which encompasses the whole of his activity: that, through himself, he brings men and God together; not by drawing them closer externally, but through his birth in the world and our rebirth into him. He *is* God and man, something that we cannot become. But by virtue of the fact that he is both, we can, in him, participate in his mystery by becoming, through his grace, containers and outer coverings of God. Outside of grace, men cannot participate in this mystery; they can, no doubt, be attractive, but only through themselves; their shell is filled with the contents of their own personality. By contrast, the Christian who lives in grace becomes, while retaining all of his undiminished personality, the shell and outer covering of the greater mystery of God, to which he is attracted and that renders him attractive himself. That is his participation in the work of the Incarnation.

A natural, mature man knows his strengths and must take account of them, he knows the limits of what he can achieve; he can estimate, for example, how far he could go were he to develop this or that particular talent. But when a man knows that God dwells in him and he in God, then he can no longer operate with such units of measure and self-defined boundaries. He can now offer himself for service to God, the Unknown, and God will make what he wishes of him. The only proviso is that this must originate in full self-surrender, in abandonment of calculation, and not, for example, in the calculating notion that one will get farther on this path than on any other. It could happen, after all, that God might leave one's natural talents unexploited. And yet the man would still become that which, according to the image of the Father and the Son, the Holy Spirit would like him to be: an instrument in the service of God.

The twofold character of the Lord reaches its fulfilment in the Eucharist, in which he exerts a perpetual influence on both God and man. He is both of these as a result of his Incarnation, and during the time that he allowed both to have their effects on men on earth, he recognized that he thereby led men to the Father. And so he decided to remain in the state of exerting this influence even after his return. He decided that the first one who would have to remain in God and in men should be himself. His words regarding John, *If it is my will that he remain* in me, presuppose that he himself will remain in men until his Second Coming. And yet his time has run out; he has to return to God so as to remain wholly in God again. But in order to remain while nevertheless leaving, he devises the Eucharist. Previously, he was one among many, a God in human form amid the crowd of men. And he succeeded in reaching those men who were available to him in his immediate environment. Now, he wants to be in all men.

The manner of his Incarnation, which had locked him into the framework of a normal human life, he now translates, in an infinite way, into a continually renewed Presence of the host that transcends time and space. In the Incarnation, he lowered himself to the level of human form and became, as subject to the Spirit and the will of the Father, almost nothing. However, what happened but once is perpetually renewed, inasmuch as he continually arises in every transubstantiation. The inconceivability of the submergence of the Son in the virtual nothingness of man acquires a kind of continuity through the inconceivability of the emergence of the Son in every host. And if he demands that we surrender ourselves to him uncomprehendingly in order to become newly formed by him, he makes this possible for us through his incomprehensible emergence and Presence in the host. We are transferred into the middle of the inconceivability of his self-renunciation and the inconceivability of his reemergence in the transubstantiation. God himself has his intrinsic inconceivability; however, he submits himself, as man, to a process of becoming within self-surrendered incomprehensibility and brings this surrenderedness to fulfilment in the host, which is, as it were, reclaimed into the Divine without being annulled as human.

Earlier, the Lord spoke of his hour, which at the same time had come and was present: for him as a man, it remained an hour whose time of arrival he left solely up to the Father. He had made himself so much a man that he adapted the scope and focus of his knowledge solely to the demands of his mission. What he knew in the context of his mission forbade him to act so long as his hour had not yet come—though without this constraint necessarily having to presuppose his positive knowledge of the hour. Precisely by repeatedly calling attention to the fact that his hour had not yet come, he alluded to its constant approach and evolvement, as well as to the fact that, in relation to it, he stood in unvarying readiness. The hour may come when it will: it will not take him by surprise even though he does not want to know its arrival time in advance. He does not live weighed down by the gravity of this hour, which would mean that he would subordinate everything to that hour, would implement none of his plans just to remain freer for its arrival; rather, he acts, works, carries out his commission and knows, too, that he will carry it out, that the hour will not interrupt what is essential but will fulfill it in some way determined by the Father and that he himself, in unity with the Father, will absorb the hour into his work. The hour—like every man, every place, every previous time that was not the hour—will become for him a part and aspect of his mission. By allowing the hour to come, by remaining aware of it in every context without letting himself be overwhelmed or hindered by it, he shows that he regards time as merely an arrangement designed to accompany him by the Father, that he knows how everything included in time belongs to eternity. That today and tomorrow, what is intended and what has been accomplished, are all equally directed toward fulfilment of the Father's will. That every instance of readiness, as long as it is nothing more than readiness, is already actual fulfilment. That it neither wanes nor longs to be fulfilled prematurely. Nothing of what he offers the Father and the Father takes from him to use according to his will has any sort of condition attached to it. He exists so completely in the will of the Father that, at every moment, he both does and recognizes what is of the Father—nothing more and nothing less.

From the omnipresence of the coming hour within his planning and readiness—which does not mean that he therefore makes it preponderant over other hours—there is a path that leads to understanding of the Son's eucharistic attitude. By refusing, while he was on earth, to anticipate the hour as a historic one, by constantly preparing himself for it while yet leaving its arrival time up to God, he remained *timeless* in the midst of his temporal life. And by becoming timeless in the Eucharist, he not only draws every moment of his temporal life into it but also remains at all times open toward the Church. He stands at the service of her time just as, when he was on earth, he stood at the service of the Father's time. He does this in order that every one of our times might become his time. To a certain extent, he overcame time for us in order to be able to bring it under his control. Natural man can, and must, organize his lifetime by making plans that have to be carried out in successive stages within that lifetime. Even the life of the Lord, when it is subsequently surveyed as a whole, appears to have been the evolvement of such a plan. And yet it was not really that, no more than is any other Christian life. For Christians, there is no such organizing; the whole organization of Christian time lies in God's hands. A Christian could not, for example, make up his mind to live for thirty years in obscurity and then to switch to a life of action. Or to develop himself religiously during the next few years in such a way that he would have reached a certain level by a certain time. Not even the Son wished, or was able, to exercise control over his time in this sense. He could only say: The hour is not here, the hour is coming, the hour has come. Amid all his human planning, a Christian must remain pliable in the hands of God. In that lies the overcoming of time. What should be imitated by us is not the external course of the Lord's life, but only the fact that, at any given time, he did what was of the Father. He would like to give this readiness to us, not as a mere teaching, but as something supremely practical and realizable; and this is the great consequence of his remaining, and coming to be, in us through the Eucharist. The Eucharist, too, knows nothing of time. We should actually always be prepared to receive it, to communicate, just as he was always prepared to receive the Father.

On the Cross, when the hour has come and the Son is dying, he offers up his Incarnation to the Father. At this moment, his acknowledgment of the Father's time is such that he does what is of the Father. His death is his last reception of the Father. His death is like a mirror-image of the Eucharist. He allows himself to be received by the Father while he simultaneously receives the Father. He enters the transtemporality of the Father, receiving, within his time, participation in eternity; thus his dying into the Father is also the beginning of his eucharistic Incarnation. (Even though the transubstantiation already occurred earlier, during the Last Supper, it is still only from the Cross that it derives its force and only on the Cross that it is finally sealed: through the entry of the spirit of the Son into the Father.) From this, it becomes clear just how much the Eucharist is a gift to us from the Father: in granting the Son permission to die, he opens up for him the way to the Eucharist. The Incarnation itself, to the mind of the Son, was already a work aimed at revelation of the Father. And in the Eucharist, the Son tightens, as it were, his tie to the Father in order to show the Father's love, through it, to the world. Consequently, there is now something like a threefold paternal relationship of the Father to the Son: first, one from time immemorial in the eternal generation of the Son; second, one since his Fatherhood became manifest to the world through the Son's Incarnation; and third, one in which he is perpetually the Father and appears as Father in the Eucharist. The Eucharist is by no means a sign of the Son's becoming independent. On the Cross, he no doubt brings the completed mission back to the Father, but in such a way that this returning enables him to receive a new mission from the Father: a permanent mission in the Eucharist. In the Cross, his commission no more reaches a conclusion than does any Christian commission. Only unbelief can understand mission in that way. For belief, every ending of a mission is in itself a new beginning.

In the Incarnation, he was the creature of God; he bore his image in the way that the Father had made it, provided with the normal attributes and powers. In the Eucharist, it is as if all this has been submerged while emphasis is given to that which, in the Incarnation, was abasement, humiliation and smallness: hence, precisely, to the divine concealed in it. To this belongs also the forgoing of any tie with time. By removing himself from the normal chronological context, he situates himself within a new kind of complete indifference: Mass can be said or not said, the host can be baked or not baked, he can be administered in Communion or not administered, he can be worthily received or not worthily. Everything remains in suspension, it nowhere intersects with the course of natural time; and yet, when it is then actualized, the whole timelessness and eternality of the Eucharist compresses itself into the temporal instant, into the now in which the Lord bestows himself and is received. And precisely in this contact between time and eternity, the Lord determines the filled time of the recipient. Through Communion, one can be invited to participate in some currently actual mystery in the life of the Lord: a mystery of love, of devotion, of taking action or of remaining silent, of waiting or of suffering. From the content of time that is now communicated, threads extend out to the temporal appearance of the Lord. And these threads are tied through the timelessness of the Eucharist.

There are also many other things which Jesus did. But he did them in such a way that, even unrecorded, they have not been lost but are still being done today, since everything is contained in his eucharistic activity and since he can grant everyone participation in them through his Eucharist. In it, however, above and beyond the Cross, he also takes over something that is God's and something that is man's—with his journey through hell. At the Last Supper, he drew us in, too, as active men, through the positive command, "Do this in remembrance of me", and then, in his suffering on the Cross, committed his spirit back into the hands of the Father and received in return the eternal affirmation of his body by the Father; but in his journey through the netherworld, by contrast, he absorbs the passivity and negativity of men into himself simultaneously with the whole night of the Father, in order, in his Resurrection and his continued life in the Eucharist, to bring all things together, from heaven to hell, in himself. In this context, the Cross is like a midpoint between the earthly part, from the Incarnation to the Passion, and the other-worldly part, the journey through the netherworld. However, it is not in his historical existence that we experience this totalness of the Son, but in his eucharistic existence, in which he grants us participation in all the mysteries of his redemption, including their summary, the Cross. This participation comes about, however, not in the Cross itself, but after the Cross in the Eucharist.

In the host, he lives as one who is bestowed. Hardly has he allowed himself to be made present through the words of transubstantiation than he dispenses himself again. In his becoming present, he causes the spirit of the priest to combine instrumentally with the Spirit of God to form a single principle, just as, in the Incarnation, the Holy Spirit had joined with the Mother to form the principle of his generation. But because this new sort of generation in the host is nevertheless a continuation of his Incarnation, not only is the Father involved in it but also the Mother, both in the priest who plays a cooperative role through his office and in the believers who, as receivers, imitate the Mother's receiving of the Child. In the Eucharist, Mary is not excluded; the Son integrates her, too, into his eucharistic life, into its becoming and subsisting. He does not deny his Mother when he becomes present for the Church in the Mass, not even when he remains reserved in the tabernacle and least of all when he dispenses himself in Communion.

However, it is not one host only that the Lord bestows, but every host, and every one contains in itself the unrestricted possibilities of his life. Thus he pours himself out endlessly over the entire world. And that is why *the world itself could not contain the books that would be written* if his whole life were to be recorded. All that he has done can be neither recounted in detail nor summarized. For although each individual deed exists as such, it is never detachable from the unlimited context of his oneness in the Father and in the Spirit. And even if an evangelist could believe himself to have recounted everything that he had seen and experienced, he would still know that he can describe only the externals, whereas the inner dimensions would have escaped him. John, who is closer to the Lord than the others and is therefore unable to describe any individual deed as something isolated, senses behind everything the ocean of love that envelops and washes over everything and cannot be captured in any words. Which means not only that he apprehends events in the way that a lover is capable of apprehending them, but primarily that we, with our standards of judgment, with our constant deficiency of love, have lost the capacity to grasp the words of love in the total fullness of their import. There where John is still representing an interconnected whole that is visible to him, we go around picking out little fragments for ourselves. The simple fact is that love, as it lives in the Lord and as he communicates it, can be grasped only by lovers who themselves participate in his ever-greater love, who are willing to dispense with measuring both his love and their own. And when John says that it is impossible for *every one of them to be written,* he wants to say that the love is too great to admit of being comprehended or delineated by breaking it down into individual elements. Every attempt to grasp any individual element would necessarily fail because of the way that each trails off into the totality of love. Relevant here is the fact that, in this love, there is no clear boundary between this world and the beyond. In the love, because it is the ever-greater, there is always a beyond. But this beyond is always something this-worldly, because it is, after all, the same love in which one lives. Thus all boundaries are dissolved. Similarly, we cannot place limits on the Holy Spirit as the bearer of the mission from the Father in the Son; he is the effacer of boundaries, the participation of time in eternity. The Son carries within him time and eternity: he carries within him the unity of the perfect love that he is in relation to the Father and the perfect love that he becomes in relation to us. He has come in order to bring eternal life to us, not once we have died, but to us believers today. Believingly, we live in eternal life today. Thus it is impossible to make plans at the temporal level, because the eternal life that is given us today is the life of the Father, Son and Spirit. And in eternal life, they have the mystery of their own planning and confer that life on us together with their time and planning. Any postponement of belief and conversion until tomorrow would be a forgoing of eternal life today, an act of placing oneself outside of eternal life. And because eternal life always exists at this very moment, it also always exerts its claim at this very moment. But this is exactly what fulfilment is. If it is alive in a man and is answered affirmatively by him, then it is fulfilled and that man lives in fulfilment, is in the process of fulfilment. In belief, eternal life is involved in fulfilling itself. In an unstoppable involvement that is realized evolvement.

Christian life is placed in the midst of this realized evolvement. The basic demand is that it should remain in fulfilment. As temporal life, it will certainly take account of temporal laws, will attempt to fulfill the eternal through temporal planning. But everything temporal remains an instrument subordinated to the planning of God, a part of Christian service to God. God leaves us with our natural powers for the purpose of serving him. He gives them back to us after we have handed them over to him and he has accepted them.

That is how the divine and the human wills are related to each other in the self-sacrificial prayer of Saint Ignatius: God gives us our liberty, our memory, our understanding, our will after we have submitted all these to him so that he might take charge of them. He gives us our will, which exists in order to do his will. There is a parallel between this prayer and the dying prayer of the Son: "It is finished." In the *Suscipe,* the prayer is that the Lord might take everything; just as, in the dying prayer of the Son, the Father has taken everything. Through this, the Lord becomes the Eucharist and we become participants in eternal life, that is, in the life of the Son. For the Son has given us his life so that we will really possess it: he has lost it to us. If the Son has died on the Cross and lost his life to us, then he no longer has any life left. He must receive anew from the

Father the life of someone who has given away, and thus lost, his own life. And in the context of this new vitality he draws all of us into the same process of giving and losing. If the Son has given everything and yet still lives, then he actually lives the fulfilment of his life: he lives the meaning of his life. And every Christian can do the same, namely, give his life away in order to become the one that he is: one who has been given to God. The simplest example is that of the martyr; in losing his life, he becomes the one that he is: a martyr, that is, a witness, a saint, a true Christian. Of the avowedly dedicated Christian, too, it holds true that whoever does the will of the Father loses his life; he perhaps loses what were, from a purely worldly perspective, his best potentialities, those in which people say that the fulfilment of his life would have lain. And even when God makes use of one's natural capacities and propensities, it is only if everything had previously been given back to him in an attitude of complete — to the point of nullity — indifference.

The point at which the life of the Lord and our life come into contact is the Eucharist and, additionally, all the sacraments. Outwardly, the sacraments appear as nothing; inwardly, they contain eternal life. Just as an eye is outwardly nothing, yet inwardly contains the entire world regardless of whether the things that it sees are near or far, so the sacraments are the point in which the divine world is compressed and by which it is mediated. They are in us, they affect us, just as the objects of sight affect the open eye: we need only open our eyes in order to see. In order to possess God, we need only receive that which he wants to give us. And just as the natural objects of sight do not withdraw from the eye as long as it remains open, so, too, the sacramental ones do not withdraw as long as we remain in the attitude of receivers, undergoing change with the open eyes of belief. And just as the field of seeable things presents itself to our eye as far too great for us to be able to take it all in, so that which is mediated by the sacraments is infinitely greater than what we think we understand and receive. To everyone to whom the Lord dispenses a sacrament — and he is always the one who ultimately dispenses — he gives his entire world; but he offers it to the individual within the communion of believers. If, then, the individual were also able to understand some measure of what he receives, there would still remain the infinite multiplication of this gift through the number of receivers; so that, from this side, too, things would go beyond all calculation—even though no one receives anything that is not simultaneously something general and no one is taken by the Lord so personally that he does not always see him as a member of the community. Everything in the reception of the sacraments is, after all, truth, and truth always presupposes generality, but equally a personal world with its own history and its own orientation. Thus truth is something open in all directions and with no possible end. The Johannine is not exhausted in the Gospel and the Letters of John; it can unfold once again, in a wholly new and unexpected way, in the Apocalypse. So, too, the truth of the sacraments is inexhaustible; even though they are always a communication of the one and only truth of Christ, no one knows the extent and coloring of this truth in another, just as no one knows how the same sort of food tastes to his neighbor. But because the Lord, as dispenser of the sacraments, always offers himself as the one who is receiving from the Father, he also confers, in every case, something of this most intimate, most personal aspect of himself, something of his way of receiving and sensing the Father. The constantly increasing element of broadening that ran through the Gospel is thus also incorporated into every sacrament, and in fact, not as something inherent in us, some natural ability to assimilate and experience, but as an always-more that the Lord in each case bestows out of himself and that enables the recipient to absorb the Ever-Greater of God in a constantly expanded way. If it is the will of the Son that the Father should really recognize the Son in the believer, then the Son must impart something of his essence to the believer so that the Father might find it present in him.

Were every one of them to be written, I suppose that the world itself could not contain the books that would be written. John could spend his whole life writing books about what he had experienced during his years together with the Lord. And if he were very diligent, he would have accumulated, at the end of his life, only a small bundle of manuscripts, something that the strength of a man can carry and that the mind of a man can comprehend. In view of this utmost that he was able to do as a man, it dawns on him how infinitely much more the Lord has brought about. And if he had written down the whole of Johannine experience, it would not coincide with the experience of the other apostles and even less with that of all believers, to whom the Lord always devotes himself personally. The number of believers at the time when John existed is still comprehensible. It would be possible for all of them to have communicated their experience. And even the number of all the believers throughout all the ages is a finite one. However, if they all wrote down what they knew of the Lord, it would still bear no proportion to that which the Lord has actually accomplished. For everything that he does is only partially disclosed to us, because we only partially believe and because his activity is simultaneously directed into eternity and undertaken from out of eternity.

He came in order to glorify the Father, and he does that from eternity to eternity. The glorification of the Father is so boundless that, in order to accomplish it, the Son must do something infinite that comes from all eternity and goes into all eternity. He accomplishes it as the Son, but in enduring unity with the Father and the Spirit. The sacraments are taken up into this activity: they effect the opening of eternal life toward us, but they effect the opening of all that is toward the eternal, triune God. They are a continuation of the life and efficacy of the Incarnation so that it might take hold of us. They are this as representations of the Son and, through him, of the Trinity. Inasmuch as the triune God opens himself, in the Son and in the sacraments, all the way to us, he encloses the entire world in himself, for in the triune God an infinite, flowing opening and the infinite closing of unity are one and the same thing.